Language, Gender, and Citizenship in American Literature, 1789–1919

Studies in American Popular History and Culture

JEROME NADELHAFT, *General Editor*

No Way of Knowing
Crime, Urban Legends, and the Internet
Pamela Donovan

The Making of the Primitive Baptists
A Cultural and Intellectual History of the Antimission Movement, 1800-1840
James R. Mathis

Women and Comedy in Solo Performance
Phyllis Diller, Lily Tomlin, and Roseanne
Suzanne Lavin

The Literature of Immigration and Racial Formation
Becoming White, Becoming Other, Becoming American in the Late Progressive Era
Linda Joyce Brown

Popular Culture and the Enduring Myth of Chicago, 1871–1968
Lisa Krissoff Boehm

America's Fight over Water
The Environmental and Political Effects of Large-Scale Water Systems
Kevin Wehr

Daughters of Eve
Pregnant Brides and Unwed Mothers in Seventeenth-Century Massachusetts
Else L. Hambleton

Narrative, Political Unconscious, and Racial Violence in Wilmington, North Carolina
Leslie H. Hossfeld

Validating Bachelorhood
Audience, Patriarchy, and Charles Brockden Brown's Editorship of the *Monthly Magazine and American Review*
Scott Slawinski

Children and the Criminal Law in Connecticut, 1635–1855
Changing Perceptions of Childhood
Nancy Hathaway Steenburg

Books and Libraries in American Society during World War II
Weapons in the War of Ideas
Patti Clayton Becker

Mistresses of the Transient Hearth
American Army Officers' Wives and Material Culture, 1840–1880
Robin Dell Campbell

The Farm Press, Reform, and Rural Change, 1895–1920
John J. Fry

State of 'The Union'
Marriage and Free Love in the Late 1800s
Sandra Ellen Schroer

"My Pen and My Soul Have Ever Gone Together"
Thomas Paine and the American Revolution
Vikki J. Vickers

Agents of Wrath, Sowers of Discord
Authority and Dissent in Puritan Massachusetts, 1630-1655
Timothy L. Wood

The Quiet Revolutionaries
How the Grey Nuns Changed the Social Welfare Paradigm of Lewiston, Maine
Susan P. Hudson

Cleaning Up
The Transformation of Domestic Service in Twentieth Century New York City
Alana Erickson Coble

Feminist Revolution in Literacy
Women's Bookstores in the United States
Junko R. Onosaka

Great Depression and the Middle Class
Experts, Collegiate Youth and Business Ideology, 1929–1941
Mary C. McComb

Labor and Laborers of the Loom
Mechanization and Handloom Weavers, 1780–1840
Gail Fowler Mohanty

"The First of Causes to Our Sex"
The Female Moral Reform Movement in the Antebellum Northeast, 1834-1848
Daniel S. Wright

US Textile Production in Historical Perspective
A Case Study from Massachusetts
Susan M. Ouellette

Women Workers on Strike
Narratives of Southern Women Unionists
Roxanne Newton

Hollywood and Anticommunism
HUAC and the Evolution of the Red Menace, 1935–1950
John Joseph Gladchuk

Negotiating Motherhood in Nineteenth-Century American Literature
Mary McCartin Wearn

The Gay Liberation Youth Movement in New York
"An Army of Lovers Cannot Fail"
Stephan L. Cohen

Gender and the American Temperance Movement of the Nineteenth Century
Holly Berkley Fletcher

The Struggle For Free Speech in the United States, 1872–1915
Edward Bliss Foote, Edward Bond Foote, and Anti-Comstock Operations
Janice Ruth Wood

The Marketing of Edgar Allan Poe
Jonathan H. Hartmann

Language, Gender, and Citizenship in American Literature, 1789–1919
Amy Dunham Strand

Language, Gender, and Citizenship in American Literature, 1789–1919

Amy Dunham Strand

Taylor & Francis Group
New York   London

First published 2009
by Routledge
711 Third Avenue, New York, NY 10017

Simultaneously published in the UK
by Routledge
2 Park Square, Milton Park, Abingdon, Oxfordshire OX14 4RN

Routledge is an imprint of the Taylor & Francis Group, an informa business

First issued in paperback 2012

© 2009 Taylor & Francis

Typeset in Sabon by IBT Global.

All rights reserved. No part of this book may be reprinted or reproduced or utilised in any form or by any electronic, mechanical, or other means, now known or hereafter invented, including photocopying and recording, or in any information storage or retrieval system, without permission in writing from the publishers.

Trademark Notice: Product or corporate names may be trademarks or registered trademarks, and are used only for identification and explanation without intent to infringe.

Library of Congress Cataloging in Publication Data
Strand, Amy Dunham.
  Language, gender, and citizenship in American literature, 1789–1919 / by Amy Dunham Strand.
    p. cm. — (Studies in American popular history and culture)
  Includes bibliographical references and index.
  1. American literature—19th century—Criticism and interpretation. 2. Politics and literature—United States—History—19th century. 3. United States—Intellectual life—19th century. 4. English philology. 5. Gender identity in literature. 6. Citizenship in literature. I. Title.
  PS201.S77 2009
  810.9'358735—dc22
                                        2008019156

ISBN13: 978-0-415-99193-3 (hbk)
ISBN13: 978-0-415-54161-9 (pbk)

Portions of the following articles are reprinted here:

"Interpositions: Hope Leslie, Women's Petitions, and Historical Fiction in Jacksonian America." *Studies in American Fiction* 32.2 (Autumn 2004): 131-64. Used by permission of *Studies in American Fiction* and Northeastern University.

"Notes at the Intersections of Language and Literature: The American Dialect Society's Early *Dialect Notes*." *American Speech* 81.2 (Summer 2006): 115-31. Copyright 2006 by the American Dialect Society. Used by permission of the publisher, Duke University Press.

For Meg and Abby

Contents

Acknowledgments xi

Introduction: "A Band of *National Union*": Literature, Gender, and American Language Ideologies 1

1 *Hope Leslie,* Women's Petitions, and Political Discourse in Jacksonian America 16

2 Vocal (Im)Propriety and the Management of Sociopolitical Mobility in *The Wide, Wide World* and *Ragged Dick* 62

3 The (Re)Construction of Dialect and African American (Dis)Franchisement in Charles W. Chesnutt's Writings 105

4 Henry James and the Linguistic Domestication of Women and Immigrants at the Turn of the Century 145

Coda: *Herland* and "The Future of English": Considering Language, Gender, and National Identity in Early-20th-Century America 184

Notes 193
Bibliography 231
Index 253

Acknowledgments

I have many institutions and individuals to thank for their generous support. The University of Washington's Walter Chapin Simpson Center for the Humanities fellowship gave me the unmatchable experience of working with an interdisciplinary group of scholars in the project's early stages. Washington's Elizabeth Kerr Macfarlane Endowed Scholarship in the Humanities and the Department of English also supported this project. To the anonymous donors to the department's travel fund, I owe thanks for the opportunities to witness the wideness of the academic community at conferences across the country. And to my readers and editors at Routledge, who saw this project through its latest iteration, I give thanks.

I am profoundly indebted to my mentors, who have provided exceptional models of the teacher and scholar I hope to be. I thank Mark Patterson for his model of mentorship, his constructive responsiveness, and his rare abilities to guide without scripting and to pose otherwise daunting conceptual questions in welcoming ways. I am grateful to Gail Stygall, particularly for first sparking my interest in gender and language, for cheering it on, and for modeling what it might mean to be an active, engaged public intellectual. To Anne Curzan and Gregg Crane I owe special thanks, for they patiently continued to work with me even after leaving Seattle. Through conversations with Anne, this project emerged, developed, and crystallized; I thank Anne for her attentive engagement and peerless vision, for her contagious enthusiasm and boundless energy, and for her exemplar of teaching and scholarship. Gregg's meticulous readings and challenging questions have reliably unfolded to me a sense of what this project might still one day become; I am extremely grateful for his incisive responses to my queries, both big and small. To Richard Veler, my undergraduate thesis advisor, I owe my passion for 19th-century American literature, my pursuit of graduate studies, and my pedagogical ideals.

From the beginnings of this study, friends at the University of Washington—Heather Easterling, Kim Emmons, Pat Linder, Nicole Merola, Colby Nelson, Alison Tracy Hale, Molly Wallace, and Christine Wooley—made graduate study collegial and modeled intellectual and personal generosity in myriad ways. Most of all, Leigh Ann Litwiller Berte, my writing partner and dearest friend, gave her time, energy, and understanding to this project. My scholarship and my teaching inevitably gain from Leigh Ann's keen mind, catalytic conversation, and thoughtful commentary; my life itself is vastly richer because of her quick wit and close friendship.

I cannot give enough thanks to my family. My parents, Don and Joyce Dunham, nurtured my early love of reading and writing and instilled in me the value of education, and my sister Alyssa has provided willing ear and wise counsel during my work on this project as throughout our lives. To Chris, Meg, Abby, and Zuzu, I owe my most heartfelt gratitude. Zuzu, a puppy when I began graduate school, has made sure that I've regularly gotten fresh air and met our neighbors. Much-loved Meg and well-adored Abby each marched exuberantly through their first years of life during final stages of this project, and they have kept me ever mindful of the present and hopeful for the future. And for Chris' tireless spirit, unfailing good humor, and ever-readiness to embrace new ventures together, I continue to be most deeply grateful.

Introduction
"A Band of *National Union*": Literature, Gender, and American Language Ideologies

> Besides this, a *national language* is a band of *national union*. Every engine should be employed to render the people of this country *national;* to call their attachments home to their own country; and to inspire them with the pride of national character. (Noah Webster, *Dissertations on the English Language* [1789] 397–98, Webster's emphasis)

> The school-ma'am has been trying since the Revolution to bring American English to her rules, but it goes on sprouting and coruscating in spite of her, like the vigorous organism it is. My guess is that it will eventually conquer the English of England, and so spread its gaudy inventions round the globe. (Henry Louis Mencken, "The Future of English" [1835] 90)

In the post-revolutionary moment, Noah Webster famously used his ideas about language to express his political opinions about national identity. Viewing American English as a unifier, Webster espoused that "Our political harmony is [. . .] concerned in a uniformity of language," such that "a *national language* is a band of *national union*" (*Dissertations* 20, 397–98).[1] Over the century-plus from Webster's *Dissertations on the English Language* (1789) to H. L. Mencken's first edition of his monumental *American Language* (1919), the practice marked by Webster's *Dissertations*—a now well-noted tradition of projecting concerns about national identity onto commentary about language—overlapped with an equally notable rhetorical tradition of inserting notions of gender into commentary about language, a practice epitomized in the writings of Mencken, whose *American Language* renewed a sense of American cultural independence in the post-World War I era. While Mencken, like Webster, ultimately envisioned the global conquest of American English, Mencken departed from Webster in his rhetoric: In his figuration of American language as a "vigorous organism"—a kind of robust and impish schoolboy resisting the feminized forces of standardization embodied in the "school-ma'am"—Mencken conceived the language's imperialistic conquest in gendered terms ("Future of English" 89).

2 Language, Gender, and Citizenship in American Literature

This project traces the transformation from Webster's commentary on language and nation to Mencken's triangulation of language, nation, and gender—a transformation enacted through literary products and language debates throughout the 19th and early 20th centuries. From Washington Irving's tyranny-tongued Dame Van Winkle to Charlotte Perkins Gilman's pleasant-voiced Herlanders, gender emerged in American discussions of language to allay a range of concerns about national identity and national citizenship produced by social and political transformations. In particular, this project examines literary and cultural texts to show how such commentary worked in four distinct 19th-century contexts—Jacksonian Indian removal and slavery, the rise of social and political mobility at mid-century, Civil War Reconstruction, and turn-of-the-century immigration—to hold in check progressive notions of citizenship. In passionate discussions about language issues—particularly petitioning, grammar/slang, dialect, and language education—the pairing of language with essentialized notions of gender enabled Americans to recast the idea of America, holding open the promise of democratic consent while diminishing, or excluding, the political voices of not only women, but also Native Americans, African Americans, and immigrants in or from the imagined nation.

As I see it, it is through the interplay among the often-naturalized terms of language, gender, and nation—defined in, through, and against one another—that a contestation of citizenship time and again occurs, and it is this contestation that constitutes the crux of *Language, Gender, and Citizenship in American Literature, 1789–1919*. Rather than characterizing language itself as necessarily "masculine" or "feminine," this project explicates how gender ideologies have been grafted onto ideas about language, and conversely how language ideologies have been grafted onto ideas about gender, in order to narrate stories about who may (or may not) perform the role of American citizen and how they may (or may not) do it—such that gendered commentary about American language, posed as consensual but in fact often understood as "natural," contributes to beliefs about how individuals might participate in a democratic nation. Discourses of language and gender worked in mutually constitutive ways to underline particular ideas about American *citizenship* 'the status of a citizen with its attendant duties, rights, and privileges' (*American Heritage Dictionary*, 3rd ed.)—a "status" contested throughout American history.[2]

Contestations of American citizenship might be seen as embracing a spectrum of visions ranging from, to borrow Werner Sollors' useful paradigm, a forward-looking, contractual, consent-based model of citizenship held out as the nation's ideal to a backward-looking, hereditary-oriented, descent-based model. Sollors' paradigm of consent/descent to comprehend American ideology undergirds my conceptualization of how discourses of language, gender, and nation might work together to regulate American citizenship. The tension between consent and descent in American history has been echoed in the tensions between contract/identity, performance/ essence, and nurture/nature—paradigms that embrace thinking about language, nation, and gender as open or closed, fluid or fixed, improvisational or pre-determined concepts and that, at different moments in American history, have conjoined linguistic and political maneuvers to define national citizenship.[3]

After the American Revolution, Webster's own rhetoric about language itself fluctuated between fluid and fixed notions of consent and descent. On the one hand, Webster conceived of language as a system akin to that of the law, declaring that "the unanimous consent of a nation, and a fixed principle of a language, coeval and coextensive with it, are like the common laws of a land, or the immutable rules of morality, the propriety of which every man, however refractory, is forced to acknowledge, and to which most men will readily submit" (*Dissertations* 28). Here, language is analogous to a political system—open, based in the "consent" of the community, and revisable. Yet at the same time, Webster's commentary—in its comparison of language to "a fixed principle" or "immutable rules"—envisions language as a closed, unchangeable, predetermined system. When such commentary about American language is combined with ideologies of gender—perhaps the most easily naturalized of categories of identity—it can invoke identitarian notions of citizenship at the same time that it appeals to contractual ideals of American community. Such commentary can thereby essentialize language, theoretically holding open the potential of democratic consent while supporting a model of citizenship based on descent.[4]

Throughout this project, then, I aim to highlight stories about the articulation of American citizenship through discourses of gender and language—stories that, like Washington Irving's classic "Rip Van Winkle" (1819), tell us something about how attitudes about gender have been repeatedly inserted into commentary on language to absorb anxieties about the process of becoming "national." Irving's "Rip Van Winkle" follows Webster in the post-revolutionary era to highlight the very triangulation of concerns in which this project is invested. "Rip Van Winkle" tells a story of how the American nation was created through a transformation of symbols. Moreover, because "Rip Van Winkle" focuses on Dame Van Winkle and her voice, it tells a story about how the declaration of national, cultural, and linguistic independence was intertwined with attitudes about gender.

In Irving's tale of "becoming American," Rip literally and figuratively awakens from his "torpor" to new signs of the "nation"—in fact, to a new national lexicon that Webster envisioned in his *Dissertations* and catalogued in his *An American Dictionary of the English Language* (1828).[5] Rip not only emerges from his sleep to discover new "signs"—"The Union Hotel" replacing the village inn; a "liberty pole" instead of a tree; a portrait of "the ruby face of King George [. . .] singularly metamorphosed" into

"GENERAL WASHINGTON" (Irving, "Rip" 436). He also awakens to new, unfamiliar words in a strangely once-familiar setting:

> He looked in vain for the sage Nicholas Vedder, with his broad face, double chin, and fair long pipe, uttering clouds of tobacco smoke instead of idle speeches; or Van Bummel, the schoolmaster, doling forth the contents of an ancient newspaper. In place of these, a lean bilious looking fellow, with his pockets full of handbills, was haranguing vehemently about rights of citizens—election—members of congress—liberty—Bunker's hill—heroes of seventy-six—and other words, that were a perfect Babylonish [Babel-ish] jargon to the bewildered Van Winkle. (436)

Rip's awakening from his twenty-year nap is simultaneously experienced as a national and linguistic transformation—bringing home to us Christopher Looby's observation of "the belief that the nation was made out of words" (*Voicing* 4). Indeed, as Looby notes, "There may be no text of the early national period in which the mysteries of time, change, and national inception were more pregnantly addressed than this ["Rip Van Winkle"]. The allegorization of historical process as semiotic substitution is acute" (95).

While Rip's uncanny awakening is certainly national and linguistic, it is simultaneously gendered. Here, by focusing on Irving's gendered use of language in figuring nation-creation, I fuse Looby's reading of the story with Judith Fetterley's interpretation. Fetterley insists on the centrality of the otherwise nameless Dame Van Winkle as both "woman" and "villain," as the spokesperson of a civilization to be escaped in order to accomplish a fantasy of "life in an all-male world, a world without women, the ideal American territory" (*Resisting* 3, 6, 11). Thus Irving tells us in "Rip Van Winkle" that Rip's newfound freedom as a citizen of the United States is experienced less as the freedom to participate in the new democracy that resulted "from the changes of states and empires" and the throwing off of "the yoke of old England" than as the freedom from his tyrannical *wife's* "petticoat government" and "the yoke of matrimony" (439).

What is more, Irving figures Rip's attainment of freedom, which parallels the nation's achievement of independence, through gendered *linguistic* images, as freedom from the "daring tongue of this terrible virago," his "termagant wife" ("Rip" 432). Irving repeatedly characterizes the domestic "tyranny of Dame Van Winkle" (439) through descriptions of her speech: She regularly delivers "curtain lectures" ("tirade[s] delivered by a wife after the curtains around the four-poster bed have been drawn for the night" [430n8]); she is "continually dinning in his ears [. . .]. Morning, noon, and night, her tongue was incessantly going, and everything he said or did was sure to produce a torrent of household eloquence" (431); she equally subjects Rip's dog Wolf to "the ever-during and all-besetting terrors of a woman's tongue" and proves true the adage that "a tart temper never mellows with age, and a sharp tongue is the only edge tool that grows keener by constant use" (431). The fact that these descriptions are meant to be humorous (Irving ironically places the story in the mouth of the comical Diedrich Knickerbocker) does not detract from, but rather reinforces, the intensity of their cultural impact. Indeed, these gendered linguistic stereotypes *are* funny precisely *because* they have cultural resonance, and it is this resonance that gives them ideological force. Rip still experiences freedom from the tyranny of the "mother country" most fully as freedom from the shrewish "sharp tongue" of Dame Van Winkle—whose death from "[breaking] a blood vessel in a fit of passion at a New-England pedlar [sic.]" fittingly marks the passage of the colonial era (438). That Irving uses such gender-laden linguistic and domestic images to characterize the political transformations of the revolution suggests the need to consider the interarticulation of American identity—and specifically the process of "becoming American," which is expressed most completely in gaining the rights of citizenship—with discourses of language and gender. Ultimately, in this case as in many others, the focus on woman's language eclipses the significance of national transformations.

The terms *language, nation,* and *gender*—three traditionally-naturalized terms that underlie this project—are also illuminated by this reading of "Rip Van Winkle." As Irving's repeated characterization of Dame Van Winkle's shrill voice suggests, *language* is often perceived as an essential extension of identity. Yet simultaneously, as Rip's experience of new signs and a strange lexicon suggests, *language* denotes a visual, written, or spoken system of representation, as well as a consensual, creative means of imagining a community and delineating membership in it. And through Rip's awakening to a "Babylonish" new national "jargon," Irving's story reveals that the political category of *nation* itself is less an organic or natural entity than a creative historical process that takes place on the contested grounds of culture and through language.

Bearing in mind Max Weinreich's famous formulation that a language is a dialect with an army and a navy, I thus understand language as contributing to the formation of nation as "less a prior determinant of nationality than part of a complex process of cultural innovation, involving hard ideological labor, careful propaganda, and a creative imagination" (Weinreich cited in Lippi-Green 43; Eley and Suny 7). Following constructionist explanations of *nation* by social historians and critical theorists alike over roughly the last four decades, I take for granted descriptions of "nation" as an affective, discursive construction by theorists since Ernest Gellner and Eric Hobsbawm. This understanding has been expressed perhaps most memorably in Benedict Anderson's idea of the nation as "an imagined political community and imagined as both inherently limited and sovereign"—and no less "real" because imagined—that emerged, in the context of 18th-century transformations, in understandings of religious community, dynastic realms, and time, and emerged on the ground paved by the rise of print capitalism and vernacular languages (Anderson 6, 27, 42–46).

As my reading of Irving may also indicate, I equally take *gender* as a necessary term in the theorization of nation—and a term, like *language* and *nation*, that has often been valued as "natural." I chiefly understand *gender* not as essence or as a collection of traits or sex roles but, in Gail Bederman's succinct expression, as "a *historical, ideological process*" through which "individuals are positioned and position themselves as men or as women" (7, her emphasis).[6] As others have described, national membership "is highly gendered," in large part because the nation has been consistently imagined through the family, thereby reproducing traditional, patriarchal family relations on a large scale—a fact that has meant most clearly "women's exclusion from citizenship, preeminently through lack of the franchise, but more extensively in a complex repertoire of silencings and disabilities, which barred them from property, education, profession, and politics—all those opportunities that qualified men for roles in the public sphere" (Eley and Suny 26). In familial figurations of the nation throughout the 19th century, alternately "natural" and "constructed" notions of gender and language made happy bedfellows, working in tandem with domestic ideology to cast men and women into roles of political or not-political participation.

In this respect, Irving's familial and linguistic characterizations of women's roles as wives and mothers in "Rip Van Winkle" reveal how ideas about gender and language together narrate a tale of becoming, in Rip's case, "a free citizen of the United States" (Irving, "Rip" 439). Irving's use of familial metaphors casts Rip's experience of the new nation as linguistic *and* gendered—wherein Rip's tongue-wagging domestic despot is replaced by a "fresh likely woman" (438), his now-very-maternal daughter, whose tone of voice awakens his memory and with whom he finds "a snug, well-furnished" home, from which he is free to "go in and out whenever he pleased, without dreading the tyranny of Dame Van Winkle" (439). Here, gendered commentary about language, such as the stereotypical tyranny-tongued wife or maternally-voiced daughter in Irving's story, persuasively scripts the nation as a domestic space and describes who and how one might become a citizen—in Irving's words, by Rip's taking a very public seat, "on the bench, at the inn door" to become "reverenced as one of the patriarchs of the village" (439). Working in tandem with the ideology of domesticity, such gendered notions about language reinforce different conceptions of citizenship for men and women, wherein Rip's "regular track of gossip" is assigned to "the village" and the tones of his wife and daughter, whether shrill or sweet, to the home (439). As well, working beyond the implications of separate domestic/political spheres, such gendered preoccupations with language can function to mask fundamental sociopolitical changes such as the "changes of states and empires" (439). In other words, gendered preoccupations with language help procure a seamless transition from one state or empire to another.

Because literary texts such as Irving's imaginatively reflect and disseminate ideologies of language, gender, and nation, literary texts comprise this project's focal points. In using literary texts to bring to light historical moments of gendered commentary about language, this project follows critical linguist Rosina Lippi-Green's suggestion that "novelists provide insight into a cultural phenomenon which is otherwise inaccessible" (186). As an historicist Americanist interested in language, and as a student of rhetoric interested in American literature and culture, I also draw on other key cultural texts that take up linguistic concerns, such as U.S. congressional records, periodicals, grammar books, etiquette manuals, and educational materials. There are strong historical and theoretical justifications for this interdisciplinary approach. Historically, 18th-and 19th-century Americans saw the nation's literature, in the broadest sense of the term, as springing from its language. For example, Webster's views on the necessity for American linguistic independence extended to his championing literary independence as well. In a letter written to John Canfield just before the appearance of Webster's first published book, *A Grammatical Institute of the English Language* (1783)—the initial part of which became popularly known as his successful "Blue-Backed Speller"—Webster moves from the subject of language reform to literature, which he conceives as "the principal bulwark against the encroachments of civil and ecclesiastical tyrants," and ends with the claim that "America must be as independent in literature as she is in politics, as famous for arts as for arms; and it is not impossible but a person of my youth may have some influence in exciting a spirit of literary industry" (*Letters* 3–4). Early-19th-century thinkers, such as Walter Channing in his "Essay on American Language and Literature" (1815), echoed Webster in their belief that an independent national literature is "the product, the legitimate product, of a national language" (Channing 307).[7] In the 19th century, American language and American literature were linked.

From a historical perspective, then, American literature and its study are arguably central to the study of national language ideologies. From a theoretical perspective as well, literature has an allusory relation to reality that offers us a glimpse of how these language ideologies might play out in our lives. As Louis Althusser suggests, "I believe that the peculiarity of art is to 'make us see' (*nous donner à voir*), 'make us perceive,' 'make us feel' something which *alludes* to reality. [. . .] What art makes us *see*, and therefore gives to us in the form of '*seeing*,' '*perceiving*' and '*feeling*' (which is not the form of *knowing*), is the *ideology* from which it is born, in which it bathes, from which it detaches itself as art, and to which it *alludes*" ("Letter on Art" 222, his emphasis). Literary texts, in the case of my study, illuminate various ways in which attitudes about gender and language were combined to express ideas about national identity and national citizenship. The novelists with whom I converse in this project—primarily Catharine Sedgwick, Susan Warner, Horatio Alger, Charles Chesnutt, Henry James—each, in Althusser's words, "give us a 'view' of the ideology to which their work alludes and with which it is constantly fed, a view which presupposes a *retreat,* an *internal distantiation* from the very ideology from which their novels emerged. They make us 'perceive' (but not know) in some sense *from the inside,* by an *internal distance,* the very ideology in which they are held" (222–23, his emphasis).[8] Althusser further elaborates an understanding of *ideology* that underpins this project: "When we speak of ideology we should know that ideology slides into all human activity, that it is identical with the 'lived' experience of human existence itself: that is why the form in which we are 'made to see' ideology in great novels has as its content the 'lived' experience of individuals" (223).[9] As products of language, literary texts are valuable to this project because they show us, in imaginative form, *how* "lived" ideologies such as race, class, gender, and nation could be deflected onto discourse on language. That is, while we all know that the 19th and early 20th centuries were variously racist, classist, sexist, and nativist, I study fiction by Sedgwick, Warner, Chesnutt, and James, among others, because they powerfully illuminate *how* these various –isms were managed *through* ideas about language.

In focusing on gendered commentary on language, this project brings the study of American literature and culture to bear on recent works in language studies and brings a consideration of the field of language studies into conversation with American literary studies. This project, then, not only intervenes among the topics of language, gender, and nation. It also bridges and extends contemporary scholarship in language and literary studies, as well as rhetoric and women's studies, in order to contribute to an understanding of the gendered politics of language in America.

Works on the politics of language by critical linguists, such as Deborah Cameron's *Verbal Hygiene* or Lippi-Green's *English with an Accent: Language, Ideology, and Discrimination in the United States,* have shaped this project in important ways by taking popular perceptions of language as the serious object of sociolinguistic study and establishing that, as Cameron puts it, "ideas about language are recruited very often to non-linguistic concerns" (*Verbal Hygiene* 11).[10] Central to my conceptualization of this study has been Cameron's *verbal hygiene,* a term which loosely denotes "the urge to meddle in matters of language" through commentary *about* language (or metalinguistic commentary) that is both "descriptive" and "prescriptive"— and therefore is practiced equally by linguists who purport objectivity and by enthusiastic "language mavens" who lament misused expressions or the "decline" of the language (vii-viii).[11] Cameron's idea that verbal hygiene is wrapped up in complex ways with issues of authority, identity, and agency— that "verbal hygiene is not just about ordering language itself, but also exploits the powerful symbolism in which language stands for other kinds of order—moral, social and political" (25)—is crucial to my understanding of how, over the course of the 19th century, concerns about national citizenship were deflected onto gendered commentary about language. Yet, whereas Cameron tends to begin with the regulatory discourse surrounding language to argue that this discourse instills social order, I show how the need for sociopolitical order often takes the form of language regulation. I focus on particular 19th-century American verbal hygiene debates in which ideologies of language, nation, and gender overlap—verbal hygiene, for example, about women's roles as destroyers, reproducers, or policers of American linguistic culture in discussions of petitioning, grammar, dialect, and language instruction that I situate within particular sociopolitical contexts. In doing so, I also hope to provide a unique view of the cultural history of English language in America.[12]

To make sense of ideological intersections between American language and literature, and between gender and American citizenship, literary scholars have also done important work in recent years. I am indebted to the work of several scholars who have shaped my thinking: In addition to Looby, David Simpson and Thomas Gustafson, among others, have amply described the importance of language to American political identity in *Voicing America: Language, Literary Form, and the Origin of the United States; The Politics of American English, 1776–1850;* and *Representative Words: Politics, Literature, and the American Language, 1776–1865*. Gavin Jones' *Strange Talk: The Politics of Dialect Literature in Gilded Age America* and Joshua L. Miller's *Lingual Politics: The Syncopated Accents of Multilingual Modernism, 1919–1948* have offered me valuable models for bringing literary and language study together. In works of literary scholarship such as *National Manhood: Capitalist Citizenship and the Imagined Fraternity of White Men; The Anatomy of National Fantasy: Hawthorne, Utopia, and Everyday Life;* and *Revolution and the Word: The Rise of the Novel in America,* Dana Nelson, Lauren Berlant, and Cathy Davidson have attended to the crucial connections between gender and national citizenship in late 18th- to mid-19th-century fictional and other cultural representations.

Language, Gender, and Citizenship in American Literature works between these literary projects, attempting to fill a historical gap between Simpson's *The Politics of American English* and Miller's *Lingual Politics,* and a conceptual gap between Looby's *Voicing America* and Berlant's *Anatomy of National Fantasy*. For example, I add an explicit consideration of attitudes about language to the production and operation of Berlant's gendered and racialized "National Symbolic," described as "the order of discursive practices whose reign within a national space produces, and also refers to, the 'law' in which the accident of birth within a geographic/political boundary transforms individuals into subjects of a collectively-held history" (Berlant 20).

While Berlant's work explores the interarticulation of discourses of race, gender, and sexuality with nation in the United States since the Civil

War, it does not examine how these interarticulations have been propagated through American attitudes about language. In considering gendered commentary on language, I thus try to tease out a particular strand—language—from Berlant's National Symbolic knot, which she says is "not merely juridical, territorial (*jus soli*), genetic *(jus sanguinis)*, linguistic, or experiential, but some tangled cluster of these" (5). Furthermore, I introduce an explicit analysis of gender into Looby's consideration of what Irving, in his Mustapha letters, called America's "pure unadulterated LOGOCRACY or *government of words.*"[13] Introducing gender into Looby's consideration of "voice"—a "strange trope" which Looby interprets as registering the "widespread American sense of nation fabrication as an intentional act of linguistic creation" (*Voicing* 4)—brings my project close to Caroline Levander's *Voices of the Nation: Women and Public Speech in Nineteenth-Century American Literature and Culture.* Yet, rather than read 19th-century commentary about the "female voice," as Levander does, as a site of consolidation and contestation of rising middle-class consciousness, I recast Looby's broader characterization of "voice" as a figure for nation-creation in 18th-century texts by re-reading its gendered relationship to the vote, which reframed the idea of the nation in the 19th century.[14] I thus take "voice" as an often-gendered linguistic figure for discourse registering concerns about citizenship in the 19th century, and I understand discussion of voices, whether male or female, as simply one manifestation of often-gendered commentary on American language.[15]

Indeed, for any understanding of 19th-century "voice" (or of commentary about voices), the trope must be situated historically, within a range of 19th-century sociopolitical transformations, and etymologically, within the term's political associations with the vote. Nineteenth-century "voice" must surely be seen within a historical context in which a powerful rising middle class transformed the nation. But it must also be seen within the context of a number of other social and political moments—including, but by no means comprehending, women's political discourse surrounding Indian removal and slavery and the ensuing fight for women's suffrage; the Civil War Amendments and Reconstruction; and the naturalization of "new" immigrants at the turn of the century. In this project, then, the period from 1789 to 1919 not only traces a linguistic path from Webster's *Dissertations* to Mencken's *American Language.* It also embraces a historical trajectory from George Washington's inauguration to Congress' approval of the Nineteenth Amendment, a trajectory in which white, middle-class men, African American men, immigrants, and finally women, gained what Rogers Smith calls "the badge of full citizenship" (232): the right to vote. It therefore examines gendered commentary about language (or, broadly, "voices") in light of particular events in the history of the American franchise (or "votes"). The connections between these linguistic and historical contexts are borne out in the etymological links between *voice* and *vote,* since the meanings of the two words have long been interrelated in Anglo-American politics, as in the following senses: *to have a voice in* 'the right or privilege of speaking or voting in a legislative assembly'; *to give voice to* 'to vote for'; *to put to voices* 'to put to the vote,' 'to vote'; and *to collect the voices* 'to take a vote.' Underlining the significance of these interconnected terms to American government, the compound *voice vote* is original to the U.S., meaning 'a vote taken by noting the relative strength of the calls of *ay* and *no*.' Further, the still-relevant sense of *voice* as 'the expressed opinion, judgment, will, or wish *of* the people [. . .] as indicated or shown by the exercise of the suffrage,' and as reflected in phrases such as the "popular voice" or "common voice," underscores the relation between "voices" and the franchise, the "badge of full citizenship" (*OED*, 2nd ed.).[16]

This inherently political connection between voices and votes, between speech and suffrage, was memorably recognized in the Declaration of Sentiments, drafted by Elizabeth Cady Stanton and presented at Seneca Falls in 1848. The fact that the Declaration of Sentiments' first-named grievance (that man "has never permitted her [woman] to exercise her inalienable right to the *elective franchise*") is immediately followed by the claim that man "has compelled her to submit to laws, in the formation of which she had no *voice*" reveals the extent to which the convention's attendees recognized that woman's "voice"—whether written or spoken—was associated with her political discourse or "vote" (Declaration 207, my emphasis). As Stanton understood, partially through the use of her "voice," a woman could become, or could be kept from becoming, "American" in the fullest sense of citizenship. Moreover, the Declaration of Sentiments suggests the extent to which ideas about the use of one's "voice"—and arguably ideas about language more broadly—could discipline the formation of American identities and manage access to the right to vote. The task of becoming American thus becomes, in part, the task of "languaging" votes and, in the words of Susan Warner's sentimental heroine, whom I discuss in chapter two, the task of "governing" voices. Yet, while women's studies scholars have done valuable work on the history of women's suffrage in America, and while the 19th-century campaign for women's suffrage is an important part of the historical course of this study, this project is less about understanding women's suffrage *per se*, than it is about attempting to understand the effect of gendered language politics on enfranchisement in America.[17] That is, I seek to understand how anxieties about national citizenship—about the political participation of Indians, the middle class, African Americans, immigrant groups, *and* women—are managed *through* commentary about language and gender together, through gendered commentary about "voices."

In the context of changes and challenges to the franchise, gendered commentary about language emerged in discussions and representations of petitioning, grammar/slang, dialect, and language education to govern, ideologically speaking, the citizenship of not only women but also Native Americans, middle-class white men, African Americans, and immigrants in particular moments over the long 19th century. As each chapter successively demonstrates, discussions of petitioning, grammar/slang, dialect, and language education were instances of wider discourses of, respectively, national political language, vocal propriety, linguistic essentialism, and linguistic domestication. In these discourses, gender surfaced in concerns about language as both institution and communication; it became attached to the prescription of national language *standards* (as in the conceptions of grammars and language manners I address in chapters two and four) as well as to the regulation and representation of language *practices* (as in the conceptions of political discourse and dialect in chapters one and three). These discussions of language ultimately invoked ideas about gender to negotiate concerns about American identity and national citizenship in specific ways. Ideas about language and gender could figure national independence, as Irving's story shows. Such commentary about language and gender also deflected divisive national debates over Indian removal and slavery, stabilized sociopolitical mobility, illuminated the dynamics of Jim Crow, and tempered the rise of the "New Woman" and the "new" immigration.

In chapter one, "*Hope Leslie*, Women's Petitions, and Political Discourse in Jacksonian America," I explore a foundational moment for gendered commentary about national language: women's mass petitioning, which represented their first collective claim to political discourse and a symbolic vote in national policies over Indian removal and slavery. This chapter shows how congressional responses to women's antiremoval and antislavery petitions helped to prompt the gag rules that not only attempted to regulate women's access to political discourse, but also deflected debate over the Indian and Slavery Questions and excluded Indians and slaves from the imagined nation. I argue that Catharine Sedgwick's *Hope Leslie* (1827) anticipates how congressional responses to women's petitions diverted racially-charged debates about Indian removal and slavery to deliberations over gendered political discourse. By explicitly bringing literary analysis into studies of these antiremoval petitions, and by bringing petitioning into a study of antebellum literature, this chapter builds on and extends Alisse Portnoy's important archival work and rhetorical analysis of women's antiremoval petitions in her *Their Right to Speak: Women's Activism in the Indian and Slave Debates*. My reading similarly supplements recent studies in women's history, such as *Signatures of Citizenship: Petitioning, Antislavery, & Women's Political Identity*—Susan Zaeske's rhetorical analysis of women's antislavery petitions in relationship to their development of political identity—by closely examining earlier petitioning efforts in conjunction with Sedgwick's fictional petition as nascent claims to a national, political language. The discussions of petitioning that take place in Sedgwick's popular novel and on the floor of Congress in this antebellum moment are, as this chapter suggests, foundational to the nation's gendered language politics that unfold into more subtly gendered discussions about language over the following century.

Chapter two, "Vocal (Im)Propriety and the Management of Sociopolitical Mobility in *The Wide, Wide World* and *Ragged Dick*," examines how discourses of gendered vocal propriety such as grammar and slang materialized in a mid-century moment of sociopolitical mobility marked by two further challenges to the franchise—the struggle for women's suffrage officially inaugurated by Seneca Falls and the gradual relaxation of property requirements that led to nearly universal white male suffrage by 1860. More specifically, when read alongside the era's publications on vocal (im)propriety—readers, elocution manuals, grammar books, and collections of slang—Susan Warner's and Horatio Alger's best-selling stories illustrate how the dual discourses of grammar and slang became, respectively, associated with domestic femininity and urban masculinity. My analysis of grammar and slang elucidates how mid-century gendered commentary on language helped to achieve and to challenge what Jane Tompkins has identified as a 19th-century "ethic of submission." Moreover, it suggests how this commentary could both impel social mobility and locate mobile voices—and votes—within clearly defined social and political arenas, consequently quelling gender- and class-charged concerns about an increasingly porous national citizenship.

In "The (Re)Construction of Dialect and African American (Dis)Franchisement in Charles W. Chesnutt's Writings," chapter three, I explore how late-19th-century discussions and representations of dialect—many of which revolved around the speech of black male storytellers epitomized by Joel Chandler Harris' Uncle Remus—took place in the context of anxieties about granting the elective franchise to black men in the Fifteenth Amendment (1870). This chapter demonstrates how the Gilded Age's proliferating scientific and literary discourses on language, such as dialect, appealed, in tandem with the law, to paradigms of consent and descent to essentialize language and to diffuse anxieties over African American political speech in an era of Jim Crow legislation. In this legal and linguistic context, Chesnutt's fictions "The Dumb Witness" (1897) and *The Colonel's Dream* (1905) introduce overtly gendered as well as racialized power dynamics that shifted focus from the era's preoccupation with the representation of dialect to the politics of speech itself. Written as Chesnutt himself contemplated issues of (dis)franchisement and moved away from the use of literary dialect, Chesnutt's depictions of gender and language illuminate the descent-bound politics of national (dis)franchisement for African Americans as well as women, and they propose consensual linguistic and legal alternatives.

"Henry James and the Linguistic Domestication of Women and Immigrants at the Turn of the Century," chapter four, shows how gender emerged in ideas about language education—specifically vocal manners and English instruction—to domesticate women's and immigrants' political voices at a time when the rise of "New Women" and "new" immigration prompted a reincarnation of mid-century concerns about class, ethnicity, gender, and national citizenship. This chapter suggests that Henry James' *Bostonians* (1886) and his cultural criticism—namely "The Question of Our Speech" (1905), "The Speech of American Women" (1906–07), and "The Manners of American Women" (1907)—tell a twofold story about how the turn-of-the-century task of dealing with the alien dramatically relocated women's social and linguistic roles from the drawing room to the national American scene. Yet the potential political impact of these new roles was tempered through discourses of linguistic domestication that were linguistic expressions of "civilization" and "Americanization." James' writings illustrate how commentary on women's linguistically domesticating role—as seen in linguistic etiquette manuals such as Richard Grant White's popular *Everyday English* (1881) and in early-20th-century texts of Americanization—blended ideas about "nature" with ideas about "nurture" to produce notions of national citizenship for immigrants as well as women.

In the coda, "*Herland* and 'The Future of English': Considering Language, Gender, and National Identity in Early 20th-Century America," I return to the linkage of language and gender to figure political unity, within "America" as well as in opposition to other nations, in the context of the achievement of women's suffrage. By reading Charlotte Perkins Gilman's *Herland* (1915) alongside Mencken's work, culminating in "The Future of English" (1935), I offer ways in which the ideological intersections among language, gender, and nation resurfaced in years surrounding the Nineteenth Amendment. Following Guyatri Spivak's distinction between "'*internal* colonization'—the patterns of exploitation and domination of disenfranchised groups *within* the United States—and the various different heritages or operations of colonization in the rest of the world" (792), the coda gestures to the potential role of gendered national language ideologies in a global framework. Gilman's and Mencken's writings on language forecast the gendered national politics of language in our day of linguistic imperialism and suggest an ongoing need to examine the role of language and gender both in negotiating national citizenship and in imagining America as a global citizen.

This exploration of American literary texts within particular linguistic and sociopolitical contexts leaves out much—for example, its scope necessarily excludes a more expanded exploration of the imperial capacity of American English or an explicit analysis of geography.[18] Despite these omissions, this study illuminates how gendered commentary on language can become a fairly thin disguise for concerns about national citizenship and illustrates, moreover, the range of linguistic and literary forms taken by concerns about national identity. That is, petitions, grammars, dialects, and etiquettes, are, in my view, unique, gender-inflected forms not only for understanding debates about political participation in America, but also for understanding the conditions of creating American literature. Petitions, grammars, dialects, and etiquettes thus emerge from this study as truly meaningful figures—figures resonating *within* and *beyond* literary texts to provide governing structures of meaning in American culture.

At the same time, fictions such as *Hope Leslie, The Wide, Wide World, Ragged Dick, The Colonel's Dream,* or *The Bostonians* emerge as the complex imaginative products of a dialogue between available rhetorical forms and contextual concerns—such that, through the project of governing voices, these texts themselves might be contemplated as fictive petitions, primers, theories of language, or verbal criticism. Perhaps finally, in an attempt to make sense of how American literature participates in gendered national language ideologies and how, in turn, these ideologies are reflected, shaped, and disseminated by literature, *Language, Gender, and Citizenship in American Literature, 1789–1919* provides one kind of explanation of the particular ways in which literature and language have been entwined in the making of America and in the managing of American citizenship.

1 *Hope Leslie*, Women's Petitions, and Political Discourse in Jacksonian America

1. INTRODUCTION

"Legal Condition of Woman." "Structure of the Indian Languages." "Hope Leslie." "Northeastern Boundary." (*The North American Review,* April 1828)

These four titles were listed in immediate succession on the content page of the April 1828 issue of *The North American Review:* a collocation of titles and topics that was not merely coincidental but reflective of their complex connections in America's consciousness. In the late 1820s and 1830s in the United States, all of these issues were key concerns—the "Woman Question"; the "Indian Question"; interest in language, not only American English but also other languages, including those of Native American Indians; the claiming of a distinct American literature; and a concern with national boundaries, geographical and cultural.[1] Perhaps it should be no surprise, then, that, independently and together, these issues were frequently discussed in the nation's periodicals, played out in multifaceted ways in novels like Catharine Maria Sedgwick's *Hope Leslie; Or, Early Times in the Massachusetts* (1827), and surfaced in congressional debates of the period. This chapter explores the constellation of cultural, literary, and political concerns signaled by this page of *The North American Review*—particularly, it focuses on *Hope Leslie* and women's antiremoval petitions to examine the larger debate over women's access to national, political language in the contexts of Indian removal and slavery.[2]

Neatly foregrounded on the first page of the April 1828 *Review,* concerns with women, Indians, language, and national boundaries—as well as American literature and literature by women—were situated within untidy political and rhetorical inheritances. These entangled concerns were worked out in part through language, and in the Early American Republic, national *language*—the collective spoken and written practices configuring the nation as a discourse community—was intimately public, political, and republican, oriented toward unification versus fragmentation. Through political discourse, citizens participated in their government: Tacitly consenting, individuals were transformed into a republic; dissenting, they could potentially transform the republic itself, reforming it into a new republic, as they had done with the American Revolution. Given this, rhetoric took on an especially important role in the young republic. Sharing a rhetoric—sharing a way of knowing the world and a way of articulating it—helped to sustain the body politic and prevent its division. The shared rhetoric of the founding fathers, like their frames of knowledge, rested on principally masculine, neoclassical rhetorical roots and helped to preserve a known political order of social rank.[3] Indeed, as Robert Connors explains, prior to 1830, the study of rhetoric itself was agonistic—athletic, combative, and oral—and it was largely limited to educated white males. Those who could not and did not participate in the highly rhetorical and political life of the early nation were not, at base, considered citizens.[4] Like the body politic it supported, a masculine neoclassical rhetorical tradition was clearly unavailable to those who were educationally disadvantaged—women, Indians, slaves, and children.

In 1830, as women began collectively using national political discourse by petitioning with men against Indian removal and slavery, this shared rhetoric and known political order were shaken. By the 1830s and beyond, Kenneth Cmiel explains, as the middle class grew and gained political entrée and as styles of speaking and writing were increasingly leveled, traditional ways of knowing and speaking were challenged. The rhetorical world of the 1820s and 1830s sat on the cusp of Revolutionary America's neoclassical rhetorical roots and the mid-19th-century development of "middling" rhetorical styles that mixed refined and raw language, that witnessed a wider range of speakers on the public podium, and that flattened deferential forms, in turn creating a backlash of anxiety about standards of decorum in a democratic culture (Cmiel 55–56). As well, as some have argued, after 1830, because of cultural changes such as coeducation in college classrooms, the study of rhetoric itself began to shift to an increasingly *irenic* model—more developmental and inclusive of both men and women—a shift possibly signaling larger changes in understandings of citizenship and of the nation as a discourse community.[5] For some, the increasing differentiation of rhetoric in 19th-century America, including the initial feminization of the agonistic marketplace, meant the decline of public debate. At the same time, the ever-widening access to national political discourse also held out the possibility of democratic transformation—of citizenship based on consent—a sometimes-worrisome possibility for those who had inherited the nation's more aristocratic reins.

Thus in 1830 when women together with men began petitioning against Indian removal and then against slavery, collectively accessing the masculinized world of national political discourse and dissenting from the social contract, many congressmen attempted to limit access to that once-unifying, now-unsettled political discourse. In collectively petitioning Congress on a national issue for the first time, women spoke for both themselves and others, called attention to the moral dimension of the nation's policies towards Indians and slaves, and hoped to effect change in national policy. At heart, women's petitions called into question ideas about national citizenship, particularly who had a "voice"—a "vote" symbolic or actual—in determining the course of the nation. In fact, the terms *petition, enfranchise,* and *suffrage* overlap in significant ways. While *enfranchise* means 'to endow with the rights of citizenship, especially the right to vote,' the word *suffrage* both denotes 'the right or privilege of voting, the franchise' and means 'a short intercessory prayer' (*OED*, 2nd ed.). As we will see, this was exactly what women's *petitions* on behalf of Native Americans Indians and slaves were: short intercessory prayers, but to political ends that initiated, if not symbolically enacted, women's enfranchisement. Alisse Portnoy thus illustrates that the complex context of the 1830s and the antiremoval petitioning campaign, rather than the 1840s, was the genesis stage of women's rights (*Their Right* 6).[6]

This chapter suggests that women's antiremoval and antislavery petitions and congressional responses to them comprise a foundational national language debate and an important, if not originary, historical moment for national gendered commentary about language. This period's journals, literature, and congressional debates about petitioning illustrate the process by which gender was inserted into notions of proper language to support ascriptive ideas about national citizenship—in this case, about who has the right to speak as a citizen on topics of national importance such as Indian removal or slavery.

At the nexus of politics, rhetorics, and ethics, literature of the period represents this process imaginatively, recasting the nation's past and its present in narrative and illuminating the form and context of gendered language debates that we cannot glean from histories of these debates alone. As I will show, when read in the context of attitudes about women and language reflected in periodicals such as *The North American Review,* women's petitions, and congressional debates on the right to petition, Sedgwick's *Hope Leslie* pre-figures how gendered language ideologies emerged in debates about national identity and race in Jacksonian America. *Hope Leslie* particularly imagines a form for women's political discourse—the petition—as well as responses to women's petitions, and thus participates discursively in white women's unprecedented petitioning campaigns against Indian removal and slavery. Moreover, Sedgwick's novel reveals the ways in which debates about petitions as women's access to political discourse could *themselves* subtly work to "remove" the "Indian Question" from the discussion and to silence, if temporarily, the congressional debate over slavery in the late 1830s, ultimately to redraw national boundaries cultural, political, and geographical.

2. THE "INDIAN QUESTION," THE "WOMAN QUESTION," AND PETITIONING AS NATIONAL POLITICAL DISCOURSE

In *Hope Leslie,* Sedgwick's Native American Indian heroine Magawisca tells a "new version of an old story" when she recounts her tribe's massacre by whites (53). "But here," Sedgwick writes of Magawisca's narration, "it was not merely changing sculptors to give the advantage to one or the other of the artist's subjects; but it was putting the chisel into the hands of truth, and giving it to whom it belonged" (53). Everell Fletcher, to whom Magawisca tells her story, "had heard this destruction of the original possessors of the soil described, as we find it in the history of the times," but the truthful hands of Magawisca "sculpt" for him "a very different picture," and a very persuasive one, "of those defenceless families of savages [. . .] exterminated, not by superior natural force, but by the adventitious circumstances of arms, skill, and knowledge" (53–54).

In this scene, Sedgwick explains Pequods' removal from Massachusetts. But she also calls attention to the formal, historical, rhetorical, and ultimately political dynamics circulating both in and around her novel; she points out the ways in which both history and fiction are forms of representation with ongoing rhetorical and political effects. In "putting the chisel into [Magawisca's] hands of truth," Sedgwick skillfully implements her novel's "design," to recast the traditional Puritan histories of William Bradford, John Winthrop, William Hubbard, and Benjamin Trumbull, among others, to illustrate "not the history, but the character of the times" (*Hope Leslie* 5), to portray the period not as a record of events, but as the moral and mental qualities attributed to the age. Indeed, in her novel's first pages, Sedgwick subtly calls attention to the politics of representing the past, to the ways in which "genuine" histories about Puritans and Indians are perhaps unavoidably constructed from the conquerors' point of view, a perspective of which her readers, or more "impartial observers," should be aware:

> These traits of their [the Indians of North America] character will be viewed by an impartial observer, in a light very different from that in which they were regarded by our ancestors. In our histories, it was perhaps natural that they should be represented as 'surly dogs,' who preferred to die rather than live, from no other motives than a stupid or malignant obstinacy. Their own historians or poets, if they had such, would as naturally, and with more justice, have extolled their high-souled courage and patriotism. (6)

Sedgwick notes here how any history, even "genuine history"—a term held out as a perhaps unachievable ideal—is a representation of events from the historian's point of view.[7]

Further, in counterposing her historical fiction to "genuine history," Sedgwick claims for *Hope Leslie* an almost non-historical space still rooted in historical events, thereby claiming a kind of timeless persuasive power for fiction in the present:

> These volumes are so far from being intended as a substitute for genuine history, that the ambition of the writer would be fully gratified if, by this work, any of our young countrymen should be stimulated to investigate the early history of their native land. (6)

That is, Sedgwick seems to say, fiction works imaginatively across what we understand as historical periods. As depicted by her sculpture metaphor, writing fiction is a creative, multi-dimensional artistic act in which the writer molds the past potentially more powerfully than "genuine history." Providing an aesthetic experience for her "young countrymen," Sedgwick's fiction possesses the persuasive power to "stimulate" readers across time, not only "to investigate the early history of their native land" but also to respond in perhaps unforeseeable ways (6). In other words, Sedgwick's historical fiction might reconstruct the past by "putting the chisel" into new hands, but it has reverberating rhetorical effects, simultaneously constructing and impacting the present, not only to re-make history, but also, perhaps, to help make history happen. Placing the subjugation of the Indians in the 17th century and couching Pequod-Puritan relations in a romance plot, Sedgwick makes a rhetorically and politically savvy move for her early-19th-century readers: By historically distancing and romanticizing these still controversial dynamics, she renders the 1820s-30s contentious debates over Indian removal less morally confrontational for her readers in their own historical moment.[8]

Nevertheless, as much as kindling interest in the nation's past from an unconventional perspective, the novel raises issues of Sedgwick's contemporary moment from an alternative standpoint. Karen Woods Weierman authoritatively describes how *Hope Leslie* registers Sedgwick's experience of three major Indian removals: the 1637 Pequot War; the 18th-century removal of Indians from Stockbridge, Massachusetts, in which her own family played a part; and the 19th-century Cherokee Indian removal, nationally debated as Sedgwick was writing *Hope Leslie*. As Woods Weierman's study begins to suggest, criticism on *Hope Leslie* has overlooked the way in which Sedgwick's novelistic commentary on Indian removal looks both backward and forward. In particular, Sedgwick calls attention in *Hope Leslie* to the fate of the Indians in Jacksonian America—the "Indian Question." As well, by keenly focusing on creating a form for women's political voices on this political topic, Sedgwick's novel calls attention to another significant concern of this era—the "Woman Question." And, through its repetitions of its heroines' petitions for justice, it takes up yet another timely political issue—the issue of petitioning. This section will survey these contexts—the Indian Question, the Woman Question, and petitioning—contexts with which, as the next section will demonstrate, *Hope Leslie* engages as surely as it does the Puritan histories treated in Sedgwick's Preface.

When women began petitioning against Jacksonian Indian removal in 1830, they entered a national political debate about the "Indian Question"—an appellation signifying an ongoing topic surrounding Indian-white relations in America and expressing itself in the late 1820s and 1830s primarily in the debate over Cherokee removal from Georgia. Although the Indian Question, of course, had been at issue long before, Indian removal was intensely debated in public at least from the mid-1820s, when Georgia began making claims to Indian Territory within the state, to 1838, when Cherokee Removal officially began. In the mid-1820s, the state of Georgia requested that the federal government move the Indians out of the state, despite the Indian Trade and Intercourse Act (1802), which had given the federal government jurisdiction in Indian Territory (Zinn 132). Desiring Indian land, the state of Georgia actively harassed the Cherokees through stringent laws that only intensified when gold was found on Indian lands in 1829. In the face of this harassment, the federal government essentially relinquished its jurisdiction over Indian-state relations and refused to provide protection for the Indians. This approach of wielding power by disclaiming power became policy when Andrew Jackson was elected president in 1828.[9]

In response, opponents of removal led by Jeremiah Evarts, corresponding secretary of the American Board of Commissioners for Foreign Missions (ABCFM), organized an antiremoval campaign in which, as we will later see, women became key participants. Evarts published a series of influential essays protesting Jacksonian Indian removal policies under the pen name William Penn, first published in the Washington newspaper the *National Intelligencer,* reprinted in newspapers throughout the country, and circulated as pamphlets in Boston in 1829 and Philadelphia in 1830.[10] Yet, despite the widespread protests pouring into Congress between January and May 1830, on May 28, 1830, Congress passed the Indian Removal Act, authorizing the federal government to exchange lands west of the Mississippi for land held by Indians living east of the great river and setting off a chain of treaty violations with the Indians.[11]

Of the debates surrounding the Indian Question, Sedgwick herself would have been aware. Although Sedgwick appears to have said little about either Indian removal or the campaign against it in her personal papers, Sedgwick's letters demonstrate that she considered it a family responsibility to keep up on national affairs; when her father Theodore, speaker of the House of Representatives under George Washington's presidency, was away from home, she wrote to him of local politics (Garvey 289; Sedgwick *Life and Letters* 80).[12] Sedgwick was well-read and well-informed, recommending to her father *Walsh's Review* for "the high integrity of its political principles" and *The Edinborough Review,* a model for *The North American Review,* for its value as a "literary journal" (*Life and Letters* 86). National affairs, including congressional debates over timely and controversial topics such as the national bank and Indian removal, were circulated widely in periodicals such as *The North American Review* and *Niles'*

Weekly Register, which published summaries of congressional debates and proceedings.[13]

Sedgwick would also have been aware of the "Woman Question"—the public debate over women's proper sphere discussed in journals of the time. As women increasingly entered the "public" and "masculine" sphere, the national discussion of "woman's sphere" became increasingly heated. In recent years the notion of such "separate [gendered] spheres" has been rightly attacked as "too crude an instrument–too rigid and totalizing," as a construct that can simply reinforce binary thinking about gender rather than aid us in understanding it as one of many subject positions taken up within relations of power (Davidson 445).[14] Yet the problem with the "separate spheres" trope may be predominantly a problem of identifying exactly what was "separate" and what was not. In the early 19th century, the domestic sphere (with its attendant roles of wife and mother) was women's socially sanctioned area of activity; the legal sphere remained decidedly off-limits to women; and the political sphere, while largely inaccessible to women, was becoming slightly more hazily so. Early 19th-century women clearly had some impact on the course of the nation's politics, for example through their increasingly public roles in benevolent societies and church organizations, but there were legal restrictions to their political activity, separating them from their male counterparts: They could not serve on juries, hold office, practice law, hold separate property; and, of course, they could not vote.[15] Women were beginning to make public speeches, but they could not make these speeches, especially on political topics, without censure.[16] That is, while the Republican Mother brought women a measure of access to republican virtue, the republican citizen was still figured as male—and a male orator.

The cordoning-off of legal issues and political rhetoric for white men was reinforced through gendered discussions of language in some of the most prestigious and influential journals of the time. In fact, what appears in a survey of articles and reviews from *The North American Review* and *The Democratic Review* from the late 1820s to late 1830s is clear praise for women's "quiet," domestic language, written or spoken, and an equally strong condemnation of their "noisy" political discourse. As James Fenimore Cooper put it, women were understood to be the "natural agents" responsible for "maintaining the [linguistic] refinement of a people" (*American Democrat* 154). Exemplifying the contradictory attitudes about women and language over the decade that this chapter examines, Cooper's characterization of the speech of American women becomes increasingly negative from his *Notions of the Americans* (1828) to *The American Democrat* (1838)—the same decade over which women's petitions to Congress steadily increased. For example, in *Notions of the Americans,* Cooper affirmed "the voices of the American females," whose "soft and silvery tones" "softened" the "harsh" edge of the English language as it was heard in Europe (367–68). Yet in *The American Democrat* (1838), he criticized American women's "utterance" as decidedly "less agreeable" than men's, a "defect" that must be remedied because of women's influential role in the nation's nurseries, "the birth-place of so many of our habits" (146–47).[17] Through gendered commentary about language much like Cooper's—whether applause or censure—antebellum pundits anxiously asserted "woman's place," such that the borders through which Americans attempted to clarify and define appropriate "spheres" of activity for women were regulated, in part, through commentary about women's linguistic behavior, ultimately also working to maintain the borders not only between "domestic" and "political" but also, to borrow Amy Kaplan's construction, between the "domestic" and the "foreign." From the late 1820s to late 1830s, characterizations of women and language, perhaps not surprisingly, increasingly aligned acceptable women's language with domestic duties and unacceptable women's language with political action.

These characterizations, confining women's positive national linguistic influence within their roles as wives and mothers and allying women's use of language to ideologies of republican motherhood, can be seen in articles addressing the Woman Question and in reviews of women writers like Sedgwick and Lydia Maria Child in periodicals like *The North American Review* and *The Democratic Review*. For example, in April 1825, Chief Justice John Marshall, in a letter to *The North American Review,* expressed his views on "the influence of the female character on society" in the context of female education (444). Marshall writes:

> I have always believed, that national character, as well as happiness, depends more on the female part of society than is generally imagined. Precepts from the lips of a beloved mother, inculcated in the amiable, graceful, and affectionate manner, which belongs to the parent and the sex, sink deep in the heart, and make an impression which is seldom entirely effaced. These impressions have an influence on character, which may contribute greatly to the happiness or misery, the eminence or insignificancy, of the individual. (445)

For Marshall, the speech of the "female part of society" positively affects "national character." Yet at the same time, such speech finally equates to the "precepts from the lips of a beloved mother." Praiseworthy American women's speech, in Marshall's view, is confined to mothers' speech—"amiable, graceful, and affectionate."

Similarly, in the April 1828 issue of *The North American Review* mentioned at the beginning of this chapter, reviewers of Sedgwick's *Hope Leslie* concentrate approximately half of the article discussing women and written language. As they put it, "the female influence in literature" remains a positive influence, but largely because of its "meliorating" touch—the grounds for the editors' praise for *Hope Leslie* (411–20). On the other hand, for "authoresses" unlike Sedgwick, who create less desirable effects in their writing, it is a different story. "Female literature," *The North American Review* asserts, is to be celebrated only as long as it remains peculiarly "female":

> That some females seem to have forgotten their sex, and to have prided themselves on throwing off their peculiar qualities, and adopting the coarser habits of men, in their literary performances, is true. But such cases are happily, and as we think, necessarily rare. The masquerade is out of nature, and gives no pleasure to those whose approbation is valuable. It is like the occasional adoption of masculine attire by heroines of the stage. All may not be disgusted with the metamorphosed individual, but certainly none can respect, and few can approve. (410)

Even for the editors of *The North American Review*—which, relative to its peer periodicals, was generally broad-minded and sympathetic to women—it is difficult to imagine women, or women's use of language, as not derivative of their sex, that is, outside the domestic sphere and its accompanying roles of wife and mother. When they do imagine "female literature" outside this sphere, it is imagined as theatrical and unnatural, disgusting and unrespectable. As Karen Halttunen has shown, such "masquerades" were widely condemned in an age that feared the hypocrisy of manipulative confidence men and painted women as destabilizing figures in American society. Such a "literary performance" of "the coarser habits of men" by women writers is considered false to their essential identity; women who adopt the "coarser habits of men" in their writing blur gender categories through artifice.

Thus in further reviews of Sedgwick's and Child's works, the editors of *The North American Review* and *The Democratic Review* praise these women's "domestic" literary language and condemn their "political" language. In reviewing the "Works of Mrs. Child" (1833), *The North American Review* applauds Child's *The Frugal Housewife* (1829), a compendium of domestic advice, more highly than any of her other works, calling it: "a more revolutionary book than any other that Mrs. Child has written,— more so even than the Rebels; for the revolution with which this busies itself, extends all over our houses. It operates like a health committee, or a committee of vigilance. [. . .] We like this. It is refreshing, once in a while, to see people really giving their money for what is useful, and letting a poor novel sink out of the market [. . .]" (142–43). The "usefulness" of Child's writing derives from its association with women's household preservation of "health" and discipline.[18] What is perhaps most interesting here is the choice of the term "revolutionary"—diction that positively aligns "revolutionary" language for women with the *status quo* and effectively disciplines women's use of political discourse. The laudable and "revolutionary" aspects of Child's writing thus come out of its association with domesticity—a rhetorical containment of women's linguistic efficacy under the household roof, following ideologies of republican motherhood.

When Child addresses the very political issue of slavery, *The North American Review* changes its tone. A July 1835 article entitled "Slavery," in part reviewing Child's *An Appeal in Favor of that Class of Americans called Africans,* begins: "We have placed the above title of a book by Mrs. Child, at the head of this article in order to express our regret that a writer capable of being so agreeable, and at the same time so useful, should have departed from that line of authorship in which she has justly acquired a high reputation" ("Slavery" 170). The writers end by chastising Child, her "pen," and "pens like hers, which may be otherwise so agreeably and beneficially employed, diverted from their legitimate spheres of action, and employed in urging on a cause so dangerous to the Union, domestic peace, and civil liberty, as the immediate emancipation of the slaves at the South" (193). The article, then, is bookended by criticism that is rooted both in the subject of slavery and in the diversion of Child's written language from its "legitimate sphere of action" to a political and national issue—by writing on behalf of "that class of Americans called Africans." These bookends linguistically drive home the disciplinary point that it is acceptable, agreeable, "useful," and even beneficial for women to produce discourse pertinent to the domestic sphere, but not to the political sphere.[19]

When *The Democratic Review* came into circulation at the end of the decade as a comparatively conservative northern journal with an ardently nationalistic, successful combination of political commentary and literature, this view of women's language as appropriate only in the domestic sphere was apparently well-established.[20] An article broadly titled "American Women" (1839) largely assesses the works of Sedgwick in an uncanny repetition of *The North American Review*'s review of Child's writing a few years earlier. This review of Sedgwick's *Means and Ends*—a positive review of one woman's writing on the domestic scene—becomes the springboard for a proscription of women's participation in the political sphere. The editors assess *Means and Ends*—a "little volume" addressed to girls between ages ten and sixteen and aimed at "the formation of the character appropriate to the social and domestic relations of *the American Woman*"—and say it "pleases us best of all of Miss Sedgwick's writings" (127–28). Above all of works, this one is "so admirably adapted, in an unaffected and quiet way, to work so much and valuable good" towards "the proper training of the American wife and mother" and is most worthy of "preservation" (128). Moreover, just as Child's reviewers commended Child's domestic writings as "revolutionary," Sedgwick's reviewers applaud *Means and Ends* for "its thoroughly *American* and *Democratic*—words that we regard as altogether synonymous—character" (128). In the end, Sedgwick's "unaffected and quiet" domestic writing amounts to an assessment of Sedgwick herself, who pleases *The Democratic Review* because she discursively reinforces domesticity and "cautions her young friends from appearing as 'the bold assertors of their own rights, and the noisy proclaimers of their own powers;' and contents herself with advising them to qualify themselves by education, self-training, and habits of self-reliance, for the exercise of higher powers than women have yet possessed, in the full assurance that then they cannot and will not be long withheld from them" (136).

Indeed, *The Democratic Review* uses commentary on Sedgwick's writing as a springboard to address the Woman Question more broadly. The editors support expanded opportunities for women in "occupations of industry" (136–38). Yet, women are still barred from "political action": "Provided that a free equality of rights is extended through all classes of society, it is difficult to perceive the benefit to result from simply doubling the actual numbers of all the respective classes, so far as the political action of the society is concerned, by admitting to a participation in it by the female half, as well as the male" (138). The editors predict that women will soon no longer desire direct participation in government because oppression will soon be destroyed, and they "think, therefore, that those champions of the 'Rights of Women' who direct their efforts to the latter object, of obtaining the recognition of their right to an equal participation in public affairs, are sailing on a wrong tack" (139). Thus, they say, "In opposing ourselves to the idea of women being admitted to take an open part in the public affairs of society, we by no means wish to discountenance their taking an enlightened interest in them" (139). Both Child's and Sedgwick's use of literary language, like women's discourse more generally, is commended as long as it does not mean their direct access to political language—particularly, as this article evidences, as long as it does not mean women's participation in government or their access to the fundamental element of political speech, the vote.

For women who were interested in having a voice on the Indian Question, and later the Slavery Question, while seeking not to inflame the Woman Question, petitioning provided an answer. Petitioning represented a religiously-resonant form of political discourse particularly persuasive for women, a form that united the Judeo-Christian religious discourse of prayer with the secular Anglo-American discourse about the justified resistance to authority based on natural rights. Petitioning was, then, a discourse attempting to use moral dissent to reframe political consent. Petitioning had particular religious and historical importance for antebellum women writers and reformers, who, well-versed in Biblical and classical history, were familiar with women who had petitioned heroically on behalf of those less powerful. One of the earliest senses of the word *petition* is prayer or supplication: The Old Testament describes petitioning as an act resembling a prayer from an individual to God, and the New Testament reinforces this sense; likewise, in his *Compendious Dictionary* (1806), Noah Webster defines *petition* in its noun form as "a prayer, request, entreaty, article," and Charles Buck's *Theological Dictionary* (1818) defines *prayer* itself as "a request or petition for mercies."[21] From an antebellum theological perspective, the term *petition* was often understood as an intervention on behalf of others, which was precisely what women who petitioned against

Indian removal envisioned themselves doing. Frequently called *intercession,* a petition was a part of prayer including "a desire of deliverance from evil, and a request of good things to be bestowed [. . .] *not only for ourselves but for our fellow creatures also*" (Buck 383, my emphasis).

In one sense, then, political petitioning was like prayer, rooted in a private act—in the earliest Judeo-Christian tradition, based on a covenant between believers and their God. Antebellum women often drew upon Biblical history in their sense of petition as a paradoxically prayerful form of political intervention by heroic *women,* like the Old Testament's Queen Esther, to whom Mrs. Fletcher compares Magawisca early in *Hope Leslie* (32) and to whom there are numerous references in antebellum literature. Esther, a prime example of the heroic petitioning woman, petitioned on behalf of the Jewish people, who were threatened by plans for their annihilation, courageously saying, "Then I will go to the king, though it is against the law; and if I perish, I perish" (Esther 4:16 RSV).[22] From Esther's petition, her people were spared, and the king issued an edict granting them the right to assemble and to defend themselves against their enemies (Esther 8:11). Through its religious associations, petitioning thus provided a socially acceptable means of moving from a decidedly "private" stance to a more "public" voice, affirming the residually reciprocal relationship between the most powerless supplicant and her sovereign. Thus, on one level, women's use of petitioning to gain a voice on issues of national moment was seen as appropriate.[23]

Yet, although petitioning contained the echo of religious language and was a logical, acceptable route for women to take to express their beliefs, the act of petitioning by human beings to other human beings also contained an element of secularity. When those possessing less power petitioned those seeking to preserve their authority, petitioning became decidedly political, dealing with the negotiation of power and its material effects—as seen in the danger of death that Esther faces when she petitions the King without first being summoned. The act of petitioning operated in an identifiably political space: for Esther, at the royal throne; for Sedgwick's Hope Leslie and Magawisca, as we will see, before the Puritan magistrates; and for 1830s women petitioners, before the nation's legislative bodies. In addition, petitioning provoked political responses, and it bore political effects: in the Old Testament, the freeing of the Jews; in *Hope Leslie,* the removal of Magawisca; and, as I will discuss below, in the 1830s, extended debates over the right to petition that ultimately challenged its very meaning.

For early-19th-century Americans, petitioning represented the most basic access to national, political discourse, and the English history of petitioning was interwoven with "American" history. Offering a comprehensive history of Anglo-American petitioning, Norman B. Smith claims that, as an "ancient right," petitioning is "the cornerstone of the Anglo-American constitutional system" and "the likely source of the other expressive rights—

speech, press, and assembly. The development of petitioning is inextricably linked to the emergence of popular sovereignty" (1154). Initially, petitioning came about in response to political needs, became institutionalized, then became a fixed right (1155). By the time of the American Revolution, petitioning in England was popular, unpunished, and often successful. In England, as Pauline Maier explains, petitions gave subjects "a way of seeking redress of wrongs done under the authority of the King, whom they could not sue in the regular courts" (51).[24] In colonial America as well as England, the right to petition was a foundational expressive right, involving a kind of dialogic contract between the governed and their governors, entailing a hearing and a response. In 1641, the 100 laws resembling the Magna Carta in the Body of Liberties adopted by the Massachusetts Bay Colony Assembly gave individuals the right to voice their grievances and to have those grievances addressed in return. It was the primary responsibility of colonial assemblies to respond to a variety of petitioners' concerns; through petitions, a direct line was maintained between public and private governance, and there was no sharp division between inhabitants and their representatives in colonial assemblies.[25] The earliest petition laws thus presumed a kind of contractual use of political discourse between governed and governors, and they relieved some of the strain of restricted colonial suffrage by granting at least minimal access to political discourse, even to unfranchised individuals, which included women, felons, Indians, and in some cases, slaves. In addition, colonial petitions were the foundation for legislative, judicial, and executive action—they often called for legislative responses in tax policy, land distribution, monopoly grants, and trade and licensing privileges; brought about debt actions, estate distributions, divorce proceedings, and criminal cases; or asked for the enforcement of existing laws (S. Higginson 145–55; N. Smith 1171–73).

Historically, then, the right to petition was a foundational expressive right, involving a dialogic contract between the governed and their governors, entailing a hearing and a response. As Garry Wills suggests, it was the breakdown in colonial petitioning's representative, dialogic functions—the failure of redress for petitions regarding the Stamp and Molasses Acts—that sparked the American Revolution, grounding the creation of the United States in the act of collectively petitioning the British People, the British Parliament, and King George III (55–57, 63–64).[26] After the Revolutionary War, both state conventions and the framers of the Constitution guaranteed the right to petition as a separate and fundamental right, not substitutable but supporting other freedoms of expression, such as the right to assemble, as seen in the First Amendment's petition clause: "Congress shall make no law [. . .] abridging the freedom of speech, or of the press, or the right of the people peaceably to assemble, and to petition the Government for a redress of grievances" (U.S. Const., Bill of Rights, Art. I). In the first few decades of Congress, petitions dealing with contested election results, the National Bank, the expulsion of Cherokees from Georgia, land distribution, the abolition of dueling, the government in the territories, the Alien and Sedition Acts, and the slave trade were received, read aloud and dealt with (typically referred to committees) at the opening of each session (S. Higginson 157–58). Literally, petitioners' words were heard and responded to at the national level in the early decades of Congress. Eventually, escalating numbers of petitions and elastic constitutional language resulted in the dispute over whether the petition clause provided for the petitioner's right simply to voice grievances to Congress, or whether it also required that Congress receive and consider petitions in return. If dialogic as such, then the act of petitioning also signified democratic participation in government.[27]

Whether monologic or dialogic, at least up until the 1830s, the right to petition was a basic right to have a voice in national political affairs. As residually religious but also historically foundational, representative, and responsive, linking the governed to government, petitioning signified a link between language and the nation. With the right to petition discursively constituting the bond between individuals and the body politic, petitioning thus worked as dissent to remake consent. Helping to highlight the ways in which petitioning worked alongside notions of consent and dissent, Enlightenment social contract theories are worth considering here. Following John Locke's account of natural rights, the founding fathers envisioned the Constitution, in part, as the social contract among citizens who pledged allegiance not to a sovereign God or monarch, but to a sovereign people. Theoretically, individuals entered the social contract in order to preserve their natural freedoms (life, liberty, property) as much as possible, and only their consent, their promise and contract, made them members of the *civitas* (Locke 74, 77). Citizens entered Rousseau's social contract for the good of the individual but also for the good of the whole, through mutual consent resting partly on individual reason but also, emphatically, on "what is right for all of us" (Bellah 279).[28] By their tacit consent, then, individuals were transformed into a republic; so, whether motivated by the more liberal principles of Locke or the more republican principles of Rousseau, by individual interest or the good of the whole, the social contract rested on a notion of consent that was worked out through a concept of political language—a kind of rhetorical contract. Through political discourse and public oratory that both implicitly and explicitly created and sustained the social contract, citizens founded the civil state and participated in their government. If they dissented through political discourse, such as petitioning, they could make over their government and re-form the republic itself—thereby reframing consent.

Individual dissent—as we see with individual petitions to the government for redress of personal grievances—would get reabsorbed into the general will, again becoming part of the whole, perhaps as a new law or judicial action. Most of the petitions in America before the early 19th century were submitted by individuals pressing a private grievance. Yet what might happen when a *group* dissented from the social contract? Theoretically, through collective dissent—through the cooperative exercise of the expressive right of petition—citizens could dissent in a way distinctly unable to be reabsorbed by the general will. They could revolutionize the body politic, calling into question the "representative" nature of the nation and the transparency of the political language through which it was imagined. As R. W. Hoyle corroborates, while petitioning was at root conservative and operated within existing political structures, mass petitioning "was viewed with apprehension by government" (365).[29] When they collectively petitioned Congress on national issues beginning in 1830, women, men, and Indians themselves exercised political discourse and dissented in efforts to reverse national policies on removal and to remake the nation consensually.[30]

When *women* petitioned collectively, they were dissenting from the social contract by exercising political discourse that had largely only been used by white men. When women petitioned, they particularly tested and unsettled the rhetorical contract—the abstract national, political discourse that had rested on neoclassical ideals of gentlemanly speech and shared decorum, upholding the social contract and supporting the American nation. Moreover, their petitions, their dissent, also implied their *consent*. Their dissent, in other words, enacted their citizenship and their symbolic vote, and demanded recognition as such. Petitions, read aloud in Congress, affected the legislative and judicial processes. If women's petitions were given a hearing at the beginning of each congressional session (or, more specifically, on Mondays, the designated day for reading petitions in the 1830s), then they were plainly political: They would literally be heard on the "national" level, in the legislature where the national "voice," the national political discourse, was gendered male. Petitioning collectively on behalf of others for the first time, even if delicately declaring the "uniqueness" of their case in prayerful language and on gendered grounds, women were nonetheless demanding collective representation in national political affairs, almost asking to be considered *citizens*—not just in the sense of a inhabitant, but in the sense of an enfranchised resident who can vote and expect protection from the nation-state in the exercise of her rights. And if largely dialogic procedures of petitioning were followed—so that Congress responded—it meant that women's voices were not only heard in Congress, but that their influence extended there, possibly effecting widespread political change. If Congress were obligated to listen and to respond, it meant that women, and those for whom they presumed to speak, were participating in a political process heretofore raced white and gendered masculine. Such a possibility was unsettling because it drew attention, to borrow Sollors' paradigm again, to the conflict between the descent-based model of citizenship latent in the founding of the nation, and the consent-based model of citizenship held out as the nation's ideal.

While petitions *per se* were not always couched in humble rhetoric, antebellum women's antiremoval petitions initially adopted a supplicating stance and combined petitioning's religious and secular senses, joining notions of God-given rights with notions of political rights, and Biblical heroines with American heroes. The remainder of this chapter will explore how Sedgwick's *Hope Leslie* initiates in literary form the 1830s petitioning campaigns against Indian removal and slavery and sheds light on the dynamics surrounding them. In *Hope Leslie,* Sedgwick self-consciously casts the petition as a figure for a religio-political discourse of dissent, proposing a form for women's political speech that pushed the bounds of propriety in her day. Through the use of its Anglo-American and Indian heroines who repeatedly appeal for justice, the novel pre-figures white women's petitions on behalf of Indians and slaves, and it informs the responses to them and the debates surrounding them. *Hope Leslie* imagines exceptional, individual Indian and Anglo women characters petitioning, but it stops short of imagining collective activism for them. It thus took the actual historical events of 1830—Sedgwick's readers and the women's antiremoval petitioning campaign—to supply this collective action, to amplify the ethic and form of political discourse in the novel. While, through the use of petitions, both *Hope Leslie* and the petitioning campaigns reached for the possibility of a consensual model of citizenship, such a revision of American citizenship was finally unsustained and unsustainable in both the text and its context, as seen in the gendered commentary about language that congressmen ultimately used in response to petitioners. As we will see, such metalinguistic strategies culminated in the gag rule, which simultaneously denied expressive liberties and natural rights, maintained the *status quo,* and preserved, if temporarily, an expansionistic agenda for the nation.

3. PETITIONING IN *HOPE LESLIE*

> 'Thou art somewhat forward, maiden,' he said, 'in giving thy opinion; but thou must know, that we regard it but as the whistle of a bird; withdraw, and leave judgment to thy elders.' (Catharine Maria Sedgwick, *Hope Leslie* [1827] 109)

Such is the Puritan magistrate Mr. Pynchon's response to Hope Leslie, Sedgwick's defiant young Anglo-American heroine, when she speaks on behalf of Nelema, an elderly Indian woman charged with witchcraft in saving Hope's tutor's life from a rattlesnake bite. In this scene, which reverberates throughout *Hope Leslie,* Hope defends Nelema's innocence before the Puritan triumvirate on the principle that "It was better to mistake in blessing than in cursing" and that "truth companies not with cowardice" (*Hope Leslie* 109). The scene is narrated by Hope Leslie, in a letter she writes to her metaphorical brother Everell Fletcher in England. Here, Hope not only voices her opinion to Mr. Pynchon, who regards her as a "rash and lawless girl" (121), but also writes her own story from her own perspective, much as Sedgwick herself rewrites Puritan-Indian relations from her own revisionist perspective in this historical romance. Furthermore, Hope's point of view, like Magawisca's perspective before, is one that Sedgwick invests with truth, as heroines Hope and Magawisca both keep their promises. Hope Leslie's testimony on behalf of Nelema, and her plea for Nelema's just treatment, is indeed "forward," as well as compassionate, open, and generous, erring on the side of sympathy. Yet Pynchon, a representative of the Puritan governing body, dismisses Hope's plea for justice as merely a minor's "opinion," carrying the insignificant weight of a "whistle of a bird" on an issue better left to "thy elders," the Puritan patriarchy.

Pynchon's statement that Hope's opinion is like a mere "whistle of a bird," when placed alongside additional bird imagery in the novel, can be read as a kind of rhetorical attempt to dismiss or to contain Hope and her potentially subversive opinions, as his bird metaphor resonates with other avian figures throughout the narrative. For example, early in the novel, prior to the Indian raid on the Fletcher's peaceful home and Hope's arrival on the scene, domesticated birds are figured as "diligent little housewifes" who "ransacked forest and field for materials for their house-keeping" (61); midway through the story, Governor Winthrop figures Hope herself as a lawless, "wild bird" on whom he is "impatient to put jesses" (155); and later in the novel, Hope is finally the "decoy bird" unwittingly "caught in the net" of the designs of the Puritan leaders who expect to arrest an Indian conspiracy but instead arrest the innocent (235). As these figures together demonstrate, whistling young American "birds" like Hope Leslie are meant to be contained within the home. Yet these alternately domesticating, dismissive, and containing avian figures also attest to the need to render Hope's "whistle"—nevertheless a challenge to Puritan authority—powerless and harmless; Hope's "whistle," however "weak," is yet undomesticated and uncontained. It represents her bold and potentially disruptive use of political speech—speech on a political topic (the Indian Question) and in a political space (before the Puritan magistrates). Together with Magawisca's voice, Hope's "whistle" challenges the governing structure by speaking out on behalf of others in *Hope Leslie*.

Taking this scene as an emblematic one, we can see how *Hope Leslie* calls attention to the fate of Indians, yet focuses even more intensely on creating a forum for women's political voices. That is to say, the novel's central concerns are with giving women—Hope Leslie, Magawisca, and Sedgwick herself—a persuasive voice on the Indian Question. Sedgwick manifests these concerns particularly by engaging the religious-yet-political form and the sympathetic content of the *petition*. Indeed, Sedgwick repeats the word *petition* and synonyms for it—supplication, entreaty, appeal, and prayer—multiple times throughout *Hope Leslie,* and she underscores the importance of the concept of petitioning by accentuating her heroines' deferent physical stance in making petitions. The novel thus pivots around the vision of women's petitioning to revise patriarchal management of Puritan-Indian relations, just as Sedgwick's contemporaries would come to petition against Jacksonian policies.

Through its repetitions of Hope's and Magawisca's petitions for justice, *Hope Leslie* imagines women having increasing access to political discourse and ultimately holds out hope for women's collective transformation of the political sphere. Throughout the novel, as I will describe in more depth below, various characters, particularly Magawisca and Hope, are pictured in positions of supplication, "petitioning" those in authority for just treatment under exceptional circumstances. Magawisca petitions her father for the Fletchers' lives, especially Everell's; Hope petitions the Puritan triumvirate for Nelema's release from prison and later pleads with Governor Winthrop for Magawisca's release (and when the magistrates fail to respond to her pleas, Hope engineers Nelema's and Magawisca's respective escapes); and finally, in the novel's climactic court scene, Magawisca pleads for her own, and her nation's, liberty.[31] In each of these cases, *Hope Leslie* advances the notion of women petitioning to have a political voice on the Indian Question. Their petitions together challenge patriarchal authority, advocating a peaceful resolution to Indian-white animosities, and effectively hold out hope that, through women, the differences between nations might be transcended.[32]

Yet *Hope Leslie* also depicts the alternately dismissive and silencing responses with which Magawisca's and Hope's petitions were met, and it thereby foresees some of the tactics that Congress uses in the face of 1830s petitions. Hope's and Magawisca's petitions are devalued, rebuked, evaded, censured, or silenced, often by critiquing the language in which their requests are couched—by inserting concerns about gender into the consideration of these women's petitions and by reading the form of their petitions as content. Such responses effectively forge otherwise unlikely alliances between white men, in Sedgwick's novel and in debates over actual petitions, to remove both the Indian Question and the Woman Question from discussion. In its portrayal, then, of women's petitions *and* of their reception, both of which I will discuss in this section, *Hope Leslie* reveals how a debate over women's political discourse obscures deliberations over the fate of an Indian woman and her nation, "removing" the Indian Question from the discussion and finally ending the debate altogether.

Despite its role in antebellum American culture and in key scenes throughout *Hope Leslie,* the subject of petitioning in Sedgwick's fiction and in 19th-century American literature has received little scholarly consideration. Based on available evidence at the National Archives, it does not appear that Sedgwick herself signed an antiremoval petition.[33] However, for Sedgwick, the possibility of the petition as a form for women's political intervention was in fact pertinent not only in the 1600s—the period in which she imagined *Hope Leslie's* protagonists petitioning Indian and Puritan authorities for others' liberties against the backdrop of the English Civil War, in which both men and women had petitioned.[34] The possibility of the petition had significance as well in Sedgwick's family history and personal life: The Stockbridge Indians had repeatedly petitioned the General Court against the seizing of their land by, among others, Sedgwick's own ancestors, particularly her great-uncle.[35] More immediately central to Sedgwick's imagination of petitioning would have been the case of her beloved childhood nurse, Elizabeth Freeman, affectionately called Mammy Bet, Mum-Bett, or Mumbet. In 1781, with the help of Catharine's father Theodore Sedgwick—prominent Berkshire lawyer, U.S. Senator, and Speaker of the House of Representatives under George Washington's presidency—Freeman appealed for and gained her freedom, an event that Catharine celebrated in "Slavery in New England" (1853) and that her brother Henry Dwight Sedgwick recounted in *The Practicability of the Abolition of Slavery: A Lecture Delivered at the Lyceum in Stockbridge, Massachusetts, February 1831.*[36]

As seen in Sedgwick's depiction of Elizabeth Freeman's post-Revolutionary appeal for freedom in "Slavery in New England," Sedgwick was interested in mirroring the nation's founders' revolutionary political action in individuals' petitions for liberty. Sedgwick explicitly links Freeman's attainment of freedom with that of the founding fathers:

> It was soon after the close of the revolutionary war that she [Freeman] chanced at the village 'meeting house' in Sheffield, to hear the Declaration of Independence read. She went the next day to the office of Mr. Theodore Sedgewick, then in the beginning of his honourable political and legal career. 'Sir,' said she, 'I heard that paper read yesterday, that says, 'all men are born equal, and that every man has a right to freedom. I am not a dumb *critter;* won't the law give me my freedom?' I can imagine her upright form, as she stood dilating with her fresh hope based on the declaration of an intrinsic, inalienable right. Such a resolve as hers is like God's messengers—wind, snow, and hail—irresistible. (Sedgwick, "Slavery in New England" 421)

This passage draws direct parallels between the colonists' Declaration of Independence and "Mumbet's" individual application for freedom. In *Hope Leslie,* Sedgwick explores a range of just such individual petitions, by both male and female protagonists, that likewise have natural rights arguments at their core, and she makes the petitions of her female characters central to the novel, demonstrating how women could use the petition to intervene politically alongside their male counterparts' slightly less humble interpositions. While an individual appeal like Freeman's is distinct from a joint petition on behalf of a group, women's collective petitions on behalf of others were indeed, as we will see, realized in Sedgwick's lifetime, magnifying and making explicit, collective written use of the supplicating rhetorical stance that Sedgwick imaginatively engages through the individual, spoken petitions of *Hope Leslie's* female protagonists.

The most heroic act of *Hope Leslie* begins with Magawisca's petitions to her father, Pequod chief Mononotto—petitions through which Magawisca seeks a political voice and challenges the patriarchal handling of Puritan-Pequod relations. Early in the novel, Magawisca begs Mononotto not to kill Mrs. Fletcher and her white children in a raid on the Fletcher home, which Sedgwick frames as provoked by whites. Sedgwick links the deferent postures and powerful pleas for mercy which supply the form and content of women's petitioning when she describes Magawisca as "sinking down at her father's feet and clasping her hands" and begging Mononotto to save the Fletchers, in a kneeling posture that submissively disguises the radical content of her grammatical imperative to "save them—save them" (*Hope Leslie* 63). Sedgwick emphasizes how Magawisca's stance is an utter formality, a "token" with its own signifying power: "Magawisca must feel, or feign submission; and she laid her hand on her heart, and bowed her head, in token of obedience" (75). Yet Mononotto, a Pequod chief whose once-pacific nature "had been changed by the wrongs he received" (56), rejects his daughter's prayers on behalf of the Fletchers. Mononotto spares only Hope's sister, Faith Leslie, and her adoptive brother, Everell Fletcher, who is to be sacrificed in retribution for Magawisca's brother's death at the hands of the colonists. Magawisca repeats the posture of petitioning when she "clasped her hands in mute and agonizing supplication," offering another "silent entreaty" on behalf of Everell's life (84). But even this does not sway Mononotto, who says in response, "think you, that now this boy is given into my hands to avenge thy brother, I will spare him for thy prayer? No—though thou lookest on me with thy mother's eye and speakest with her voice, I will not break my vow" (84). Magawisca again "threw herself on her knees [. . .] entreated [. . .] wept—but in vain [. . .] again she appealed to her determined keeper, and again he denied her *petition* [. . .]" (91, my emphasis). Only after she has gone through the "formality" of petitioning multiple times does Magawisca escape from her guard to rescue Everell on the sacrifice rock—a heroic and physical intervention appropriate to the moment only because her previous efforts have failed. When Mononotto is just about to kill Everell on the sacrifice-rock at the Housatonick River, Magawisca resorts to action; she springs from the high side of the rock and "interposes" her body between the chief and the victim, saving Everell, but losing her own arm (93). Magawisca's action here decidedly resonates with the heroic intervention of Sedgwick's beloved Elizabeth Freeman, who had, in Sedgwick's words in "Slavery in New England," "interposed" her own arm between her slave mistress's "large iron shovel red hot from clearing the oven" and her innocent "sister in servitude," Lizzy ("Slavery" 418).[37]

Over the course of *Hope Leslie,* women from both Anglo and Indian "nations" heroically speak and often act for justice, as Magawisca does, thus undermining the patriarchal notion of divided nations with an equal commitment to justice—or, as Sedgwick puts it, to the "rights of innocence"—and effectively suggesting that, through women, the differences between nations can be bridged. After Magawisca has been imprisoned on charges of conspiracy against the Puritans, Hope's petitions on her behalf echo Hope's earlier testimony on behalf of Nelema, with which this section begins. Hope's petition on behalf of Magawisca follows a discussion with the Winthrop family, in which she claims an independent voice to speak out against the intrusion in her affairs by the imposter Sir Philip Gardiner, who is, at this point, a character associated with and trusted by the Puritan patriarchy, since his impostures have not yet been discovered. Hope says, "I was persecuted by Sir Philip Gardiner, whose ungentlemanly interference in my concerns, will, I trust, relieve me from his society in the future," adding, "Sir Philip strangely mistakes me [. . .] if he thinks anything could console me for apparently betraying one who trusted me [Magawisca] to sorrowful, fearful imprisonment" (270). Here, Hope claims for herself the right to speak out, despite Governor Winthrop's interruption that "our friend, Sir Philip, hath deserved your thanks rather than your censure" (270). After speaking for herself, Hope then, "clasping her hands with earnest supplication," petitions Governor Winthrop for "our poor Indian friend" (273). Exemplifying several aspects of women's petitioning, Hope's petition is worth quoting at length:

> When the door was closed, and he had seated himself, and placed a large arm-chair for her, all the tranquility which she had just before so well sustained, forsook her; she sunk, trembling, on her knees, and was compelled to rest her forehead on the Governor's knee: he laid his hand kindly on her head, "what does this mean?" he asked; "I like not, and it is not fitting, that any one should kneel in my house, but for a holy purpose,—rise, Hope Leslie, and explain yourself—rise, my child," he added in a softened tone, for his heart was touched with her distress; "tyrants are knelt to—and I trust I am none."
>
> "No, indeed, you are not," she replied, rising and clasping her hands with earnest supplication; "and therefore, I hope—nay, I believe, you will grant my petition for our poor Indian friend."
>
> [. . .]
>
> "Well, what would you have, young lady?" asked the Governor, in a quiet manner, that damped our heroine's hopes, though it did not abate her ardour.
>
> "I would have your warrant, sir," she replied boldly, "for her release; her free passage to her poor old father, if indeed he lives."
>
> "You speak unadvisedly, Miss Leslie. I am no king; and I trust the Lord will never send one in wrath on his chosen people of the new

world, as he did on those of old. No, in truth, I am no king. I have but one voice in the commonwealth, and I cannot grant pardons at pleasure; and besides, on what do you found your plea?"

"On what?" exclaimed Hope. "On her merits, and rights."

"Methinks, my young friend, you have lost right suddenly that humble tone, that but now in the parlour graced you so well. I trusted that your light afflictions, and short sickness, had tended to the edification of your spirit."

"I spoke then of myself and humility became me; but surely you will permit me to speak courageously of the noble Magawisca."

"There is some touch of reason in thy speech, Hope Leslie," replied the Governor, his lips almost relaxing to a smile. (273–74)

Hope's "petition for our poor Indian friend" clearly draws on a religiously-resonant posture (Hope "sunk, trembling, on her knees," and "clasp[ed] her hands with earnest supplication" in a stance that Winthrop himself aligns with "holy purpose") and is thus an effective way for her, as a young woman in a patriarchal, hierarchical culture, to gain a hearing for her request to her superior (he "laid his hand kindly on her head [. . .] for his heart was touched with her distress"). The petition, Sedgwick suggests, creates the possibility that the patriarchal authority just may "relax his lips to a smile," so that this particular form of "open intercession" must be exhausted before pursuing other forms of political expression. This "possibility of a smile" comes partly because the petition works conservatively within the power structure to attempt change. As we see in Hope's petition to Winthrop, petitioning's posture of genuflection physically recognizes the power differential between Hope and Winthrop, lending the form of humility to the natural-rights content of her request on behalf of Magawisca—a form especially appropriate for Hope to gain an audience on an issue of "national" moment. Hope's "holy" posture of genuflection helps to temper her politically far-reaching request by deflecting attention away from the petitioner to the authority figure, such that when Hope kneels, her posture leads Winthrop to respond to his own position of authority ("tyrants are knelt to—and I trust I am none"). Indeed, this *genuflected* posture calls attention to the *deflected* form of petitioning; sharing the same root (flectĕre 'to bend'), *deflection* signifies a turning aside, change in direction of, or deviation from a straight course (*OED*, 2nd ed.). This form is strategic—in Sedgwick's words, Hope's "graceful humility enabled her to start with her story from vantage ground" (270). Sedgwick includes Hope's petition—even lingers upon it—to explore the potential of the petition as a still-deferential form for interposing and effecting change.

Yet Winthrop's response to Hope's petition equally indicates the joint power play at work to subdue women's political discourse. The fact that Winthrop's rebuke ("Methinks, my young friend, that you have lost right suddenly that humble tone") immediately follows Hope's natural rights argument for Magawisca (grounding her plea in "her merits, and rights") reveals Winthrop's desire to diminish the political substance of the petition by deflecting it onto Hope's "tone." If Winthrop responds to Hope's petition to grant Magawisca personhood, based on Hope's egalitarian, natural rights argument for Magawisca's "merits, and rights," then Winthrop by extension grants Hope a voice in the commonwealth—a slippery slope for patriarchal authorities in that it implies that other young women, as well Indians, just may have a similar voice, an implication that Sedgwick draws to its fullest extent in Magawisca's trial scene, below. In the meantime, we see how Winthrop deflects the focus of discussion from these objectionable possibilities to the impudent and graceless "tone" of Hope's speech, a common strategy used in response to antiremoval and antislavery petitions. In turn, Hope employs her own rhetorical strategy, justifying her right to speak in the integrity of her intentions, and using Magawisca's captivity as a platform for her own purposes. Moving beyond a critique of Hope's "tone" by adding, "I am no king. I have but one voice in the commonwealth," Winthrop dismisses Hope's petition in a different way—he appeals to the legal structure to disavow his responsibility for Magawisca's case. To claim a lack of executive authority would become a familiar rhetorical strategy to early-19th-century readers, as Winthrop's response to Hope reverberated in policies under Jackson, who bypassed federal treaties and laws and instead supported states' rule over Indian nations in Georgia, Alabama, and Mississippi, paradoxically exerting power by disowning responsibility.[38]

Through Hope's alliances with the Indian women Nelema and Magawisca, then, *Hope Leslie* tells a story about one white woman's efforts to petition on behalf of Indian women, and Hope's own defense of her right to do so. Sedgwick also tells of Magawisca's speaking for her white "sisters," Hope and Faith. Yet *Hope Leslie* goes even further by giving Magawisca her own voice, allowing her self-representation within the Puritan legal system and revealing the possibilities and limits of an Indian woman's political speech. Near the end of *Hope Leslie,* Magawisca is tried for facilitating a long-promised reunion between Hope and her biological sister Faith, who was captured by the Pequods in the raid on the Fletcher home many years before. With the help of an egotistically-scheming Sir Philip Gardiner, the Puritan patriarchs have interpreted this reunion as Magawisca's aid in a conspiracy against the colonies. But at her trial, Magawisca's bold self-defense elicits the crowd's sympathy, generating a new political consensus and potentially destabilizing Puritan legal authority. In the courtroom, a skeptical Magawisca refuses to allow others to represent her case. Magawisca disregards Everell's instructions to "Say [. . .] that you are a stranger to our laws and usages, and demand some one to speak for you" (286).[39] Instead, Sedgwick writes, this is Magawisca's rather bold response:

Hope Leslie, Women's Petitions, and Political Discourse

> Magawisca bowed her head to both advisers, in token of acknowledgement of their interest, and then raising her eyes to her judges, she said,—"I am your prisoner, and ye may slay me, but I deny your right to judge me. My people have never passed under your yoke—not one of my race has ever acknowledged your authority" (286).

Magawisca goes on to petition on her own behalf in a scene that conveys and subsequently contains the threatening potential that women's petitions may lead not only to their own political voice but also to that of racial others.

While the novel's preceding petitions work within the power structure, Magawisca's courtroom petition for liberty is substantially different. While she "prays" to the magistrates for her freedom, she "prays" for such rights without acknowledging her place in the Puritan chain of authority. Moreover, her performance of a supplicating posture when her words deny such deference makes her act of petitioning one of pure form, unreflective of hierarchies of authority. In the dramatic courtroom moment:

> She paused—passed unresisted without the little railing that encompassed her, mounted the steps of the platform, and advancing to the feet of the Governor, threw back her mantle, and knelt before him. Her mutilated person, unveiled by this action, appealed to the senses of the spectators. Everell involuntarily closed his eyes, and uttered a cry of agony, lost indeed in the murmurs of the crowd. She spoke, and all again were as hushed as death. "Thou didst promise," she said, addressing herself to Governor Winthrop, "to my dying mother, thou didst promise, kindness to her children. In her name, I demand of thee death or liberty."
>
> Everell sprang forward, and clasping his hands exclaimed, "In the name of God, liberty!"
>
> The feeling was contagious, and every voice, save her judges, shouted "liberty!—liberty! grant the prisoner liberty!"
>
> The Governor rose, waved his hand to command silence, and would have spoken, but his voice failed him; his heart was touched with the general emotion, and he was fain to turn away to hide tears more becoming to the man, than the magistrate. (293)

Preceded by identifiably forceful actions—she "passed unresisted," "mounted," "advanced," and "threw back her mantle"—Magawisca's petition is not a humble request couched in selfless religious language, but a political "demand" referencing her own nation. For Magawisca, then, the petition is an "unveiled" form refusing to cloak a radical request in the garb of humility on behalf of others and insisting on fulfillment of past promises. When Magawisca throws back her mantle in this petition, she unveils and cites the absent presence that is the corporeal marker of her interposition to save Everell's life. Even the audience's response echoes the scene two hundred pages earlier when "The voice of nature rose from every heart, and responding to the justice of Magawisca's claim, bade [Everell] 'God speed!'" (93). For, Magawisca's revolutionary plea for herself, like the speech of the most practiced Revolutionary orator, provokes a "contagious" sympathy, "touching" even the Governor's heart, moving him to tears, rendering him speechless, and causing most of those who hear her to rally to her defense—and it forces a consensual re-negotiation of national identity to accommodate an Indian woman who holds "American" values. Sedgwick writes that Magawisca's words leave "in the breasts of a great majority of the audience, a strange contrariety of opinion and feelings. Their reason, guided by the best lights they possessed, deciding against her—the voice of nature crying out for her" (294). Here allying sympathy with a kind of "true" voice, "the voice of nature," Sedgwick makes a natural rights argument for Magawisca that she casts in "strange contrariety" to the Puritan "rational" legal system.[40] Magawisca's cry of "death or liberty," validated by the very political rhetoric of Patrick Henry, but rooted in a maternal promise and directed against the Puritan forefathers, destabilizes the white, patriarchal authority of the courtroom.[41] In the end, the American "nation" does not have room for Magawisca—she is removed. But in the interim, Sedgwick envisions the possibility for her inclusion. In addition, Sedgwick reveals *how* Magawisca becomes excluded, through the silencing of the courtroom debate.

Indeed, in this scene, Sedgwick imagines the limitations to women's antiremoval and antislavery petitions by portraying the strategies by which Magawisca and her champions are silenced in the courtroom. Allying readers' sympathies with honest Hope and noble Magawisca, Sedgwick depicts the responses of their antagonists, like the odious imposter Sir Philip Gardiner, who fear the extreme democratization of the "nation" inherent in Magawisca's insistence on speaking for herself in the courtroom. When John Eliot defends Magawisca, converting "a prayer into an *ex parte* statement of the case" (284)—a phrase that calls attention to the interarticulation of religious and political discourse—Sir Philip's reactive and self-interested strategy to protect "his own interest" foreshadows strategies of 1830s congressmen to silence women petitioners. He works "to inflame the prejudices of Magawisca's judges, and by anticipation to discredit her testimony" (285) by playing on the stereotypes and fears of the people, in particular, "the notion that the Indians were the children of the devil [. . .] and the belief in a familiar intercourse with evil spirits" (286). Gardiner fabricates lies about Magawisca's "diabolical writhings" at the burial ground on the night of her meeting with Hope (286). When Magawisca finally does have the opportunity to speak for herself and her people, she appeals to truth, with dignity and calm (287), and proposes that Sir Philip swear on the telltale crucifix that he had dropped in her prison cell, the symbol of his religious belief that threatens to unravel his "true" identity as a Romish worshipper: "'This crucifix,' she said, 'thou didst drop in my prison. If, as thou saidst, it is a charmed figure, that hath power to keep thee in the straight path of truth, then press it to thy lips now, as thou didst then, and take back the false words thou hast spoken against me'" (289). When confronted with Magawisca's evidence that will betray him as both a fraud and a religious outsider to the Puritan magistrates, Gardiner responds by feigning ignorance, charging Magawisca with insulting him with her "uttered malignities," and calling upon the court to silence her:

> "I know not [what this woman means]; but I should marvel if this heathen savage were permitted, with impunity, to insult me in your open court. I call upon the honourable magistrates and deputies," he continued, with a more assured air, "to impose silence on this woman, lest her uttered malignities should, in the minds of the good people here assembled, bring scandal upon one [himself] whose humble claims to fellowship with you, you have yourselves sanctioned." (289)

In this scene, we see reactions similar to the congressional responses we will see to women petitioners who were likewise accused of "minister[ing] to political malignity" (Benton 10:535). Here, Sir Philip aligns himself with "the honorable magistrates" against "this woman" whose "uttered malignities," he claims, may scandalize them all. Again, as in Winthrop's response to Hope, the focus is shifted from the matter at hand—Sir Philip's identity and credibility—to Magawisca's "insulting" speech, identity, and, finally, *her* credibility. Magawisca is permitted to speak for the moment—as we have seen, she requests "death or liberty," and her powerful rhetoric elicits the crowd's sympathy and sets in motion a new consensus (293). But she is finally, effectively, silenced when, much as some congressmen will do, the "same gentleman who, throughout the trial, had been most forward to speak, [. . .] a man of metal to resist any fire," invokes a rhetoric of brotherhood and forges a white patriarchal alliance among Sir Philip and the magistrates by shouting: "Are ye all fools, and mad! [. . .] ye that are gathered here together, that like the men of old, ye shout 'great is Diana of the Ephesians! [. . .] I call upon you, my brethren [. . .] and most especially on you, Governor Winthrop, to put a sudden end to this confusion by the formal adjournment of our court" (293–94). Ultimately, the debate is ended. The court is adjourned. And Magawisca is removed from the courtroom and returned to jail.

As such, Sedgwick portrays how a deflection of the debate onto Magawisca's political speech—her "uttered malignities"—and ultimately onto her gendered and racialized status as a political rhetor, effectively shuts down the trial and suppresses discussion altogether. Sedgwick illustrates that, although women may speak out together, creating a web of transnational women's voices speaking for justice, their political language is unsustained and unsustainable within a racialized national patriarchal system, and it has varying effects for those who speak it, and for those for whom it is spoken.

Hope and Everell—those for whom Magawisca has petitioned—are not only saved, bodies intact, but are to be happily united in marriage. In contrast, Hope's petitions on behalf of Magawisca, and Magawisca's pleas for herself, are rendered ineffectual. Although Everell and Hope can resort to action, courageously rescuing Magawisca from jail in the face of the failure of the justice system, she, like her father and the rest of the Pequods, is finally removed from the land and from the text—"lost in the deep, *voiceless* obscurity of those unknown regions" (339, my emphasis).

Thus, as some have argued, *Hope Leslie* ends with a troubling focus on resolving gender relations more so than race relations. Moreover, *Hope Leslie* importantly depicts *how* this happens—how a concern with women's political discourse, and with its suppression, mediates the shift in focus, particularly in the court scene sketched above. To a greater and more provocative extent in *Hope Leslie* than in Child's *Hobomok* (1824) or Cooper's *The Wept of Wish-Ton-Wish* (1829), the novels to which *Hope Leslie* is most often compared, Sedgwick elucidates how Indian removal succeeds through gendered commentary about language, encapsulated in the responses to Hope's and Magawisca's petitions. Unlike Child's and Cooper's similarly sympathetic portraits of Indians, which engage some but not all of these concerns simultaneously, Sedgwick's historical romance ultimately shows how political discussions of women, language, and Indians work together to negotiate cultural and geographical boundaries—how concerns with women's political discourse could disfranchise not only women but also the Indians for whom they claimed to speak. Thus Sedgwick's setting is historically-oriented to the 17th-century, but her plot and themes are steeped in early-19th-century debates, while Child's and Cooper's plots and themes are well-steeped in 17th-century conflicts. Child and Cooper equally suggest pertinent reasons for the disappearance of Indians—for example, the failure of intermarriage and the outright violence of western expansion. But Sedgwick shows us the complex ways in which the governing body itself diverted discussion from the fate of Indians to the petitions on their behalf, petitions that envisioned a contractual political discourse or a symbolic vote and underwrote a consensual vision of citizenship. Such a diversion ultimately involved using debate about gendered political language to front national expansion both on and off the prairie.[42]

Sedgwick thus stands out in her depiction of women's petitioning as the highly politicized topic it was in Jacksonian America. Sedgwick registers the dynamics at play both in 1630, when the novel was set, and in 1830—when American women began an unprecedented petitioning campaign against Jacksonian Indian removal. While not depicting collective petitioning action for women, by dwelling upon the heroic, individual petitions of its female characters and by appealing to the sympathies of a wide-ranging group of readers, *Hope Leslie* may have helped to pave the way for predominantly white, middle-class Jacksonian women to expand the religiously-resonant but politically-geared rhetoric of the fictional petitions

Sedgwick had imagined in *Hope Leslie*. As her peers attested, Sedgwick's writing possessed the power of galvanizing the country's sympathies: In Lydia Sigourney's words, Sedgwick "moved her country's heart" with *Hope Leslie,* whose popularity Sigourney memorialized in the last stanza of her poem "The Stockbridge Bowl." Sigourney's tribute not only commemorates Sedgwick's reputation, but also documents the connection between her fiction and the women, like Sigourney, who read and may have been "moved" by her to speak on behalf of Indians and slaves.[43]

As women collectively entered deeply entrenched, race-charged debates about Indian removal and slavery, the meaning of petitioning was transformed alongside these racialized issues. The gag rules enacted between 1836 and 1844, as we will see in the next section, functioned to transform the right to petition to a mere right to complain, a right without its original political efficacy, a somewhat diluted right increasingly aligned with the "quiet" voice of the domestic sphere—a right that was indeed, to invoke Pynchon's words to Hope Leslie, "but as the whistle of a bird."

4. THE ANTIREMOVAL AND ANTISLAVERY PETITIONING CAMPAIGNS AND THE GAG RULE

Within three years after *Hope Leslie's* publication, Lydia Maria Child and Angelina Grimké had opposed Jacksonian Indian removal, and together with Catharine Beecher, Harriet Beecher Stowe, and other women of Hartford, Lydia Sigourney, who had apparently read Sedgwick's widely-acclaimed novel, had generated a host of women's antiremoval petitions to Congress. *Hope Leslie's* fictional petitions thus soon resounded in the supplicating rhetoric of women's actual, historical petitions.

On December 1, 1829, with Sigourney and other women of Hartford, Beecher outlined the plight of the southern Indians in an anonymous "Circular, Addressed to Benevolent Ladies of the U. States," printed on the first page of the December 25, 1829 *Christian Advocate and Journal and Zion's Herald,* a publication of the Methodist Episcopal Church.[44] Beecher appeals to women's moral position and calls directly for women's prompt, widespread petitions to Congress against Jacksonian removal. In its heavy reliance on the prayerful posture of the petition, the "Circular" echoes the form that *Hope Leslie* had imagined:

> Have not then the females of this country some duties devolving upon them in relation to this helpless race? [. . .] They have nothing to do with any struggle for power, nor any right to dictate the decisions of those that rule over them.—But they may *feel* for the distressed; they may stretch out the supplicating hand for them, and by their prayers strive to avert the calamities that are impending over them. It may be, that female petitioners can lawfully be heard, even by the highest rulers

of our land. Why may we not approach and supplicate that we and our dearest friends may be saved from the awful curses denounced on all who oppress the poor and needy, by Him whose anger is to be dreaded more than the wrath of man; who can "blast us with the breath of his nostrils" and scatter our hopes like chaff before the storm [sic.]. It may be this will be *forbidden* [sic.]; yet still we remember the Jewish princess [Esther] who, being sent to supplicate for a nation's life, was thus reproved for hesitating even when *death* stared her in the way: "If thou altogether hold thy peace at this time, then shall deliverance arise from another place; but thou and thy father's house shall be destroyed. And who knoweth whether thou art come to the kingdom for such a cause as this?" ("Circular, Addressed to Benevolent Ladies of the U. States," Beecher's emphasis)

Here, Beecher justifies women's intervention in the Indian Question as a sympathetically-motivated interposition on behalf of another "helpless race" versus women's own rights. Carefully negotiating women's position by emphasizing that they have no interest in the "struggle for power," nor the right to "dictate" political decisions themselves, Beecher claims that it is precisely women's extra-political position that grants them the right to intervene on behalf of others in this exceptional situation—as Beecher later emphasizes, to "*sway the empire of affection*"—or, as Sigourney put it in her poetic tribute to Sedgwick, to "move [the] country's heart" ("The Stockbridge Bowl" 201). By repeating the word *supplicate* three times within six sentences, Beecher highlights the humble stance of the petition as an appropriate form for women's intercession on behalf of the Indians—as we have seen, a deflected form of appeal. Invoking the inspirational Queen Esther, Beecher's words moreover have Biblical reverberations, couching a politically-fraught issue within a religious allusion and emphasizing the element of divine intervention in women's involvement. Yet Beecher's heightened attention to the religious roots of women's petitions and her apparent anxiety over their "lawfulness" also belies the politically sensitive nature of these petitions; Beecher is well aware that women's requests "may be . . . *forbidden*" by those in positions of political authority, and she is aware of the politically time-sensitive nature of the issue itself. At the end of the "Circular," Beecher attests that it was written "solely by the female hand" and directly begs her audience to petition on behalf of the Indians, providing a model for the campaign to come:

> Let every woman who peruses it, exert that influence in society which falls within her lawful province, and endeavor by every suitable expedient to interest the feelings of her friends, relatives, and acquaintances, in behalf of these people, that are ready to perish. *A few weeks* must decide this interesting and important question, and after that time sympathy and regret will all be in vain.

Beecher here recognizes the time-sensitive nature of Indian removal at the turn of the decade and appeals to women, in their privileged positions outside the political realm, to yet "lawfully" exert their influence over the issue.

As they had responded to Sedgwick's novel, readers apparently responded warmly to Beecher's appeal: In a major change in the history of U.S. petitioning, hundreds of women's antiremoval petitions began arriving in Congress just weeks after the circular, and 1830 and 1831 brought hundreds more on behalf of Native American Indians and slaves. Prior to this moment, American women had not petitioned both separately and collectively on an issue addressed by men and undergoing national legislation. Although women in America had submitted petitions prior to this point, they had typically done so on a small scale and on personal, familial matters (such as pensions, compensation for war losses, or divorce) or on local benevolent activities (such as the legal incorporation of female charitable societies). While women had signed temperance petitions as early as 1818, the predominantly white, middle-class, northern women who participated in the antiremoval campaign departed from previous efforts by abandoning male intermediaries and by joining together from various states to petition Congress directly in opposition to national policies.[45] Rather than have others intercede on their behalf, these petitioning women justified their own right to political speech and spoke on behalf of others. In the context of Indian removal, petitioning, then, was the first civil right that American women collectively justified and achieved—that is, the right to political expression (Portnoy 6).

Just as Hope had entered a political discussion about Puritan-Pequod relations by following the dictates of her heart, when women like Sigourney and Stowe began, in Beecher's words, to "*feel* for the distressed" and to "stretch out the supplicating hand for them" by petitioning against Indian removal, they entered a national political debate over the Indian Question. In their echo of Beecher's "Circular's" supplicating stance, these petitions rhetorically magnified the postures of petitioning physically depicted in *Hope Leslie*. While not always successful in effecting their aims—the women's antiremoval petitioning campaign did not finally prevent the removal of the Cherokees from Georgia, nor do Magawisca's petitions sway Mononotto's purpose or Hope's petitions bring Magawisca's freedom—petitions nevertheless established a form through which women could gain a hearing by speaking deferentially yet no less politically on topics of national moment.

This section, after briefly outlining the arguments of representative antiremoval petitions from women then men, will show that early 1830s antiremoval petitions and congressional responses to them set a rhetorical precedent for the debates over antislavery petitions later in the decade—in which, ultimately, the debate over slavery became deflected onto a debate about gendered political discourse that congressmen finally used to assert a shared, white, masculine national identity between North and South. Rather than focusing on the request at hand, typical congressional responses to antiremoval petitions pivoted first on questions of the petitions' language

46 *Language, Gender, and Citizenship in American Literature*

and reception and finally on concerns with petitioners' gender to avert larger national and racial concerns. Because petitioning itself represented access to political discourse, congressional commentary about women's petitions became less about Indian removal and more about who could access the political discourse signified by debate of these national issues. With the intensification of women's antislavery petitions around 1835, these prototypical responses intensified. Anxieties about gender emerged in congressmen's concerns about the language of petitions and of petition-*ers* to parallel the cultural proscription of women's language to "quiet" domestic "uses." More exactly, concerns about gender emerged in discussions of petitioning to force a reconsideration of the terms of language and nation—the rhetorical contract underlying the social contract—thereby pitting contractual notions of citizenship against ascriptive ones. Simultaneously, concerns about gendered political discourse intervened to quell anxieties over the relationship between nation and race and forged an otherwise unlikely coalition between northern and southern men to preserve a union of sorts. Inadvertently, then, the petitioning debate itself effectively silenced discussions of Indian removal and slavery, stalling antiremoval and antislavery efforts, such that the controversial issues of the late 1830s became not only the natural rights denied Indians or slaves but also the expressive civil rights filtered through the political discourse of predominantly white women and denied through the gag rule.

Likely motivated by the call for women's petitions in the anonymous "Circular" attributed to Catharine Beecher, the "Memorial of Sundry Ladies of Hallowell, Maine, praying that certain Indian tribes may not be removed from their present places of abode" was the first women's petition on behalf of Indians, submitted to Congress on January 8, 1830, and endorsed January 18, 1830 (Portnoy 1n1). Just over a month later, on February 15, 1830, the petition "Memorial of the Ladies of Steubenville, Ohio, Against the forcible removal of the Indians without the limits of the United States," was submitted by 63 women and read in the House of Representatives. As a characteristic women's petition against Indian removal, the Steubenville petition was followed by hundreds more like it, then thousands against slavery.[46]

Roughly two-thirds of the Steubenville memorial—the first three of four paragraphs—justifies women's "speaking" out in public, grounded in four key arguments: (1) Christian obligation, the petitioners argue, requires them to appeal to a higher law and to speak on behalf of other "fellow Christians"—the 50,000 Indians to be removed under the contemplated Removal Act; (2) the issue's "pressing importance" demands that women advise the public representatives of their brothers and husbands; because of the issue's extraordinary nature, women's role in the private sphere justifies their action in the public sphere; (3) petitioners' female sympathy allows them entrance into the discussion for "the cause of mercy and humanity"; and (4) America's reputation for generosity and deference toward women, as recognized by foreign observers, should induce their congressional audience to hear their prayers and thus to uphold a national tradition of tolerance for women. The time spent justifying their entrance into the discussion of Indian removal reveals the ways in which considerations of gender impacted women's basic right to petition and was a strategy that, arguably, eventually backfired, as women had to use racialized debates to establish their own relationship to the nation. These justifications acknowledge the "small voice of *female* sympathy" that the memorialists reference earlier in the petition when, at the end of paragraph two, they ask, "and if we approach the public representatives of our husbands and brothers only in the humble character of suppliants in the cause of mercy and humanity, may we not hope that even the small voice of *female* sympathy will be heard?" This question, evoking the religiously resonant, prayerful posture of petitioning, figures these Steubenville women as kneeling suppliants and draws on the humble language of prayer in line with the approved images of women's pious speech circulating in 19th-century American culture. As Portnoy shows, women began petitioning as just such an acceptable extension of their moral authority. Thus these women cast themselves in the "humble character of suppliants," claiming that moral obligation and the dictates of the heart require "*all* who can feel for the woes of humanity, to solicit, with earnestness, your honorable body," and that the exceptionalism of the case excused what might otherwise be perceived as women's "presumptuous interference" or "unbecoming" decorum. These petitioners accentuate their own position as "the feeblest of the feeble": They "implore," "appeal," and "pray" to those who "should be the representatives of national virtues as they are the depositaries of national powers." One can almost see them kneeling, "stretching out the supplicating hand," as Hope and Magawisca did.

Yet, embedded within their moral and gendered justifications, lay a much less unassuming natural rights argument. After the first paragraphs justify their right as women to discuss the Indian Question, the Steubenville petitioners set out their main request in one long paragraph, whose argument centers on two points: (1) America's national virtues need to be protected by the nation's representatives, those with national power, thus the U.S. should honorably uphold their treaties with the Indians to avoid lasting curses upon the nation; and (2) the Indians had a natural right to the lands of their forefathers and should not be compelled to go into the wilderness—a natural rights argument that stressed "the *undoubted natural right* [sic.] which the Indians have to the land of their forefathers," and that implied a censure of "the peculiar guardians of our national character." The immediacy of this argument is brought home by the final sentences of the petition which appeal to Congress "to shield our country from the curses denounced on the cruel and ungrateful, and to shelter the American character from lasting dishonor." Women's petitions thus provided the opportunity to voice not only their religious beliefs, but also their political and philosophical arguments.[47]

A representative men's petition, "Memorial of Certain Inhabitants of Pennsylvania, Praying that the Indians may be protected in their rights, &c." was read in the Senate on January 7, 1830, referred to the Committee on Indian Affairs, and ordered to be printed. The twelve men who address this petition "To the Senate and House of Representatives of the United States in Congress assembled" use a much less deferential address than do the women's petitions. Perhaps not unexpectedly, they spend no time establishing their rationale for speaking on the issue and immediately get to the crux of their argument, that: (1) Indian removal violates existing treaties with the Indians, especially the Act of 1802, which should be considered sacred promises; (2) Removal not only violates treaties, but violates history, particularly the heroes of the Revolution; (3) Removal violates Indians' rightful inheritance, as they are legitimate owners of their land; (4) Removal constitutes sanctioned tyranny (akin to England's tyranny over the colonies, to one nation's tyranny over another), the oppression of another people by force; and (5) Removal is a breach of national faith and an implication of national honor; to protect the national honor, the petitioners charge that the nation must scrupulously adhere "to the path of justice and humanity" (4). The emphases, then, in the men's petitions and the women's petitions are slightly different. As seen here, the men's petitions make more legal and natural rights arguments, yet they still invoke the moral idea of national honor, as the women petitioners do; conversely, the women rely on a moral argument about national virtue, yet they still reference the dishonorable violation of treaties and inheritance that Indian removal would constitute.[48]

Interestingly, despite their separate signatures and varying rhetorical emphases, both men's and women's petitions against Indian removal were initially received very similarly. As congressional records show, early women's petitions were discussed then ordered to lie on the table, just as men's petitions were. And, at the beginning, antiremoval petitions presumably signed by men met with the ire of Congress as much as women's petitions did. For instance, the reaction of particularly southern congressmen to a petition submitted to the House of Representatives on January 11, 1830 from "citizens of New York," likely men, foreshadowed the reaction to women's antiremoval and antislavery petitions, in that these responses equally deflected the conversation from Indian removal to the "indecorous language" of the petitions. Before this petition "from a meeting of citizens of New York, praying the interposition of the General Government to protect the Southern Indians from injustice and oppression" was referred to the Committee on Indian Affairs, the House of Representatives wrangled over whether the petition's language was decorous or indecorous, objectionable or respectful, and how to deal with the petition (Benton 10: 607–08). As *Niles' Weekly Register* reported in its January 16, 1830 issue, the New

Hope Leslie, *Women's Petitions, and Political Discourse* 49

York memorial "gave rise to a debate on the character of the memorial and the propriety of referring it, which occupied the house for two hours," in which nearly a dozen Representatives took part (37: 351).[49] According to the *Register's* summary of the two-hour debate:

> By most of the gentlemen from Georgia, and by Mr. Drayton, of South Carolina, particularly, it was contended that the *language* of the petition was *highly disrespectful* and *indecorous* towards a sovereign state of the union, and that it would be sanctioning the *indecorum* to *receive the petition* and dispose of it in the ordinary mode, which they strenuously opposed. [. . .]
>
> On the other hand, it was argued that the *language* of the petition was not *indecorous* towards Georgia, because the injustice which it deprecated and invoked the government to avert, was hypothetical and suppositious; that the *language* was strong indeed, but such as freemen had a right to address to their representatives on a subject which they deemed of national concernment; that, even if it were *indecorous* towards one of the states of the union, that was not sufficient to justify the *rejection of the memorial,* inasmuch as indecorum in its *language* towards congress could alone justify congress in refusing to receive it; that *the right of petition was a sacred right,* and should not be curtailed or denied without the clearest and most indisputable grounds for such a step, &c. &c. (37: 351, my emphasis)

As seen here, the debate over this early antiremoval petition focused on two main sets of issues: the decorum/indecorum of the petition's *language,* rather than its request; and the question of whether to (or how to) receive the petition, embedded in conflicting understandings of the right of petition itself. In the response to this early petition, then, we glimpse the linguistic and procedural issues that became central to the continuing debates over Indian removal and antislavery petitions, particularly those from women, throughout the decade.

In addition, the initial response to this early petition reflects several specific tactics used to silence discussion of the petitions, if not to silence the petitioners themselves, with the effect of further diverting attention from the actual "content" of the petitions to their "form." As reported by *Niles' Weekly Register* and detailed by Thomas Hart Benton's *Debates of Congress,* the heated debate in the House about the reception of the January 11, 1830 New York memorial reflects four loose categories of tactics used repeatedly over the decade to divert the discussion from the petitions' content, all tactics that dramatize the relationship between nation and language: (1) accusing the petitions of having disrespectful language, the most popular tactic, echoing Winthrop's rebuke of Hope's lack of humility; (2) charging the petitions and petitioners with nonseriousness, akin to Pynchon's dismissive "whistle of a bird" metaphor; (3) stalling for time, often by appealing to legal process, as did the Puritan magistrates in calling for adjournment of the court, and as did Winthrop in disclaiming authority; and (4) contending that the petitioners were meddling in issues not directly concerning them. Once increased petitions began arriving from women, these responses only intensified, as the discussion became caught up with anxieties over *gendered* political discourse—a discussion that ultimately forged, as it did in Magawisca's courtroom, a patriarchal alliance through gendered commentary on language. Although scholars have thoroughly analyzed the congressional response to antislavery petitions, the response to these early Indian removal petitions has been under-attended to. Just as women's petitions against Indian removal foreshadow later petitions against slavery, the congressional reception of these petitions likewise anticipates that of subsequent petitions. Because the debate over the New York petition anticipates amplified congressional responses to later petitions, I will briefly discuss the responses to this particular memorial.

Diverting attention from the substance of the petition, the first general tactic is to object to the memorial's disrespectful *language*. Following Representative Richard Wilde of Georgia, who first uses this strategy in rising not to "oppose the reference of this memorial, however objectionable he considered its language" (Benton 10: 608), other southern representatives also took up this line of argument:

> Mr. [William] Drayton, of South Carolina, said, *the sole ground upon which he opposed the commitment of this memorial was the language in which it was couched.* The memorialists, in common with other citizens, said Mr. D., have the constitutional right to petition Congress for the redress of grievances. As they possess the right, it is for them to decide what are the proper occasions for its exercise. The only limitation which has been, and which, in my judgment, ought to be imposed upon those who address the Legislature, is, that *their language should not be indecent or disrespectful. But this memorial so plainly offends against decorum, that we should, it appears to me, be wanting in what is due to ourselves and to those whom we represent, were we to permit it to be referred to any committee of the House.* (Benton 10: 609, my emphasis)

Accusing the petition of "indecorous," offensive language is one way of refusing to listen to those who speak it, of shutting down the discussion of the topic at hand by focusing on "how" before even getting to the "what." Drayton continues to object to the petition's language, diverting attention from its substance, by charging that the "constitutional right" to petition has been transformed into a vehicle for "opprobrious epithets" (610).

As with the other three consistent responses to the memorial, with this most pervasive response—to attack the petitioners' language—the segment of the House against the petitions (largely southern representatives) forced a defensive position for congressmen like William Storrs (NY), whose argument in defense of the petitioners similarly focused not on the substance of the petitions, but on their language and, more basically, on their right to petition no matter what their language (612). While Storrs' argument is passionate, and on the side of the petitioners, it is forced to respond to the metalinguistic commentary of congressmen who equate the House of Representatives with a national body potentially threatened by "disrespectful" language. Likewise, Rep. William Archer (VA) must respond, on behalf of the memorialists, not to their grievances themselves, but to the linguistic value of their petition and to their right to petition: "It was said that the memorial contained language disrespectful towards one of the States of the Union. He confessed he did not perceive it. He had read the petition, and did not find anything disrespectful; and he quoted the language deemed exceptionable, to show that it was so" (613). In effect, both sides focus on the potential power of disrespectful language to do damage to the government, whether state or national; and the argument becomes one about linguistic issues rather than Indian rights.

A good example of tactic two is Georgia Representative Wiley Thompson's initial response to the petitioners: a blatant accusation of the nonseriousness of the petitions, extending to a more general claim that not every petition must be considered by Congress. Thompson, immediately after moving to refer the petition to the Committee on Indian Affairs, "rose and said, that, disclaiming all intention of opposing the reference proposed, he would, however, question the propriety of entertaining every petition or memorial which may be addressed to Congress, whether it be the result of an accidental meeting at a grog-shop or not" (608). Thompson's disdainful insinuation that the petition came from "a grog-shop" is tantamount to an attack on the petitioners' character, a dismissive charge of the signers' foolhardiness.[50]

The third general response to the petitioners' concerns is to claim that it is not the proper stage or the proper time to discuss the removal of the Indians from their lands. Representative Thompson rallies this strategy when he states that "he did not wish to provoke discussion upon the subject alluded to, because that was not the proper stage for its discussion" (608). Other representatives, such as John Bell of Tennessee, use a similar argument about ill timing, dissuading fellow legislators from entering "a discussion, *which was premature,* which could result in no good, and *for which the House could not then be prepared*" (609, my emphasis). Thompson's and Bell's responses highlight the silencing strategies within the political process—stalling in response to a petition, or moving the petition to a House Committee in order to avoid the "excitement" of discussing it. Indeed, the consequences of such discussion were writ large in the minds of these congressmen; given the importance of shared rhetoric to national harmony in early America, they feared that intense debate would lead to national division and vulnerability—again, a dramatization of the relationship between language and nation.

The fourth tactic, charging petitioners with meddling with issues not their own, an argument easily transferred to gendered separate spheres, rested on an understanding of petitioning's restriction, historically, to voicing one's personal grievances. Yet Georgia's Mr. Wilde exaggerates this valid concern. Using strikingly hyperbolic language, Wilde asks why, if the Indians are so aggrieved, they were not complaining for themselves:

> Whence, then, the necessity of the petitioners' interference? Might they not be told that every one was ready enough to detail his own grievances? Was it less true now than formerly, that, if everybody would take care of themselves, and of their own business, everybody and everybody's business would be well taken care of? Give me leave, sir, said Mr. W., to ask, why, according to their own statement, these petitioners came before this House? They set forth no grievance of their own or of their fellow-citizens. They suggest no remedy resting in the action of this House for the real or imaginary grievances of others. Why may we not as well entertain supplications in behalf of the suffering people of Ireland or Hindostan? In what character, he inquired, did the memorialists present themselves? Was it as self-constituted guardians of the public faith? Were they voluntary superintendents of the treaty-making power? Curators by assumption of the persons and property of the Southern Indians? or censors—he knew not by what right—of the Legislatures of sovereign States of the Union? (608)

Here, Wilde invokes an inflammatory string of absurd rhetorical questions to argue against the petitioners' "interference" with the Indians' business, placing it as politically and geographically "outside" their jurisdiction as the concerns of far-off Ireland or Hindostan. Issued as an offensive, it is on the shoulders of the petitioners' supporters to defend their right to speak on behalf of the Indians.[51]

These four general congressional responses to the January 11 antiremoval petition are prototypical of more vehement responses and silencing strategies to forthcoming petitions, particularly those from women. As soon as a mere few months after the January 11 petition debate—in fact, in the month prior to the passage of the Indian Removal Act—concerns with gender enter discussions of petitioning. As the Thursday, April 15, 1830 entry, "Removal of the Indians," in Benton's *Debates of Congress* reveals, Georgia Senator John Forsyth defends Georgia's position and actions and comments particularly on the delusionality of female antiremoval petitioners to defend his position:

> Recently great efforts have been made to excite the public mind into a state of unreasonable and jealous apprehension in their [the Indians'] behalf. The evidences of these efforts are before us in petitions that have been pouring in from different parts of the country. The clergy, the laity,

the lawyers, and the ladies, have been dragged into the service and united to press upon us. But these efforts have been unavailing: the people are too well informed to be deluded; they have too much confidence in the justice and wisdom of the administration to be misled by persons who have united, at this eleventh hour, in opposition to a project which has been steadily kept in view by three administrations. [. . .] That many respectable persons have been deceived, is not disputed. They have been the unresisting instruments of the artful and designing, and ministered to political malignity, while they believed themselves laboring in the cause of justice and humanity.

Two evidences of such delusions are before me. A circular printed for the signature of the ladies, and forwarded to me with a note, "read with a view to eternity," as if I were in danger of eternal punishment if I did not abandon the defence of the position taken by Georgia, on which I have already periled my reputation as a politician, and stand responsible as an accountable being. (Benton 10: 535)

This response illustrates how, as early as April 1830, as "ladies" publicly become part of the cause of antiremoval "excitement," concerns about gender emerge in congressional responses to petitioning to complicate—or perhaps, rather, to oversimplify—the debate over Indian removal.[52] Moreover, in alleging that the clergy and the ladies have been equally deluded to enter into politics and "minister to political malignity," Forsyth invokes an opposition between politics and religion that undermines the very grounds upon which women claimed their authority to speak against removal. In aligning delusional clergy and ladies in an era that, as Ann Douglas has shown in *The Feminization of American Culture*, barred both from the political realm, Forsyth works to question the credibility of the petitions in order to justify their dismissal. Here, we see that concerns about not only language but also gender and social role deflect substantial conversation about Indian removal, as responses to petitions become increasingly concerned with not only *how* the language of petitioning is used but also *who* has access to this language.

When petitioners' "indecorous language" came from women antislavery petitioners, congressional responses resulted in the gag rule. Indeed, the focus on gender in both antiremoval and antislavery petitioning campaigns provided, in one respect, a smooth transition from one to another, for both heated issues of removal and slavery were protested by women and elicited a shift in attention to gendered political discourse. Thus when women began submitting petitions against slavery in unprecedented numbers in 1835, congressional anxieties about gender and gendered spheres intensified—as seen in Representative Garland's vehement response to women's antislavery petitions.[53] In a speech on December 23, 1835, Representative Garland prescribes marriage to control the women petitioners "madly shooting out of their proper sphere, and undertaking to control national politics":

Permit me, sir, to make one further remark on this subject [the antislavery petitions presented from a Northern Representative] before I approach the question [the abolition of slavery in the District of Columbia] itself; and that is, *who are these petitioners?* [. . .] one portion of these petitioners [is]—the *females;* I beg pardon—the *ladies.* Now, sir, there is no man on the floor who has a higher admiration of the female character than I have; but I must confess *I do not like to see them madly shooting out of their proper sphere, and undertaking to control national politics. I do not like to see them become politicians.* Sir, I was very much interested and amused at the sublime and beautiful description of the character and virtues of these ladies, with which the gentleman [Mr. Granger, in an earlier address] entertained the house. They are all gentleness, all kindness, all benevolence. Oh, yes, sir, and their objects are all designed for good; and so absorbed are they in their benevolent designs, that they have not brought themselves to contemplate the awful consequences of their rash proceedings. Now, sir, I have one single recommendation for the gentleman. It would seem, from his remarks, that one of the peculiar virtues of these females is, to disturb his slumbers; and, as I understand the gentleman [a congressman who spoke on behalf of the petitioners] is a bachelor, and these female petitioners are, I do not doubt, old maids, not exceeding twenty-five—for they never get beyond that age—*I would recommend him to take one of these interesting, charming ladies for his wife; and, in so doing, I have no doubt he would lessen the ranks of the abolitionists one,* at least, and secure himself against any further disturbance of his midnight slumbers; for, be assured, Mr. Speaker, it is a most powerful soporific, and a very pleasant one into the bargain, as you and I can testify. (*Register of Debates* 2064, my emphasis)

Representative Garland's speech, continuing for several pages, invokes all of the responses to antiremoval petitions, and these are clearly intensified when they are coupled with his concerns about gender and separate spheres. For example, he charges petitioners with intolerable, even seditious, language that threatens the nation: "Have they not declared, in print, that they would pull down and destroy the very arch of the Union, rather than they would fail to effect their purposes? Sir, is this language, in the midst of our northern friends, to be tolerated?" (2068). According to Garland, these antislavery petitioners lack seriousness and credibility; they are "fanatical," "devilish," and "hypocritically canting" "disturbers of the tranquility of the nation" (2065–66). In addition, for Garland, the petitioners meddle with others' affairs. Garland declares, "*when pious and godly-given ladies,* in some few portions of the North, are petitioning to redress my grievances, when I feel no grievance, when I know of no grievance at all, I humbly conceive it to be *an improper and impertinent interference with my rights*" (2074, my emphasis). Garland explicitly calls for decisive action to silence the petitions; in an uncanny echo of the Puritan magistrates,

Garland invokes a rhetoric of brotherhood, stating that he "hope[s] this question will now end; that our northern brethren will meet it in the most decisive form, and give such an explicit expression of their sentiments as will tranquilize the South on the one hand, and silence the fanatics on the other" (2075). Although the "decisive" action Garland advocates—an outright rejection of the petition and those like it—was not achieved until several months later, Garland's "incendiary" speech effectively won the day. The women's petition in question was ordered to lie on the table by a vote of 144–67 (2077)—a sign of the gag rule to come in the months ahead.

In May 1836, in response to massive numbers of antislavery petitions and after yet another controversy in the House over the question of whether to receive them, the 25th Congress approved, by large margins, three resolutions to silence the petitions by "receiving" them but sending them to the table without consideration. The three resolutions, effective through July 1836 and called the Pinckney gag, held that Congress had no power to interfere with slavery in the states, that Congress should not interfere with slavery in the District of Columbia, and that all petitions, memorials, resolutions, propositions, or papers at all relating to the subject of slavery or the abolition of slavery would be tabled without any further action, and without being printed or referred to committee. This set of resolutions became the first of several renewed annually, culminating in an 1840 House Rule that prohibited petitions from being introduced at all; together, these resolutions and rules became collectively known as the gag rule over the period from 1836 to 1844.[54] This gag rule effectively transformed the right to petition (S. Higginson 144–45). In other words, petitioning became a decisively monologic use of political language.

Legal historians such as Stephen Higginson have attended to how the problem of the sheer volume of antislavery petitions, combined with the highly-charged, deeply-entrenched issue of slavery, helped lead to the gag rule (158–59). Yet they overlook the ways in which gender entered into and shaped the congressional response to these petitions—petitions submitted by women. After the initial 1836 gag rule, abolitionists, particularly women, redoubled their efforts. Petitions asking for the abolition of slavery in the District of Columbia continued to flood Congress; and antislavery, anti-gag congressmen like John Quincy Adams insisted on presenting them in the House, where they met with vehement response.[55] In 1837, as a result of numerous appeals to women by abolitionists like the Grimké sisters, and through the organizational efforts of the first national convention of the women's American Anti-Slavery Society in New York City in May, women stimulated another deluge of petitions to Congress.[56] The increased numbers of petitions and signers at the outset of the second session of the 25th Congress (December 4, 1837–July 9, 1838) began it in controversy yet again. The arguments were similar: Southerners and many northern democrats argued that although abolitionists had the right to petition, Congress was not obligated to receive or to consider their petitions; a handful of northerners, especially those sympathetic to abolition, continued presenting petitions and insisted that petitioning was an absolute right, entailing the guarantee of reception and consideration. And concerns with gender continued to emerge in discussions of appropriate political language, putting pressure on the consensual model of citizenship held out by petitioning and finally forging an ascriptive alliance between northern and southern white men.

Eventually, as seen in the sustained anti-petition argument given by Representative Bynum on January 9, 1837, gendered commentary about language realigned the "sides" of the slavery debate, effectively pitting all congressmen against women and clergy and anxiously asserting a masculine identity for national politics. Bynum's response to antislavery petitions centers on the gender of the petitioners, whom he calls "a set of low, ignorant fanatics, united with some boys; and, he was sorry to say, with women. Yes, sir, the women of Massachusetts had become legislators, and were urging their imbecile, timid men to action" (*Register of Debates* 1329). Indeed, what seems most offensive to Bynum is that these "deluded," "ignorant," and "fanatical" petitioners—adjectives he repeats throughout his speech (1335–38)—had "stepped into the political theatre" to "call on men to act": "he thought it a portentous foreboding, an awful omen, when women were stepping into the political theatre, and calling on men to act, and recommending what subjects they should legislate on. He felt no disposition to go further into the investigation of the character of these women; *it was enough for him to know that they were females;* he felt a disposition towards them of the kindest nature, and was ready to say, 'Father, forgive them, for they know not what they do'" (1329, my emphasis). Bynum's statement here that "it was enough for him to know that [the petitioners] were females" reveals the extent to which gender and gendered spheres entered into this particular national language debate. He continues:

> He could not conceive a more degrading condition than this House would be placed in, by consuming its time, an enormous expense to the Treasury, in receiving and listening to the petitions and memorials of old grannies and a parcel of boarding-school misses, in matters of state and legislation. What light could they throw on the subject? When grannies and misses become legislators, he thought it time for the men of New England to fold up their arms and to go home. The Congress of the United States was no place for them. (1330)

Here, the cause of "degradation" to the House becomes "listening" to "old grannies" and "boarding-school misses." Bynum views the "officious interference" of the "ladies [. . .] who had made themselves conspicuous in their petitions" as "degradation" to Congress; as well, it is "a national insult" (1333). Indeed, women's political discourse imperils the nation; their petitioning threatens, to use Bynum's word, "dissolution"—a threat against which the entire body of representatives should equally unite to raise their voices (1333).[57]

Thus Bynum calls on congressmen across regions of the nation to oppose the petitions, revealing the extent to which the "insulted nation," as well as the nation's legislative body, is gendered masculine and requires a manly rhetorical defense. Appealing to "the sons of those revolutionary fathers of New England," Bynum asks, "is it possible that these hardy sons of the North and East should be so delinquent in duty as to require now to be spurred on by the petitions of adults, women, and school children?" (1335). Through a series of deft rhetorical maneuvers and a reassertion of separate, gendered spheres that aligns both northern and southern men together against petitioners, rather than pitting northern representatives against their southern "brethren," Bynum thus changes the terms of the debate and asserts the political sphere as men's:

> To a New England man human nature cannot conceive a project more suicidal and self-immolating than that now agitated by the religious fanatics and priesthood of the Eastern and Northern States. But such a policy could only be expected, when politicians were prompted to action by the exhortations of women and children. It is not in the field, nor is it in the cabinet, where the counsel of lovely woman has been found most potent; to adorn her sex, she is destined for a different sphere; and it is for the want of men, "That women become most mannish grown, /And assume the part that men should act alone." He would tell the abolitionists, not a single object that they contended for could they accomplish, short of a civil war, and one, too, that would drench the fairest fields of this great republic with brothers' blood; and that they are stupid, silly, idle, creatures who dream of the contrary. Where, then, will be found their women and children, who crowd this House with silly petitions? Where their priests? In the tented field? No, sir, but skulking, shivering, shrinking from danger and responsibility, and even then denying the part that they had once taken in getting up this tragic drama. Will their women then be seen in the field, amid the clanger of arms and the shouts of victory, or heard in the cabinet with the cries of their children around them? Let the hardy sons of New England, who have had little or nothing to do with getting up this excitement, but on whom alone the brunt of war would rest, if acted out, answer this! (1337)

In effect, Bynum dynamically re-maps the sides of the dispute. Northern, southern, and eastern men—and everything they represent (manliness, intelligence, reason, action, bravery)—are allied together against the war brought about by abolitionists' libelous words, and everything the abolitionists represent (femininity, stupidity, silliness, idleness, weakness). The "real" enemy both northern and southern representatives need to fight, in other words, is the war of words that Bynum's antislavery "grannies" and "boarding-school misses" ignited in their petitioning campaign.

Such inflammatory anti-petition responses from congressmen like Bynum worked alongside equally provocative pro-petition responses to shift the focus of debate away from the abolition of slavery. Tension over the petitions in the House culminated in March 1838, when the House referred all memorials protesting the Annexation of Texas to committee without consideration. In the aftermath, John Quincy Adams gave his famous speech defending the right of both men and women to petition and occupying the mornings of House proceedings from June 16 to July 7, 1838. In the course of defending abolitionists' right to petition, Adams sustained a defense of women's right to petition and virtually proposed women's suffrage.[58] While Bynum's speech represents the extreme anti-petition stance, focused particularly on women's and clergy's delusional political discourse and men's necessary opposition to it, Adams' speech defends women's right to petition. Both substantially focus on the political discourse of petitioning and the gender of its users. Together, these positions reveal the extent to which gender mediated the debate over petitioning on both sides; and gender and political language mediated the debate over slavery. Thus the petitioning debate itself, as Adams seems to imply in his speech, finally enabled an economic and cultural imperialism, just as it did with the ultimately successful removal of the Cherokees from their lands (Adams 58).

In his "Speech Upon the Right of the People, Men and Women, to Petition," Adams volleys a defense of women's petitioning in response to the charge from another congressman that, in departing from their proper sphere by petitioning, women discredited national character—a claim which, Adams states, "is fundamentally wrong" (67). Adams staunchly defends women petitioners' departure from the "duties of the domestic circle" on the basis of their virtues and purity as women, claiming that "women are not only justified, but exhibit the most exalted virtue when they do depart from the domestic circle, and enter on the concerns of their country, of humanity, and of their God" (68). Adams continues his argument via historical precedent—Biblical, Roman, Greek, Anglo-Saxon, and European examples of women, including Esther, who brought honor to their times and their countries, and then women of the American Revolution (71–73, 75).

Moreover, Adams clearly links the right to petition with the ultimate right of citizenship, the right to vote, using his defense of women's right to petition to imply women's right to vote: "And the right to petition, according to the gentleman [Mr. Howard], (said Mr. A.,) is to be denied to women because they have no right to vote! Is it so clear that they have no such right as this last? And if not, who shall say that this argument of the gentleman's is not adding one injustice to another?" (Adams 77). Adams soon tempers his argument for women's suffrage by returning to the religious nature of the petition and, hence, its propriety for women:

I do not, however, mean to be understood as countenancing the general idea that it is proper, on ordinary occasions, for women to step without the circle of their domestic duties. I do not so consider it: and I say that, when they do so depart from their ordinary and appropriate sphere of action, you are to inquire into the motive which actuated them, the means they employ, and the end they have in view. I say further, that, in the present case, all these, as well the motive as the means and the end, were just and proper. It is a petition—it is a prayer—a supplication—that which you address to the Almighty Being above you. And what can be more appropriate to their sex? (81)

While couching his political remarks within a return to a softened rhetorical stance, invoking women's piety, and revealing the extent to which gendered concerns constrained the petitioning debate, Adams remains one of the few to speak in defense of women antislavery petitioners, and the only man in either House in the 1830s to speak at length in defense of women's right to petition; he quickly became their hero (Portnoy, *A Right* 177). And while the remainder of Adams' speech focuses on issues of annexation (first, the precedent of Louisiana under Jefferson, now Jackson's dealings with Mexico for the attainment of Texas), it is no small matter that these issues revolve around Adams' four-day defense of women's right to petition—his defense of women's access to political language, even bordering on their right to vote.

Adams' defense reflects the extent to which the debates over petitioning were embedded within removal and slavery debates, and the extent to which these very debates were deflected onto regulation of women's political discourse. These petitioning debates, circuited through discursive concerns about gender and nation, obscured the vexed relationship between nation and race, particularly with Indian removal and slavery, in which national ideals and actions starkly conflicted. Culminating in the gag rule and in Adams' 1838 speech, the debates in Congress about women's petitioning finally reveal the ways in which discussions of gender and language intervened in national issues such as the accession of Cherokee lands in Georgia (taking place over the 1830s), the annexation of Texas (which finally occurred in 1845, officially connecting the politics of expansion and slavery), and slavery itself (not abolished for another almost-30 years, with the Thirteenth Amendment finally appearing on December 18, 1865). The petitioning debates' byproducts included a shift in attention to expressive rights and their basic denial—to the ways in which denial of human rights spilled into the denial of civil rights, and vice-versa. The debates also assured women's voices a political presence for the first time, and can be seen as the locus of the women's movement, with petitioning as women's foundational political right. At the same time, however, the debates diverted attention from Indian removal and slavery, and placed it on women's political discourse, enabling a U.S. expansionist stance through this diversion.

Purified of the political voices of women, Indians, and slaves, the gag rule "ended" the debates within the nation's legislature, as within Sedgwick's Puritan courtroom. Put another way, the gag rule rejected the possibility of consensual citizenship held out through women's petitioning, instead retrenching to an ascriptive model of citizenship based on white masculinity and in conflict with founding American principles. By mid-century, as we will see in the next chapter, these gendered language ideologies determining *who* should speak, based on *how* and *where* they should speak, would become particularly entrenched, as congressmen's concerns about linguistic "decorum" were seen in wider cultural concerns with gendered vocal propriety.

Catharine Beecher herself seemingly recognized how debates over women's petitions could become all-consuming when she reconsidered her December 1829 "Circular." In her *Essay on Slavery and Abolition with Reference to the Duty of American Females* (1837), Beecher, again drawing on Queen Esther, writes that women should *not* petition for the abolition of slavery:

> If petitions from females will operate to exasperate; if they will be deemed obtrusive, indecorous, and unwise, by those to whom they are addressed; if they will increase, rather than diminish the evil which it is wished to remove; if they will be the opening wedge, that will tend eventually to bring females as petitioners and partisans into every political measure that may tend to injure and oppress their sex, in various parts of the nation, and under the various public measures that may hereafter be enforced, than it is neither appropriate nor wise, nor right, for a woman to petition for the relief of oppressed females. (103–04)

For Beecher, anxious about whether women's petitions for others would lead to women's petitions for their own political rights, if women's petitions "will be the opening wedge," a kind of slippery slope leading to increased political involvement, then women should not petition. For Beecher and indeed for many of her contemporaries in the 1830s, the limits of petitioning and the limits of enfranchisement were, ostensibly, the limits of gender ideologies, but they were moreover the limits of ideologies of race and nation.[59] As such, concerns about gender and language would ultimately negotiate race-charged national issues, from removal to slavery.

5. CONCLUSION: FICTIONS AND/AS PETITIONS

Taking up the theme of women's petitioning and portraying the politics of petitioning, Sedgwick's novel "ends" in both a similar and different place from the antiremoval and antislavery campaigns. Just as congressional debates over the right to petition "ended" in the gag rule and worked to sustain various kinds of removals, attention to Magawisca's "scandalous" utterance in Sedgwick's Puritan courtroom shuts down deliberations altogether. In addition, the routes to these conclusions are similar: Hope's "whistle of a bird" and Magawisca's "uttered malignities" elicit charges of disrespect, nonseriousness, or intermeddling and expose the gendered linguistic manipulation through which the nation's elect worked to maintain their power. Through Hope's and Magawisca's persistently heroic speech, Sedgwick suggests that women's political discourse is worth imagining, as is a nation that might make room for the equally dissenting and consenting voices of women, Indians, and slaves; Hope, like white women petitioners, still speaks out, even if she presumes to speak on behalf of Indian women. Yet also because of this ventriloquism, the novel doesn't follow the potential of petitioning to its conclusion; Sedgwick stops short, not only by imagining the possible as past, but also by removing Magawisca and marrying Hope. We have to rely on the realities of petitions in the 1830s to supplement Sedgwick's story—to see the ways in which women continually petitioned and were gagged, real Indians removed, and abolition stalled.

In addition to their "stories" ending in similar and yet different places, there are important formal similarities and differences between *Hope Leslie* and 1830s women's petitions. Shuttling between prayer and political discourse, women's petitioning invites us to examine the blurring of the line between fictional and political representation. *Hope Leslie* draws on many elements of petitioning—but it is not a petition. Instead, *Hope Leslie* is a trope for petitioning, like but decidedly unlike the petition. Read by wide audiences of both men and women, like petitions, *Hope Leslie* may dissent from masculine historiography, "putting the chisel into the hands of truth and giving it to whom it belonged"; it may give public voice to Sedgwick's private stance; it may gain a fame predominantly confined to male writers at the time; it may work to shape a new moral, and even political, consensus. Yet in *Hope Leslie,* Sedgwick constructs a self-consciously fictional world without legal constraint; women petitioners, in contrast, adopt a self-consciously non-fictional stance, taking pains to negotiate a rhetorical and political position on the Indian Question that will be acceptable to the nation's representatives and will consequently gain a hearing.

Yet precisely because Sedgwick's novel is *not* overtly "political," because it is distinctly *unlike* a petition, because it *is* "imaginary," *Hope Leslie* allows Sedgwick to cast her own "vote" on the Indian Question—but without officially petitioning, without receiving the reprimand an actual petition would have engendered, and without raising the responses that anxiously betrayed the need to render her "uttered malignities" as utterly apolitical as "the whistle of a bird." It is from its position on the boundary of petition and not-petition that *Hope Leslie* highlights the persuasive ways in which fiction can blend "literary" and "political" language and gain imaginative power. While Hope Leslie's voice, similar to those of women who petitioned, can be rendered "but as the whistle of a bird," *Hope Leslie's* cannot.

2 Vocal (Im)Propriety and the Management of Sociopolitical Mobility in *The Wide, Wide World* and *Ragged Dick*

1. INTRODUCTION: GOOD READERS AS GOOD SPEAKERS

> How much happiness was Ernestine the means of bestowing through her good elocution, united to the happy circumstance that brought it to the knowledge of the King! (William McGuffey, "The Good Reader" [1879] 179)

At mid century, William McGuffey's popular *Fifth Eclectic Reader* featured a story entitled "The Good Reader," in which Ernestine, the young daughter of a royal gardener, outshines two boy pages in reading aloud a petition from a poor widow to the King of Prussia. Although the fact that Ernestine reads a petition testifies to the cultural resonance of the form of the petition in the mid 19th century, what is particularly notable here is that Ernestine's reading of the widow's petition signifies the proper engagement of her *voice*. While one of the boys reads the widow's story with "a dismal monotony of voice" and the other with "a good share of self-conceit" and "great formality," Ernestine reads "with so much feeling, and with an articulation so just, in tones so pure and distinct, that when she had finished, the King, into whose eyes the tears had started, exclaimed, 'Oh! Now I understand what it is all about; but I might never have known, certainly I never should have felt, its meaning had I trusted to these young gentlemen,'" whom he dismisses for a year, advising them to spend the time in learning to read (177–78). Through "her good elocution," Ernestine bestows much happiness, not only on the King, whose eyesight is weak, but also on the widow who sent the petition, and on her son, the two pages, her father, and the neighbors who often assembled at her father's house to hear her read: Ernestine has "the satisfaction of aiding her father to rise in the world, so that he became the King's chief gardener"; and "As for the two pages, she was indirectly the means of doing them good, also; for, ashamed of their bad reading, they commenced studying in earnest, till they overcame the faults that had offended the King. Both finally rose to distinction, one as a lawyer, and the other as a statesman; and they owed their advancement in life chiefly to their good elocution" (179).

In addition to presenting the petition as an appropriate and perhaps familiar form for female literate engagement, "The Good Reader" highlights the extent to which, in mid-19th-century America, "good reading" was an oral activity associated with "good speaking," with the proper use of one's voice. As Samuel Kirkham's popular *Essay on Elocution,* first published in 1833, states: "The first object of elocution is, to make a good *reader;* its second object is, to make a *good* reader; its third object, to make a *good reader;* its last and grand object is, to make an *accomplished* and *powerful* SPEAKER" (16, Kirkham's emphasis).[1] In fact, sandwiched between poems and stories like "The Good Reader," throughout McGuffey's readers are the exercises in distinct articulation and correct pronunciation that books like Kirkham's explicitly drilled and that Ernestine's "good elocution" taught by example. For example, McGuffey directs: "Pronounce correctly and distinctly. Do not say *laughin* for laugh-in*g; casmunt* for case-ment; *chryslis* for chrys-*a*-lis; *some-thin* for some-thin*g; wonderin* for won-der-ing; *dyin* for dy-ing" (*New Fourth Reader* 109 in Minnich 112). Such instructions, like the stories themselves, worked to make Kirkham's good *readers and speakers,* and they manifested language ideologies of which conceptions of gendered social role were no small part. Stories like "The Good Reader" and the extremely popular McGuffey readers in which they were published—readers that were arguably "the most influential manifestation of American popular culture of the era"—transport us to "the ideological heart of America" (Gorn 2–3).

Like other stories and manuals on "good speaking" that this chapter explores, McGuffey's "The Good Reader" and his popular readers are thus valuable introductory lenses into ideologies of language, gender, and nation that were intertwined in mid-19th-century American culture.[2] Taken as commentary about a young girl's role as a consumer, producer, and policer of linguistic culture, Ernestine's story invokes overlapping ideologies of language and gender in its telling of a very "American" 19th-century success story in condensed fictional form: notably, how a young girl's "good elocution" prompts the happiness and prosperity of all those around her, even while her vocal skills are confined to socially acceptable roles for white, middle-class women, such as helping others, speaking for the poor, or reading with feeling. "The Good Reader" thus attributes to a young girl the responsibility of upholding and disseminating values of proper speech to promote others' social, political, or economic success outside the home.[3] Such stories championed ideologies promoting an "American" identity via linguistic practices that were not only classed (with ideas about proper use of one's voice prompting social mobility), but also gendered (with "true womanhood" producing separate social and linguistic roles for boys and girls, men and women) and "national" (with hegemonic middle-class, white, Protestant values often presented as "American" values). In the case of "The Good Reader," Ernestine's vocal propriety worked to advance the social and political prosperity of some (such as the King's pages, who become a lawyer and a statesman) and locate others (such as Ernestine herself) in their (quite apolitical) places.

We might, then, see Ernestine's story in "The Good Reader" as the story of McGuffey's "good" readers, and we might view them together as a story of mid-19th-century America: a story that this chapter aims to tell about how what I call gendered vocal propriety—a subset of linguistic propriety that took up gendered notions about the proper use of one's voice—could both motivate and quell mid-century sociopolitical mobility. Within the context of other publications on vocal propriety, such as grammar books, pronunciation guides, or elocution manuals, and alongside some of the era's most popular fiction, such stories give us insight into how conceptions of gendered vocal propriety emerged to help Americans manage mid-19th-century social and political transformations. More precisely, this chapter argues that conceptions of gendered vocal propriety helped to manage changing notions of citizenship that challenged traditional conceptions of American piety and property and that created increased social and political mobility. Manifest partly in linguistic and literary discussions about "grammar" and "slang," discourses of gendered vocal propriety checked mid-century anxieties about the changing franchise by recuperating notions of piety and property within discourse on language, making American identity a linguistic product of both morality and hard work associated with white, middle-class, gendered, Protestant values.[4] These discourses figured American identity in distinctly gendered ways that had singular effects for women and men, such as Ernestine and the two pages. In addition, through rhetoric that associated language with mid-19th-century conceptions of gender, grammar itself often became associated with feminized, middle-class domesticity and slang with urban, lower-class masculinity.

When read alongside mid-century manuals addressing vocal propriety, two of the period's most popular book-length "success" stories—Susan Warner's best-selling *The Wide, Wide World* (1850) and Horatio Alger's famous *Ragged Dick* (1867)—indicate how girls and boys could "become" American women and men through their gendered linguistic labors in distinct ways. For both protagonists Ellen Montgomery and Dick Hunter, the attainment of vocal propriety via the often feminized discipline of grammar successfully opens the way to "upward" mobility in the dual senses of moral uplift and middle-class refinement. Yet like that of the "The Good Reader," whose elocutionary success is contained, Ellen's education results in her submission and domesticity, while Dick's attainment of vocal propriety grooms him for citizenship in both private and public spheres, giving him access to a feminized, middle-class domesticity without the loss of the romanticized individuality, mobility, or "freedom" of the streets.

While recent scholars have blurred the distinctions between urban and domestic spaces as uniquely masculine and feminine ones—demonstrating persuasively that 19th-century streets were spaces for women as well as men—the depictions of language and gender in these popular mid-19th-century cultural and literary texts ultimately reinforce domestic ideology's distinctions between gendered spaces, assigning women to the domestic realm and men to the political through their social and linguistic roles.[5] The stories of Ellen's and Dick's becoming "good speakers" finally show us how grammar and slang, as two mid-19th-century manifestations of gendered vocal propriety, invoked conceptions of property and piety to quell gender-, ethnic-, and class-charged anxieties about national citizenship, not only by propelling social mobility, but also by locating mobile mid-century voices and votes within clearly defined social and political spheres. Before turning to these stories, this chapter will first address the mid-century historical and linguistic contexts from which discourses of gendered vocal propriety emerged.

2. GENDERED VOCAL PROPRIETY: GRAMMAR AS FEMINIZED AMERICAN PIETY AND DOMESTICITY

In a historical moment of incredible social mobility, popular textbooks like McGuffey's readers emphasized elocution because, as Oliver Wendell Holmes observed in *The Autocrat of the Breakfast Table* (1858), "There are single expressions, as I have told you already, that fix a man's position for you before you have done shaking hands with him" (107). Holmes' text reveals and raises important notions about speech and social identity, reflecting the idea that, according to Holmes, a person's speech expresses their history, as well as contributing to the 19th-century drive to watch one's vocal expressions. Holmes' description of an "indigenous" country speaker, for example, broadly indicates how even a brief statement from a person could deliver "a delicious, though somewhat voluminous biography, social, educational, and aesthetic" (*Autocrat* 110–11). Mid-19th-century commentary about language, such as that in McGuffey's *Readers* and Holmes' *Autocrat*, reflects a heightened attention to speech; it further suggests the importance of ideas about speech to "fixing" social "positions" at a time when, as I discuss below, social and political identities were increasingly open to revision. When coupled with ideas about social class, ethnicity, gender, and nation, distinctions in speech came to signal identity in sharp ways, differentiating "good" speakers from "bad," sorting out the privileged from the riffraff, the genteel from the vulgar, and the "lady" from what Holmes would call the "suffragist."[6]

Moreover, ideas about *gender* and proper speech could gently mask other concerns, as a brief overview of Holmes' commentary on women's voices throughout the *Autocrat* demonstrates. Indeed, Holmes' reflections on women's voices show how he worked out anxieties about issues such as national identity, class status, ethnicity, or women's suffrage through his own gendered commentary on language. For example, Holmes describes the voices of American "young persons of the female sex" who "have bustled in [aboard a train] full-dressed, engaged in loud strident speech, and who, after free discussion, have fixed on two or more double seats, which having secured, they proceed to eat apples and hand round daguerreotypes"; for Holmes, these female voices come to stand in nationally for "generally not agreeable voices" of "our [American] people," absorbing his concerns about national identity (221–22). Another voice—the "delicious," bewitching voice of a German chambermaid who searched for a lost key with "soft, liquid inflections, and low, sad murmurs"—actually "frightens" Holmes, not because of its ethereality, but because it leads him to contemplate the very material horror of "a *mesalliance,* that lasts fifty years to begin with, and then passes along down the line of descent (breaking out in all manner of boorish manifestations of feature and manner [. . .] until one came to beings that ate with knives and said 'Haow!)" (223–24). Likewise, Holmes remarks on another German woman's "ravishing" voice that, Holmes declares, "could not have come from any Americanized human being." Holmes' commentary about this voice deflects anxieties about class, gender, and national identity: He contrasts the "*muliebrity*" and "*femineity*" [Holmes' emphasis] of this German woman's voice, which is "subdued by the reverential training and tuned by the kindly culture of fifty generations," to the "self-assertion, such as free suffrage introduces into every word and movement" of American voices, as well as to the "ten to one" Americans who speak with a "hard, sharp, metallic, matter-of-fact business clink in the accents [. . .] that produces the effect of one of those bells which small trades-people connect with their shop-doors, and which spring upon your ear with such vivacity, as you enter, that your first impulse is to retire at once from the precincts" (224). While there are, of course, differences among these commentaries on women's voices, what is striking about all of Holmes' contemplations is that they absorb anxieties about, and provide a forum for Holmes to discuss, the much wider issues of national character, ethnic intermarriage, "free suffrage," and an expanding class structure.

As this section will suggest, discourses of gendered vocal propriety, such as Holmes' commentary on the "loud strident speech" of young American women, emerged to referee anxieties about the theoretically mobile lines of social and national identity at mid-century. By discourses of gendered vocal propriety, I mean discourses of propriety that combined ideas about governing one's voice with 19th-century gender ideologies such as true womanhood, which emphasized purity, piety, domesticity, and submissiveness for women.

In recent years, the topic of linguistic propriety—in terms of its instantiations as concerns with areas of linguistic study like accent—has been provocatively explored in historically-focused studies of the English language.[7] Yet while such historical treatments of the English language may briefly mention literary examples of linguistic propriety, there is little room in these treatments for literary analysis; and linguistic propriety has been altogether under-explored in literary and composition-rhetoric studies. Thus one goal of this chapter is to apply a more sociolinguistic understanding of the mid 19th century to historicist literary treatments of the period, and to bring into dialogue studies in language, literature, and composition-rhetoric as they pertain to a historicized 19th-century linguistic propriety. This chapter, and this section in particular, aims to historicize grammar, for instance, as a cultural concern with gendered vocal propriety, and to consider it as an abstraction taking on larger ideological force in 19th-century America.[8]

In the years surrounding the first major revision to McGuffey's reader in 1857, Americans witnessed enormous geographical, economic, social, and political changes that reformulated both religious and secular cornerstones of American culture, or what Elliot Gorn identifies as American piety and property. Over the two middle quarters of the 19th century, the Protestant church's official role in state governments was disestablished, and Protestantism became increasingly secularized, displacing the cultural, intellectual, and religious force of Calvinism with what Ann Douglas has seen as a feminized, anti-intellectual, consumer-obsessed sentimentalism (25, 85). At the same time that the dwindling cultural force of Calvinism remapped the religious landscape of American piety, the nation experienced westward geographic expansion, marked also by the acquisition of the Southwest from the war with Mexico (1846–48); an expanding middle class; the birth of new political parties and the consolidation of antislavery factions such as the Barnburners, Liberty party, and Free-Soilers in the Republican Party (1854); and increased immigration from Germany and Ireland. Indeed, from 1840 to 1860, the U.S. population came close to doubling, with a huge influx of easily-naturalized immigrants, particularly from Ireland, arriving between 1846 and 1856 (Bode, *Anatomy* 38).

While a staggering array of sociopolitical transformations such as these occurred in the middle decades of the 19th-century, focusing on the era's expanded franchise conveys how these religious and secular changes were felt in new understandings of American citizenship, the contours of which were shifting in tandem with the nation's expanding geographic and economic borders. That is, focusing on the era's expanding franchise—what Elizabeth Cady Stanton called the "first right" of citizenship—gives an overarching sense of how ideas about American citizenship changed over this period in conjunction with changes in conceptions of piety and property.

Two key changes occurred to the franchise between the Revolution and the Civil War that signified expanding notions of citizenship in America: the gradual relaxation of property requirements that led to nearly universal white male suffrage by 1860, and the official inauguration of the fight for the franchise by white women at the Seneca Falls convention in 1848.[9] Before the Revolution, property ownership was the primary requirement for the endowment of the rights of national citizenship, particularly the right to vote. After the Revolution, as the nation expanded westward and property ownership became increasingly widespread, it was no longer the primary requirement for citizenship. Between 1790 and 1860, the electorate expanded to include almost all white adult male suffrage.

If property were no longer a requirement to vote, then the "first right" of citizenship could theoretically be open to all; thus political capacity became attached to gender and race. As Rogers Smith writes: "The Jacksonian sense of American civic identity was fully revealed in the era's franchise laws. Though in 1828 fourteen states still had property or taxpayer requirements for voting, by 1860 only South Carolina still retained a version of the restrictions that had long built class hierarchies into American voting laws" (213). Thus between 1824 and 1840, active participation in presidential elections rose from 29 to 80.2 percent of white adult males (201). Yet, as Smith also points out, "to analyze these years solely through the prism of scholars' 'republican revival' is dangerously incomplete" (201): "once wealth restrictions that had disfranchised most free blacks and assimilated Native Americans were abandoned, Jacksonian racism made it imperative to make such ascriptive disqualifications explicit. And as women began to voice their demands for the franchise more widely, Democratic officials almost universally rejected them" (213).

While women, as we have seen in the previous chapter, began using political discourse in 1830 with the antiremoval petitioning campaign, the Woman's Rights Convention that gathered July 19–20, 1848 in Seneca Falls, New York formally articulated women's demands for the vote and officially challenged traditional patriarchal notions of citizenship, officially blurring lines between "separate spheres" and inciting their entrenchment.[10] The Declaration of Sentiments, prepared by Stanton, debated by Seneca Falls conveners, and signed there by 68 women and 32 men, borrowed rhetoric from the Declaration of Independence and drew—as women's antiremoval and antislavery petitions had—on both natural rights and religious language. This document reverberated with the injury of a failed contract—with "the conviction that the Revolution had made implicit promises to women which had not been kept" (Kerber and De Hart 207). Of course, the most controversial aspect of the Declaration of Sentiments was the first grievance listed: the claim that man "has never permitted her [woman] to exercise her inalienable right to the elective franchise."[11] This was followed by the grievance that "Having deprived her of this first right of a citizen, the elective franchise, thereby leaving her without representation in the halls of legislation, he has oppressed her on all sides," which led to the Declaration's resolution demanding the "first right" of citizenship: "That it is the duty of the women of this country to secure to themselves their sacred right to the elective franchise" (207, 209). As many historians and Stanton herself have claimed, although this controversial resolution to pursue the vote was Stanton's "most important original contribution," it was the only resolution not approved unanimously at the convention (Lerner, "Meanings" 204).

That both men and women attendees rejected the resolution and that it took another 71 years for women to win the vote give us some indication of the extent to which women's claim for the elective franchise challenged prevailing gender norms and drew out ascriptive traditions of citizenship. These challenges generated the women's rights movement but also led to the entrenchment of gender ideologies such as domesticity and true womanhood. Just as congressmen had raised their prohibitions against the propriety of women's political discourse when women petitioned on behalf of Native American Indians and slaves in the 1830s, during the 1840s and 50s, as Rogers Smith describes, women gained some new economic rights, "but the few explicit changes made in their civic status brought them even more in line with the limiting doctrines of republican motherhood, buttressed now by stronger biologically based claims for the propriety of their political subordination" (230). Continues Smith, "As many scholars have noted, the Jacksonian era instead [of a liberal egalitarian view of women's status] saw the further entrenchment of beliefs that women were especially suited for the domestic sphere, concerned primarily with child-rearing, housekeeping and hygiene, and religiously based personal morality" (234–35).[12]

In this context of these expanding notions of citizenship for white men, and potentially for white women, discourses of gendered vocal propriety arose to reinforce the entrenchment of domestic ideology and to provide more subtle ways of preserving past notions of citizenship. Pairing gendered social and linguistic roles with the religious and secular values of piety and property, gendered vocal propriety emerged during this era of sociopolitical mobility to ground ideas of American identity in laws of language. This development is strikingly marked by the fact that the definition of *propriety* itself moved, over the 19th century, from its long-time sense of *property*, as in something owned or possessed, to the sense of *proper* 'fitness, appropriateness, aptitude, suitability; appropriateness to the circumstances or conditions; conformity with requirement, rule, or principle; rightness, correctness, justness, accuracy,' and became attached to notions of morality, as in 'conformity with good manners or polite usage; correctness of behaviour or morals; becomingness, decency. *The proprieties:* the things that are considered proper; the details of conventionally correct or proper conduct' (*OED*, 2nd ed.). Discourses of propriety thus enfolded notions of property (propriety was a self-possession, a manifestation of possessive individualism) and notions of piety (propriety became an expression of moral character, a secular expression of religious observance).[13] Propriety—of which gendered vocal propriety was a part— offered a different means of culturally preserving the Whiggish hierarchy, distinction, moral integrity, and personal diligence that many felt would lead to the progress of American civilization as the borders of American citizenship were expanded and contested.

Discourses of propriety gave people access to both social success and moral character and propelled them to learn to read, write, and speak "properly" through a wide a range of 19th-century self-improvement and educational activities, including a linguistic self-improvement movement that eagerly expressed itself in a range of elocution manuals, pronunciation guides, and grammar books, on which the remainder of this section is focused.[14] The linguistic self-improvement movement that began in the 1840s emphasized, as Robert Connors notes, "proper usage and grammatical correctness in speech and writing" and sprang, in part, from "the eastern reaction against the roughness and crudeness of frontier America, an attitude that wished to set standards of propriety in language as in all other aspects of life; and the desire for self-improvement and getting ahead" (120). Linguistic self-improvement, as a facet of education, was also seen as a safeguard against the moral corruption caused by the nation's prosperity and geographic, political, and economic expansion. For example, much of Lyman Beecher's jeremiad, "A Plea for the West" (1835), reprinted under the title "Necessity for Education" in *McGuffey's Sixth Eclectic Reader* (1879), articulates how some perceived education in general as needing to keep pace with, or to provide a moral restraint on, an expanding population, commerce, manufacturing, agriculture, *and* citizenship, or "we must perish by our own prosperity" (L. Beecher 99):

> The great experiment is now making, and from its extent and rapid filling up, is making in the West, whether the perpetuity of our republican institutions can be reconciled with universal suffrage. Without the education of the head and heart of the nation, they cannot be; and the question to be decided is, can their nation, or the vast balance power of it, be so imbued with intelligence and virtue, as to bring out, in laws and their administration, a perpetual self-preserving energy? (100)

For Beecher, as well as for many other Americans of his day, amidst the instability of "universal suffrage" and attending threats of republican disintegration, education emerges as the nation's life preserver.[15] In the context of such educational fervor, linguistic self-improvement activities such as conversational and grammatical correctness could become means of both social advancement and social discipline.

Codified in readers like McGuffey's and in linguistic self-improvement texts of mid-century, notions of vocal propriety stepped in to give ambitious-yet-anxious Americans rhetorical access to national identity through both property and piety, both to promise more fluid social identities and to curb them. Further, ideas about vocal propriety were distinctly gendered to delimit realms of national participation. The ways in which discourses of gendered vocal propriety invoked notions of property and piety to locate women's speech squarely in the domestic sphere can be seen explicitly in texts addressing proper uses of voice—manuals on conversation and elocution, pronunciation guides, and grammar books—that proliferated at mid century.

Two texts—Andrew P. Peabody's "Address Delivered Before the Newburyport Female High School, Dec. 19, 1846" and Parry Gwynne's "A Word to the Wise, or Hints on the Current Improprieties of Expression in Writing and Speaking," both included in Peabody's *Conversation, Its Faults and Its Graces*—exemplify how ideas about vocal propriety were gendered to support (white, middle-class, Protestant) ideologies of true womanhood, particularly domesticity.[16] Both Peabody and Gwynne blend ideas about gentility with ideas about morality in discourse on language that buttressed domestic ideology.

According to Peabody in his address to young ladies, his auditors "do more than any other class in the community towards establishing the general tone and standard of social intercourse. The voices of many of you already, I doubt not, strike the key-note of home conversation"; and such conversation "interweaves with a never-resting shuttle the bonds of domestic sympathy" (10). "Speech, too," reiterates Peabody, "is the sole medium of a countless host of domestic duties and observances," and nine-tenths of all domestic unhappiness "can be traced to no other cause than untrue, unkind, or ungoverned speech" (21, 24). Given that their voices "strike the key-note of home conversation," these young ladies are charged with observing vocal proprieties: adopting the characteristics of "graceful, elegant, and profitable conversation," including correct and easy pronunciation, and "shun[ning] all the *ungrammatical vulgarisms* which are often heard, but which never fail to grate harshly on a well-tuned ear," vulgarisms that include *hain't* for *has not, done* for *did,* and *won't* and *ain't,* or filler words, such as "I'm sure," "You know," "I declare," or "Did you ever?" (14–16). Reflecting how vocal propriety invoked gendered notions of social class and moral character, Peabody emphasizes how young women's speech habits not only can reveal them as "coarse and vulgar" or "give unfavorable impressions as to the good breeding of the person that uses them," but also can have "a very bad moral bearing" (14–16). Peabody further emphasizes a kind of vocal piety among young ladies, as the habit of using "exaggerated, extravagant forms of speech" like *splendid* and *magnificent* is a "crying sin among young ladies": "Our words have a reflex influence upon our characters," and young ladies risk the loss of their "reputation for veracity" because of a "habit of overstrained and extravagant speech" (14–16). Indeed, "Higher considerations [. . .] should govern our conversation; and the divine Teacher assures us that even for our idle words we are accountable to Him who has given us the power of speech" (18). To drive his moral point home to his impressionable female audience, Peabody stresses that religion is necessary as "the guiding, controlling element in conversation. All conversation ought to be religious," such that even "Common subjects" should be "talked of religiously" because "our words are all uttered in the hearing of an unseen Listener and Judge" (25–26). Such discourse on vocal propriety thus incorporated flagging national values of piety and property into gendered language ideologies.

Parry Gwynne's "A Word to the Wise, or Hints on the Current Improprieties of Expression in Writing and Speaking," similarly reveals how vocal propriety invoked gendered notions of gentility to absorb larger concerns about women's potentially mobile social identity. He overtly brings gender to bear on vocal propriety:

> Never speak of 'lots' of things. Some young men allow themselves a diffusive license of speech, and of quotation, which has introduced many words into colloquial style that do not at all tend to improve or dignify the language, and which, when heard from *ladies'* lips, become absolute vulgarisms. A young man may talk recklessly of 'lots of . . . ' [. . .], but a lady may *not*. Men may indulge in any latitude of expression within the bounds of sense and decorum, but woman has a narrower range—even her mirth must be subjected to the rules of good taste. It may be naive, but must never be grotesque. It is not that we would have *primness* in the sex, but we would have refinement. Women are the purer and the more ornamental part of life, and when *they* degenerate, the Poetry of Life is gone. (103, Gwynne's emphasis)

Gwynne reveals how gendered vocal propriety linguistically locates men and women in precise spheres: Young men may "talk recklessly" and have certain "latitude of expression," while "ladies" have "a narrower range." Via such notions of gendered vocal propriety, mobile mid-century American identities were effectively located in comparatively wide or confined spheres of activity.

Joining with advice in such conversation manuals, discourse on *grammar* was perhaps the most pervasive national manifestation of vocal propriety. What Rollo Lyman calls the "heyday" of grammar that capped the second quarter of the 19th century coincided in important ways with rising consciousness of propriety. As Richard Bailey puts it, "With the unprecedented emphasis on gentility, grammar was viewed as a prerequisite to polite behavior, and etiquette books urged particular forms of English, often in excruciating detail" (*Nineteenth* 253). Bailey further claims that "During the nineteenth century, young people studied grammar assiduously—doubtless more intensively than any time before or since. Since grammar as a school subject had long been in place, there was little need to justify the time spent studying it" (253).[17] Capitalizing upon anxieties about self-presentation and pivoting on notions of vocal propriety, 19th-century understandings of *grammar* increasingly embraced not simply the scientific study of language *grammar* had once denoted (orthography, etymology, syntax, and prosody) but also, as Lindley Murray's exceptionally popular *English Grammar* put it, "the *art* of speaking and writing the English language *with propriety*" (Murray [1824] 13, my emphasis).[18] Goold Brown, too, in his *Institutes of English Grammar* (1849) pointed out that "he who is desirous either of relishing the beauties of literary composition, or of expressing his sentiments *with propriety* and ease, must make the principles of language his study" (iii, my emphasis). At this moment, grammar thus dealt not with what linguists today regard as grammar—either the internalized rules that speakers of a language share or the more scientific study of structural relationships in language—but with broader questions of *usage,* with ways of speaking with *propriety* within a speech community.[19]

Long linked to religious study, national identity, and the training of good citizens, grammar as propriety incorporated American values of property and piety in distinct ways, thus serving, like other discourses of vocal propriety on conversation or pronunciation, not only to motivate but also to clarify mobile sociopolitical identities, eventually lending itself as a natural partner to the cult of true womanhood. As an expression of vocal propriety, grammar was cultural capital and moral authority for the era's ambitious. Seth Hurd's volume, *A Grammatical Corrector* (1847), serves as an exemplar of mid-19th-century grammar books that both reflected and conveyed ideas about linguistic propriety as a kind of property. Hurd describes the object of his volume:

> Such is the office of the "Grammatical Corrector." It is a perpetual memento of what is to be avoided; a manual adapted to the wants [. . .] of *all* [Hurd's emphasis] who wish to avoid the common *improprieties of speech;* a method of counteracting bad habits by an efficient and practical establishment of good ones. In short, with respect to the errors of language, *this little book is precisely what a counterfeit detector is in money matters!* (vi, my emphasis)[20]

Like many grammar manuals of the 1840s and 1850s, Hurd's *Grammatical Corrector* preached an odd mix of self-denial and self-potentiality, of verboten language use and possibilities for self-improvement and class mobility. It preached a doctrine of linguistic reform and accessibility to "*all*," reflecting an open notion of performable social identity and permeable social lines: Readers could use books like Hurd's to correct their grammatical faults and rise in social status. Yet at the same time, it implied that, at root, one's social identity was static and intrinsic, even authenticable: Books like Hurd's could help speakers use grammar as a tool, like "a counterfeit detector [. . .] in money matters," to detect, through speech, if someone were not "the real thing." Hurd's use of the phrase "a counterfeit detector" at this time is noteworthy, reflecting that language, like money, has value, and needs to be guarded by those who use and "possess" it. *McGuffey's Sixth Eclectic Reader* echoed this notion in saying that words should be pronounced "as beautiful coins, newly issued from the mint, deeply and accurately impressed, perfectly finished; neatly struck by the proper organs, distinct in due succession, and of due weight" (qtd. in Gorn 28). While such comparisons between proper speech and money may have been unconscious, they "made explicit that education [. . .] had as much to do with social class and professional status as with learning to read and write the English language" (Gorn 28). In short, mid-19th-century grammar, a manifestation of vocal propriety, was a prized possession, regarded as personal property.

Given its history and its context, it was perhaps no coincidence that mid-19th-century grammar also integrated the era's religious sentiment and emphasized grammatical instruction as a route to piety. The 18th century's Webster and Murray were both devout, as were Murray's mid-19th-century followers Samuel Kirkham and Goold Brown. Good grammar, as in Murray's text, was equated with clear communication, but also piety and virtue, purity and precision (Murray [1826] 6, 250, 304). Kirkham saw grammar as "that learning which lifts the soul from the earth, and enables it to hold converse with a thousand worlds" (Kirkham 13).[21] Indeed, Kirkham—who "did as much as any textbook writer to promote an absolutist view of correct English" (Finegan 375)—explicitly linked mid-century grammatical principles with both patriotic and religious duty, urging his readers to study grammar to prevent that "you should ever be so unmindful of your duty to your country, to your Creator, to yourself, and to succeeding generations, to be content to grovel in ignorance" (Kirkham 15). Grammar thus became a kind of "moral barometer" (Mathews 60 qtd. in Bailey, *Nineteenth* 216). And thus many grammar books, like G. P. Quackenbos,' first published in 1851, read much like sermons, emphasizing the "essential properties" of expressing thoughts in the vernacular: "purity, propriety, precision, clearness, strength, harmony, and unity" (Quackenbos 5).

Such "essential properties," however, embodied laws of language that were often less about language than about norms of gendered vocal behavior. Like Peabody's and Gwynne's commentaries about conversation, discourse on grammar invoked piety and property to place male and female speakers in specific ways. In a culture that celebrated true womanhood even while debating the Woman Question, grammatical ideals were easily gendered to overlap ideals of true womanhood such as purity, piety, domesticity, and submissiveness. Thus, although notions of vocal propriety expressed in discourse on grammar motivated women and men in some similar ways, when these discourses were combined with gender ideologies such as true womanhood, vocal propriety located women in the domestic sphere. As Emerson said in 1856, "The keeping of the proprieties is as indispensable as clean linen," reflecting the association of propriety with often-gendered domestic labor (*Eng Traits, Manners* qtd. in *OED*, 2nd ed.). It takes no stretch of the imagination to see how notions of propriety could be combined with ideas about gendered social and linguistic behavior (ideas about women's domestic "voice") to help regulate political behavior (ideas about the "vote")—a recipe that the Seneca Falls signers certainly recognized and a process that cultural texts usefully illuminate.

The fundamental paradox that, through gendered commentary about her "proper" voice a woman could become, or could be prohibited from becoming, a citizen in the fullest sense was specifically recognized in two resolutions of the Seneca Falls Declaration of Sentiments. In one resolution, the signers recognize that "the objection of indelicacy and *impropriety,* which is so often brought against woman when she addresses a public audience, comes with a very ill-grace from those who encourage, by their attendance, her appearance on the stage, in the concert, or in the feats of the circus" (209, my emphasis). In the final resolution, they also state that "it is self-evidently her [woman's] right to participate with her brother in teaching [the great subject of morals and religion], both in private and in public, by *writing and by speaking,* by any instrumentalites *proper* to be used, and in any assemblies *proper* to be held" (209, my emphasis). In noting "the objection of indelicacy and impropriety" perceived in women's public address, the Declaration references the wide spectrum of gendered metalinguistic criticism leveled against women's speaking in public, and especially speaking on political matters, at the time of Seneca Falls.[22] Yet in noting the "right to participate . . . both in private and public, by writing and speaking," Stanton also acknowledges the importance of a "public" voice—one exercised outside the domestic realm—to the gaining of political "rights." Thus the Declaration of Sentiments pinpoints precisely how notions of gendered vocal propriety tied views of gender to "proper" uses of language within particular arenas of activity. These notions could be equally used to release (as in the Declaration itself) or to repress voices and votes—to articulate and to locate mobile social and political American identities at a time when the religious and secular laws governing and clarifying such identities had apparently been challenged.

Ideas about grammar as a path to both middle-class prosperity and personal piousness thus overlapped neatly with mid-century gender ideologies, which had long perpetuated sex differences in language.[23] In the context of mid-19th-century America, when true womanhood stressed women's purity, piety, domesticity, and submissiveness, gender ideologies coupled "naturally," and nationally, with language ideologies that associated "good speech" such as grammar with the very values of feminized middle-class domesticity. Together, Susan Warner's *The Wide Wide World* and Horatio Alger's *Ragged Dick*—to which I will now turn—aptly illustrate how education in grammar, as just such a manifestation of gendered vocal propriety, prompted two very "American" success stories. Through their respective educations in grammar, Ellen Montgomery and Dick Hunter successfully attained middle-class piety and property, but in quite distinct arenas of national participation.

3. *THE WIDE, WIDE WORLD* AND *RAGGED DICK*: STORIES OF GENDERED GRAMMAR EDUCATION, DOMESTICATION, AND AMERICANIZATION

Just as grammar was one of the most-discussed linguistic topics of the second quarter of the 19th century, Susan Warner's *The Wide, Wide World*

(1850)—what Jane Tompkins calls "the Ur-text of the nineteenth-century United States" (Afterword 585)—was the most-discussed American novel of the early 1850s, not eclipsed in popularity until *Uncle Tom's Cabin* (1852) gained wide readership (Bode, *Anatomy* 172).[24] Generally recognized as the first best-seller in America, Warner's sentimental novel moreover makes the process of attaining gendered vocal propriety a central theme. By the end of the novel, Warner's orphaned Ellen Montgomery finds a home in feminized, middle-class domesticity, appreciably via her achievement of linguistic self-discipline.

Indeed, Ellen Montgomery's first encounters with Alice Humphreys, her surrogate mother-sister, begin to "place" Ellen not only within the Humphreys family but also in middle-class society. Teaching Ellen "good English" is one of Alice's priorities, as seen in their introduction to one another:

> "Permit me to ask if you know English?" [asked Alice]
> "Oh, yes, ma'am, I hope so; I knew that a great while ago."
> "Did you? I am very happy to make your acquaintance then, for the number of young ladies who *do* [Warner's emphasis] know English is in my opinion remarkably small. Are you sure of the fact, Ellen?"
> "Why yes, Miss Alice."
> "Will you undertake to write me a note of two pages that shall not have *one fault of grammar,* [my emphasis] nor one word spelt wrong, nor any thing in it that is not *good English* [my emphasis]? You may take for a subject the history of this afternoon."
> "Yes, ma'am, if you wish it. I hope I can write a note that long without making mistakes."
> Alice smiled.
> "I will not stop to inquire," she said, "whether *that long* [Warner's emphasis] is Latin or French; but Ellen, my dear, it is not English."
> Ellen blushed a little, though she laughed too.
> "I believe I have got into the way of saying that by hearing aunt Fortune and Mr. Van Brunt say it; I don't think I ever did before I came here." [...]
> "[...] Ellen, I will make a bargain with you,—if you will study English with me, I will study French with you." (Warner 171)

As Alice makes clear here, "knowing English" is not the same as Ellen's speaking her native tongue; "knowing English" means speaking "good" *British* English. For Alice hails from England and holds up a different national linguistic standard as well as a different class standard: She displays British English as "Standard" English—which it was in Ellen's day, when the rural "Yankee" English of Ellen's Aunt Fortune and Mr. Van Brunt had not proven itself either "refined" enough or "English" enough to be considered an appropriate model. Ellen's knowledge of this standard is to be "tested" in her writing of it, but Ellen's *speech* (her expression "that long") is what gives away her lack of proper linguistic knowledge. Ellen's blush—an indication of her embarrassment—also betrays the extent to which this knowledge is socialized, classed knowledge, as does her attempt to distance herself from the mistake. "That long," she explains, is an expression that results from the company she keeps with hard-working, unrefined country Yankees, not part of her "own" language, or her "own" class identity. As Ellen's friend Ellen Chauncey will later say, such country manners need some "brushing up," and such "brushing up" of her language is exactly what Ellen Montgomery pursues throughout the novel (285). *The Wide Wide World* thus bears out critiques of grammar instruction as reinforcing ideologies of standardization. What's more, Warner's phenomenally popular novel speaks to the mid-19th-century moment—Rollo Lyman's "heyday of grammar"—as a complex "scene" of American vocal education, a scene around which, as Deborah Brandt might put it, "hangs" some significant "ideological congestion" (207).

Warner's *The Wide, Wide World* together with Horatio Alger's *Ragged Dick* (1867)—two popular mid-19th-century stories that imagine the achievement of American identity in part through linguistic labors—help us to locate Ellen Montgomery's ideologically-saturated "scene" of language learning within 19th-century American discourses of vocal propriety. These discourses of vocal propriety, as discussed in the previous section, arose within the context of an expanded franchise, a rapidly growing middle class, heightened debates about women's rights, and shifting immigrant populations, as well as increased literacy education. In giving their protagonists access to gendered vocal propriety in this context, Warner's and Alger's narratives give us a valuable glimpse into how mid-19th-century ideologies of gender and language—particularly grammar as gendered vocal propriety—could work together to promote American identities for their child protagonists, identities that ultimately locate them in different places.

While critics have attended to these stories, particularly *Ragged Dick*, as articulations of mid-19th-century white, middle-class, Protestant values, they have overlooked the specific interarticulation that I explore here—the process by which gendered language ideologies are intertwined with these values to produce national identity.[25] While scholars too have noted themes of discipline and submission, particularly in *The Wide, Wide World*, I am interested in probing more in-depth the *linguistic*—or, more precisely, *vocal*—facets of discipline in these works.[26]

This section thus argues that the education in grammar by which these two orphaned children, Ellen Montgomery and Dick Hunter, attain middle-class propriety and consequently become respectable potential American citizens are, to no small degree, gendered processes of linguistic self-discipline. By the finale of *The Wide, Wide World,* Ellen is placed in middle-class domestic culture, considerably via her successful linguistic self-discipline, a trajectory that makes her not only the sentimental heroine critics have long dubbed her, but also a kind of heroine of mid-century vocal propriety who linguistically achieves social mobility. Over the course of the novel, Ellen's study of English—geared toward the attainment of vocal propriety, or what Alice and most Americans called "good English," or "good grammar"—offers her a mobile, performable social identity through language. Ellen's labor in language is ultimately rewarded by her attainment of property, piety, and national identification; as Ellen gains grammar, she loses her socially unplaced status and becomes an ideal 19th-century American woman, a wife who is given entrée into middle class American culture. Like Ellen, the orphaned Dick Hunter—who begins taking care of himself at age seven by becoming a newsboy, match-boy, and boot-black (51–53)—becomes place-able within middle-class American culture. By the end of *Ragged Dick*, Alger's hero gains access to feminized middle-class domesticity, and with it, to "American" values of piety and property.

Yet for Ellen and Dick, education through grammar has different effects, leading them to inhabit particular spaces in each narrative. From one perspective, Ellen successfully becomes a middle-class American wife through her attainment of "good grammar." But from another perspective, Ellen's discipline in grammar also *im*mobilizes her. For, the space in which we leave her at the end of the novel is the thoroughly privatized, feminized space of "*her room* [Warner's emphasis]" in the Humphreys house that her now-husband John (not incidentally, the brother of Alice, her grammar tutor) has meticulously outfitted for her—a room "so delightfully private" that it has "no entrance but through other rooms," and a room in which she finally claims herself fully "satisfied" (Warner 574, 577, 583). Ellen's grammar education thus results in, and aids, her internalization of a 19th-century ethic of submission and ultimately locates her within the domestic sphere—a domain in which, as Tompkins and others have suggested, she could claim some cultural power, but a compromised sense of power, and certainly not political power. Alger, in contrast, depicts Dick Hunter's grammar education as less absolute. It allows him to retain a linguistically flexible social identity, one that gives him access to the feminized domestic spaces of the middle class, but also, potentially, to the masculinized public, and political, world.

Although published in book form nearly two decades apart, *The Wide, Wide World* and *Ragged Dick* are equally relevant to this chapter's concerns because, in the conditions of their creation, in their popularity with readers, and in the lessons they give, they have become synonymous with important aspects of 19th-century America. Both books were the source of their authors' respective "rises" from economic or moral failures, composed amid their respective connections with New York City. The Warner family's worsening financial situation after losses from the Panic of 1837 led Susan, a volunteer with the New York City Tract Society, to turn to writing to earn a living; she began writing *The Wide, Wide World* in 1848 at age twenty-nine, when the family had to sell all of their belongings to pay a mortgage on

Vocal (Im)propriety and the Management of Sociopolitical Mobility   79

one of her father's properties (Tompkins, Afterword 592; Argersinger 385). A Unitarian minister, Alger composed *Ragged Dick; Or, Street Life in New York with the Boot Blacks* in New York after hitting "rock bottom" in 1866, when he narrowly escaped prosecution for "performing 'unnatural' acts with several boys in his congregation in Brewster, Massachusetts" by vowing "never again to seek or accept a ministry" (Trachtenberg vi). Although neither Warner's nor Alger's subsequent works reached the popularity of *The Wide, Wide World* or *Ragged Dick*, both started their authors in new directions and gave them reliable income as writers. Warner's *The Wide, Wide World*, as mentioned above, is generally recognized as the first best-seller in America. And Alger's bestseller gave him a formula for success in the literary market, much as McGuffey's readers had.[27] Both successes led their authors to extend their works for a juvenile audience; the Warner sisters, in response to reader requests, wrote several children's books for a series called "Ellen Montgomery's Bookshelf," and Alger created an entire series of Ragged Dick stories culminating in *Rufus and Rose* (1870) (Damon-Bach 48n2, Trachtenberg x-xiii). And over time, both books, if not their authors, have become identified with characteristics of "American" identity—*The Wide, Wide World* with sentimentality and *Ragged Dick* with the "rags-to-riches" formula of the Franklinian success story.[28] Eerily like the biographies of their authors, each fiction can be read, as Jane Tompkins reads *The Wide, Wide World*, as different but equally recognizable versions of "an American Protestant *bildungsroman*" (*Sensational* 184). As Tompkins suggests, stereotyped characters like Ellen Montgomery and, I would add, Ragged Dick:

> are the instantly recognizable representatives of overlapping racial, sexual, national, ethnic, economic, social, political, and religious categories; they convey enormous amounts of cultural information in an extremely condensed form. As the telegraphic expression of complex clusters of value, stereotyped characters are *essential* [Tompkins' emphasis] to popularly successful narrative. Figures like [. . .] Ellen Montgomery operate as a cultural shorthand, and because of their multilayered representative function are the carriers of strong emotional associations. Their familiarity and typicality, rather than making them bankrupt or stale, are the basis of their effectiveness as integers in a social equation. (*Sensational* xvi)

Yet the ways in which these stories have come to stand in for larger cultural narratives can also occlude our analysis of perhaps other stories of which they are a part—such as the coming-of-age stories about language, gender, and national identity I want to highlight.

As for many mid-19th-century grammarians, for Warner and Alger, moral character and future destiny were essentially linked through one's behavior, a linkage that required the self-discipline of one's habits, including linguistic ones. Andrew Peabody had foregrounded just such an essential relation between speech and character to motivate linguistic discipline in young high school women when he told them that "by speech you adopt thoughts, and the voice that utters them is a pen that engraves them indelibly on the soul. If you can suppress unkind thoughts, so that, when they rise in your breast, and mount to your very lips, you leave them unuttered, you are not on the whole unkind,—your better nature has the supremacy. But if these wrong feelings find utterance . . . there is reason to fear that they flow from a bitter fountain within" (19–20). Peabody further observes how blessed might many delinquent young ladies be if, when they were exercising their tongues, what he calls "unruly members," they only believed that "they were writing out their own characters in their daily speech! [. . .] To say nothing of the social effect of such a [bad] life, is not the tongue thus employed working out spiritual death for the soul in whose service it is busy? I know of no images too vile to portray such a character" (22). The logic of this linkage of linguistic behavior, character, and destiny might be most simply expressed in the words of a still-popular proverb, sometimes attributed to Frank Outlaw: "Watch your thoughts; they become words. Watch your words; they become actions. Watch your actions; they become habits. Watch your habits; they become character. Watch your character; it becomes your destiny."

In such a chain of linkages, one's good character is indicated by one's habits, actions, words, and thoughts, such that the goal is to bring one's "self" in line with one's "outer" behavior, linguistic and otherwise, a goal that requires the highest mode of discipline: self-surveillance, or "watching" one's own thoughts, words, actions, and habits to internalize discipline.[29] As the Preface to *The Primer of Politeness* put it, "He is best taught who has learned the secret of self-control. *He is best governed who is self-governed*. Other things being equal, that school is the best where the government is the result of moral and not of physical force" (Gow n. pag., my emphasis). More specifically, Kirkham's observation on elocutionary training aptly illustrates the *vocal process* of linguistic self-discipline in stating that "the vocal powers, like those of the mind or the other powers of the body, are strengthened and matured, and brought under *subjection* [my emphasis], only by a long and persevering *exercise* [Kirkham's emphasis] of them" (*Elocution* 16–17). Thus in *The Wide, Wide World*, Ellen Montgomery's exterior, good manners emanate in part from her interior, essential goodness, and in part from her "persevering exercise" of them, as an exchange later in the novel shows: The young Ellen Chauncey describes her young friend Ellen Montgomery, "I do not think Ellen is so polite because she is so much with Alice and John, but because she is so sweet and good. I don't think that she could *help* being polite" (418). To which Mrs. Gillespie adds, "mere sweetness and goodness would never give so much elegance of manner. As far as I have seen, Ellen Montgomery is a *perfectly* well-behaved child," and Mrs. Chauncey responds, "That she is, [. . .] but neither would any cultivation or example be sufficient for it without Ellen's thorough good principle and great sweetness of temper" (418).

Warner's narrator gets the final word here: "Ellen's sweetness of temper was not entirely born with her; it was one of the blessed fruits of religion and discipline. Discipline had not done with it yet" (418).

In addition, in Ellen Montgomery's world, the ideology by which one's behavior links one's "character" to one's "destiny" is powerfully situated within a Christian belief system, in which God's authority reigns supreme and "destiny" means not only one's success on earth but also spiritual survival in the world beyond. Thus the "arena of human action" in sentimental literature like *The Wide, Wide World* is not only the world, but "the human soul" (Tompkins, *Sensational* 151). And thus Ellen's challenge is not simply to discipline herself in order to earn *others'* love—as Ellen's mother tells her early in *The Wide, Wide World,* "It will be your own fault if she [Aunt Emerson] does not love you, in time, truly and tenderly" (21). Her challenge is also to earn *God's* love, a goal that continually renews itself. From the moment of her Christian conversion on the steamboat—from her literal and spiritual journey from her mother's child to orphaned child to God's child—Ellen must make herself "be a servant of God," who, as Warner's Mr. Marshman puts it, "has given you every good and pleasant thing you have enjoyed in your whole life" (74, 72). For although God's love is unconditional, it is also something Ellen is always unworthy of receiving, always humbly graced to receive. Thus it makes sense that Alice gives Ellen both linguistic and religious standards, as Alice situates all aspects of Ellen's behavior within Christian duty—in Warner's words, "the faithful, patient, self-denying performance of every duty as it comes to hand—" (239).

Such Christian duty, together with humility, discipline, and self-sacrifice, comprise what Tompkins calls an "ethic of submission," an ethic of the utmost importance in Ellen Montgomery's world.[30] Tompkins provides valuable insight into ideas about the process of developing Christian self-submission, a process that, as I will show, dovetails with Ellen's project of linguistic self-discipline: "Since self-submission does not come naturally, but is a skill that can only be acquired through practice, the taking apart and putting back together of the self must be enacted over and over again, as each new situation she meets becomes the occasion for the heroine's ceaseless labor of self-transformation" (*Sensational* 176). Although Tompkins does not attend to vocal aspects of Ellen's self-discipline, within this religious framework of self-submission, learning to discipline her vocal behavior helps Ellen claim a higher, spiritual form of power at the same time that it prepares her to become an acceptable ambassador of American pure womanhood and an ideal American wife.

Warner makes clear throughout the novel that Ellen's vocal behavior and consequent linguistic discipline are situated within the 19th-century Christian "ethic of submission." Over the course of the novel, Warner linguistically charts Ellen's development from external discipline to self-discipline and from rebellion to submission. Warner calls attention to the vocal aspects of this trajectory by placing it within mid-19th-century discourses of vocal propriety. Specifically, through her characters' voices, Warner indicates whether characters are "good" mentors to Ellen. "Good" voices, like "good" readers or "good" grammar, thus materialize the essential connection between language and character in the world of *The Wide, Wide World*.

All of Ellen's mentors in *The Wide, Wide World* have beautiful, spiritualized voices. Perhaps the most memorable and idealized voices in the novel belong to Ellen's most influential friends and mentors—Alice and her brother John Humphreys.[31] Indeed, it is no more than Alice's *voice* that first acquaints an unhappy, lonely, weeping Ellen with Alice herself:

> In one of these fits of forced quiet, when she lay as still as the rocks around her, she heard a voice close by say, "What is the matter, my child?"
>
> The silver sweetness of the tone came singularly upon the tempest in Ellen's mind. She got up hastily, and brushing away the tears from her dimmed eyes, she saw a young lady standing there, and a face whose sweetness well matched the voice looking upon her with grave concern. She stood motionless and silent. (148)

As Warner indicates here via Alice's voice, Alice is almost pure abstraction, pure spirit—a kind of angel—until we, like Ellen, see that her face "matches" her voice's sweetness, revealing a connection between Alice's appearance, Alice's sound, and her essential goodness. Even upon Alice's deathbed, her "clear sweet voice" rings in Ellen's ears as an indication of her ideal character (429). Indeed, throughout the novel, Alice and her brother John are held up as models of morality, and their voices convey them as such.[32]

Singing hymns at the beginning of the novel, Ellen herself possesses a "clear childish voice" that transports her listening mother, Mrs. Montgomery, beyond the earth and "to that city where sorrow and sighing shall be no more" (56). Ellen's voice is also described in relation to Alice's and John's voices:

> Alice and her brother were remarkable for beauty of voice and utterance. The latter Ellen had in part caught from them; in the former she thought herself greatly inferior. Perhaps she underrated herself; her voice, though not indeed powerful, was low and sweet and very clear; and the entire simplicity and feeling with which she sang hymns was more effectual than any higher qualities of tone and compass. She had been very much accustomed to sing with Alice, who excelled in beautiful truth and simplicity of expression; listening with delight, as she had often done, and often joining with her, Ellen had caught something of her manner. (451)

As this passage reveals, not only is "beauty of voice" a quality essential to one's good character; it is also to an extent perfectable. "Utterance" is perhaps even more disciplinable, socially manageable, and performable. As Warner makes clear, training Ellen's already-clear "voice" and disciplining her "utterance" is part of her grooming for her national role as an ideal American woman, and eventually her domestic role as John's wife: "She [Ellen] had an admirable teacher [John]. He taught her how to manage her voice and manage the language; in both which he excelled himself, and was determined that she should; and besides this their reading often led to talking that Ellen delighted in" (464). Warner's pronouns are important here: John teaches Ellen to "manage *her* voice," with the possessive pronoun indicating voice as an *a priori* quality of self, and to "manage *the* language," with the article indicating an external property made her own through her linguistic labors. Over the course of *The Wide, Wide World*, Ellen's voice and "the language"—a grammatical, correct utterance—become part of her identity, a self-possession that she uses to distinguish herself when she travels outside the nation's geographic boundaries to live with her Scottish relatives.

Situated within Warner's essentialized descriptions of characters' voices, Ellen's attainment of vocal propriety as the incorporation of both piety and industry—a kind of Puritan-laden possessive individualism—is the linguistic trajectory of the novel. Ellen's possession of proper speech is one of her major challenges in the novel, and learning vocal propriety from Alice and John is part of her journey to it. Once at her Aunt Fortune's house, Ellen continually embarks and re-embarks upon her plan to teach herself the self-restraint, self-discipline, self-possession of a Christian lady—particularly when it comes to her linguistic behavior: "She earnestly prayed that if she could not yet *feel* right toward her aunt, she might be kept at least from acting or speaking wrong" (157). She is constantly provoked, however, into what she considers rash, passionate speech in response to her unsympathetic aunt—at one point even talking back to her: "'Stop! stop!' said Ellen wildly,—'you must not speak to me so! Mamma never did, and you have no *right* to! If mamma or papa were here you would not *dare* talk to me so.' The answer to this was a sharp box on the ear from Miss Fortune's wet hand" (159). After such everyday episodes, Ellen characteristically launches into self-reprimand and into interior battles:

> "Oh," said Ellen, "why couldn't I keep still!—when I had resolved so this morning, why couldn't I be quiet!—But she ought not to have provoked me so dreadfully,—I couldn't help it." "You are wrong," said conscience again, and her tears flowed faster. And then came back her morning trouble—the duty and the difficulty of forgiving. Forgive her aunt Fortune!—with her whole heart in a passion of displeasure against her. Alas! Ellen began to feel and acknowledge that indeed all was wrong. But what to do? There was just one comfort, the visit to Miss Humphreys in the afternoon. "She will tell me," thought Ellen; "she will help me. [. . .]" (160)

In the context of mid-19th-century heightened linguistic self-consciousness and Christian self-submission, Ellen's awareness of her language reflects her own hyper-self-awareness. Controlling her self, in many ways, becomes the task of managing her speech. As she later tells Alice: "I get very angry and vexed, and sometimes I say nothing, but sometimes I get out of all patience and say things I ought not. I did so to-day; but it is so very hard to keep still when I am in such a passion" (165). In contrast to her foil—the rebellious Nancy Vawshe, who admits "it's of no use to hold my tongue. I do try, sometimes, but I never could keep it long" (231)—Ellen repeatedly berates herself for her vocal outbursts and launches into self-reform: "'Why couldn't I be quiet?' said Ellen. 'If I had only held my tongue that unfortunate minute! what possessed me to say that?'" (181).[33] But, initially at least, she can not do so on her own; such a challenge as holding her tongue requires the help of Alice and John, who adopt her as a part of the Humphreys family.

Ellen's continued interactions with Alice over the course of the narrative demonstrate Ellen's progress in achieving the goal of making Alice's "good English" her own. Alice perpetually holds up her "English" standard, as when they discuss a rocking-chair Mr. Van Brunt has made for Ellen. Ellen says:

> "[. . .]—you see the back is cushioned, and the elbows, as well as the seat;—it's queer-looking, ain't it? but it's very comfortable. Wasn't it good of him?"
>
> "It was very kind, I think. But do you know, Ellen, I am going to have to quarrel with you?"
>
> "What about?" said Ellen. "I don't believe it's any thing very bad, for you look pretty good-humoured, considering."
>
> "Nothing *very* bad," said Alice, "but still enough to quarrel about. You have twice said '*ain't*' since I have been here."
>
> "Oh," said Ellen, laughing, "is that all?"
>
> "Yes," said Alice, "and my English ears don't like it at all."
>
> "Then they shan't hear it," said Ellen, kissing her. "I don't know what makes me say it; I never used to. [. . .]" (221)

Each time Ellen disciplines her voice, she loses a little more of her own will. This point is reinforced here through Ellen's symbolic kiss; while at the beginning of the novel, Ellen *receives* kisses (from her mother, from Mr. Marshman), by the end, she has fully developed the habit of giving them away. And Alice and John, who consistently receive her kisses, continue to discipline Ellen's speech by British standards, as seen in another exchange centering on the regulation of Ellen's vocal improprieties. Ellen:

> "Oh, nicely now! Where's Mr. John? I hope he won't ask for my last drawing to-night,—I want to fix the top of that tree before he sees it."

"*Fix* the top of your tree, you little Yankee?" said Alice;—"what do you think John would say to that?—*un*fix it you mean; it is too stiff already, isn't it?"

"Well, what *shall* I say?" said Ellen laughing. "I am sorry that is Yankee, for I suppose one must speak English.—I want to do something to my tree, then.—Where is he, Alice?" (404)

Similar to her use of expressions *ain't* and *splendid*, about which Alice likewise mocks Ellen (404), Ellen's use of the word *fix* in this passage is a focal point of metalinguistic commentary throughout the novel, and the novel's prohibitions on it notably echo mid-19th-century prohibitions in grammar and usage manuals. For example, as discussed in the previous section, Andrew Peabody in his 1846 Newburyport address considers *ain't* "absolutely vulgar" and terms like *splendid* and *magnificent* a "crying sin among young ladies" (14). In addition, like many other mid-century grammarians, Seth Hurd specifically includes *fix* in his list of errors to be avoided in his *A Grammatical Corrector*. According to Hurd, Ellen's use of *fixed* for 'repaired' is blatantly incorrect; *fixed* "should be to make permanent or prepare or arrange—neither of which means to mend or repair," a usage for which Hurd emphatically finds no authority (33–34). The use of *fix* as a noun for 'state, situation, or condition,' as in "He is in a bad fix," is another particularly forceful 19th-century grammatical prohibition: "*Fix*," says Hurd, "cannot be correctly employed as a noun in any instance" (34). Beyond Hurd's prohibitions, the American verb *to fix* was continually remarked upon by English travelers to the U.S. throughout the mid-1800s, including Marryat, Godfrey Thomas Vigne, and Charles Dickens, as Mencken notes in *The American Language* (26). Later in *The Wide, Wide World*, the prohibited word *fix* comes back to haunt Ellen when she explains to John that she had not exercised because "I had fixed myself so nicely on the sofa with my books; and it looked cold and disagreeable out of doors" (477). John replies, "Since when have you ceased to be a fixture?" to which Ellen declares, laughing, "What!—Oh [. . .] how shall I ever get rid of that troublesome word? What shall I say?—I had *arranged* myself, *established* myself, so nicely on the sofa" (477).

By the time Warner's orphaned Ellen is exported to her guardian, Uncle Lindsay in Scotland, she has become a successfully-educated, linguistically-disciplined young American woman by British standards. But Ellen now faces a new challenge: to submit obediently, but as a young lady with American loyalties and religious principles, to her unsympathetic Scottish relations. At this point in the novel, Ellen's national identity explicitly complicates her gendered linguistic behavior. From the Humphreys, she has "learned self-command in more than one school" (437), such that people would say of her, "I never saw a more perfectly polite child" (475). At the same time that Ellen's correct English grammar has become her "own," she has become an American patriot; as Ellen tells Miss Sophia before leaving for Scotland, she "had a great deal rather be an American" than a Scotchwoman (494). In fact, the extent to which her language is wrapped up in not only her proper gender role but also her nationality—the extent to which her "good English" has become her very "American" property—surprises her wealthy Scottish aunt and uncle, who are astonished by her "very sweet voice" and "very nice English," yet put off by her patriotism.

The connection between Ellen's "good English" and her national identity (or, from her relatives' perspective, the dissonance between them) becomes clear in a pivotal scene in which Ellen defends American heroes from the attacks of her Scottish relatives:

> "To think," said the latter [her uncle] the next morning at breakfast,—"to think that the backwoods of America should have turned us out such a little specimen of—"
>
> "Of what, uncle?" said Ellen, laughing.
>
> "Ah, I shall not tell you that," said he.
>
> "But it is extraordinary," said Lady Keith [her aunt],—"how after living among a parcel of thick-headed and thicker-tongued Yankees she could come out and speak pure English in a clear voice;—it is an enigma to me."
>
> "Take care, Catherine," said Mr. Lindsay, laughing,—"you are touching Ellen's nationality;—look here," said he, drawing his fingers down her cheek.
>
> "She must learn to have no nationality but yours," said Lady Keith somewhat shortly.
>
> Ellen's lips were open, but she spoke not.
>
> "It is well you have come out from the Americans, you see, Ellen," pursued Mr. Lindsay;—"your aunt does not like them."
>
> "But why, sir?"
>
> "Why," said he gravely,—"don't you know that they are a parcel of rebels who have broken loose from all loyalty and fealty, that no good Briton has any business to like?"
>
> "You are not in earnest, uncle?"
>
> "*You* are, I see," said he, looking amused. "Are you one of those that made a saint of George Washington?"
>
> "No," said Ellen,—"I think he was a great deal better than some saints. But I don't think the Americans were rebels."
>
> "You are a little rebel yourself. Do you mean to say the Americans were right?"
>
> "Do you mean to say you think they were wrong, uncle?"
>
> "I assure you," said he, "if I had been in the English army I would have fought them with all my heart."
>
> "And if I had been in the American army I would have fought *you* with all my heart, uncle Lindsay."

"Come, come," said he laughing;—"*you* fight! You don't look as if you would do battle with a good-sized mosquito."

"Ah, but I mean if I had been a man," said Ellen.

"You had better put in that qualification. After all, I am inclined to think it may be as well for you on the whole that we did not meet. I don't know but we might have had a pretty stiff encounter, though." (505–06)

Warner here reveals how the 18th-century American-British revolutionary "encounter" survives in the 19th century as a war of words, an encounter of language and linguistic standards, into which Ellen's gendered social role enters.[34] Moreover, at the heart of this scene is Warner's revelation of the extent to which the disciplinary processes of feminine domestication, grammar education, and becoming American go hand-in-hand. Ellen *can* and *does* participate in this "national" rhetorical battle, showing herself rhetorically adept, much to the discontent of Lady Keith, who hopes "Ellen will get rid of these strange notions about the Americans" (506). Yet Ellen's speech is not nearly as threatening as her more political participation might have been. Ellen recognizes this fact when she notes that she could only have participated in that very public Revolutionary battle "if I had been a man," and Mr. Lindsay reinforces it when he declares to Ellen, "if your sword had been as stout as your tongue, I don't know how I might have come off in that same encounter" (506). Finally, the scene reveals that, while Ellen has proven her vocal propriety and grammatical acceptability, she has not yet completely mastered her passion. The processes of attaining feminine decorum, linguistic discipline, and an American identity continue to be interarticulated as Ellen and her uncle continue to have some "pretty stiff encounters" of a spoken sort, wherein Mr. Lindsay provides his own "schooling" of Ellen's speech in the prohibition of certain kinds of speech (such as discussing her American friends) and the encouragement of others (such as calling him "father") (520, 530).

While commentary on Ellen's "pure English" reflects the extent to which her speech and her social identity as a young American woman are disciplined via notions of vocal propriety, perhaps the most overt and graphic instances of disciplining Ellen's speech are the occasions when Mr. Lindsay and Mrs. Lindsay (Ellen's grandmother) physically touch Ellen's lips, "a way of silencing her that Ellen particularly disliked, and which both Mr. Lindsay and his mother was [sic] accustomed to use" (541). For instance, when Ellen, "with uncontrollable feeling," defends her friends Alice and John to Lady Keith, "Instantly, Mr. Lindsay's fingers tapped her lips," after which, "Ellen coloured painfully, but after an instant's hesitation, she said, 'I beg your pardon, aunt Keith. I should not have said that'" (530). The episode launches Ellen into familiar self-reprimands for her unbridled vocalizations. She goes to her room, "and sitting down on the floor, covered her face with her hands. 'What shall I do? what shall I do?' she said to herself. 'I never shall govern this tongue of mine. Oh, I wish I had not said that! they never will forgive it. What *can* I do to make them pleased with me again?'" (530). Ellen's inability to "govern her tongue" leads to the withdrawal of her Scottish relations' love—"a cool air of displeasure about all they said and did" (530). Ellen's choice of words here is important, suggesting that this young woman's need to "govern" her speech again arises most acutely—and with the most emotionally painful of consequences—in the expression of her national identity.

The importance of "governing her tongue" to the interarticulation of Ellen's gendered domestic role, linguistic discipline, and American identity is even more forcefully seen in another scene, when Mr. Lindsay forbids Ellen from visiting Mrs. Allen, the old Scottish housekeeper with whom she likes to converse. Warner writes that Ellen begins "a remonstrance. But only one word was uttered; Mr. Lindsay's hand was upon her lips," and he takes away *Pilgrim's Progress,* a gift from John that she had been reading (551). In this noteworthy scene, Lindsay physically silences Ellen at the same time that, in confiscating *Pilgrim's Progress,* he attempts to remove the elements of her American, middle-class, Puritan roots represented by the book.[35] The ideological implications of this scene are intense. While the real problem is that the Lindsays want to make Ellen less "American" and more "Scottish," to make her forget her nationality and to make her socially acceptable to their Scottish acquaintances, Ellen internalizes the problem and sees the struggle as a problem, again, of self-control:

> She had been a passionate child in earlier days; under religion's happy reign that had long ceased to be true of her [. . .]. She was surprised and half frightened at herself now, to find the strength of the old temper suddenly roused. [. . .] In vain she would try to reason and school herself into right feeling; at one thought of her lost treasure [her book] passion would come flooding up and drown all her reasonings and endeavours. (553)

From Ellen's point of view, the battle is with her own "conscience" and with mastering her voice and the passions that arouse it. Thus the challenge is to "school herself" to self-disciplined vocal propriety: "'How long is this miserable condition to last!' she said to herself. 'Till you can entirely give up your feeling of resentment, and apologize to Mr. Lindsay,' said conscience. 'Apologize!—but I haven't done wrong.' 'Yes, you have,' said conscience; 'you spoke improperly; he is justly displeased; and you must make an apology before there can be any peace'" (553). Ultimately, Ellen "laid down care and took up submission" (555), and her reformed, proper, dispassionate language reflects this; she speaks no more of the Humphreys and calls Mr. Lindsay "father," just as he wishes. As Warner finally puts it, "Three or four more years of Scottish discipline wrought her no ill; they did but to serve to temper and beautify her Christian character; and then, to her unspeakable joy, she went back to spend her life with the friends and guardians she best loved, and to be to them, still more than she had been to her Scottish relations, 'the light of the eyes'" (569).

As Warner charts through the attainment of Ellen's vocal self-discipline, Ellen finally becomes a linguistic model of 19th-century American ideal womanhood: She is vocally, and essentially, pure, pious, submissive, domestic—and "American." *The Wide, Wide World* is thus in many ways complicit in 19th-century gendered and national linguistic socialization. It also, significantly, illuminates the process by which this socialization occurs. Through a process of "self-schooling" and "governing" her tongue, Ellen is filled with gendered vocal propriety. Indeed, by the time that Ellen marries her adoptive brother, finding a permanent domestic place in forging her own family with John Humphreys, she no longer needs her lips touched to silence her passionate voice. Ellen and her "guardians" have together schooled her to vocal submission, even silence. As Ellen observes to John, "There is one comfort—you will not touch my lips if I say anything you do not like" (572); but this, perhaps, is less because John would not do so than because Ellen no longer needs such physical silencing. Now filled with gendered vocal propriety instead of passion, she can silence herself. She is so perfectly filled with vocal propriety, vocal piety and vocal property, that John trusts her with his material property, giving her money for housekeeping and "other purposes" and assuring her that he "would a great deal rather not" know how she spends it, for he should know if she spends foolishly, not by words but by "eyes and mouth," which "have their own language" (582–83). When we last see Ellen, she is precisely located in the Humphreys' home. Ellen's domestication, and the self-silencing that attends it, is depicted as absolute, for she says in the last lines of the novel, "'I am satisfied [. . .] that is enough. I want no more'" (583). Warner's novel thus valuably illuminates how the very national process of domestication can occur through gendered notions of linguistic discipline.

In many ways, Dick Hunter's grammar education in Alger's *Ragged Dick* is similar to Ellen Montgomery's. Like Ellen's, Dick's attainment of grammar performs his essentially honest character, and his increasing linguistic self-discipline is accompanied and reinforced by his accruing self-discipline in religious, economic, and even physical matters, shoring up an increasingly respectable "American" identity. In addition, Dick's incorporation of vocal propriety into his already upstanding character is attended by the attainment of piety and paves the way for his future prosperity. And while the process of linguistic refinement does not feminize Ragged Dick *per se*, it does open the doors—quite literally—to a middle-class domesticity that is distinctly feminine in contrast to the urban street scene from which he comes.

Like Ellen, what Dick Hunter needs to gain propriety is simply a certain disciplining of his behavior, not the complete overhaul of an already sound character, as Peter Carafiol has pointed out (171). Dick's character, we learn from the beginning, is innately good, reflected in his face, which

Alger repeatedly describes in *Ragged Dick* as "frank" and "honest": "Some of his companions were sly, and their faces inspired distrust; but Dick had a frank, straight-forward manner that made him a favorite" (4–5). In contrast to the questionable characters of the book like Micky Maguire, Dick "looks honest," "has an open face," and "can be depended upon" (21); he is not a lad who "look[s] as if he would steal" (61); and "He had a frank, honest expression, which generally won its way to the favor of those with whom he came in contact" (119). Dick's face, in short, evidences his essential goodness: He was "above doing anything mean or dishonorable. He would not steal, or cheat, or impose upon younger boys, but was frank and straight-forward, manly and self-reliant. His nature was a noble one, and had saved him from all mean faults" (8).

Yet, we are told at the beginning of the tale, despite his honest core, "our ragged hero," is in need of behavioral refinement, as he smokes, swears, and speaks slang. Dick Hunter, says Alger, "wasn't a model boy in all respects. I am afraid he swore sometimes, and now and then he played tricks upon unsophisticated boys from the country, or gave a wrong direction to honest old gentlemen unused to the city" (6–7); he was extravagant with his money and "However much he managed to earn during the day, all was generally spent before morning. He was fond of going to the Old Bowery Theatre, and to Tony Pastor's, and if he had any money left afterwards," he would treat his friends to dinner or gamble it away (7, 8); to top it off, Dick "had formed the habit of smoking. This cost him considerable, for Dick was rather fastidious about his cigars, and wouldn't smoke the cheapest. [. . .] But of course the expense was the smallest objection. No boy of fourteen can smoke without being affected injuriously. Men are frequently injured by smoking, and boys always" (7–8).

Dick's linguistic behavior particularly marks him as an unrefined, if experienced, lower-class masculine urban figure. Throughout the narrative, Dick speaks a nonstandard, "improper" language, sprinkled with slang terms, characterized by imprecise pronunciation such as the dropping of final consonants, and associated with the talk of other boys of the street. Dick's slovenly-pronounced speech greets us on Alger's first page: "I oughter've been up an hour ago," "My guardian don't allow me no money for theatres, so I have to earn it," and "Lots of boys does it [stealin'], but I wouldn't" (3). Dick's slang vocabulary is also decidedly gendered. As Alger comments, a word like "hunky" is not "to be found in either Webster's or Worcester's big dictionary; but *boys* will readily understand what it means" (10, my emphasis). Such "boys'" slang peppers the text and provides a platform for commentary on Dick's peculiarity and difference from his more domesticated, middle-class friends.[36] For example, when he meets Frank Whitney, staying in a "pleasant chamber" at the refined Astor House at the beginning of the tale, he calls Frank "a brick"—a term Frank does not understand (22, 24). When Dick has his "First Appearance in Society," Alger's title for chapter seventeen, at a dinner at the Greyson family's "elegant house with a brown stone front," he characterizes the name of the only female character depicted at any length—Ida Greyson—as "bully" and "tip-top," terms that make her "break into a silvery laugh" (116–17). Indeed, it is through his language that Dick most feels his undomesticated difference from these characters. At this "first appearance in society"—during which Ida Greyson's mother gently quells her inquisitiveness with the maxim "Little girls should be seen and not heard"—Alger tells us that "Dick seated himself in an embarrassed way. He was very much afraid of doing or saying something which would be considered an impropriety, and had the uncomfortable feeling that everybody was looking at him and watching his behavior" (118). Dick sorely lacks the vocal propriety that will put him at ease in social settings such as the Greysons' feminized home. Dick's challenge is thus to shape his ragged, dirty, low-class appearance and improper vocal behavior to conform to (and confirm) his character—so that, in contrast to the counterfeit bill that appears in Alger's third chapter, Dick's "face" truly reflects his worth, and so that he will "rise" to become suitable companions for, and to be at home with, his child-mentors Frank Whitney and Ida Greyson in the feminized, middle-class domestic spaces they inhabit.

Like Warner in *The Wide, Wide World,* Alger linguistically charts Dick's self-disciplined rise and domestication in large part through his vocal attainment of grammatical speech. Dick's clean new clothes from Frank's uncle, Mr. Whitney, start the process and cue the linguistic transformation that follows. Dick is inspired by his conversations with Frank and the example of Mr. Whitney, who "get[s] up in the world," as Dick puts it, through a Franklinian narrative of self-improvement by working as an apprentice at a printing-office, inventing a machine, and pursuing his "taste for reading and study" (77). Dick soon begins "getting ambitious" (97): He hires lodging for himself, refrains from fighting (partly in an effort not to "hurt" his clothes [95]), saves money in a bank account, attends Sunday School, and enterprisingly exchanges lodging for tutoring from his friend Henry Fosdick, who, "though only twelve years old, knew as much as many boys of fourteen" and "had always been studious and ambitious to excel" (107). As Dick says, "I'll make a bargain with you. I can't read much mor'n a pig; and my writin' looks like hens' tracks. I don't want to grow up knowin' no more'n a four-year-old boy. If you'll teach me readin' and writin' evenin's, you shall sleep in my room every night. That'll be better'n door-steps or old boxes, where I've slept many a time" (105). Dick makes rapid progress in his studies—studies that notably occur in the confines of the lodging house, which has become a safe, appealing, domestic alternative to the Old Bowery:

> A new life had commenced for Dick. He no longer haunted the gallery of the Old Bowery; and even Tony Pastor's hospitable doors had lost their old attractions. He spent two hours every evening in study. His

progress was astonishingly rapid. He was gifted with a natural quickness; and he was stimulated by the desire to acquire a fair education as a means of "growin' up 'spectable," as he termed it. Much was due also to the patience and perseverance of Henry Fosdick, who made a capital teacher.

"You're improving wonderfully, Dick," said his friend, one evening, when Dick had read an entire paragraph without a mistake.

"Am I?" said Dick, with satisfaction.

"Yes. If you'll buy a writing-book to-morrow, we can begin writing to-morrow evening." (123)

Over time, Dick's accession of linguistic propriety is attended by his acquisition of not only piety, as he continues attending Sunday School, but also property, as he saves up a considerable sum of money, prompting his dream to "live on Fifth Avenoo" (137): "He was beginning to feel the advantages of his steady self-denial, and to experience the pleasures of property. Not that Dick was unduly attached to money" (147). For, as Alger writes, "Dick had gained something more valuable than money. He had studied regularly every evening, and his improvement had been marvellous [sic.]. He could now read well, write a fair hand, and had studied arithmetic as far as Interest. Besides this he had obtained some knowledge of grammar and geography" (137). His very properly-speaking mentor Henry Fosdick continues to help Dick correct his speech and attain "good grammar." For example, when Dick says, "I didn't think I could have wrote such a long letter, Fosdick," Henry replies, "Written would be more grammatical, Dick" (173). By the end of the narrative, much like Ellen Montgomery, Dick is able to check his own improper speech, and his self-discipline signals his attainment of vocal propriety.

Dick's vocal propriety, as the lesson goes, finally leads, much as Ellen's does, to his acquisition of piety and property—to moral behavior, self-possession, ten-dollar-a-week pay, and a tidier domestic space. When Dick applies for a position at a large warehouse, the merchant Mr. Rockwell asks him, "'How would you like to enter my counting-room as clerk, Richard?' [. . .]. Dick was about to say 'Bully,' when he recollected himself, and answered, 'Very much'" (183). With his new position and new income, Ragged Dick sets his sights on a new, "neater" house in a "nicer quarter of the city" and renames himself Richard Hunter. Esq., which prompts Fosdick to describe him as "a young gentleman on the way to fame and fortune" (185).

Yet, while there are certainly striking convergences in Dick's and Ellen's experiences of grammar in attaining vocal propriety, their similar experiences ultimately have different effects. While Dick's vocal propriety, like Ellen's, gives him entrée to middle-class culture and may help him to feel comfortable in Ida Greyson's company, his process of linguistic discipline differs from Ellen's in some important ways. Perhaps most significantly, Dick's education in grammar is incomplete, putting him in a different place than Ellen. By the end of the narrative, Dick's speech has been in Alger's words, "somewhat modified"—and *he* is able to modify *it* to obtain the situation he desires—but it is not thoroughly purged of the expressions of his previous street life. Alger writes: "It should be added that Dick's peculiar way of speaking and use of slang terms had been *somewhat modified* by his education and his intimacy with Henry Fosdick. Still he continued to indulge in them to some extent, especially when he felt like joking, and it was natural to Dick to joke, as my readers have probably found out by this time" (176, my emphasis). Dick's retention of slang terms—previously associated with and understood by "boys" and now associated with "joking"—continues to give him considerable linguistic flexibility and some degree of social mobility.[37] While attaining linguistic discipline, then, Dick also has linguistic freedom, giving himself access not only to feminized, middle-class domestic spaces like the Greyson home, where his achievement of vocal propriety will now put him at ease, but also to a much wider, masculinized, and multiply-classed public sphere where he will continue to earn his living—an arena in which he will potentially be able to participate, in George Foster's words in the next section, in the political role of *citizen*.

4. GENDERED VOCAL (IM)PROPRIETY: SLANG AS MASCULINIZED AMERICAN IRREVERENCE AND LICENSE

> Compared with the performances in the audience, the ranting and bellowing and spasmodic galvanism of the actors on the stage, are quite tame and commonplace. "Hello, Bill Swipes! You up in the second tier! Who de ——— guv yer de extra shillin'?" "Come out of that, you Jo Brewer! Why don't yer come along!" "I say, Jim! Ain't this high? Have yer salooned yer gal yet?" "Get off my toes! Keep yer ———sharp elbows out o' my ribs! Take that be J——— ! Watch! murder! Take him off! Hyst der rag! Go it! Sh-sh-sh-h-h!" and so up goes the curtain, the orchestra blows and kicks, and the actors go on in perfect dumb-show—not a syllable nor a squeak being heard by the uproarious, joyous audience. (George Foster, *New York in Slices* [1849] 120)

In his descriptions of the unrefined Ragged Dick, Horatio Alger may well have brought to fictional life one of the rowdy, street-wise, rough-speaking "Newsboys" or "B'hoys" whom George Foster described in his *New York Tribune* sketches in the late 1840s and collected in his *New York in Slices* in 1849.[38] Moreover, in *Ragged Dick,* Alger may well have fulfilled Foster's fantasy of transforming these rowdy mid-19th-century street figures—the Newsboy and the B'hoy—into articulate, domesticated, presentable, but no less "free," citizens. These mid-19th-century figures expressed both the misfortune and the promise of the era's rapid urbanization and industrialization. Generally heard in the Bowery—"the grand parade-ground of the b'hoys," where "the b'hoys are so plenty"—they were particularly heard, as in the passage above, at one of Ragged Dick's old haunts, the Bowery Theatre, to which Foster devoted a section of his collection ("Slice 33," 120–21). According to Foster, the speech of the B'hoys, like their other behavior, is unrestrained, mischievous, and strikingly aggressive in quality, such that it drowns out even "the ranting and bellowing and spasmodic galvanism of the actors on the stage," which appear comparatively "tame and commonplace." As we have seen in the transformation of Ragged Dick into Richard Hunter, Esq., such a transformation of these speakers into citizens happens, in no small part, through the linguistic conversion of such slang into proper speech via the influence of grammar's feminized, domesticating vocal propriety. As Alger's *Ragged Dick* and George Foster's sketches show, part of the appeal of mid-19th-century urban slang—and those who spoke it—was that, while associated with boyish irreverence, it was also shapeable into the respectable, domesticated speech of manly citizenship.

Works like Foster's "slices" reflected and propagated associations of slang with urban masculinity. Alongside a burgeoning body of 19th-century scholarship and commentary on slang, they show us how grammar and slang can be viewed as contemporaneous gendered linguistic responses to concerns about American social and political mobility—interdependent instances of gendered vocal propriety that helped to locate mobile sociopolitical identities through gendered ideas about language. Through its associations with rowdy behavior in masculinized urban spaces, in a range of mid-19th-century literary and linguistic works discussed in this section, slang was a manifestation of gendered vocal *im*propriety that, as the flip side of propriety's coin, expressed irreverence and had a different kind of currency among its users.[39] Because women were well-socialized to preserve the purity of language, it was assumed "that women would be both innocent and ignorant" of slang—that women would not understand the slang words being spoken around them (Bailey, *Nineteenth* 179). Thus while grammar—that is, grammar in the popular sense of linguistic propriety—placed otherwise unplaced voices, such as Ellen Montgomery's and Dick Hunter's orphaned voices, slang released these voices and celebrated their mobility.[40] While grammar was associated with feminized domestic spaces, slang was associated with mid-19th-century liminal spaces, like the frontier or the city, where Davy Crockett's "frontier screamers" evolved into George Foster's B'hoys who "slung" urban street slang. In addition to sketches such as Foster's in the *Tribune*, influential humor publications like *The New York Picayune* (1847–60) featured their own comically exaggerated B'hoy, who soon became a familiar character type in popular fiction, as in Ned Buntline's (Edward Z. C. Judson's) *The B'hoys of New York* and *The G'hals of New York*, both published in 1850.[41]

Vocal (Im)propriety and the Management of Sociopolitical Mobility 95

The mid-19th-century associations of slang with lower-class masculinity and New York street life can be vividly seen in George Foster's depictions in *New York in Slices* of the Newsboy's and the B'hoy's dress and behavior, descriptions that reinforced representations of slang as "ragged" speech and that were echoed in literary renderings such as Alger's *Ragged Dick*. Dick wears pants that "were torn in several places and had apparently belonged in the first instance to a boy two sizes larger than himself" and "a coat too long for him, dating back, if one might judge from its general appearance, to a *remote antiquity*," justifying Dick's claim that it was George Washington's through the Revolution (Alger 4–6, my emphasis). Alger's description of Dick's dress replicates Foster's description of the Newsboy's dress as

> descended to the 19th Century from a *remote antiquity* [. . .] fragments of the costume of a remote period, artfully reconstructed; and it is not impossible (and the heathen manner in which they are freely riddled gives plausibility to the conjecture) that some of them have figured in the Crusades. Find us the Tailor who makes the Newsboy's Uniform, and we will tell you when the American Union is going to be dissolved. (104, my emphasis)

The Newsboy's behavior, like the unrefined Ragged Dick's, is also questionable: "We are afraid Tom Newsboy is a trifle profligate; he swears, we know, freely; drinks, fights, and very often stays out all night. This last we must not dwell on too strongly as a vice, for it is often a necessity. Tom having no home to go to, and not thinking it worth while to be at a charge for lodgings, takes up his quarters for the night in a box or a bunk, under a stoop or in an entryway [. . .]" (Foster 104). Besides possessing a "profound passion for the Theatre," the Newsboy possesses "speed of foot, power of vociferation, rapidity of utterance, force of character" (105), and "bold and startling cries" that happily "bellow out" the downfall of the "Royal Families of Europe" with "the greatest satisfaction" (106). The Newsboy clearly resembles another of Foster's characters—the B'hoy—who is even rougher around the edges and more representative of New York urban life than the Newsboy in his glad embrace of "the career of vulgar rowdyism" (44). As Foster says, "one cannot be said to really know New-York—to understand in what way its human nature is different from other human nature—without studying the habits and character of the B'hoys" (43). Like the Newsboys who must sleep outdoors and huddle together with shaggy dogs, the B'hoys are associated with the wild: "Thrown into the world in childhood without guide or protector, and with no means of education, or worse still, no one to inspire in them the desire for education, they grow up like wild weeds and must inevitably produce bitter and unwholesome fruit"; they are "Full of rough play, and uncouthly sociable as a company of young bears" (44). As seen in the epigraph above, their *speech* is equally "rough," "wild," and "uncouthly sociable."

What is striking about Foster's descriptions of both the Newsboy and B'hoy is that, while their disorderly, mobile behavior borders on the "dangerous" and raises a threat to "public peace," both of these figures, like Alger's Ragged Dick, are innately good and thus reformable. These figures possess a courage, frankness, magnanimity, fun, and friendship that is simply repressed and stunted under "unfavorable auspices." As Foster writes of the B'hoys:

> They are brave, easily led astray, but not naturally wicked. They are good, unselfish, frolicsome creatures, whose misfortune is that a rude contact with society, under unfavorable auspices, has served to ripen and bring out only a certain class of functions and attributes, while the intellectual and moral faculties which could alone have given them value or useful direction, have been repressed and stunted. Thus, their courage is quarrelsomeness; their frankness is vulgarity; their magnanimity subsides to thriftlessness; their fun expands to rowdyism; their feelings of friendship and brotherhood seeks dangerous activity in mobs and gangs who conspire against the public peace. (44)

Indeed, within both of these slang-speaking figures is the potential for reformation into citizens who can contribute to, rather than threaten, "the public peace."

Foster envisions specific plans, including feminine influence and discipline, for reformation of the B'hoy and the Newsboy alike, such that the "B'hoy—whom we are now compelled to regard as the disgrace of the times—would become a cheerful, industrious, well-to-do, and valuable member of the community" (47). To become a potential citizen, the B'hoy, according to Foster, particularly needs feminine associations: "respectable associations—and especially of the refining influence of cultivated female society" that would encourage "his ambition, his desire to struggle and shine, which he shares in common with all man and woman kind" instead of leading him "to the rum-shop and to the haunts of the vicious and vile" (44). According to Foster, the B'hoy also needs discipline, the ideal instillation of which he imagines through "an army of Volunteer Agriculturists," in which the B'hoy could be sent out to labor in the purifying air of the countryside, "armed with hoes, rakes, scythes, and cradles, artilleried with ploughs and harrows [. . .] what a glorious chance would this be for the B'hoy and how much less national money and national crime it would cost, and how much happiness instead of death and mourning it would entail!" (45). For Foster, perhaps not surprisingly, the reformative force of the countryside, its "pure skies" and "virtuous freshness," is identified with the "moral purity" of ideal womanhood, as, in another sketch, he cautions "real" women to remain in the countryside rather than venture into the vices of the city (53).[42]

Foster stretches his fantasy of the B'hoy's reformation even further in his vision of the transformation of Newsboys into citizens: "What kind of citizens these Newsboys will make—what kind of creatures will spring from these mixed elements of turmoil, street-running, precocious activity of body and mind, and precocious profusion of cash, no one can guess; for the system—started some ten years since—has not been long enough in operation to bring any of them of age. Our best wishes are with the Boys" (107). In writing the story of *Ragged Dick,* Alger seems to have fulfilled Foster's fantasies, transforming newsboy and shoe shine boy Ragged Dick into Richard Hunter, partially through what Foster names as the "refining influence of cultivated feminine society"—an "influence" that Ragged Dick, as we have seen, obtains through exposure to the Greyson family's home, and moreover through the domesticating discipline of grammar as vocal propriety.

At the time Alger and Foster were writing, a scholarly interest in slang first appeared and grew up alongside the obsession with grammar—testament to the interdependence of slang and grammar as twin discourses of gendered vocal propriety. Mid-19th-century anxiety about grammar was concurrent with the rising use of, and interest in, slang (Bailey, "Democracy" 9–11).[43] Although the word *slang* was first used in the mid-18th century, "*slang* in the modern sense is very much a 19th-century word" (Bailey, *Nineteenth* 177)—and, perhaps, an "American" one. Noah Webster's *American Dictionary* (1828), "the first standard dictionary in the world to be advertised as American, was also the first to make room for the word *slang* as a part of the recognized English vocabulary" (Lighter, Intro xxv). According to Jonathan Lighter, slang likely did not become noticeably American until the 1830s and 1840s ("Slang" 243); according to Eric Partridge, it was around 1850 that *slang* became an "accepted term for 'illegitimate' colloquial speech" (Partridge 3).[44] While the first dictionaries of "vulgar" English appeared in the late 1700s, it was not until the 1820s—again, the same era that saw an increased interest in grammar books—that compilations of slang really began to be produced and consumed by "that portion of the book-buying public fascinated by the doings of bucks, swells, Corinthians, and demireps" (Bailey, *Nineteenth* 177). George Cruikshank's cant dictionary of London appeared in 1848, followed in 1851 by *A Collection of College Words and Customs,* with an enlarged edition appearing in 1856.[45] John Bartlett of Massachusetts published four editions of his "trail-blazing" *Americanisms* between 1848 and 1877 (Lighter, Intro xxv). According to Irving Lewis Allen, an important record of New York street speech—George Washington Matsell's *Vocabulum*—was published in 1859 (23); a similar source of mid-19th-century street speech, entitled *Leaves,* was comprised of stories told in cant and was published in the *National Police Gazette* in the 1860s (262n44). Perhaps most significantly, in the same year that *Vocabulum* appeared, John Camden Hotten, an Englishman who had lived for a short time in America, produced the first *Slang Dictionary*. Other slang dictionaries soon followed in the wake of its several editions. Thus, "Fortified by comparative philology and conversant with the discoveries of new-word collectors like J. C. Hotten and John Bartlett, intellectuals of the late nineteenth century came to take a more moderate view of what was called slang, finally transforming the label into a less disdainful synonym for the nonstandard informal vocabulary, especially in its urban manifestations" (Lighter, Intro xxv).[46]

Characterizations of slang as masculinized nonstandard speech standing in opposition to feminized vocal decorum were obvious in the studies of slang that rose in the mid-1800s. Growing out of early studies of cant, later slang studies were based in the groups from which slang was observed to have come most commonly—the military, college students, cowboys, sports reporters, and the film industry—groups that have traditionally tended to be male and/or dominated by men. To study its history is to learn that slang has, from its beginnings, been associated with undomesticated speech and largely masculine, "outlaw" speakers.[47] This tendency has been followed by the conventional observation that men use more slang than women. As the 1868 middle-class monthly *The Ladies' Repository* observed: "if it were not for our women there would be danger of having our English smothered in slang. They seldom use it—a well-bred woman never uses it" (qtd. in Cmiel 129). A century later, Stuart Flexner, in his *Dictionary of American Slang* (1960), restated even more strongly the connection between slang and men in observing "that most American slang is created and used by males" (xii). While they may have reflected the cultural climate of the 1960s, Flexner's comments on slang—which extended to the observations that men in particular tend to avoid "weak" or "feminine" words, use slang to shock, and enjoy the hyperbole in slang—also indicate the extent to which slang continued in the 20th century to be associated with an urban or out-of-doors masculinity, in contrast to grammar's association with domestic femininity. Indeed, Flexner makes these associations explicit when he remarks that a couple may

> live under the same roof, the wife in her *home*, the man in his *house*. Once outside of their domesticity the man will begin to use slang quicker than the woman. She'll get into the *car* while he'll get into the *jalopy* or *Chevvie*. And so they go: she will learn much of her general slang from him; for any word she associates with the home, her personal belongings, or any female concept, he will continue to use a less descriptive, less personal one. (xii)

The stereotype of men as slang speakers and women as slang avoiders has thus been supported in writings on slang since it first arose as a serious object of study in the 19th century—as we have seen, a historical and literary context carrying complex ideological freight.[48]

Although it may be true that slang has come to be associated with masculinity and/or rebelliousness simply because men use more slang than women—and more studies are needed on this subject—*rhetoric* about slang has tended to heighten this potentiality, just as, we have seen, rhetoric about grammar has tended to capitalize on its associations with feminine domestic virtues such as piety and purity, not to mention domesticity and submissiveness. Nineteenth-century commentary on slang, as well as definitions of slang in our day, are revealing in this respect. In the 1850s, Oliver Wendell Holmes characterized the slang he heard around Boston as "commonly the dishwater from the washings of English dandyism, schoolboy or full-grown, wrung out of a three-volume novel which had sopped it up" (*Autocrat* qtd. in Lighter, Intro xxxiii). Holmes' figuration of slang as the common "dishwater" of dandies and schoolboys reveals its disreputable association not only with popular comic literature but also with certain masculine English types, a move that interestingly distances it from American soil for Holmes. Harvard professors James Bradstreet Greenough and George Lyman Kittredge echoed Holmes when they figured slang as "a peculiar kind of vagabond language, always hanging on the outskirts of legitimate speech, but continually straying or forcing its way into the most respectable company"—a figuration that evokes slang as an unwanted guest or a pesky child hanging on his mother's skirts (Greenough and Kittredge qtd. in Lighter, Intro xxvi). As the commentaries of Holmes and Greenough and Kittredge show, the rhetoric describing slang could be as colorful as slang itself, often reinforcing its opposition to grammar as an expression of gendered vocal propriety.[49]

The fact that slang continued throughout the 19th and early 20th centuries to be identified with the brawn and liberty that many have perceived as particularly American is likewise noteworthy; the fact that slang has often been seen as particularly "American" indicates how descriptions of slang can promote or critique or otherwise express ideas about national identity. While he approached language from a distinctly different perspective than Holmes, Greenough, or Kittredge and was clearly one to scorn the reinforcement of sexual differences, Walt Whitman in 1855 particularly celebrated the "brawny" characteristics of the "limber" and "full" English language and applauded its ability to attract the "terms of daintier and gayer and subtler and more elegant tongues" (*Leaves of Grass* 1018). And in "Slang in America," Whitman associated American slang, just as he did the English language itself, with notions of liberty and resistance, describing slang as "the wholesome fermentation or eructation [belching] of those processes eternally active in language" and celebrating its "lawless germinal element," its "certain freedom and perennial rankness and Protestantism in speech" (54–55). As Mencken would observe in *The American Language:* "With the possible exception of the French, the Americans now produce more slang than any other people, and put it to heavier use in their daily affairs. [. . .] American slang, says George Philip Krapp, 'is

100 *Language, Gender, and Citizenship in American Literature*

the child of the new nationalism, the new spirit of joyous adventure that entered American life after the close of the War of 1812'" ("Archaic" 302 qtd. in Mencken, *AL* 567). Mencken also notes that: "Not a few agree with Horace Annesley Vachell that 'American slanguage is not a tyranny, but a beneficent autocracy. . . . *Lounge-lizard,* for example, is excellent. . . . It is humiliating to reflect that English slang at its best has to curtsey to American slang" (572–73). Vachell's image of English slang as "curtseying" to American slang, "the child of the new nationalism," highlights the way in which rhetoric about slang could associate it with both gendered linguistic propriety and national identity.

Such descriptions of slang, as we have seen, were born in a mid-19th-century moment, in which interests in both slang and grammar rapidly accelerated alongside a changing socioeconomic structure and reformulations of national citizenship. Indeed, in this context, slang seems to have arisen as a kind of masculinized linguistic embodiment of an Algeresque "American Dream." Slang, when tempered by grammar, gave young newsboys like Ragged Dick access, both rhetorical and real, to masculine urban frontiers as well as feminized middle-class domesticity—and, strikingly, to American identity. In a sense, grooming young girls and boys for citizenship depended on upholding these very distinctions between masculine and feminine behavior, nonstandard and standard speech, lower-class and middle-class culture, urban and domestic spaces, and American or un-American identity—but allowing Alger's boys and Foster's B'hoys potential access to both.

In the end, then, we might see the dialectic of gendered vocal (im)propriety, manifest through the mid-19th-century discourses of (feminized) grammar and (masculinized) slang, as itself disciplining anxieties about an American citizenship that was being challenged at this time along both class and gender lines. Such interdependent discourses of gendered vocal propriety dealt linguistically with changing notions of national citizenship by locating certain types of speech, and their speakers, in particular places—urban and domestic, masculinized and feminized—places that were also, quite clearly, political or nonpolitical realms of potential national participation.

5. CONCLUSION: LITERARY DISCIPLINE AND RESISTANCE: THE "IRREVERENT SPEECH" OF *THE HIDDEN HAND*

> "Demmy, you New York newsboy, will you never be a woman?"
> (E.D.E.N Southworth, *The Hidden Hand* [1859] 376)

Of course, as discipline invites resistance, not all 19th-century Americans internalized the era's gendered language ideologies, just as not all the era's popular fictional "orphans" allowed themselves to be "placed" by these ideologies in domestic or political spheres. To be sure, the popular fictional orphan Capitola Black, the heroine of E. D. E. N. (Emma Dorothy Eliza Nevitte) Southworth's *The Hidden Hand. Or, Capitola the Madcap,* came to literary life in 1859, seemingly as a direct challenge to the equally well-disciplined—in terms of both gender and language—Ellen Montgomeries and Ragged Dicks who preceded and followed her. Writing her first novel, *Retribution,* a year after Seneca Falls, Southworth consciously recorded and reflected upon 19th-century attitudes about gender (Dobson, Intro xxi-xxii). Moreover, as the above quote shows in its puzzlement over the blurring of newsboy's slang with womanly identity, Southworth had her finger on the pulse of the gendered politics of language in her day.[50]

In *The Hidden Hand,* Southworth imaginatively resists the dialectical discipline of gendered vocal propriety. Through its depiction of Capitola's speech, which intermingles domesticated, feminized grammar with masculinized, urbanized slang, much as Cap's behavior more generally blends separate arenas of gendered activity, *The Hidden Hand* reveals how discourses of gendered vocal propriety could divert larger national issues to gendered linguistic concerns, and how these gendered discourses could together govern perceptions of identity.

For example, *The Hidden Hand's* opening scene marks the introduction of Ira Warfield, fondly called Old Hurricane, to the young orphaned Capitola, disguised as a newsboy in order to successfully peddle penny papers like *The Herald, Tribune,* and *Express* in Rag Alley, 1845 New York City. In this scene, Capitola manipulates her orphan's voice in order to stay alive on the streets of New York. Yet, for her guardian-to-be Old Hurricane, the immediate puzzle is not Capitola's poverty, but her *gendered* identity—one which he must decipher through her voice:

"Please, Sir, do you want your carpet-bag carried?" asked a voice near.

Old Hurricane looked around him with a puzzled air, for he thought that a young *girl* had made this offer, so soft and clear were the notes of the voice that spoke.

"It was I, sir! Here I am, at your's and everybody's service, sir!" said the same voice.

And turning, Old Hurricane saw sitting astride a pile of boxes at the corner store, a very ragged lad, some thirteen years of age.

"Good gracious!" thought Old Hurricane, as he gazed upon the boy, "this must be crown-prince and heir-apparent to the 'king of shreds and patches.'"

"Well, old gent, you'll know me next time, that's certain!" said the lad, returning the look with interest.

It is probable Old Hurricane did not hear this irreverent speech, for he continued to gaze with pity and dismay upon the ragamuffin before him. He was a handsome boy, too, notwithstanding the deplorable state of his wardrobe. Thick, clustering curls of jet black hair fell in tangled disorder around a forehead broad, white, and smooth as that of a girl; slender and quaintly-arched black eyebrows played above a pair of mischievous, dark gray eyes, that sparkled beneath the shade of long, thick, black lashes; a little turned-up nose, and red, pouting lips, completed the character of a countenance full of fun, frolic, spirit, and courage. (Southworth 33)

Here, Southworth shows, the fact that Capitola has had to perform a newsboy's identity in order to survive on urban New York streets, gets displaced by a concern with her gender and language. Old Hurricane is puzzled less by the problem of Cap's urban poverty than the problem of her gender, which he attempts to solve *through* attention to Cap's voice, whose clear "notes" "sound" like a girl's, but whose "irreverent speech" "looks" like a boy's. There is a conspicuous slippage between the identity of the individual Old Hurricane initially hears and that which he sees: His first impression is guided by Capitola's voice, "for he thought that a young *girl* had made this offer, so soft and clear were the notes of the voice that spoke." Not only is the sound of this first-heard voice "soft and clear," but its proper speech is also correct and polite, initially offering, "Please, Sir, do you want your carpet-bag carried?" Capitola's "girl's" voice initially betrays her identity as a girl, bringing home the chapter's epigraph from Sir Walter Scott's "Marmion," which tells us, "Her sex a page's dress belied, / Obsured her charms, but could not hide" (33). But only momentarily—for Old Hurricane soon discards his aural first impressions, trusting his eyes more than his ears, to decide that the girl's voice "really" belongs to a boy, a "handsome" boy who speaks slang reminiscent of Foster's Newsboys and B'hoys. Capitola's slangy, "irreverent speech" finally governs Old Hurricane's impressions of her gendered identity. Capitola's "newsboy's" slang—seen in phrases like "Well, old gent," "Oh, crickey," "Oh, Lor'!" and "Oh, Gemini!"—confirms the "very ragged lad" he sees (33–34).

Through Old Hurricane's puzzled perceptions of Cap's intermingled and mobile speech, Southworth reveals, however playfully, the ways in which larger socioeconomic and political issues might be circuited through discourses of gendered vocal propriety, and she contemplates the ways in which social identities were disciplined by such discourses. As Southworth shows, gendered vocal differences are, in part, manifestations of very material factors with which readers are never directly confronted; controversial national problems such as class or race are thus Southworth's own "hidden hand," one that she plays, subtly, through depictions of gender and language in the novel.[51] Throughout the novel, Cap's bursts of such irreverent speech continually addle Old Hurricane's ideas of her appropriate gendered behavior, causing him at various points to explode, "Cap! how often have I told you to leave off this Bowery boy talk *Rum!* bah!" (173). Mischievous Cap has "no reverence, no docility, no propriety" (186), according to

Old Hurricane, who exclaims, "Demmy, you New York newsboy, will you never be a woman?" (376).

Taking Cap off the street indeed results in a modification of her speech—she loses much, but not all, of her slangy "Bowery boy talk." After Capitola's sex is discovered and she recounts her story to the city court judges, Old Hurricane remarks, in particular, that "the language used by the poor child during her examination was much superior to the slang she had previously affected, to support her assumed character of newsboy" (41). Her removal to Hurricane Hall is, further, a substantial change in material circumstances, a change that Southworth initially signals by Capitola's transformation in dress as well as speech. For, under the influence of Old Hurricane's *property,* Capitola attains discernible *propriety.* Taken from Rag Alley to the dress shop, Capitola is "indeed transfigured" (50) from "the king of shreds and patches" (33): "Her bright black hair, parted in the middle, fell in ringlets each side her blushing cheeks; her dark gray eyes were cast down in modesty at the very same instant that her ripe red lips were puckered up with mischief. She was well and properly attired in a gray silk dress, crimson merino shawl, and a black velvet bonnet" (50). Through close attention to Capitola's dress and language, Southworth shows how the attainment of 19th-century gendered propriety is entwined with performances of piety and property: Cap's "dark gray eyes were cast down in modesty" as her silk, merino, and velvet "properly" outfit her.

Southworth is therefore aware of 19th-century gendered rules/roles of propriety, and *The Hidden Hand* becomes the story of how Capitola breaks these conventions, through speech and action. Capitola is both "rhetorical" and "real" soldier in Southworth's novel, as we come to find out through her many adventures. She captures the bandit Black Donald; daringly disguises herself to rescue her friend Clara Day from a doomed marriage; consistently breaks Old Hurricane's prohibition of riding her horse Gyp rampantly over the countryside; fights the menacing Craven Le Noir in a duel, during which she showers his face with a mixture of dried peas and gunpowder; and, after unsuccessfully circulating a petition in Black Donald's favor, orchestrates his escape from prison on the eve of his hanging. With Capitola Black, sentimental conventions (her orphaned status, her trajectory from puberty to marriage, her domestic location under a tyrannical guardian) "are raised only to be violated. When a female protagonist is introduced as having been born 'squalling like a wild cat' (18), she is guaranteed never to grow up to be another Ellen Montgomery" (Dobson, "Subversion" 234).

In further contrast to Ellen Montgomery, Capitola's linguistic behavior also resists final domestication. By the end of the novel, Capitola Black marries Herbert Greyson, fulfilling one expectation of the sentimental heroine. But her voice is not self-disciplined or happily contained. In fact, as Southworth writes in the story's penultimate paragraph: "I wish I could say, 'they all lived happily ever after.' But the truth is, [. . .] I know for a positive fact, that our Cap sometimes gives her 'dear, darling sweet Herbert,' the benefit of the sharp edge of her tongue, which of course he deserves" (485). Southworth resists characterizing Cap's speech here as a function of either Ellen Montgomery's pure womanhood or Dame Van Winkle's shrewhood. While Capitola's voice is spoken within the domestic sphere, there is nothing really pure, pious, or submissive about it; "the sharp edge" of likable Capitola's tongue simply compels Herbert's attention because he "deserves" it, but neither is this "sharp edge" objectionable. In Capitola, Southworth thus evokes but also subverts the linguistic conventions of sentimental heroines like Ellen Montgomery, using her language to reinforce her resistance to feminized middle-class domesticity. Though married at the end of the novel, Cap is not quiet. Her domestic setting may be familiar, but she refuses to be classed as a familiar sentimental heroine whose voice is contained by it.

In linguistically subverting gender conventions in her popular novel *The Hidden Hand,* Southworth thus illuminates just how conventional the discourses of gendered linguistic (im)propriety really were. Indeed, in its very mixing of grammatical and slangy speech and its subversion of sentimental and rags-to-riches linguistic formulae, Southworth's book reveals the cultural consensus surrounding ideologies of gendered vocal (im)propriety, particularly discourses of feminized grammar and masculinized slang, that arose in an era that saw the expansion of the franchise to white men and the glimmer of its expansion to white women. And ultimately, *The Hidden Hand* shows us how popular literary works themselves might perform and challenge the work—to use Ellen Montgomery's words—of "governing" the voices of American girls and boys.

3   The (Re)Construction of Dialect and African American (Dis)Franchisement in Charles W. Chesnutt's Writings

1. INTRODUCTION: RECONSTRUCTION, REPRESENTATION, AND REPRODUCTION

> The active participation of the masses, and the extension of the right of suffrage to the very lowest and most ignorant classes have, moreover, favored the admission of so many vulgar and cant terms that in politics, above all, the line between slang and solemn speech is not always perceptible. Where appeals are made at every election to vast assemblies, not unfrequently consisting largely of so-called Mean Whites, and of Blacks but recently emancipated from slavery and all its blighting consequences, strong colors must be used to paint the adversary, and still stronger language to impress the dull minds. (M. Schele de Vere, *Americanisms* [1872] 249)

Two years after the Fifteenth Amendment granted the elective franchise to African American men, writer M. (Maximilian) Schele de Vere focused on the relation between "the extension of the right of suffrage to the very lowest and most ignorant classes" and the fluctuation, even corruption, of speech, in particular the blurring of "the line between slang and solemn speech." As the last two chapters have shown, antebellum Americans often turned to discussions of language—for example, debates about political language or vocal propriety—to manage anxieties about national citizenship, particularly concerns about whose voices could count in the body politic and whose could not. After the Civil War, too, ideas about language similarly emerged to manage concerns about citizenship in new ways, as indicated by Schele de Vere's commentary. For, at the same time that Schele de Vere expresses linguistic concern about the destabilization of the "line between slang and solemn speech," he places this concern within the context of a more sweeping sociopolitical concern about "the extension of the right of suffrage to the very lowest and most ignorant classes," a right which had indeed been extended to "so-called Mean Whites" and "Blacks but recently emancipated from slavery."

The legislation following the Civil War inscribed a consensual, forward-looking vision of American citizenship, the most revolutionary leveling of ascriptive conceptions of citizenship in the nation's history. After the Thirteenth Amendment (1865) illegalized slavery, the Civil Rights Act (1866) opened the way for the federal government to protect former slaves and to enlarge the goals of Reconstruction by "making African Americans full United States citizens and guaranteeing certain rights of citizenship" (Thomas, Intro 7). Together, the Civil War Amendments represented the legal inscription of a consensual vision of citizenship: The Fourteenth Amendment (1868) overturned the *Dred Scott* case (1857) to guarantee national citizenship to all African Americans, and the Fifteenth Amendment (1870) prohibited states' interference with voting rights for African American men, as based on "race, color, or previous condition of servitude" (U.S. Const., Amend. 15).[1] While the passage of the Thirteenth Amendment was relatively uncontroversial, many opposed the Fourteenth and Fifteenth Amendments because they reversed traditional ways of life in the South, violated beliefs in white supremacy and states' rights, and tapped into fears of racial intermixture and a miscegenous nation (Thomas, Intro 7–9).

Lawmakers would attempt to curb the fears about racial intermixture prompted by the Civil War Amendments in part through antimiscegenation laws prohibiting marriage between whites and people of other races. For many Americans, Reconstruction legislation created what Eva Saks, in her analysis of the American case law of miscegenation, calls a "crisis of representation," in which social form deviates from legal form and "makes social form an unreliable sign of legal form (and vice versa)," ultimately destabilizing those subjects "most central to social life: language, family, property, and race" (41).[2] In addition, by destabilizing these subjects, Reconstruction created what could be called a crisis of reproduction. Through the antimiscegenation laws that proliferated in the wake of the Civil War Amendments, the courts attempted to solve these representative and reproductive crises—to regulate sociopolitical relations by appealing to the essentialist metaphor of blood, a fictitious, descent-oriented figure that antimiscegenation discourse itself created (Saks 48, 40). As Saks argues, the retention of "blood" in legal discourse itself bespoke the crisis of representation at the heart of legislation that was "entailed in litigating a crime in which legal definitions [of 'blood'] contradict physical signs ['skin'] and social codes"—the discrepancy "between 'looked like' and 'was,' between representation and identity in the logic of miscegenation" (39–40, 56).

In appealing to signifiers of descent such as blood, these antimiscegenation laws prohibiting "mixed-blood" marriages sought to secure the nation, and its white patriarchy, at the site of the family—the racialized and gendered site of both representing *and* reproducing the nation. Antimiscegenation laws relied upon the same logic that reversed the Civil War Amendments and that anticipated future Jim Crow legislation. Such antimiscegenation laws, by regulating the mythic flow of "blood," attempted to regulate both race relations and relations of gender and sexuality. For, as recent scholars have shown, racialized political images of blood, a metaphor of descent, have never been "completely dissociated from a metaphorics of sex, vitality, and gender. [. . .] Issues of blood, race, and motherhood [have] converged in a political obsession with the life-giving body of women" (Linke 37).[3] Although women were not represented in the law, as the racialized reproducers of family and nation, women had an overdetermined status under the law. As Laura Doyle portrays in *Bordering on the Body,* "A historical and cross-cultural consideration of the racial-patriarchal economy reveals the absolute interdependence of ideologies of race and sex," such that the regulation of marriage is at the center of the preservation of kinship patriarchy and "the race or group mother is the point of access to a group history and bodily grounded identity, but she is also the cultural vehicle for fixing, ranking, and subduing groups and bodies" (20, 26, 4).[4] Thus invoking the gendered and racialized descent-based figure of blood, antimiscegenation cases like *Pace v. Alabama* (1882) would serve as "an important symbolic antecedent for the 'separate but equal' rhetoric of the United State Supreme Court's decision upholding the constitutionality of segregated passenger trains" in *Plessy v. Ferguson* (1896) and in other Jim Crow legislation that would reverse the Civil War Amendments in part by similarly invoking metaphors of descent (Saks 44).

As foretold by these antimiscegenation laws that aimed to solve a national "crisis of representation" by regulating national reproduction, the consensual vision of citizenship extended in the Civil War Amendments was reversed by legislation that rewrote citizenship as an extension of ascribed traits such as race and gender by appealing to metaphors of descent such as blood, nature, or tradition. This legislation ultimately preserved political rights—particularly the franchise—for white patriarchy. For, the crucial issue, as Mark Twain recognized and Saks reminds us, was "how this blood would vote" (Saks 67)—that is, how (or whether) African Americans, and women, would achieve representation in the body politic. As Saks suggests, this is partly why anxieties about miscegenation and racial intermixture lay at the heart of debates over the Civil War Amendments and the Civil Rights Acts. The fear in all of these cases was similar: that broadly interpreting the Civil War Amendments would create a slippery slope in which blacks and women could enjoy the same citizenship rights as white men.

Thus, as antimiscegenation cases regulated the family by invoking the metaphor of blood to prohibit racial intermixing, the decision in *Bradwell v. Illinois* (1873) similarly invoked the metaphor of nature to prohibit the intermixing of gendered spheres. When Myra Bradwell, who had studied law with her husband, claimed her right to practice law as a citizen of the United States on the basis of the Fourteenth Amendment's protection of the "privileges and immunities of citizens of the United States," Chief Justice Joseph P. Bradley asserted that

> the civil law, as well as nature herself, has always recognized a wide difference in the respective spheres and destinies of man and woman.

Man is, or should be, woman's protector and defender. The natural and proper timidity and delicacy which belongs to the female sex evidently unfits it for the occupations of a civil life. The constitution of the family organization, which is founded in the divine ordinance as well as in the nature of things, indicates the domestic sphere as that which properly belongs to the domain and functions of womanhood. The harmony, not to say identity, of interests and views which belong or should belong to the family institution, is repugnant to the idea of a woman adopting a distinct and independent career from that of her husband. [. . .] a married woman is incapable, without her husband's consent, of making contracts which shall be binding on her or him. [. . .] The paramount destiny and mission of woman are to fulfill the noble and benign offices of wife and mother. This is the law of the Creator. And the rules of civil society must be adapted to the general constitution of things, and cannot be based on exceptional cases. . . . (*Bradwell v. Illinois* qtd. in Kerber and De Hart 243)

As with Bradley's recourse to "nature herself" and "the nature of things" to curb Bradwell's rights of citizenship and to locate her "paramount destiny and mission" solidly in "the domestic sphere," the retention of metaphors of descent had similar effects for African Americans, likewise curbing citizenship rights for black men in the Jim Crow legislation that culminated in the *Plessy* decision. As Rogers Smith puts it, the story of the last quarter of the 19th century thus becomes one of "the mounting repudiation of Reconstruction egalitarianism and inclusiveness in favor of an extraordinarily broad political, intellectual, and legal embrace of renewed ascriptive hierarchies"—ascriptive hierarchies that made participation in the political sphere "unnatural" for both blacks and women (347).[5]

As Schele de Vere's comments at the beginning of this chapter suggest and as the remainder of this chapter will show, the crises of representation and reproduction occasioned by Reconstruction played out not only in debates about political representation, but also in linguistic and literary discussions of language—just one dimension of the "intellectual [. . .] embrace of renewed ascriptive hierarchies" to which Smith refers above. Through similar appeals to the paradigm of consent/descent, then, conversations about language and the law played out the issue of (dis)franchisement for African Americans and women in parallel ways.

Particularly in discussions and representations of *dialect,* a wide range of writers and critics at the end of the 19th century invoked metaphors of consent/descent to deflect anxieties about the nation's racial patriarchy and to manage the conflicts of representation and reproduction at the heart of Reconstruction legislation, but in a less fraught space. More specifically, discussions of dialect by the American Dialect Society, William Dwight Whitney, and William Dean Howells often relied on metaphors of descent to ascribe essential traits such as race or gender to language practices in

The (Re)Construction of Dialect 109

a way that, despite their broad-minded intentions, subtly paralleled the court's ascription of essential traits to the political practices of citizenship.

In such a sociopolitical and linguistic context, literary representations of dialect, such as those in Joel Chandler Harris' "A Story of the War" (1880) and Charles W. Chesnutt's "The Dumb Witness" (1897) and his *A Colonel's Dream* (1905), likewise operated within paradigms of descent or consent to reconstruct the national family. Both Harris' and Chesnutt's texts project back to the antebellum era, to a historical moment before the Fifteenth Amendment when, strikingly, blacks had no vote. In this chapter, I read their very different uses of dialect—their varying depictions of black "voices"—as yet similar imaginary manipulations of language to manage post-war debates about enfranchisement. Harris' story, built around the representation of the black male storyteller's language, illuminates how literary representations of dialect might retain essentialized notions of descent and affirm the era's legal logic. In contrast, Chesnutt's representation of a mulatta woman's silence and speech uses an explicitly gendered and racialized figure for language to introduce a paradigm of linguistic consent and to resist the era's legal logic. By introducing gendered as well as racialized power dynamics into his representations, Chesnutt shifts attention from a debate over essentialized political and linguistic representation to the era's inherent racialized and gendered *politics of speech,* and in the process, he exposes the assumptions that undergirded the disfranchisement of both African Americans and women in the post-Reconstruction period. In taking up these texts, this chapter follows Chesnutt's lead in attempting to move contemporary critical conversations about dialect—conversations that tend to focus on region, race, or class in isolation from issues of gender and language—to a consideration of the gendered politics of language that, in the late-19th-century context, illuminate the larger politics of national (dis)franchisement for African Americans as well as women.[6]

2. DISCUSSING DIALECT, INVOKING DESCENT: THE AMERICAN DIALECT SOCIETY, WILLIAM DWIGHT WHITNEY, AND WILLIAM DEAN HOWELLS

> The efforts, as has been shown, to reverse the natural order of things— to force the negro into the position of the white man—are not merely failures, but frightful cruelties—cruelties that among ourselves end in the extinction of these poor creatures, while in the tropics it destroys the white man and impels the negro into barbarism.
>
> In conclusion, therefore, it is clear [. . .] that any American citizen, party, sect, or class among us, so blinded, bewildered, and besotted by foreign theories and false mental habits as to labor for negro 'freedom'—to drag down their own race, or to thrust the negro from his normal condition, is alike the enemy of both, a traitor to his blood

and at war with the decrees of the Eternal. (John Van Evrie, *White Supremacy and Negro Subordination* [1868] 339)

In 1868, in the midst of Reconstruction and in the same year as the passage of the Fourteenth Amendment, Northern doctor John Van Evrie published his *White Supremacy and Negro Subordination,* invoking powerful descent-bound figures such as "the natural order of things," "blood," and "Eternal decrees" to argue against reconstructing "American society on a Mongrel basis" and to argue for "the stupendous truth of white supremacy and negro subordination" (339, vi-vii). Moreover, as in his popular *Negroes and Negro 'Slavery'* (1853), Van Evrie dedicates an entire chapter of his later work to establishing linguistic differences between whites and "negroes," unambiguously associating language with racial essence. In *White Supremacy and Negro Subordination,* for example, Van Evrie claims that "the voice of the negro, both in its [physical] tones and its [grammatical] structure, varies just as widely from that of the white man as any other feature or faculty of the negro being"—a broad swath of varying features that Van Evrie takes pains, throughout the book, to establish. According to Van Evrie, God has provided the negro with an essentially different and lesser "vocal apparatus or organism" such that "no actual or typical negro will be able—no matter what pains have been taken to 'educate' him—to speak the language of the white man with absolute correctness" (110, 112–13). Therefore, he reasons, just as the pigeon's notes differ from the canary bird's, the owl's song from the nightingale's, the serpent's hiss from the tiger's growl, and the ass's "uncouth utterances" from the lion's "mighty roar or majestic voice," the "vocal organs of the negro differ widely from those of the white man, and of course there is a corresponding difference in the language" (110–11). According to Van Evrie, it is only because God has given the negro extraordinary "imitative instinct" that the negro might rapidly but only temporarily be able to speak the white man's language; thus, Van Evrie asserts, if removed from white society, negroes would, by a compelling "organic necessity" quickly lose "the words of their former masters, and in this as well as every other respect" regress to their "native Africanism" (114).[7] In starkly associating "negroes'" language with "an organic necessity" that "compels" them to speak it—an association of language that clearly aligns it with "nature"—Van Evrie overtly essentializes language, attributing language practices to race.

Van Evrie's text as a whole demonstrates how discussions of linguistic difference could invoke the paradigm of descent to absorb wider anxieties occasioned by the Civil War and Reconstruction, for according to Van Evrie, the same essential differences that make it impossible for the black man to speak the white man's language make it "evidently impossible" for the black man to vote, to marry, or to participate in any other civil or legal contracts of civil society. For instance, just as Van Evrie invokes "nature" or "organic necessity" to establish racialized linguistic difference, in a chapter devoted to marriage later in the book, Van Evrie uses the logic of descent to argue against negroes' "real" capacity to participate in marriage contracts or to vote in civil society. As Van Evrie contends, because "the natural affinity, the union of affection, the perfect adaptation so essential to a true marriage in our [white] race, is substantially imitated" by those negroes who marry in the South,

> to seek to force the negro beyond this—to force upon him the social responsibilities that attach to white people; or, in other words, to make marriage a legal contract in the case of negroes, *would be as absurd as to force him to vote at an election, or to perform any other high social duties, and which are evidently impossible.* In regard to his own wants, the well-being of his offspring, every thing connected with the best welfare and highest happiness that his race is capable of, he now enjoys, and any attempt to force him to marry as white people marry—that is, to make marriage a civil or legal contract—is not merely impossible, but it would be a crime and a monstrous outrage upon the nature God has given him. (240, my emphasis)

In the context of his comments about marriage and enfranchisement, Van Evrie's essentialization of language—his attribution of race to language practices as well as civil and legal practices—is a blatant example of how postbellum discussions of language could rely upon descent-based signifiers of race, gender, blood, or nature to express larger social and political concerns about Reconstruction's visions of consensual citizenship.

Although decidedly not to Van Evrie's obviously racist ends—rather, to inclusive if often racialized ends instead—other late-19th-century discussions of language, particularly discussions of dialect, also relied upon terms of descent. As this section will show, the prevalence of figures of racial or gender essence in professional discussions of language by the American Dialect Society and by the era's foremost linguists and literary critics, such as William Dwight Whitney and William Dean Howells, demonstrate the extent to which the paradigm of descent was translated into otherwise radically forward-looking cultural agendas at the moment of the founding of the disciplines of American language and literary study. Equally pioneering in their respective academic, scientific, and literary foci, the work of the American Dialect Society, Whitney's linguistic studies, and Howells' literary criticism, in clear contrast to Van Evrie, moved as far as possible outside the era's assumptions about "blood" and the "natural" yet still retained these descent-bound notions in their commentary on language. Such descent-bound notions could work to undermine their otherwise relativistic and progressive linguistic and literary endeavors by, at times, essentializing identity to language practices—an effect not without some sociopolitical resonance. For, the retention of tropes of descent within discourse on language enabled linguistic constructs such as dialect to operate analogically to blood. In turn, attitudes about language were fundamentally politicized in an era, obsessed with race and gender essence, whose legislation retained the descent-based logic of the "natural" and of "blood" to maintain racial patriarchy in America.[8]

One of a host of professional organizations dedicated to the study of language and literature, the American Dialect Society, formed in 1889, indicates the cultural centrality of discussions of language—particularly dialect—alongside debates about the law at the end of the 19th century.[9] A scan of the bibliographies printed in the first volumes of the society's *Dialect Notes*—extensive listings of works on language that the editors claim are still far from complete—testifies to the surge of publications and the range of interests that circulated around dialect study and that were cross-fertilized by various professional organizations at the time.[10] And a glance at the Society's membership lists likewise reveals how the organization came to reach a wide audience that included famous literary figures of the era: Its first-year membership of 158, which boasted a host of university-affiliated professors like Yale's William Dwight Whitney, whose popular work is discussed below, expanded in just a few years to include historical societies and public libraries across the country, as well as J. Bertram Lippincott, youngest son of publishing giant J. Ballinger Lippincott, and well-recognized writers like Thomas Wentworth Higginson, Sarah Orne Jewett, James Russell Lowell, and Brander Matthews.[11] The early work of the American Dialect Society reflects the wide reach and the overlapping linguistic *and* literary interests centered on language study at the end of the century.[12]

As well, the American Dialect Society's early discussions and publications, grappling with the term *dialect* itself, reveal how the era's descent-based views could become translated into discussions of language despite the most objective of scholarly intentions. In the late 19th century, *dialect* itself was a term whose meaning was contested, and it provided immense imaginary power in its very flexibility.[13] As Edward S. Sheldon, first secretary and later president of the American Dialect Society reflects in "What is a Dialect?" in the society's first volume of *Dialect Notes*, the defining of *dialect* in this era required a certain amount of mental gymnastics: "It is clear to me that we should start with the ordinary idea of the meaning of the word *dialect,* limiting or modifying it [. . .]. We must avoid any attempt to draw too definite lines; it is not a definition like that of a mathematical term, such as *circle* or *square,* that we shall find most useful, and our definition must rest on observation of the facts as we find them" (296).[14] Sheldon's essay also demonstrates how efforts to define *dialect* drew a range of often-hazy linguistic distinctions and relied upon ideas of the "natural." Sheldon's reiteration of his definition of dialect in the last few paragraphs of the essay relies upon the distinction between the "natural" and "artificial." Although Sheldon distances his understanding of the "natural" from understandings of it as "from nature," he repeatedly aligns dialect with what is "natural." For instance, Sheldon states, "a dialect is a form of speech actually in *natural* use in any community as a mode of communication"; and "If in ordinary use the standard language is contrasted with dialects the distinction is one which we may express by contrasting the somewhat artificial or acquired speech with the *natural* speech [. . .]" (296–97, my emphasis). Sheldon's piece shows the extent to which scientific definitions of dialect invoked the powerful idea of the "natural" and constructed an entire range of distinctions that became naturalized, or made natural; *dialect,* itself an "artificial" construction, thus contradictorily came to bear the weight of the "natural."

The broad-minded, judgment-free study of such "natural" speech was at the heart of the American Dialect Society's mission.[15] Yet, perhaps unavoidably, studies of dialect often blended with perceptions of social identity that could work against goals of avoiding value-laden linguistic judgments. As other early essays in *Dialect Notes* reveal, the study of phonology—a study itself hinging on the difficulty of aural perception, a problem that Sheldon himself seemed to recognize (287)—was often entangled in identitarian perceptions of social differences, such as those of gender or race, whether positive or negative. For example, J. P. Fruit's phonetic transcription of an Uncle Remus story, originally made for the Phonetic Section of the Modern Language Association, fondly and sanguinely recalls the language of his childhood, "the language of the negroes when they were parts and parcels of our households" (Fruit 196). Moreover, in John Uri Lloyd's recollection in "The Language of the Kentucky Negro," Lloyd's commentary about language forcefully merges with his selectively negative perceptions of racial and regional identity. Lloyd describes the "dialect of the Southern people" as the "charming and peculiar accent and modulation of words" and the "rich special mode of speech" which "carries no sense of vulgarity and no touch of ignorance, but rather the stamp of an accomplishment to be envied" (Lloyd 179–80). In contrast, he characterizes "the talk of the old slave, as well as the language of ignorant whites raised among the negroes," as speech in which "words were beheaded, curtailed, conglomerated, broken," sentences were run together, and "Barbarisms that came from illiteracy were mixed with expressions peculiar to himself. [. . .] With the negro the aim seemed to be either to shorten and simplify words and to drop letters which require an effort, or to show his 'smartness' by using words too big for his comprehension, and thus to torture them" (179–80). For Lloyd, then, dialect itself is not simply substandard, but some dialects (such as the "charming and "rich" southern dialect) are valued more than others (in this case, the "ignorant," "degraded tongue" "peculiar to" the Kentucky negro). Indeed, for Lloyd, these two ways of speaking were polarized and hierarchized, strikingly coupled with his feelings about the "Southron" and "the old Southern negro" (179). While Lloyd's commentary about black dialect is a relatively obscure and, like Van Evrie's, an extreme case of how identitarian notions were inserted into linguistic study, other more popular scholars of language, such as William Dwight Whitney, also used terms of descent to discuss dialect, while in less obvious ways.

Instrumental in the formation of the American Dialect Society, America's leading 19th-century linguist William Dwight Whitney held relativistic and progressive ideas for his time about language as a social institution.[16] Explicitly severing the long-held connection between language and race, Whitney saw language as a historical product and foregrounded the importance of human conventions in its study: The "action of the human will" in linguistic change, he says, "refuses scientific treatment" (*Life and Growth* 73). Thus in his most famous work, *The Life and Growth of Language: An Outline of Linguistic Science* (1875), he would deny outright that language, though acquired in childhood, is a product of blood, or "a race-characteristic, and as such, inherited from one's ancestry, along with color, physical constitution, traits of character, and the like; and that it is independently produced by each individual, in the natural course of his bodily and mental growth" (8). Whitney's ideas about language as a social institution are quite evident throughout *Life and Growth*, in which he seems to echo Noah Webster in elaborating the comparison of language to political institutions, a comparison that Whitney had made in *Language and the Study of Language* (1867), in which he states that speakers of a language "constitute a republic, or rather, a democracy, in which authority is conferred only by general suffrage and for due cause" (38). In these works, Whitney formulates language as consensual, choice-based, community-rooted—a revolutionary formulation for the time.[17]

While explicitly departing from long-held beliefs about language, Whitney yet remained a man of his historical moment, and his novel linguistic formulations at times retained biological metaphors to figure language and language mixing—revealing how, even for the most ground-breaking linguists, biological analogies were difficult to avoid and require awareness of their use within historical context. Whitney's biological analogies to discuss language included Darwinian evolution, genealogy, and blood—all metaphors that indicated his era's prevailing conceptual paradigm of descent and that essentialized, rather than socialized, linguistic difference in ways that could rhetorically undercut Whitney's progressive social and political figurations of language as consensual or contractual.

Although Whitney saw language as a human institution and linguistics as a historical science and denied outright any internal connection between language and biological givens, he still saw language as analogical to a living organism, thus retaining the analogical power of the natural in his writing on language in the moment of the discipline's founding—powerful analogies that remain in rhetoric about language to this day.[18] Whitney was a naturalist who went on geological expeditions with his older brother, Josiah Whitney, who became Professor of Economic Geology at Harvard, and Whitney's writings were pervaded by geological metaphors (Silverstein xi-xii). Whitney was "excited by the Darwinian hypothesis," and, while he felt that linguistics could not prove or disprove Darwin's notion, *The Life and Growth of Language* capitalized on Darwinian analogy (Hockett xvii; Silverstein xi). We can see the influence of Darwin's hypothesis in his thoughts on the nature and origin of language, in which Whitney views the voice as one of several tools developed for communication and states that "it is simply by a kind of process of natural selection and survival of the fittest that the voice has gained the upper hand, and come to be so much the most prominent [natural means of expression, such as tone, gesture, and grimace] that we give the name *language* ('tonguiness') to all expression" (*Life and Growth* 291). Also evidencing his reliance on Darwinian analogy, in "Languages and Dialects," Whitney compares the linguistic difficulty of distinguishing between dialect and language to the difficulty in natural history of distinguishing between "variety" and "species": "Transmutation of species in the kingdom of speech is no tempting hypothesis merely, but a patent fact, one of the fundamental and determining principles of linguistic study" (56). Although Whitney was cautious to delimit it as analogy only, the Darwinian analogy was a powerful one among Whitney's late-19th-century readers, as were the tropes of genealogy and blood, which equally held analogical power in Whitney's writings.

Particularly in discussions of dialect and of language and ethnology in *The Life and Growth of Language,* Whitney's analogies of genealogy and blood converge with notions of descent. In his discussion of the dialect divergence of the Romanic languages, Whitney specifically adopts an analogy of descent in noting the general principle that "genuine correspondences, of whatever degree, between the words of different languages, are to be interpreted as the result of derivation from one original: relationship, in words as in men, implies descent from a common ancestor" (169). Thus while on the one hand broadly comparing etymology to political institutions to acknowledge the effect of the human will on language, on the other hand, Whitney's comparison of etymology to genealogy, in this foundational moment of American linguistics, retains a culturally-resonant notion of blood and nods to "nature's" impact on language.

Whitney's retention of descent-based figures for language is seen even more clearly in his discussion of language and ethnology. Whitney is careful, again, to point out "that there is no necessary tie between race and language; that every man speaks the language he has learned, being born into the possession of no one rather than another" and to dissociate language from "a physical characteristic" (271–72). Yet his rhetoric nevertheless relies on a descent-bound notion of blood in his conception of language as a "transmitted institution," a figuration that straddles notions of "nature" and "nurture": "The testimony of language to race is thus not that of a physical characteristic, nor of anything founded on and representing such," says Whitney, "but only that of a transmitted institution, which, under sufficient inducement, is capable of being abandoned by its proper inheritors, or assumed by men of strange blood" (271–72). It is because of the "inducement" of "external circumstances" such as "[p]olitical control, social superiority, superiority of culture," that speech changes: "Or rather," he explains, "these are the added circumstances which, in the case of a mixture of communities, decide which element of population shall give, chiefly or wholly, its tongue to the resulting community. If there were no such thing as mixture of blood, then there would at least be next to nothing of the shifting of speech. Borrowing there would still be, but not substitution" (272). In this passage's movement from the idea of the "mixture of blood" to "the shifting of speech," Whitney's notion of language moves from that of a "human institution" to a "transmitted institution" akin to "blood"; thus the powerful retention of the figure of blood borders on naturalizing Whitney's social institution of language. To say that Whitney retains the analogical power of "blood" in his ideas about language is not to say that he sees language as equivalent to blood, but as operating both like *and* unlike blood, still a powerful descent-governed figuration. Whitney's final chapter maintains this analogical power of blood again even while delineating how language could be *unlike* blood: "Race-characteristics can only go down by blood; but race-acquisitions—language not less than religion, or science—can be borrowed and lent" (281).

The descent-based signifier of blood thus enables Whitney to shuttle conceptually between notions of language as inheritance and as exchange, both to express and deflect his era's widespread anxieties about racial miscegenation—or, as Whitney puts it, "the mixture of communities which creates the great intricacy of the ethnological problem, on its linguistic side as on its physical" (*Life and Growth* 272). As he notes in another passage entering into a debate over the mixture of languages and registering anxiety over "mixed blood," Whitney makes the case that the fact that "a language can be exchanged" is "by no means to deny its value as a record of human history, even of race-history" (274). For, he asserts, "It still remains true that, upon the whole, language is determined by race, since each human being usually learns to speak from his parents and others of the same blood. [. . .] It is not the wild and obscure races which are, or have ever been, mixing blood and mixing or shifting speech upon a grand scale; it is the cultivated ones" (274). Here, Whitney plainly analogizes mixture in language through the mixture of blood. And in the particular case of American English, *dialect* itself comes to function for Whitney as blood had functioned in American law, to sort out the mixture among American races: "There lies before us a vast and complicated problem in the American races; and here, again, it is their language that must do by far the greatest part of the work in solving it. American ethnology depends primarily and in bulk on the classifications and connections of dialects; till that foundation is laid, all is uncertain [. . .]" (275–76). In its appeal to descent, dialect thus functions as the blood imaginary does in the Reconstruction and post-Reconstruction contexts, becoming a kind of decoder for the "vast and complicated problem in the American races." Whitney severs the essential relation between signifier and signified; yet, given his era's retention of the analogy of blood, particularly within ideas about dialect, the essential relation between racial identity and speech is unable to be severed. Potential social referents of "dialect" in Whitney's work thus collapse with recourse to "blood," a common descent-bound signifier of racial identity in Whitney's day.

Like America's foremost late-19th-century linguist William Dwight Whitney, America's foremost late-19th-century editor, critic, and author retained descent-bound notions of language in an otherwise politically progressive literary and cultural agenda. Familiar with Whitney's writings during his editorship at *The Atlantic Monthly* (1871–81), William Dean Howells helped to professionalize the study of American literature, giving it the early legitimization it would need to become a discipline of its own, much as Whitney paved the way for the discipline of American linguistics.[19] In addition, a supporter of the NAACP, Howells famously worked to create a decentralized national literary forum for the "voices" of many previously un- or under-represented American writers—a broad-minded and inclusive embrace of diverse regional, women, and African American writers that, for Howells, meant newly championing the use of literary dialect.

In his first "Editor's Study" column, "The New 'Study' and the Use of American English" (January 1886), for example, Howells focuses on the topic of American English, which he hopes will constantly refresh "our inherited English" from "the native sources which literary decentralization will help to keep open" (4). In this one of many statements on American language, Howells favors novelists who write what they hear, for "without asking that our novelists of the widely scattered centres shall each seek to write in his local dialect, we are glad, as we say, of every tint any of them gets from the parlance he hears; it is much better than the tint he will get from the parlance he reads"; and, from this discussion of dialect, proceeds Howells' urging writers to write "true American":

> For our novelists to try to write Americanly, from any motive, would be a dismal error, but being born Americans, we would have them use 'Americanisms' wherever these serve their turn; and when their characters speak, we should like to hear them speak true American, with all the varying Tennesseean, Philadelphian, Bostonian, and New York accents. If we bother ourselves to write what the critics imagine to be 'English,' we shall be priggish and artificial, and still more so if we make our Americans talk 'English.' (5–6)

Howells echoes these views in his *Criticism and Fiction* (1891) and in his column "Dialect in Literature" (June 1895), which he concludes by saying, "I am not sure that I always like to read it [dialect]; but I think I should have lost much without some effects which it has accomplished in the representation of our national life" (223). For Howells, the literary use of dialect as "the racy thought and vital feeling of the characters who naturally express themselves in dialect" serves as a vital alternative to "dry and lifeless paraphrase" (223). Howells thus encourages American literature that eschews the worshipping of "standard" speech and urges a broader, more open illustration of national life—a forward-looking vision reaching toward a literary culture of consent enacted, in large part, through language.

Yet, while seeking politically progressive ends, such an embrace of dialect writing could often do so through contradictory means. Situated within the realist aesthetic's valuing of the real, the natural, and the true, discussions of literary dialect could appeal to backward-looking notions of descent in ways that might essentialize language, attributing traits such as race, class, gender, or region to language practices.[20] Thus Howells' idea that novelists should "write Americanly" as an extension of their "being born Americans," and his celebration of the "racy thought and vital feeling" of literary dialect, beg a second look. Valuing the "unpretentious" and "true," as Howells put it in "The Grasshopper: The Simple, the Natural, the Honest in Art" (1887), the realist aesthetic was grounded in the distinction between the "real" and the "artificial" and presumed a commensurability between "reality" and "representation" (71). Within this aesthetic, discussions and representations of literary dialect could appeal to notions of descent to make dialect bespeak the "natural," the "real," or "blood" itself. In *Criticism and Fiction* (1891), for example, Howells would explicitly link dialect with "what is true" in literature, saying: "But let fiction cease to lie about life; let it portray men and women as they are, actuated by the motives and the passions in the measure we all know . . . let it speak the dialect, the language, that most Americans know—the language of unaffected people everywhere" (328).

Thus when African American poet Paul Laurence Dunbar's *Majors and Minors,* what Howells called "a foundling of the press," came into Howells' hands in 1896, he particularly praised Dunbar's "Minors"—his dialect poems. Despite the fact that Howells himself recognized the "mischievous" character of a "parallel" between Dunbar's dialect poetry and his racial identity, Howells nevertheless seemed to find it difficult to separate his praise of the dialect poems from notions of Dunbar's racial essence. As the linguistic expression of the portrait of Dunbar's "woolly hair" and "thick outrolling lips" to which Howells' attention is drawn, Dunbar's "Minors" express his "real" racial identity:

> [. . .] I do not think one can read [Dunbar's] negro pieces without feeling that they are of like impulse and inspiration with the work of Burns when he was most Burns, when he was most Scotch, when he was most peasant. When Burns was least himself he wrote literary English, and Mr. Dunbar writes literary English when he is least himself. But not to urge the mischievous parallel farther, he is a real poet whether he speaks a dialect or whether he writes a language. He calls his little book Majors and Minors; the Majors being in our American English, and the Minors being in dialect, the dialect of the middle-south negroes and the middle-south whites; for the poet's ear has been quick for

the accent of his neighbors as well as for that of his kindred. I have no means of knowing whether he values his Majors more than his Minors; but I should not suppose it at all unlikely, and I am bound to say none of them are despicable. [. . .] It is when we come to Mr. Dunbar's Minors that we feel ourselves in the presence of a man with a direct and a fresh authority to do the kind of thing he is doing. (630)

Howells sees Dunbar as "most himself" in the dialect poems, equating Dunbar's racial identity with his use of dialect, and he further describes the Minors as communicating "vivid picturesqueness," "broad characterization," and "the simple, sensuous, joyous nature of his race"; in Dunbar's treatment of his material, Howells asserts, "he has been able to bring us nearer to the heart of primitive human nature in his race than any one else has yet done." The poem "When Malindy Sings," for instance, Howells calls "purely and intensely black [. . .] in its feeling," with "the strong full pulse of the music."

The paradigm of descent governing Howells' equation of "the strong full pulse" of Dunbar's dialect with the musicality of his poetry and the "black blood" coursing through the poet's veins becomes increasingly clear in Howells' introduction to *Lyrics of Lowly Life,* published in December 1896. Here, Howells dwells on authenticating the purity of Dunbar's "blood" even while claiming that the author's "race, origin, and condition" were irrelevant to his previous assessment of Dunbar's work: "Still, it will legitimately interest those who like to know the causes, or, if these may not be known, the sources, of things, to learn that the father and the mother of the first poet of his race in our language were negroes without admixture of white blood [. . .] So far as I could remember, Paul Dunbar was the only man of pure African blood and of American civilization to feel the negro life aesthetically and express it lyrically" (vii-viii). While Howells strains against praising Dunbar's poetry on the basis of race, like many of his era—though certainly to a much lesser extent than most—he remains preoccupied by the late-19th-century imaginary of blood, by metaphors of descent that were translated into language, here through the logic of realism. Even while he "accepted [Dunbar's black poems] as an evidence of the essential unity of the human race, which does not think or feel black in one and white in another, but humanly in all," Howells preserves a measure of racial difference through the essentialization of language: "What I mean is that several people might have written [the poems in literary English]; but I do not know any one else at present who could quite have written the dialect pieces" (viii-ix).[21]

The essentialization of language to racial identity through dialect was not unrelated to the essentialization of language to gender identity, just as descent-bound notions of blood or nature conjoined discourses of race and gender. As Elsa Nettels shows in *Language and Gender in American Fiction,* Howells' discussions often united with the influence of magazines, sociologists, and others in the era's construction of gender as natural and hierarchical difference.[22] And, like his contradictory characterizations of Dunbar's dialect poems—as bespeaking the "essential unity of the human race" while at the same time expressing "a race life from within the race"—Howells was contradictory in his accounting for gender differences in language. In an interview in 1895, for example, he expressed the belief that most of the generally accepted differences between men and women were the result of education and social upbringing—"very much exaggerated" (Halfmann, "Interviews" 326–27). Yet, as Nettels states, Howells' "references to the 'Eternal Womanly' and the 'Ever-Womanly' imply belief in a universal female nature to which women's virtues and deficiencies can be referred" (30).[23] Thus in his second "Editor's Study," titled "American English; W. H. White; Balzac; American Criticism" (February 1886), Howells emphasizes the disparity between "young-lady American" speech and "masculine American" speech in his critique of a British novelist Mr. Black, whose novel *White Heather* has "a character who speaks perceptible American; only, he is a man, and he speaks young-lady American as often as masculine American" (7). While these gender differences may have in fact existed in American speech, it is significant that Howells' criticism of Mr. Black's unstudied Americanisms pivots on Mr. Black's unawareness of them. Howells' criticism draws attention to the importance of perceptions of gendered linguistic differences to an "authentic" knowledge of American English and to the "reality" of literary representation.

The essentialization of language to identity that often occurred within literary realism and within late-19th-century studies of language ultimately had ambivalent effects for notions of race and gender difference. While aiming for inclusivity and reaching toward democratic consent in linguistic study and in literary representations of American life, discussions of African American dialect, or of "young-lady American" and "masculine American" English, could make language bear the descent-bound weight of the "real," much as "blood" or "nature" might in legal discourse, thereby embedding race and gender difference within language in an era that underwrote such difference in the law. In this context, literary representations of dialect and of gender and language—to which I will now turn—took up the terms of descent and consent in ways that could either idealize the sociopolitical relations of the past or reveal the regressive logic by which these relations could operate.

3. REPRESENTING DIALECT, IMAGINING (DIS)FRANCHISEMENT: JOEL CHANDLER HARRIS' AND CHARLES W. CHESNUTT'S STORIES OF THE WAR

> I am advised by my publishers that this book is to be included in their catalogue of humorous publications and this friendly warning gives me an opportunity to say that however humorous it may be in effect, its intention is perfectly serious; and, even if it were otherwise, it seems to me

that a volume written wholly in dialect must have its solemn, not to say melancholy, features. With respect to the Folk-Lore series, my purpose has been to preserve the legends themselves in their original simplicity, and to wed them permanently to the quaint dialect—if, indeed, it can be called a dialect—through the medium of which they have become a part of the domestic history of every Southern family; and I have endeavored to give the whole a genuine flavor of the old plantation.

[. . .] The dialect, it will be observed, is wholly different from that of the Hon. Pompey Smash and his literary descendants, and different also from the intolerable misrepresentations of the minstrel stage, but it is at least phonetically genuine. Nevertheless, if the language of Uncle Remus fails to give vivid hints of the really poetic imagination of the negro; if it fails to embody the quaint and homely humor which was his most prominent characteristic; if it does not suggest a certain picturesque sensitiveness—a curious exaltation of mind and temperament not to be defined by words—then I have reproduced the form of the dialect merely and not the essence, and my attempt may be accounted a failure. (Joel Chandler Harris, *Uncle Remus, His Songs and His Sayings* [1880] vii-viii)

Despite their loose ties to actual speech, or perhaps *because* of them, literary representations of language, never quite "real," are powerful linguistic renderings of particular visions of the world. The slave tales that Joel Chandler Harris popularized in literary dialect after the Civil War thus highlight the importance of language in articulating, in this case, a particular vision of 19th-century social relations. As seen in his introduction to *Uncle Remus: His Songs and His Sayings* (1880), quoted above, Harris took his dialect depictions of slave tales absolutely seriously. Harris intended to avoid "the intolerable misrepresentations of the minstrel stage" and instead to depict sympathetically what he called the "certain picturesque sensitiveness of the negro." Yet Harris' emphasis on the "phonetically genuine" nature of his representations of dialect could nonetheless perpetuate a myth of "authentic" black language, particularly a black speech that could be rendered "picturesque" and visibly differentiated from the speech of his white characters. Assuming that it was possible to reproduce both "the form" and "the essence" of black speech, Harris' conjunction of the aural ("dialect" and "phonetics") and the visual ("the minstrel stage," "vivid hints," the "picturesque") in this passage thus serves as a good illustration of the way in which literary dialect, such as the eye dialect I will discuss below, could work to create visible linguistic difference on the page, to connect social perceptions of race (via skin color or "form") with identitarian conceptions of race (via biological substance, natural "essence," or blood).[24] In this way signaling the speaker rather than the speech, Harris' literary use of dialect, then, could reinforce and disseminate notions of essential racial difference as authenticated through language. Such representations of language worked nostalgically, alongside other elements of fiction such as plot and character, to reconstruct, using Harris' introductory words, "the domestic history of every Southern family" during the post-Reconstruction era (vii).

Yet other writers, as this section will also show, complicated this logic. Indeed, in "The Dumb Witness" (1897) and *The Colonel's Dream* (1905), Charles W. Chesnutt introduces gendered as well as racialized power dynamics into his representations of language. Through his depiction of the speech of mixed-blood women, Chesnutt draws attention not simply to the form of dialect itself but to the overarching paradigm of consent/ descent in which discussions and representations of language participated. In doing so, Chesnutt represents gender and language to shift the terms of the era's linguistic and legal discussions to the overarching dynamics of discourse and power—to the importance of political speech itself—at the heart of (dis)franchisement. As Chesnutt's writings show, it is by recognizing these larger governing terms of consent and descent, terms taken up in both linguistic and legal debates about voices and votes, that invocations of dialect can avoid sustaining notions of essential difference, and potentially trouble these notions instead.

The centrality, even overrepresentation, of the black male dialect speaker's voice in popular literature at the end of the 19th century is perhaps nowhere more evident than in Harris' Uncle Remus tales, studied by the American Dialect Society and avidly consumed by American readers.[25] First published in the late 1870s in the *Atlanta Constitution,* which was founded in 1868 to unify the South during Reconstruction and was thereafter one of the largest circulating newspapers in the country, the tales were initially collected by Harris from slave folklore and then gathered in the enduring *Uncle Remus, His Songs and His Sayings,* titled as such because they were told by Harris' lovable character Uncle Remus, a freed black slave who, in Harris' words, "has nothing but pleasant memories of the discipline of slavery" (xvii), to the young, enrapt son of Remus' now-employers, Miss Sally and Master John. Perhaps most remembered and most debated as to their complex origins and multiple meanings are the slave stories that Harris grouped together as the animal legends in *Uncle Remus, His Songs and His Sayings*—legends such as the famous "Tar Baby" story in which the trickster hero "Brer Rabbit," most often interpreted as the black slave, outwits and triumphs over "Brer Fox." Yet distinct from these animal legends, and unambiguously pertinent to the context of Reconstruction discussed in this chapter, is a singular short story that Harris placed apart from Uncle Remus' "Legends," separate from his "Songs," and distinct from his "Sayings": Directly in the middle of *Uncle Remus, His Songs and His Sayings,* Harris' "A Story of the War" powerfully analogizes the reconstruction of the nation—and the national "family"—around the nostalgic regulation of the black male dialect storyteller's voice.[26]

"A Story of the War" is set in 1870, the same year in which the Fifteenth Amendment was passed. Through Uncle Remus' narration, it looks back to the war, a historical moment in which African Americans clearly had no vote. In it, Miss Theodosia Huntingdon of Burlington, Vermont decides to go south to visit her brother, John Huntingdon, otherwise known as "Mars John." When she arrives at the depot in early October 1870, a "somewhat picturesque," dialect-speaking Uncle Remus greets her (202). Once they reach the plantation, Master John convinces Uncle Remus to tell Theodosia his version of the story of "how you went to war and fought for the Union," volunteering for one day and commanding "an army of one" (205). In the story he tells, Uncle Remus stands by Ole Miss and Miss Sally while the southern white men fight in the Confederate army and the Yankee soldiers ransack the house. After they depart, Uncle Remus discovers "dey wuz a live Yankee up dar in dat tree," poised to shoot his master, who approaches the plantation on his horse who "wuz a prancin' like a school-gal" (211). As Uncle Remus recounts, he "know'd dat man wuz gwineter shoot Mars Jeems ef he could, en dat wuz mo'n I could stan.' Manys en manys de time dat I nuss dat boy, en hilt 'im in dese arms, en toted 'im on dis back, en w'en I see dat Yankee lay dat gun 'cross a lim' en take aim at Mars Jeems I up wid my ole rifle, en shet my eyes en let de man have all she had" (212). Uncle Remus shoots the Union soldier, much to the "indignant" surprise of Miss Theodosia, who declares, "Do you mean to say [. . .] that you shot the Union soldier, when you knew he was fighting for your freedom?" (212). Uncle Remus responds that he "des disremembered all 'bout freedom en lammed aloose" when he saw the man take aim at Mars Jeems. Uncle Remus and Miss Sally nurse the soldier back to health, and the soldier, who turns out to be Master John Huntingdon himself, marries Miss Sally. When Theodosia finally comments that Uncle Remus' shot cost John an arm, Uncle Remus responds that he has given him his bride, his children, and "his own brawny arms," and "ef dem ain't nuff fer enny man den I done los' de way" (212).

Clearly, this "story of the war" recounts the black slave retainer's loyalty to the southern—indeed, *national*—white family. It furthermore uses the popular trope of romantic reconciliation, in which the problems of the war are solved neither politically nor economically, but sentimentally, when the northern white soldier marries his southern nurse-bride.[27] But also strikingly, the story manages problematic postbellum relations through linguistic representations that reinforce the story's romanticized racialism.

Uncle Remus' stories are told in eye dialect, which serves as a helpful analogy for the wider overrepresentation of the black male's speech in Harris' and other dialect stories of the day. Opposed to Master John's speech, which is represented in Standard English, Uncle Remus' speech, represented in eye dialect, merges visual and aural difference on the page, associating perceptions of racial difference with linguistic difference. *Eye dialect* denotes the spelling of a word phonetically, but a case in which spelling does not reflect an actual dialect difference; for example, a word like *dicshunary* might represent what most speakers of American English, educated or not, would say, but its eye dialect spelling—d-i-c-s-h-u-n-a-r-y—"heightens the effect of illiteracy" (Nettles, *Language, Race* 75; Wolfram and Schilling-Estes 352).[28] When Uncle Remus says that he shoots the Union soldier to protect "Mars Jeems," Harris uses eye dialect to represent *knowed* as "know'd" and *was* as "wuz." Certainly, so-called standard spelling does not necessarily correspond to pronunciation. Neither is the complex literary use of dialect inherently flawed or racist; as scholars have pointed out, writers like Harris importantly paved the way for further necessary representations of black dialect, helping to overcome what Eric Sundquist sees as a long-time cultural "sound-blindness."[29] Yet the literary use of eye dialect, as in the Uncle Remus tales in which *was* is spelled w-u-z, could also perpetuate a myth of a non-dialectal, unaccented speech and visibly heighten the effect of Uncle Remus' linguistic deviance, and his racialized difference, when alleged Standard English speakers would pronounce "was" no differently. Within the context of Harris' post-Reconstruction day and its navigation of sociopolitical difference based on essentialized notions of identity, this is not insignificant.

Moreover, the fact that it is the Standard-English-speaking Master John who directs the newly freed Uncle Remus to tell the family's "story of the war" in Remus' black dialect allegorizes how the treatment of black dialect itself attempted to bring together the white patriarchal national family through particular descent-bound representations of language, representations both racialized and gendered. It is Master John—the northern-turned-southern and pervasively "national" white male—who prompts Uncle Remus to tell his tale in dialect: "before you go, I want you to tell Sister here how you went to war and fought for the Union.—Remus was a famous warrior [. . .] he volunteered for one day, and commanded an army of one. You know the story, but you have never heard Remus' version" (205). In response, Uncle Remus "shuffled around in an awkward, embarrassed way, scratched his head, and looked uncomfortable," protesting that "Miss Doshy" didn't have time for his stories. But the "upshot of it was that, after many ridiculous protests, Uncle Remus sat down on the steps and proceeded to tell his story of the war," in thick dialect and from the standpoint of a southerner (205). Uncle Remus here becomes an "authentic" spokesperson of the war and its aftermath for Master John, for Harris, and for Harris' readers, bringing North and South together through his storytelling, just as Uncle Remus' family loyalty brings Master John and Miss Sally together in the first place and establishes the new Huntingdon line of descent. John's war-time "castration" is rewarded with his new family, which insures the further reproduction of his power. For, as Harris tells us in his introduction, it is to the little boy who is the offspring of Master John and Miss Sally that Uncle Remus tells his animal fables throughout *Uncle Remus, His Songs and His Sayings*:

> If the reader not familiar with plantation life will imagine that the myth-stories of Uncle Remus are told night after night to a little boy by an old negro who appears to be venerable enough to have lived during the period which he describes—who has nothing but pleasant

memories of the discipline of slavery—and who has all the prejudices of caste and pride of family that were the natural results of the system; if the reader can imagine all this, he will find little difficulty in appreciating and sympathizing with the air of affectionate superiority which Uncle Remus assumes as he proceeds to unfold the mysteries of plantation lore to a little child who is the product of that practical reconstruction which has been going on to some extent since the war in spite of the politicians. Uncle Remus describes that reconstruction in his Story of the War, and I may as well add here for the benefit of the curious that the story is almost literally true. (xvii)

Harris' discussion here of "A Story of the War" as an example of that apolitical postbellum "practical reconstruction" explicitly frames Uncle Remus' story as about the reconstruction of the family, a family both southern and national. And by placing Uncle Remus' dialect at the center of its telling, Harris' "A Story of the War" reveals the central role of dialect, and of the dialect story, in benignly reconciling the national family not around the black man's vote, but around the black man's voice—a dialect-speaking voice that is nostalgically loyal to and proud of his white family. Given their historical climate, the dialect of Harris' stories and others like them worked through language to reconstruct postbellum sociopolitical relations as antebellum domestic relations rather than political ones, romanticizing the past social order, and allowing white, northern-and-southern men to direct the war's story.[30]

In calling our attention to Uncle Remus' role in ensuring the Huntingdon line of descent and in entertaining the little boy who is the offspring of "practical reconstruction," the above passage from Harris' introduction also draws our consideration to the unmentioned and often-overlooked mother figure who has reproduced the Huntingdon family: Miss Sally. In "A Story of the War," Miss Sally has no lines of dialogue but is a felt presence, "crooning softly as she rocked the baby to sleep" (204). At the same time, then, that Harris' literary representations of dialect depict the black male storyteller via a kind of heightened linguistic representation, they also under-represent the female speaker, figuring her as a comparatively silent presence in the story and linguistically reinforcing, in Chief Justice Bradley's words in *Bradwell v. Illinois*, "the natural and proper timidity and delicacy which belongs to the female sex [and] evidently unfits it for the occupations of a civil life."

"A Story of the War" thus gestures to the ways in which racialized *and* gendered depictions of language might aim to unite the country, not only through the often-noted marriage plot, but also through the equally nostalgic, "domestic," descent-bound voices of the dialect-storytelling brawny black man and the softly crooning, maternal white woman. It is by taking this gesture a step further and by overtly introducing considerations of gendered as well as racialized power dynamics into considerations of dialect—by making the dynamics of a mulatta woman's speech central to the stories of "The Dumb Witness" and *The Colonel's Dream*—that Charles W. Chesnutt complicates these literary representations and unravels the era's descent-bound linguistic and legal logic. As the discursive dynamics in Chesnutt's stories show, the future of the national family ultimately depends upon women's reproductive and representative capacity, as much a capacity of consent as it is one of descent.

From 1887 to 1889, Chesnutt's dialect tales, told by Uncle Julius—his alternative to Harris' Uncle Remus—were printed in *The Atlantic,* and they were soon collected in *The Conjure Woman,* published in 1899.[31] In "The Dumb Witness" (1897), originally omitted from publication in *The Conjure Woman,* and in the story's later version at the center of *The Colonel's Dream* (1905), Chesnutt offers an alternative figure to the dialect-speaking black male storyteller in his portrait of the central character Viney, whose speech radically departs from the dialect formula.[32] In a story narrated mainly by the white, Standard-English-speaking, northern-come-southern John, Viney, a mixed-blood housekeeper, does not tell her white master, Old Malcolm Murchison, the whereabouts of the family will that contains his inheritance after he physically impairs her ability to speak; through her equally inarticulate babble and articulate silence, which we eventually learn is a linguistic performance, Viney discursively rejects the means of white patriarchal control and reverses the relations between white master and slave woman, between the most and least powerful figures in American life, and instead links their social and political fates together. In part through her inscrutably mixed blood and incomprehensible language, Viney thus complicates the figures of the black male storyteller and of the softly crooning white mother in Harris' "A Story of the War." When Viney babbles, she speaks a language that absolutely refuses to be represented literarily—a literary use of language through which Chesnutt reveals language itself as dependent upon social conventions. Moreover, in his unambiguously politicized extension of "The Dumb Witness" in *The Colonel's Dream,* Chesnutt uses Viney's voice—a gender-infused model of language based on consent versus descent, on contract versus identity—to expose the descent-bound logic of dialect and disfranchisement in the post-Reconstruction era. At the same time, Chesnutt proposes the "secret" of literary and political representation, and of national reproduction, to which we may all be dumb witnesses: an alternative logic of consent, in both language and the law, in both voice and the vote.

Unlike Chesnutt's popular first conjure tales, told in dialect by Uncle Julius, "The Dumb Witness" places the subject of Viney's linguistic conjure—the issue of *her* voice, rather than Julius'—at the very heart of the story. By placing Viney's speech at the center of "The Dumb Witness," Chesnutt ultimately uses the wider representation of gender and language, rather than the representation of dialect, to negotiate anxieties about the political voices enfranchised by the Fourteenth and

Fifteenth Amendments. As a mulatta housekeeper, Viney can be read as the lowest on the sociopolitical ladder, in some sense the most removed from the immediate political context and thus least threatening to the white patriarchy and to Chesnutt's readers: a likely, diversionary character to avoid addressing anxieties about the Fifteenth Amendment, which were, at least overtly, about the voices/votes of black *men* moreso than women. But in another sense, the denial and use of this mulatta's voice, as the presumably least powerful voice in the sociopolitical spectrum, has the most startling implications; for the denial of Viney's voice ultimately implies that the liberties denied to the least powerful are those denied to the most powerful.

Chesnutt's various versions of "The Dumb Witness"—whose frame, like Harris' "A Story of the War," is set in the Reconstruction era and whose narrative recounts antebellum days—were revised as Chesnutt was considering issues of (dis)franchisement in several essays, including "Liberty and the Franchise" (ca. 1899), "The Negro's Franchise" (1901), "The Disfranchisement of the Negro" (1903), "The Courts and the Negro" (ca. 1908), and "Women's Rights" (1915).[33] The fact that Chesnutt rewrote "The Dumb Witness" at least twice, and that he did so as he was considering post-Reconstruction threats to the Civil War Amendments, calls our attention to the story's importance to Chesnutt and its relation to these issues. As does his fiction, Chesnutt's essays, to which I will next turn, complicate a descent-based representational logic.

Indeed, in "The Courts and the Negro" (ca. 1908–11), in looking back on the *Plessy* decision—to Chesnutt's mind "the most important and far reaching decision of the Supreme Court upon the question of civil rights"— Chesnutt focuses on the portion of the majority's decision that reversed the Fourteenth Amendment via essentialized notions of "the nature of things" and "racial instincts" (Chesnutt, "Courts" 155–56; *Plessy* 44, 51). Chesnutt saw what he called the "far-reaching effect of this decision" ("Courts" 157), including the "calamity" of the repeal, "by judicial construction" of "the uniform application of the Fourteenth and Fifteenth Amendments" (160). Indeed, this situation had already effectively if not nominally begun, as Chesnutt noted, many years before: "The colored people are left, in the States where they have been disfranchised, absolutely without representation, direct or indirect, in any law-making body, in any court of justice, in any branch of government [. . .]. [. . .] They have no direct representation in any Southern legislature, and no voice in determining the choice of white men who might be friendly to their rights" ("Disfranchisement" 182). Widespread anxieties about the social and political equalities granted by the Civil War Amendments that were expressed in their Jim Crow reversals culminated, then, as Chesnutt saw, in anxieties about the Fifteenth Amendment—about political representation and the elective franchise itself—and its threatened repeal at the turn of the century. As he would write in "Women's Rights" (1915), the right to a voice in government entailed the right to the vote even for the "least" powerful in the sociopolitical spectrum:

I believe that all persons of full age and sound mind should have a voice in the making of the laws by which they are governed, or in the selection of those who make those laws. [. . .]

Experience has shown that the rights and interests of no class are safe so long as they are entirely in the hands of another class—the rights and interests of the poor in the hands of the rich, of the rich in the hands of the poor, of one race in the hands of another. And while there is no such line of cleavage in other social classes, yet so far as women constitute a class as differentiated from men, neither can their rights be left with entire safety solely in the hands of men. [. . .] Their [women's] rights need protection, and they should be guarded against oppression, *and the ballot is the most effective weapon by which these things can be accomplished.* (383–84, my emphasis)

For Chesnutt, clearly, blacks' *and* women's having a *voice* meant their having a *vote* in the making of the laws that affected them.

Chesnutt particularly saw how figures of descent such as blood provided justifications for black disfranchisement. As such, he destabilizes blood as a signifier for political representation, thereby dismantling post-Reconstruction arguments for African American disfranchisement. By the time *The Conjure Woman* was published, the justificatory use of blood-based "natural laws" in post-Reconstruction disfranchisement "policies" would be one of the uppermost concerns in Chesnutt's mind. In "Liberty and the Franchise" (c. 1899), for example, Chesnutt locates the problem of blood and the fear of mixed blood at the root of race prejudice and the center of the problem of African American voting rights:

It is well, in dealing with an evil, to get, if possible, at the root of it. And the root of this evil, it must be apparent to the most casual observer, is the race prejudice, not unknown at the North, but which hovers over the South like a nightmare, warping all judgments, darkening counsel, and confusing all standards of right and wrong, of justice and equity. [. . .] *As one of the wisest and most progressive men of the South once said in substance, the white people of the South have stooped so long to the old Negro in the dust that they have never been able to rise to the full stature of manhood. Their thoughts by day, their dreams by night, are haunted by the fear that in some distant future one of their remote descendants may contain a drop of Negro blood.* Hence such drastic legislation as that by which in Georgia a few days since a colored man and a white woman were sentenced to a fine of $3,000.00 and three years in the chain gang for the crime of being husband and wife. By virtue of this same prejudice railroads must have double equipment; there must be a dual school system, at enormously additional expense. People of mixed blood, no matter how white, must be classed as black; to hold an office is a crime punishable with death.

Instead of a harmonious forward movement of the whole people, there is the constant friction of opposing elements. Scorn and contumely on the one side foster fear and hatred on the other, and as the colored people rise in the scale of life, they come in contact with the whites at more different points, each new one of which contacts is the signal for a new manifestation of an old prejudice. [. . .]

This is the root of the whole evil. The Constitution of the United States proclaims in spirit if not in words, equality before the law. Before the Civil War this was construed to apply to white men, but the 13th, 14th, and 15th Amendments make it perfectly clear that it applies to all white and colored men born or naturalized in the United States. The white people of the South have declared, as they did once before to their sorrow, that they are superior to the Constitution, *and that the Negro shall not vote*. [. . .] (105–06, my emphasis)

For Chesnutt, the descent-based myth of blood, which formed the basis for representation based on identity rather than contract, legally justified the denial of political representation for blacks.

Chesnutt saw how "blood" could provide justifications for black disfranchisement; likewise, he understood literary dialect as an often descent-based conceptualization of language and worked to destabilize it. Chesnutt recognized in particular how attitudes about dialect could work alongside attitudes about "blood" to, in Howells' words reviewing Chesnutt's work in 1900, "exclude" or to "fortify"—to distinguish or differentiate—black writers like Chesnutt from "ordinary American" art and to reinforce a view of language based on the logic of identity.[34] In other words, Chesnutt saw the problem with a representational logic that, via dialect, might attribute race to language practices—and perhaps this is why, soon after he gained access to the literary establishment, he wanted to stop writing dialect in his tales.

On September 26, 1889, not long after publishing the first of his dialect stories and in his earliest known letter to Albion Tourgée—editor, novelist, and lawyer for the defense in *Plessy*—Chesnutt indicates his interest in giving up dialect. In his letter to Tourgée, enclosing a copy of the October *Atlantic* containing his story "Dave's Neckliss," Chesnutt writes that he thinks he has "about used up the old Negro [Uncle Julius] who serves as mouthpiece, and I shall drop him in future stories, as well as much of the dialect" (qtd. in McElrath and Leitz 44). In another letter, addressed to Walter Hines Page, dated May 20, 1898, and submitting the stories that would comprise *The Conjure Woman*, Chesnutt exposes "dialect"—which he sees as "a despairing task to write"—as a fiction:

> The fact is, of course, that there is no such thing as a Negro dialect; that what we call by that name is the attempt to express, with such a degree of phonetic correctness as to suggest the sound, English pronounced as an ignorant old southern Negro would be supposed to speak it, and

at the same time to preserve a sufficient approximation to the correct spelling to make it easy reading. (qtd. in McElrath and Leitz 105)

A "Negro dialect," according to Chesnutt, does not exist. As Chesnutt recognizes, it is merely suggestive of an idea of the sound of "an ignorant old southern Negro," always an attempt, a supposition, an approximation.[35]

In "The Future American: What the Race is Likely to Become in the Process of Time" (1900), quoted below, Chesnutt further troubles any essential tie between language and race that literary dialect might be seen to support:

> [. . .] language, so recently lauded as an infallible test of racial origin, is of absolutely no value in this connection, its distribution being dependent upon other conditions than race. Even color, upon which the social structure of the United States is so largely based, has been proved no test of race. The conception of a pure Aryan, Indo-European race has been abandoned in scientific circles, and the secret of the progress of Europe has been found in racial heterogeneity, rather than in racial purity. (93–94)

Here, alongside unreservedly dismantling a descent-based view of language, Chesnutt also disrupts the idea of racial purity. He instead proposes "that the future American race—the future American ethnic type—will be formed of a mingling, in a yet to be ascertained proportion, of the various racial varieties which make up the present population of the United States" (94). More exactly, Chesnutt continues:

> It is then in the three broad types—white, black, and Indian—that the future American race will find the material for its formation. Any dream of a pure white race, of the Anglo-Saxon type, for the United States, may as well be abandoned as impossible, even if desirable. (94)

For Chesnutt, myths about language and myths about race were intimately connected; thus the reality of "dialect" and the purity of "race," similarly governed by notions of descent, become equally "impossible" dreams.

In "The Dumb Witness" and *The Colonel's Dream*, too, Chesnutt exposes the fictions of both blood and dialect underlying disfranchisement by bringing gendered as well as racialized power dynamics into the representation of Viney's speech. The general question of the literary use of dialect was surely part of Chesnutt's composition of "The Dumb Witness," but it was particularly at the heart of his considerations of how to represent Viney's speech. In the three different versions of the story, when Viney finally speaks at the conclusion of the tale, Chesnutt "apparently hesitated as to whether Viney should speak 'perfect' English or black dialect English" (Brodhead, *Conjure Woman* 171n3). In the first version of the story, she speaks in Standard English; in the second, she speaks in black dialect English; in the third version in *The Colonel's Dream,* she again speaks Standard English. In locating the dilemma of the literary use of dialect squarely in the mouth of this central mulatta woman, Chesnutt's representation of language drew attention to and took on descent-based notions of gender as well as race, and thus doubly troubled the notions of biological essence that could reinforce conceptions of dialect—a point that critics have missed in their focus not on Viney's voice but John's narration.[36] Thus while Chesnutt's Uncle Julius stories had departed a good deal from Harris' Uncle Remus and the narrative conventions of the plantation tale, in "The Dumb Witness," Chesnutt departs from these conventions even further by placing Viney's voice at the center of the tale.

Through his characterization of Viney in "The Dumb Witness," Chesnutt destabilizes the descent-based logic of blood and of dialect simultaneously: Viney's blood, like her dialect, has no fixed, pure, or stable referent and is, rather, the very mixture of blood in Chesnutt's imagined future American—a combination of white, black, and Indian intimately related to her master. Viney resembles Malcolm Murchison in appearance: "She seemed but little younger than the man, and her face was enough like his, in a feminine way, to suggest that they might be related in some degree, unless this inference was negatived by the woman's complexion, which disclosed a strong infusion of darker blood" (159–60); she is "a tall, comely young quadroon" with "a dash of Indian blood, which perhaps gave her straighter and blacker hair than she would otherwise have had, and also perhaps endowed her with some other qualities which found their natural expression in the course of subsequent events—if indeed her actions needed anything more than common human nature to account for them" (163–64); and, as Malcolm's uncle later reveals, Viney "is devoted to you and to the family—she ought to be, for she is of our blood—and she only knows the secret" of where to find the family will (166).

Just as her blood is no reliable signifier of racial identity, neither is Viney's speech, as Chesnutt describes in the scene when John first witnesses its dynamics. Viney either remains silent in reaction to Malcolm's threats, or responds in "a meaningless cacophony":

> She rose from her seat, and drawing herself up to her full height—she was a tall woman, though bowed somewhat with years—began to speak, I thought at first in some foreign tongue. But after a moment I knew that no language or dialect, at least none of European origin, could consist of such a discordant jargon, such a meaningless cacophony as that which fell from the woman's lips. And as she went on, pouring out a flood of sounds that were not words, and which yet seemed now and then vaguely to suggest words, as clouds suggest the shapes of mountains and trees and strange beasts, the old man seemed to bend like a reed before a storm, and began to expostulate, accompanying his words with deprecatory gestures. (160)

The "discordant jargon" which falls from this woman's lips resembles "no language or dialect"—a description similar to Chesnutt's description of "negro dialect" itself as vaguely suggestive of shifting forms. Indeed, Viney's language seemingly defies representation altogether, as her miscegenated body itself does—perhaps one reason why the larger discursive themes of language and power, of speech and silence, pervade the text rather than particular dialect representations. Through Viney's mixed-blood character and garbled tongue, Chesnutt thus consciously detaches both "race" and "dialect" from any firm, essential referents.

Although the central portion of "The Dumb Witness" takes place before the Civil War, by tracing its effects through and after the war, and by stretching it into the frame of the narrative, Chesnutt shows the ongoing relevance of the story's dynamics to the post-Reconstruction era in which it was written: The racialized *and* gendered power dynamics, played out in the discursive exchanges between Murchison and Viney, are liable to be replayed in the dilution of the Civil War Amendments. Perhaps most significantly for Chesnutt's disruption of descent, in the core story of "The Dumb Witness" reconstructed by John in its frame, Malcolm Murchison impairs Viney's ability to speak precisely *because* she uses language as reciprocal, as contractual, to represent her own interests. When Malcolm Murchison breaks the news to Viney to prepare the house for his new fiancée, "Some passionate strain of the mixed blood in her veins—a very human blood—broke out in a scene of hysterical violence. She pleaded, remonstrated, raged. He listened calmly through it all—he had anticipated some such scene," and at the end told her she "had better be quiet and obedient" (164–65). While, in the prevailing antebellum legal and social order, her "blood" would have dictated her silence, Viney overcomes whatever legal custom exists in order to represent her own interests in the relationship—a use of language that rests not on an idea of descent or identity, but on a notion of consent and contract, much as Hope Leslie's petition to Governor Winthrop does in Sedgwick's earlier work.[37]

In other words, on the hope of reciprocal communication, Viney petitions Murchison: She protests his decision to marry Mrs. Todd—a protest that, like Hope Leslie's and antebellum women's petitions, has pronounced political resonance. Murchison denies her claim, urging her to be "quiet and obedient." Thus the "mixed blood" dictating Viney's subordinate place becomes less relevant as her presumption of a contractual use of speech becomes more important. Viney continues to bespeak some claim to Murchison that displaces the potential marriage and causes Mrs. Todd to call off the wedding. It is this presumptuous, contractual use of language that inflames Murchison to punish her:

> In the afternoon he came home with all the worst passions of weak humanity, clad with irresponsible power, flaming in his eyes.

"I will teach you," he said to his housekeeper, who quailed before him, "to tell tales about your master. I will put it out of your power to dip your tongue in where you are not concerned."

There was no one to say him nay. The law made her his. It was a lonely house, and no angel of mercy stayed his hand. (165)

As Viney and, likely, Murchison both know, Viney is, in fact, intimately "concerned" with where she has "dipped her tongue," despite the fact that "the law"—which Chesnutt aligns here with "irresponsible power"— "made her his" and justifies his merciless act. (The fact that Murchison comes from a long line of jurists and politicians further connects his act with the law in this scene and subtly politicizes the story itself.) Although Chesnutt never explicitly describes Murchison's act—a significant elision, in that it leaves the act up to the reader's imagination—we soon realize that it is extreme, for even Murchison later feels "in some measure, that there was no sufficient excuse for what he had done" (166). We deduce that Murchison has impaired Viney's ability to speak, whether by beating her or cutting her tongue. About a week later, Murchison receives a letter from his dying Uncle, naming Malcolm his sole heir and referring him to numerous papers and valuables, whose location, undisclosed in the letter, is on the property: "I do not say here where they are, lest this letter might fall into the wrong hands; but your housekeeper Viney knows their hiding place. She is devoted to you and to the family—she ought to be, for she is of our blood—and she only knows the secret" (166). But because of Murchison's punishment of Viney's "dipping her tongue" where she is indeed concerned, Viney cannot tell where the papers are.

If Murchison punishes Viney for her presumptive use of language as contractual, then the punishment *itself*—Viney's loss of voice—also bespeaks a contractual use of language that undermines notions of descent. Viney's presumptuous speech had invoked a tie between the mulatta slave and white master that had real, binding, and political, if illegal, effects. Even more forcefully, her silence after her punishment indicates a contractual use of speech that has real, binding, and political effects: Murchison's inheritance—his livelihood and his social, economic, and political position and future—rests upon Viney's ability *and consent* to communicate with him. Given Murchison's recourse to the "law" that had "made her his," rather than to the "contract" that Viney had invoked in her protest of his new marriage, perhaps it should come as no surprise that Viney is unable and/or unwilling to communicate with Murchison. When Malcolm takes his Uncle's letter to Viney and asks her, in an ambivalent litotes, "not unkindly" to show him where old Master Roger's papers are, Viney can not, or will not, answer (167). Viney, into whose black eyes "there sprang a sudden fire," only repeatedly points to her mouth, nodding positively when Malcolm asks if it will require words to tell him: "When he had exhausted his ingenuity in framing questions he went away very much disappointed.

He had been patiently waiting for his reward for many years, and now when it should be his, it seemed to elude his grasp" (168).[38] Murchison returns Viney to the house and gives attentive care to her "wound," which eventually heals, but "she did not even then seem able to articulate, even in whispers, and all his attempts to learn of her the whereabouts of the missing papers, were met by the same failure. She seemed willing enough, but unable to tell what he wished to know" (168).

As we later learn, Viney is, in fact, *able* but *unwilling* to tell. The "mystery" is not the location of the will but the importance of Viney's "voice" as contractual—her "vote" and the representation of her interests, in the household's affairs, a say in which has been curbed by Murchison's cruelty and which now reciprocates in curbing his fate. It occurs to Murchison that Viney might be taught to write, and although "Slaves were not taught to write, for too much learning would have made them mad," Murchison hires a free black man to teach her to read and write. But "somehow she made poor progress. She was handicapped of course by her loss of speech" (168). Whatever the explanation for her inability to learn, "she manifested a remarkable stupidity while seemingly anxious to learn; and in the end Malcolm was compelled to abandon the attempt to teach her" (168). Here, Chesnutt explores the disastrous effects of withholding voice to Viney's education. As he writes in the earlier version of the story, "Ignorant people learn with their voices as well as with their minds" (168n2). Education, then, becomes a false corrective to an already intolerable situation for Viney, no substitute for the equality of exchange in her relationship with Murchison, and no substitute for the representation of her interests within his household—a denial of representation that, Chesnutt shows, acutely affects the white man as much as, or perhaps more than, his housekeeper.

Interestingly, Murchison's attempts to get Viney to communicate the will's secret location are the same insufficient substitutes that, in "The Disfranchisement of the Negro" (1903), Chesnutt sees attempted by the advocates of delayed enfranchisement, or outright disfranchisement, for African Americans: education and time (186–89). As Chesnutt writes

> All the education which philanthropy or the State could offer as a *substitute* for equality of rights, would be a poor exchange; there is no defensible reason why they should not go hand in hand, each encouraging and strengthening the other. The education which one can demand as a right is likely to do more good than the education for which one must sue as a favor. ("Disfranchisement" 189)

For Chesnutt, the only solution, which Murchison does not see, is the full restoration of Viney's physical voice and political voice—her "vote"— within the household. This solution implies her original claim to the representation of her rights that Murchison continues to view, until the very end of the story, as "tak[ing] liberties that cannot be permitted" ("Dumb

Witness" 160). For Chesnutt, a restricted political voice via restricted vote means nothing less than the complete loss of representation: "a restricted suffrage [. . .] at present means [. . .] nothing less than the complete loss of representation," and going slowly "in seeking to enforce [. . .] civil and political rights [. . .] in effect means silent submission to injustice" ("Disfranchisement" 188). Without granting representation to the least powerful of the household—with respect to "The Dumb Witness," without granting representation to Viney—no one's interests, least of all Murchison's, are ultimately served.

Neither is time the great healer or righter of wrongs in Murchison's and Viney's case, Chesnutt shows. For, years passed, and Murchison's "affairs did not prosper" ("Dumb Witness" 169). In the absence of the will, Viney's very "private" silence reaches into his very "public" affairs, completely blurring the distinction between Murchison's social and political lives; over time, Viney's lost voice becomes increasingly intertwined with Murchison's loss of legal standing, personal health and happiness, and economic fate:

> Every legal means of delay was resorted to, and the authorities were disposed, in view of the remarkable circumstances of the case, to grant every possible favor. But the law fixed certain limits to delay in the settlement of an estate, and in the end he was obliged either to compromise the adverse claims or allow them to be fixed by legal process. And while certain of what his own rights were, he was compelled to see a large part of what was rightfully his go into hands where it would be difficult to trace or recover it if the will were found. [. . .] His worry interfered with proper attention to his farming operations, and one crop was almost a failure. The factor to whom he shipped his cotton went bankrupt owing him a large balance, and he fell into debt and worried himself into a fever. The woman Viney nursed him through it, and was always present at his side, a mute reproach for his cruelty, a constant reminder of his troubles. Her presence was the worst of things for him, and yet he could not bear to have her out of his sight; for in her lay the secret he longed for and which he hoped at some time in some miraculous way to extract from her. (169)

Chesnutt emphasizes how Viney's and Murchison's lives are indissolubly tied together in a kind of mutual "gruesome attraction" (170). When the Civil War comes, Viney is freed, but she stays on to do housework (human society "did not possess the same attraction for her as if she had not been deprived of the power of speech"), sitting on the porch with "the old man commanding, threatening, expostulating, entreating her to try, just once more, to tell him his uncle's message—she replying in the meaningless inarticulate mutterings that we had heard; or the old man digging, digging furiously, and she watching him from the porch, with the same inscrutable eyes [. . .]" (170).

Ultimately, "The Dumb Witness" reveals that the "secret" that lay in Viney—the secret that Murchison "longs for" and that is momentarily betrayed by the flash in Viney's "inscrutable" eyes—is not only the whereabouts of the written will itself, but the will*power,* exerted by both Murchison and Viney, that has governed the use and loss of Viney's voice, and the discursive power relations implied therein. The reciprocality of a language based on mutual consent would have offered both Viney and Murchison an alternate future to their experience of retribution and frustration, by which Murchison is kept "digging, digging furiously" in the dirt—or, as Chesnutt says in "Liberty and the Franchise," by which he is kept stooping "so long to the old Negro in the dust that [he has] never been able to rise to the full stature of manhood" (106). Sadly, it is only after Murchison's death—the great equalizer itself—that this "secret" is revealed. John narrates the tale's conclusion, in which he approaches Viney:

> She seemed intelligent enough, and I ventured to address her.
> "Is Mr. Murchison at home?"
> "Yas, suh," she answered, "I'll call 'im."[39]
> Her articulation was not distinct, but her words were intelligible. I was never more surprised in my life.
> "What does this mean, Julius?" I inquired, turning to the old man, who was grinning and chuckling to himself in great glee at my manifest astonishment. "Has she recovered her speech?"
> "She'd nebber lost it, suh. Old Viney could 'a' talked all de time, ef she'd had a min' ter. Atter ole Mars Ma'colm wuz dead, she tuk and showed Mistah Roger whar de will an' de yuther papers wuz hid. An' whar yer reckon dey wiz, zuh?"
> "I give it up, Julius. Enlighten me."
> "Dey wa'n't in de house, ner de yah'd, ner de ba'n, ner de fiel's. Dey wuz hid in de seat er dat ole oak a'm-cheer on de piazza yander w'at ole Mars Ma'colm be'n settin' in all dese yeahs." (171)

While John had narrated most of "The Dumb Witness," it is up to Julius to "enlighten" him as to Viney's speech at the end of the story and as to the power dynamics at work throughout the story. Thus, in the end, "the dumb witness" becomes not Viney but John—who, even after telling Viney's story, remains dumbfounded as to its meaning, particularly dumb as to the reversal of power at work in Viney's muteness. Uncle Julius must "enlighten" him. And "enlighten" him Julius does—through a literary use of dialect that Chesnutt does not waver on.

It is fascinating that Chesnutt uses Julius' black dialect, the only dialect in the story, to make John, and his readers, aware of what Julius has known all along—that language itself is consensual, and subject to our own perspectives, prejudices, and blind spots. In "orderly sequence" and in Standard English, John weaves together "Some of the facts in this strange story—circumstances of which Julius was ignorant, though he had the main facts correct" ("Dumb Witness" 162). But the revelation of Uncle Julius' ending is that these "circumstances" are less important than the fact that Viney could have chosen to talk all along, if she had desired to. Thus Viney, John, and Julius are all tied together in their uses of language; Viney's illegible, unrepresentable language, John's hypercorrect Standard English, and Julius' overrepresented black dialect work together to disguise and to reveal not secret treasure or buried inheritance but the very failure and promise of contractual, reciprocal language—the importance, or perhaps, rather, the relative *un*importance of form when discourse and power are concerned.

Thus the type of language—Standard English or dialect—becomes much less central, Chesnutt shows, than powerful strategies of silencing and speaking. Viney recognizes this fact but uses it to effect a power reversal and to seek revenge; the two white men, Malcolm and John, recognize it, but only after it is too late; and the black slave retainer Julius seems to know it all along. Julius' ability to reveal the secret of Viney's story, and Viney's will to keep the will secret, are both forms of conjure—forms of "power available to the powerless in mortally intolerable situations" (Brodhead, Intro 9), but, Chesnutt finally reveals, forms that rely not on the mystical but the political to work their magic.

If there is any doubt that, through Chesnutt's portrayal of the gendered and racialized discursive dynamics surrounding Viney's disfranchisement, "The Dumb Witness" plays out the politics of language and the law, of voices and votes, then we need only turn to Chesnutt's explicitly politicized novel *The Colonel's Dream* to see how Chesnutt rewrote and extended the story a third time, placing it directly in the middle of a plot involving convict labor camps, unfair trials, lynching, and the campaign against the black vote. In *The Colonel's Dream,* Chesnutt again sets the antebellum story of Viney's voice within the post-Reconstruction era, directly amid the overturn of the Civil Rights Amendments and Civil Rights Acts that concerned him. Yet in *The Colonel's Dream,* Chesnutt overtly politicizes the plot of "The Dumb Witness," partly by replacing John with his politically progressive protagonist Colonel French—a white northern businessman gone south to his birthplace, the town of Clarendon, where he becomes another kind of "dumb witness," gradually losing his own voice of reform as white supremacists keep race relations in regressive fetters. In addition, Chesnutt consciously embeds this version of Viney's story—one that even more clearly than "The Dumb Witness" references the close relations between "white" and "black," and between men and women—within conversations about black disfranchisement. Thus framed by unequivocal debates about the black vote, Chesnutt's representation of Viney's voice in *The Colonel's Dream,* even more explicitly than in "The Dumb Witness," linguistically subverts the logic of descent that underwrote Jim Crow.[40]

Chesnutt takes conscious pains in the novel to mark broadly the 1890s racialized sociopolitical context in *The Colonel's Dream*. For example, Chesnutt writes that the people of Clarendon were "quick to resent criticism. If some of them might admit, now and then, among themselves, that the town was unprogressive, or declining, there was always some extraneous reason given—the War, the carpetbaggers, the Fifteenth Amendment, the Negroes" (108). Additionally, Chesnutt bitingly alludes to *Plessy v. Ferguson* in describing a forty-mile train ride that took his protagonist Colonel French three hours, in part because the train made a stop

> in the middle of a swamp, to put off a light mulatto who had presumed on his complexion to ride in the white people's car. He had been successfully spotted, but had impudently refused to go into the stuffy little closet provided at the end of the car for people of his class. He was therefore given an opportunity to reflect, during a walk along the ties, upon his true relation to society. (109)

Finally, Chesnutt marks the political context of *The Colonel's Dream* through the development of the perspectives of Colonel French, who becomes increasingly politically invested over the course of the novel. While French is initially satisfied with social and economic solutions to race relations—is "content to await the uplifting power of industry and enlightenment" (195)—Chesnutt's protagonist eventually "reached the conviction that the regenerative forces of education and enlightenment, in order to have any effect in his generation, must be reinforced by some positive legislative or executive action, or else the untrammeled forces of graft and greed would override them" (230). In addition to marking this broad political context, Chesnutt highlights his specific concerns with black disfranchisement in the novel and relates the story of Viney's voice to them.

Chesnutt places Viney's story between two particular conversations about fears of black domination through enfranchisement, fears exemplified in the attitudes of two leading citizens of Clarendon—General Thornton and Henry Clay Appleton, editor of the local paper the *Anglo-Saxon*, who informs French that "The suffrage in the hands of the Negroes had proved a ghastly and expensive joke for all concerned, and the public welfare absolutely demanded that it be taken away" (75). In the first illustrative conversation, General Thornton tells French how he had determined "to vote the other ticket in the last election" until, once again, "the race question assume[d] an importance which overshadow[ed] the tariff and the currency and everything else" (166). Thornton relates how he had made up his mind "toward a change of attitude [. . .] and political and intellectual independence, at the cost of many friends" (166), until he went to the polls and stood in line next to an old black man, Sam Brown, whom he had sentenced to jail for stealing:

"'Well, Gin'l,' he [Sam Brown] said, 'I'm glad you is got on de right side at las,' an' is gwine to vote *our* ticket.'"

"This was too much! I could stand the other party in the abstract, but not in the concrete. I voted the ticket of my neighbors and my friends. We had to preserve our institutions, if our finances went to smash. Call it prejudice—call it what you like—it's human nature, and you'll come to it, colonel, you'll come to it—and then we'll send you to Congress." (166–67)

Through General Thornton's remarks, Chesnutt clearly conveys the descent-bound logic of "human nature" that upheld opposition to the black vote.

Chesnutt sets up the second discussion about fear of black enfranchisement that frames Viney's story, by telling how French's political and economic reforms were met with increased resistance in a political context in which an "ambitious politician in a neighbouring State had led a successful campaign on the issue of Negro disfranchisement. Plainly unconstitutional, it was declared to be as plainly necessary for the preservation of the white race and white civilization" (193). Ultimately, as Chesnutt reveals in this politician's speech, the fear was that one black vote, like one drop of black blood, would taint the white tide:

"So long," said the candidate for governor, when he spoke at Clarendon during the canvass, at a meeting presided over by the editor of the *Anglo-Saxon,* "so long as one Negro votes in the State, so long are we face to face with the nightmare of Negro domination. For example, suppose a difference of opinion among white men so radical as to divide their vote equally, the ballot of one Negro would determine the issue. Can such a possibility be contemplated without a shudder? Our duty to ourselves, to our children, and their unborn descendants, and to our great and favoured race, impels us to protest, by word, by vote, by arms if need be, against the enforced equality of an inferior race. Equality anywhere, means ultimately, equality everywhere. Equality at the polls means social equality; social equality means intermarriage and corruption of blood, and degeneration and decay." (194)

Raising the specter of mixed blood, this candidate's speech likewise demonstrates the descent-based logic that reversed the Civil War Amendments. When read as framed by these pervasive anxieties about black (dis)franchisement, Chesnutt's story of Viney's silencing/speech becomes even more revealing of descent-based notions of citizenship as inherently flawed.

While Chesnutt changes some of the names in *The Colonel's Dream* version of Viney's story—Malcolm Murchison, for instance, becomes Malcolm Dudley—many of the story's details are the same as in "The Dumb Witness." The Dudley family's first great man, an ardently patriotic General, had distinguished himself in the War of Independence "and held high place in the councils of the infant nation," and his son "became a distinguished jurist, whose name is still a synonym for legal learning and juridical wisdom" (170). The descendant of these men, Malcolm Dudley, "kept bachelor's hall" in his uncle Ralph's house, with the only women in the house a black cook and the housekeeper, "known as 'Viney'—a Negro corruption of Lavinia—a tall, comely young light mulattress, with a dash of Cherokee blood, which gave her straighter, blacker and more glossy hair than most women of mixed race have, and perhaps a somewhat different temperamental endowment" (171). Again, because Chesnutt makes Viney an important woman of mixed blood, he highlights the importance of both gender and race to his story. When Dudley announces the news to Viney of her new mistress, Viney again reacts hysterically; again, she goes to town and tells Mrs. Todd a secret which causes Todd to cancel her engagement to him.

Yet, while many of the details of Viney's story remain the same in this version, Dudley's punishing of Viney and Viney's unraveling of the treasure's whereabouts depart from the short story in ways that further emphasize the importance of a consensual view of language. In *The Colonel's Dream,* Dudley's overseer, not Dudley himself, punishes Viney for protesting Dudley's engagement, and when Viney is found unconscious, the doctor "curtly" tells him, "'The woman has had a stroke [. . .] brought on by brutal treatment. By G-d, Dudley, I wouldn't have thought this of you! I own Negroes, but I treat them like human beings. And such a woman! I'm ashamed of my own race, I swear I am! If we are whipped in this war and the slaves are freed, as Lincoln threatens, it will be God's judgment" (172). Dudley is remorseful, treats Viney to the best of care, and the next day discovers the letter from his Uncle Ralph, dated the morning of the previous day—before Viney's beating. The letter, a modified version of the one in "The Dumb Witness," makes the buried treasure "government money"—another overt politicization of the story—and states that Uncle Ralph has confided the secret of this money's keeping in "our girl Viney, whom I can trust." An hour after reading the letter, Malcolm Dudley learns of his uncle's death, and like Malcolm Murchison of "The Dumb Witness," goes to the recovering Viney to plead with her to tell him where the money is hidden. Yet, since one side of her face was "perfectly inert" from the stroke, "and any movement of the other produced a slight distortion that spoiled the face as the index of the mind," he has trouble reading her expressions (173–74). Here, in stressing that Dudley was "accustomed to command" and that his request for information "came awkwardly to his lips," Chesnutt emphasizes Dudley's refusal of the contractual view of language that Viney had invoked in her protest of his impending marriage (174).

The significance of this contractual view of language is finally underscored by the "secret" of the consensual relationship Viney exposes when she ultimately divulges the mystery of the treasure's whereabouts on Dudley's deathbed. An exchange overheard by Dudley's nephew Ben reveals that Viney was punished because her resistant speech had declared a forbidden intimacy between Viney and Dudley, a *de facto* if not *de jure* marriage contract. We learn—from Viney herself, whose speech Chesnutt represents this time in clear Standard English—that there was no money to be found, only an intimate relationship to be discovered:

> [. . .] marvellous to hear, Viney was talking, strangely, slowly, thickly, but passionately and distinctly.
> "You had me whipped," she said. "Do you remember that? You had me whipped—whipped—whipped—by a poor white dog I had despised and spurned! You had said that you loved me, and you had promised to free me—and you had me whipped! But I have had my revenge!"
> Her voice shook with passion, a passion at which Ben wondered. That his uncle and she had once been young he knew, and that their relations had once been closer than those of master and servant; but this outbreak of feeling from the wrinkled old mulattress seemed as strange and weird to Ben as though a stone image had waked to speech. Spellbound, he stood in the doorway, and listened to this ghost of a voice long dead.
> "Your uncle came with the money and left it, and went away. Only he and I knew where it was. But I never told you! I could have spoken at any time for twenty-five years, but I never told you! I have waited—I have waited for this moment! I have gone into the woods and fields and talked to myself by the hour, that I might not forget how to talk—and I have waited my turn, and it is here and now!"
> Ben hung breathlessly upon her words. He drew back beyond her range of vision, lest she might see him, and the spell be broken. Now, he thought, she would tell where the gold was hidden!
> "He came," she said, "and left the gold—two heavy bags of it, and a letter for you. An hour later *he came back and took it all away*, except the letter! The money was here one hour, but in that hour you had me whipped, and for that you have spent twenty-five years in looking for nothing—something that was not here! I have had my revenge! For twenty-five years I have watched you look for—nothing; have seen you waste your time, your property, your life, your mind—for nothing! For ah, Mars' Malcolm, you had me whipped—*by another man!*" (273–74)

The importance of Viney's consensual use of language within a contractual relationship—the "ghost of a voice long dead"—is reinforced here by the fact that Viney's rage centers not on Dudley's actual punishment of her, but on his choosing "another man," "a poor white dog I had despised and spurned!" to do the whipping for him—a poor substitution that, to her, clearly misrepresented their true relations. Through Viney's repeated emphasis on "another man" throughout the passage, Chesnutt stresses the sanctity of their relationship; substituting another man to punish her was a further breakdown of the implicit contract between them. The *de facto* marriage contract that Viney had invoked when she protested Dudley's engagement to Mrs. Todd is further brought home by Viney's reaction upon his death: Viney burst "into tears—strange tears from eyes that had long forgot to weep" and "threw herself down upon her knees by the bedside, and seizing old Malcolm's emaciated hand in both her own, covered it with kisses, fervent kisses, the ghosts of the passionate kisses of their distant youth" (274). When the doctor comes soon after, he and Ben discover them both dead, with their hands clasped together, an evocative image of their intertwined destinies. The doctor, unsurprised, confirms Viney's story: "My father attended her when she had the stroke, and after [. . .]. He always maintained that Viney could speak—if she had wished to speak" (275).

Viney's story—the story of the gendered and racialized dynamics of discourse and power within the close but strained relationship between a mulatta woman and a white man—comes to signify more broadly the post-Reconstruction situation that squelches consensual relations as well as contractual views of language and the law. Within the larger plot of *The Colonel's Dream,* what Viney's story shows us is that Colonel French's dream of regeneration fails because of an insistent cultural investment in the logic of descent that makes miscegenation a nightmare, illegalizes interracial marriage, undermines black suffrage, and replaces forward-looking discussions of consensual political speech with backward-adhering debates about dialect. It is in part by representing Viney's speech and her silence as contractual that Chesnutt exposes the mythical investment in such descent-based difference. Ultimately, we should see the gendered politics of language in "The Dumb Witness" and at the heart of *The Colonel's Dream* as central to Chesnutt's critique of "blood" and of black disfranchisement. Through his foregrounding of dynamics of both gender and race in his literary representations of Viney's silence and speech, Chesnutt at once exposes the fiction of blood and the fiction of dialect, highlighting the logic of descent operating in both language and the law—a logic that, as we see in the conjoined fate of Malcolm and Viney, equally dooms everyone to "digging, digging furiously" in the dirt.

4. CONCLUSION: GENDER AND LANGUAGE IN FICTIONS OF LAW AND CUSTOM

> From Roxy's manner of speech a stranger would have expected her to be black, but she was not. Only one sixteenth of her was black, and that sixteenth did not show. [. . .]
>
> To all intents and purposes Roxy was as white as anybody, but the one sixteenth of her which was black outvoted the other fifteen parts and made her a negro. She was a slave, and saleable as such. Her child was thirty-one parts white, and he, too, was a slave and, by a fiction of law and custom, a negro. (Mark Twain, *Pudd'nhead Wilson* [1894] 63–64)

Though, in his fundamentally more deterministic attitude, Mark Twain diverges from Chesnutt, the two writers both deconstruct descent-governed notions of linguistic and political representation through the fictional renderings of the speech of their memorable mulatta characters.[41] In this passage in *Pudd'nhead Wilson* (1894), Mark Twain recognizes with his characteristic satirical edge the "fiction of law and custom" that made his white-appearing Roxy, arguably his most provocative female character, a slave. Moreover, through his description's progression from Roxy's speech, to her appearance, to her blood, to her condition as a slave, Twain depicts how interarticulated linguistic and legal conceptions of "dialect" and "blood" could underline or determine racial and sociopolitical status—how social conceptions made Roxy a black slave. Through the unstable descent-based signifiers of his heroine's dialect and blood, Twain, like Chesnutt, disrupts any essential equation between Roxy's "manner of speech" and her race, instead showing how Roxy's language depends not on blood but on the community in which she participates according to her social and legal status, and how Roxy's status depends on social and legal fictions, by which her one-sixteenth drop of black blood "outvoted the other fifteen parts and made her a negro." Here, Twain's use of the term "outvoted" reverberates in a historical context within which, as we have seen, conceptions of descent determined the negro's "natural" inferiority, undermined the Civil War Amendments, and legalized segregation.

It is within the social fiction of law and custom that the "doting fool of a mother" Roxy swaps her child's "coarse tow-linen shirt" with her master's child's "ruffled soft muslin" and catalytically sets in motion the remainder of *Pudd'nhead Wilson* (77, 64). As Twain reveals, Roxy's own "fiction created by her self, [in which her son] was become her master," relies upon her diligent and faithful *linguistic* performance of "the forms required to express the recognition [of her new master]" until the practice of these forms "soon concreted itself into habit" (77). Twain writes, "steadily and surely the awe which had kept her tongue reverent and her manner humble toward her young master was transferring itself to her speech and manner toward the usurper," and she became "similarly handy [. . .] in transferring her motherly curtness of speech and peremptoriness of manner to the unlucky heir of the ancient house of Driscoll"; eventually these habits "became automatic and unconscious," and "the mock reverence became real reverence, the mock obsequiousness real obsequiousness, the mock homage real homage" (73, 77). Thus highlighting how Roxy's performance of social and linguistic "forms" contributes to the construction of the identities and relations of master, slave, and slave mother, Twain uses this mother's speech to "nurture" into being what were perceived as "natural" relations and identities.[42]

Twain fascinatingly sets the plot of *Pudd'nhead* in motion through Roxy's role as a reproducer of heirs. Twain's story brings home how Chesnutt, by similarly making Viney's role as a bearer of family inheritance central to "The Dumb Witness" and *The Colonel's Dream,* highlights what has become increasingly clear to contemporary scholars: that gender and race are *inter*dependent structures of sociopolitical power that converge on women's roles in reproducing the nation, roles that the next chapter will further explore.[43] Moreover, by making Viney's garbled language central to his stories—by making her performance of speech and silence the *raison d'etre* of "The Dumb Witness"—Chesnutt creates a female character whose *voice* is responsible for representing (or not representing), for reproducing (or not reproducing) family secrets, and equally reveals that gender and language are interdependent structures of power in representing and reproducing the nation. By drawing our attention to Viney's voice itself, Chesnutt uses gender and language to draw our attention to how crucial a paradigm of consent is—for black men, women, and white men alike—for truly reproducing *and* representing the "nation," and for reconstructing it, in Chesnutt's day and beyond.

4 Henry James and the Linguistic Domestication of Women and Immigrants at the Turn of the Century

1. INTRODUCTION: LINGUISTIC DOMESTICATION AS "CIVILIZATION" AND "AMERICANIZATION"

What is it that has so vitiated the voices of most "American" men, and still more of most "American" women? For there is no doubt that the fairer sex are in this respect the least to be admired. Among fifty men you will find perhaps ten or a dozen who will open their mouths and speak clearly and freely; but among fifty women not more than two or three.

This it is chiefly which here so diminishes the charms of that sex which in England delights the ear even more than it does the eye. Among the general public here, the public of the railway car and the hotel, the woman who has not this vice is a rare exception. You shall see a lovely, bright creature, with all the external evidences of culture about her, a woman who will carry you captive so long as she is silent; but let her open her pretty lips, and she shall pierce your ear with a mean, thin, nasal, rasping tone, by which at once you are disenchanted. An English-woman, even of the lower classes, will delight you with the rich, sweet, smooth, and yet firm and crisp tones in which she utters what may perhaps be very bad "grammar." (Richard Grant White, "'American' Speech" in *Every-Day English* [1880] 93–94)

What is going to become of the language now it is thus dispersed abroad and freed from all control by a central authority [King's English] and exposed to all sorts of alien influences? Is it bound to become corrupted and to sink from its high estate into a mire of slang and into a welter of barbarously fashioned verbal novelties? What, more especially, is going to be the future of the English language here in America? (Brander Matthews, "The English Language in the United States" [1899] in *Parts of Speech* [1901] 49–50)

Even as the discussion of dialect reached new heights after the Civil War, additional commentary about language arose to express apprehensions about the changing social landscape of America at the end and turn of the 19th century, such as Richard Grant White's and Brander Matthews' emblematic questions about the status of the English language in America, above. Though writing for different audiences—White for a more popular readership than Matthews' elites—these verbal critics shared the strategy of using such commentary to navigate larger social concerns.[1] White's criticism of American women's disenchanting, poorly-bred voices—more specifically, their "mean, thin, nasal, rasping tone"—here deflects his awareness of women's increasingly public presence in the late-19th-century railway car and hotel world. Alternatively, Matthews uses his question about "the future of the English language" falling prey to barbaric influences to express yet another anxiety about the alien presence in America—and he turns to English language education to reassure his readers that all will be well.[2]

At the same time that Jim Crow was legislated throughout the nation, other historical developments were taking place in America that called again for the recasting of the idea of the nation, often in ascriptive terms of national citizenship: among them, what some historians have called the Woman's Era, or the rise of the "New Woman," alongside new immigration trends. Between 1880 and 1920, predominantly white, middle-class women increasingly entered the public arena as what some scholars have called, in a recasting of republican motherhood, "political mothers" or "maternalist politicians" who joined social and political organizations to enlarge "their sphere in public life where once only men had acted" (Kerber and De Hart 265–66). These women behaved in increasingly public and political ways, moving from submitting petitions to conducting surveys to participating in the actual drafting of bills to impact the nation's legislation (266). At the same time that the era saw the rise of the "New Woman," there was a perceived influx of immigrants from new geographical sources. According to the Dillingham Commission set up by Congress in the 1907 Immigration Act to study immigration, "new" immigrants from Southern and Eastern Europe and Asia, comprised of largely unskilled, transient, urban male workers, increased from 1883 onward.[3] The expansion, or perceived expansion, of the immigrant population alongside women in public life created new national challenges for white patriarchy. As Gail Bederman summarizes:

> Immigrant and working-class men were not the only ones challenging middle-class men's claims on public power and authority. Concurrently, the middle-class woman's movement was challenging past constructions of manhood by agitating for women's advancement. "Advancement," as these New Women understood it, meant granting women access to activities which had previously been reserved for men. Small but increasing numbers of middle-class women were claiming the right to a college education, to become clergymen, social scientists, and physicians, and even to vote. Men reacted passionately by ridiculing these New Women, prophesying that they would make themselves

ill and destroy national life, insisting that they were rebelling against nature. (Bederman 14)[4]

Together, the seemingly pervasive presence of so-called new immigrants and New Women occasioned new anxieties about American citizenship and who would have access to the political discourse upholding the nation.

The concern caused by the increasingly public presence of women and immigrants overtly resulted in legislation that attempted to curb their claims on American citizenship, in part through the regulation of language practices such as literacy. Women were still barred from the franchise, the fullest badge of national citizenship. In addition, under the 1907 Expatriation Act, they could lose what rights of citizenship they did have when they married men of other nationalities, as American-born Californian Ethel MacKenzie lost her U.S. citizenship when she married a British subject in 1909 (R. Smith 457; Kerber and De Hart 339). From the 1880s onward, Congress also worked to restrict immigration and naturalization. Among the first of these laws were the Chinese Exclusion Act (May 1882), which suspended Chinese immigration for a decade and forbade Chinese naturalization, and the Federal Immigration Law (August 1882), the first general federal immigration law, which imposed "a head tax of fifty cents upon every alien passenger and excluded convicts, lunatics, idiots, and those liable to become a public charge" (M. Jones 250–51). In the 1890s and 1910s, Congress increasingly struggled to link immigration and literacy, and Congress' renewed attempts to enact literacy bills were repeatedly vetoed by Presidents Cleveland, Taft, and Wilson—until in 1917, when the 64th Congress overrode Wilson's veto to pass Public Act No. 301. This comprehensive immigration bill not only specified a head tax of eight dollars per alien but also widened the range of excluded persons to "All aliens over sixteen years of age, physically capable of reading, who can not read the English language, or some other language or dialect, including Hebrew or Yiddish" (qtd. in Gere 20).[5] Since literacy, acquired by language education, is a social and political skill rather than an inherent personal quality, these repeated and ultimately successful efforts to incorporate literacy into the baseline qualifications for national admission suggested how lawmakers would define—expand and limit—the scope of what it meant to be American through language. And they signaled another way that ideas about language could govern national identity.[6]

At the same time that legislators sought to redraw the lines of national citizenship, in part through literacy requirements, Americans turned to discourses of civilization and projects of Americanization to manage the increased public presence of women and immigrants. Central to imagining both American "civilization" and immigrant "Americanization" were gendered notions of the (traditional white, middle-class "American") family—and, as I will show in this chapter, gendered conceptions of language. Scholars such as Gail Bederman in *Manliness and Civilization* and Louise

Michele Newman in *White Women's Rights* have convincingly explained how the discourse of civilization responded to, among other things, anxieties about the changing face of America's population. "'Civilization,'" says Bederman, "simultaneously denoted attributes of race and gender. By invoking the discourse of civilization in a variety of contradictory ways, many Americans found a powerfully effective way to link male dominance to white supremacy," using the discourse in a wide variety of ways to "legitimize different sorts of claims to power" (23). By around 1890, Bederman argues, the discourse of civilization had adopted particular meanings circulating around religion—specifically, a "Darwinist version of Protestant millennialism"—as well as race and gender (25). As a step up from "savagery" then "barbarism," "civilization" meant a specific, advanced stage in human racial evolution, one that only the white races had yet achieved; in addition, civilizations were ranked according to how sexually differentiated they were, wherein "Civilized women were womanly—delicate, spiritual, dedicated to the home. And civilized white men were the most manly ever evolved—firm of character; self-controlled; protectors of women and children" (25).

Overlapping with the discourse of civilization were projects of Americanization that worked to assimilate newcomers into "America." Americanization, like "civilization," revolved around a gendered family structure and a reincarnation of domestic ideology in which women were dedicated to the home and played key social and linguistic roles. Borrowing Anne Ruggles Gere's sense of the term, *Americanization* is "sometimes used to describe projects carried out by the National Americanization Committee under the leadership of Frances Kellor between 1916 and 1920, but here it refers to the longer-term and more complicated projects that over a period of several decades attempted to (re)connect individuals with the abstract construct of the nation state" (Gere 58).[7] As Priscilla Wald observes, such efforts to assimilate immigrants "used the traditional American family as both metaphor and medium" (246). And as we have seen, the regulation of the "American family" was circuited through the gendered figure of the mother.

While scholars have importantly shown how the discourse of civilization, with its preservation of a traditional patriarchal family structure, was buttressed by evolutionist theories that enabled women's entrance into the public sphere as "civilizers," what has frequently been overlooked is how "civilization" as well as "Americanization" worked through *commentary on language* that invoked gender as both rhetorical figure and linguistic role. As one early-20th-century Americanization text succinctly put it, because "every civilization worth while rests upon the solidarity of the home as the unit of society," it is "the business of the community and the individuals composing it to offer the mother in the home a reasonable opportunity to learn English, to understand the life of her children and the meaning of America, in order to help her to establish American standards in the home" (Winkler and Alsberg 49). Speaking about the *immigrant* "mother in the home" in a larger text addressed to her *native-born* female teacher, this passage certainly speaks to the centrality of the gendered family structure in Americanization efforts for immigrant women and for the "civilized" white, middle-class women who sought to help her in the home. It furthermore speaks to the centrality of *learning English* to understanding "the meaning of America." Here, we see how discourse on language was combined with the gendered tenets of domesticity, as both "metaphor and medium," effectively to contain the citizenship of white women and immigrants at the end of the century.

As this chapter suggests, such discourses of linguistic domestication were manifestations of "civilization" and "Americanization" efforts that worked to reshape the idea of "America" in a historical context in which the increased public presence of women and immigrants threatened white patriarchal notions of the nation. In these discourses of linguistic domestication, topics such as manners and education linked "civilization" and "Americanization" through ideas about gender and language. Henry James' work in particular illuminates the process by which discourses of gendered linguistic domestication—in which "domestic" again becomes opposed to "political" and "foreign"—could work to reinforce ascriptively gendered and racialized ideas of the nation both by gendering language itself and by gendering social and linguistic roles. James' writings valuably reflect how perceived threats to white patriarchy could be reframed in gendered terms as threats to the English language itself. These perceived threats also resulted, as James' criticism reveals, in two apparently contradictory impulses in matters of commentary about gender and language: The critique of women's speech, even down to matters as specific as vocal "tone," existed alongside the claim that women bore important and irreplaceable social roles as linguistic civilizers and educators—in short, as linguistic domesticators.[8]

Particularly attentive to language, gender, and the American scene, James' novel *The Bostonians* (1886) and his criticism (1905–07) tell a two-part story about how discourses of linguistic domestication such as manners and education created a spectrum of "private" and "public" social and linguistic roles for white middle-class American women in "civilizing" Americans and "Americanizing" aliens. Specifically, in the context of gendered commentary about language in manners manuals and verbal criticism of the day, *The Bostonians* suggests how white, middle-class women assumed central roles as upholders and reproducers of American linguistic civilization through the development of vocal tone and good linguistic breeding. As well, in the context of the Americanization efforts that followed, James' essays suggest how these women were assigned roles as bearers of American culture in the linguistic Americanization of immigrants. Thus James' fictional and nonfictional texts together tell a story about how gendered linguistic strategies could "soothe"—to use the diction of *The Bostonians'* heroine Verena Tarrant (432)—the anxiety occasioned by the

150 *Language, Gender, and Citizenship in American Literature*

public presence of women and aliens. Ultimately, discourses of linguistic domestication such as manners and education governed women's and immigrants' voices together by relocating women's political speech from the lecture platform to the dining-table, and by commissioning women as linguistic "models, missionaries, and martyrs," to use James' phrasing, in the broadly domestic, Americanizing spaces of settlement houses, classrooms, and immigrants' own homes.

2. DINING-TABLE PLATFORMS: LANGUAGE MANNERS, *THE BOSTONIANS*, AND THE DOMESTICATION OF WOMEN'S VOICES

> Taken on the whole by surprise it [the English language] may doubtless be said to have behaved as well as unfriended heroine ever behaved in dire predicament—refusing, that is, to be frightened quite to death, looking about for a *modus vivendi*, consenting to live, preparing to wait on developments. I say "unfriended" heroine because that is exactly my point: that whereas the great idioms of Europe in general have grown up at home and in the family, the ancestral circle (with their migrations all comfortably prehistoric), our transported maiden, our unrescued Andromeda, our medium of utterance, was to be disjoined from all the associations, the other presences, that had attended her, that had watched for her and with her, that had helped to form her manners and her voice, her taste and her genius. (Henry James, "The Question of Our Speech" [1905] 53)

Manifesting the era's widespread interest in primitive versus civilized cultures, James apparently turned to the language of the "civilized soul" in his cultural criticism, such as "The Question of Our Speech," quoted above, to which I return throughout this chapter. First delivered as a graduation address to the women of Bryn Mawr College on June 8, 1905, "The Question of Our Speech" focuses on caring for American speech as a marker of national civilization. Our speech and our language, taken as symbols of civilization that form the basis for "so sacred a flame" as "good breeding" (45), James says, "migrated together, immigrated together, into the great raw world in which they were to be cold-shouldered and neglected together, left to run wild and lose their way together" (52). James continues:

> Keep in sight the so interesting historical truth that no language, so far back as our acquaintance with history goes, has known any such ordeal, any such stress and strain, as was to await the English in this huge new community it was so unsuspectingly to help, at first, to father and mother. It came *over,* [sic.] as the phrase is, came over originally without

fear and without guile—but to find itself transplanted to spaces it had never dreamed, in its comparative humility, of covering, to conditions it had never dreamed, in its comparative innocence, of meeting; to find itself grafted, in short, on a social and political order that was both without previous precedent and example and incalculably expansive. (53)

James' comments reveal how language could not only "find itself grafted" on an unprecedented "social and political order," as he puts it, but also how that order could be grafted onto commentary about language. For, throughout his speech, James himself is concerned with how modern forces such as the newspaper, the common school, and immigration have cheapened American speech and thereby called into question American civilization. James' comments begin to indicate how other verbal critics turned to language to manage concerns about what they saw as an "expansive" social and political order, expanding in part through more women in public and immigration.

The fact that James feminizes the English language in his speech's next paragraph, the epigraph quoted above, reveals how ideas about *gender* might moreover be attached to ideas about national language to manage anxieties about American civilization in James' historical moment. Strikingly, James uses the gendered structure of the family to figure the "adventure of our idiom." Here, the English language is depicted as both orphaned female and immigrant—this language "came *over*," as "unfriended heroine," without home and family, to help to "mother and father" a "huge new community." That James turns to gendered domestic images not only to figure but also to displace concerns about national identity shows how they were managed in and through gendered commentary on language. For, at the end of his speech, James remarkably urges his female auditors themselves to become cultural guardians and reproducers of national speech—to sound "the clearer notes of intercourse as only women can" and become "models and missionaries, perhaps a little even martyrs, of the good cause" (56). In doing so, James' gendered commentary on language—as both symbol and means of American "civilization"—expresses the era's social and political concerns even as it attempts to make sense of them.

In Henry James' novel *The Bostonians* (1886), Basil Ransom's verbal criticism about the decline of the era's "masculine tone" further brings into focus how gendered commentary on language was a salient aspect of American social life at the time. Basil Ransom pronounces:

The whole generation is womanized; the masculine tone is passing out of the world; it's a feminine, a nervous, hysterical, chattering, canting age, an age of hollow phrases and false delicacy and exaggerated solicitudes and coddled sensibilities, which, if we don't soon look out, will usher in the reign of mediocrity, of the feeblest and flattest and the most pretentious that has ever been. (*Bostonians* 322)

While a fictional character in a novel, Basil's commentary about the feminine denigration of "masculine tone" is similar in character to the nonfiction commentary of White and Matthews, in that Basil's ideas about language—here, notably, gendered ones—become the locus for his more sweeping concerns about the decline of civilization; they linguistically analogize his larger anxieties about a possible "reign of mediocrity" in American culture. This famous passage has been the subject of much critical notice, but critics commonly focus on its terms of *gender* versus its terms of gendered *language*.[9] Through Basil's gendered commentary on "tone" and his wider reflections on heroine Verena Tarrant's voice throughout *The Bostonians,* one of the most fascinating things that James' novel shows is how gendered and racialized anxieties about national "civilization" could be borne out in ideas about language and gender, particularly ideas about American women's voices.

In this section, then, I read James' novel itself as intervening in the gendered language politics of his day to reflect the ways in which ideologies of language and gender could express late-19th-century concerns with both women's and immigrants' place in American "civilization." To again quote Althusser's formulation, novelists like James can "give us a 'view' of the ideology to which their work alludes and with which it is constantly fed, a view which presupposes a *retreat,* an *internal distantiation* from the very ideology from which their novels emerged" ("Letter on Art" 222–23).[10] While James' novels were not "popular" texts like Warner's or Southworth's novels, they were no less immersed in a 19th-century context that was preoccupied with language, a culture saturated with ideas about the governing of voices, which was one of the many cultural phenomena to which James' writings responded and about which James puzzled. The subject I pursue here, then, is not whether James endorses or does not endorse Basil Ransom's rather sexist commentary about language or Basil's equally sexist action at the end of this open-ended novel—indeed, James himself ironically veils his own position. Rather, my interest is in exploring how, in his writing, James—whose famously serpentine sentences and careful revisions witness his own attentiveness to language—reveals, whether consciously or unconsciously, *how* ideas about language and gender, such as Basil Ransom's ideas, might play a wider cultural role or roles. Entering into the era's discourse of civilization and registering the period's anxieties about gender, race, and national identity, *The Bostonians* subtly tells a story about how notions of gendered linguistic domestication, notions that were explicitly manifest in verbal criticism and manners manuals of James' day, could regulate women's political voices. Alongside popular texts of verbal criticism and manners manuals, to which this section will first turn, James' novel suggests how discussions of women's linguistic—indeed, vocal—domestication could work to sweep women off the lecture platform. It also begins to "allude to" how these discussions might work in similar ways for others.

James' novel was published at a time when verbal criticism and manners manuals flourished, expressing the era's discourse of civilization, and *The Bostonians* can be read in light of them, as well as in light of James' own cultural criticism on women's voices and national speech. According to one incomplete list, between 1870 and 1917, new etiquette books were issued at the rate of five or six a year, significantly surpassing even the high record that existed before the Civil War; women's magazines collected their discussions of etiquette in books such as *The Bazar Book of Decorum* (1870), *The American Code of Manners* (1880), and *Social Life* (1889); magazines beyond women's journals, such as *The Atlantic, Lippincott's,* and *Putnam's,* discussed behavior; and the daily press launched advice columns (Schlesinger 32–34).[11] Unlike the propriety of mid-century, which had been largely geared toward individual success and focused on rules, manners manuals of the late 19th and early 20th century saw themselves as broader contributors to American culture and "civilization." The extent to which manners were seen in this broader sense after the Civil War is perhaps best revealed by the way in which the writer of *Etiquette for Americans* (1898) framed her manual as *exceptional:* "Other books on similar subjects have gone deeply into the aesthetics of good breeding—the subtlety of kindness: it is the purpose of this [book] only to disclose, not so much the morals nor the philosophy of good manners, as the formulated rules for their observance" (13–14). In point of contrast, as Mrs. Charles Harcourt puts it in *Good Form for Women* (1907), most manners manuals emphasized the wider "philosophy" of good manners: "Mere conformity to the rules of etiquette is of comparatively little consequence" (2–3). And as Richard A. Wells would state on the first page of his Preface to *Manners, Culture, and Dress of the Best American Society* (c.1890), "True politeness is not a code of superficial rules, arranged and trimmed up for particular occasions, and then set aside at our pleasure." More importantly, as Wells' manual also reflects, the emphasis on the wider "philosophy" of manners pointed to the idea that manners were now seen as a larger issue of "civilization." Indeed, as he says, the "uses of etiquette" are the ends of "civilization": "We are not all equally civilized; some of us are scarcely more than savage by nature and training, or rather lack of training. Yet we all wish to put on the regalia of civilization that we may be recognized as belonging to the guild of ladies and gentlemen in the world" (22). Such manners manuals took up verbal criticism like Richard Grant White's, and together, verbal criticism and manners manuals were invested in upholding national civilization through language—particularly through commentary regulating women's voices.[12]

As dual markers of the extent of the development or decline of late-19th-century Anglo-American "civilization," both language and women were tasked in verbal criticism and manners manuals with upholding American culture, though again in different ways than at mid century. White's popular verbal criticism in *Words and Their Uses* (1870) and

Every-Day English (1880) can be seen as part of the widespread interest in American manners that prospered at the end of the 19th-century as never before. As seen in White's subordination of "grammar" to the "rich, sweet, smooth, and yet firm and crisp tones" of an Englishwoman in the quote above, verbal critics like White focused less on grammatical correctness as propriety than on notions about the regulation of the voice through ideas such as tone, articulation, or pronunciation, around wider concerns with manners.[13] Such notions of language manners were more reflective of morals in the broad sense of social customs, rather than the narrower, mid-19th-century sense of "right" and "wrong," or "good" or "bad," usage. An apt illustration of this transformation is how, over the decade from *Words and Their Uses* to its sequel, *Every-Day English,* White distances himself from concerns with grammar and spelling, becomes progressively more interested in discriminating among various pronunciations, and at the same time, takes on an increasingly Anglophilic attitude in describing "right pronunciation" as "the pronunciation of cultivated London" (*Every-Day English* 77; see also 81–82). White's evaluation of American speech in fact comes to center on very descent-based notions of tone of voice and inflection, reflecting how very specific ideas about women's voices would become the linguistic measure of American "civilization":

> Moreover, as to pronunciation, "American" observation is very untrustworthy; for it is in this respect that the speech of the "average American," however "polite" and "intelligent" he may be, is most likely to deviate from the true English standard. The greater number of "Americans" speak vilely; they have a bad tone of voice, and very unpleasant inflections, in great variety of unpleasantness, according to the place of their birth and breeding. It is only in a comparatively small, although actually numerous, circle of people of high social culture, in New England and New York, and in the latter place among those of New England birth, or very direct descent, that the true standard of English speech is found in this country. (*Every-Day English* 90)

Such notions of "the true standard of English speech," stratified into ideas about intonation and inflection, were deftly coupled with notions of ideal womanhood; "the best" American women were given the "civilizing" role of upholding language manners, even as they were criticized for not being as "civilized" as their English counterparts, as we also see in White's writing. White pronounces that "the speech of a well-bred woman, accustomed all her life to the best society, may be of more value than the opinions of a whole faculty of professors, although she may not know a vowel from a consonant. There is but one proviso,—that the society in which she has grown up shall be the best English society" (*Every-Day English* 88). This paradigm of "the speech of a well-bred woman" upholding American speech becomes even more potent when White contrasts it, in the same essay on "'American' Speech," with the voice of a "Western actress of some celebrity" whose tone "propelled me from the door like a pellet from a pop-gun" (95). Notwithstanding his regional impressions, White's negativity, like his general assessment of American speech, centers on the woman's "tone," which he compares to "a pellet from a pop-gun"—a strong and startling image granting potentially explosive power to the female voice. Thus for verbal critics like White, American "civilization" would be upheld largely by the language manners of American women.

The reason why verbal critics and manners commentators looked to women and language to uplift national civilization and to make good manners more permanent than some perfunctory performance of rules is readily apparent in the repeated concerns with "good breeding" in White's commentary. Here White's valuing of "the speech of a well-bred woman" is telling: "Well-bred" connotes both nature (or birth) and nurture (or culture), both good "blood" ("very direct descent") and good education (an upbringing among the "very best society"). Invoking breeding and women together makes linguistic habits appear as natural characteristics of "descent," as White puts it. In the context of concerns about "civilization," this was important to those of White's day; for the fact that manners writers like Harcourt or Wells emphasized manners as something "deeper," more "subtle" than a "code of superficial rules," yet simultaneously stressed them as matters of "training, or rather lack of training," evidences the need to make manners something achievable yet permanent, something inheritable that, as Wells says above, could definitively set the "ladies and gentlemen" apart from the "savage." Thus Henry James would explain "the idea of good breeding" as "the idea of *secure* good manners":

> The idea of good breeding—without which intercourse fails to flower into fineness, without which human relations bear but crude and tasteless fruit—is one of the most precious conquests of civilization, the very core of our social heritage [. . .]. It is an idea, the idea of good breeding (in other words, simply the idea of *secure* good manners), for which, always, in every generation, there is yet more, and yet more, to be done; and no danger would be more lamentable than that of the real extinction, in our hands, of so sacred a flame. Flames, however, even the most sacred, do not go on burning of themselves: they require to be kept up; handed on the torch needs to be from one group of patient and competent watchers to another. ("Question" 45)

Giving women the responsibility of "securing" good manners through vocal training—of keeping up the "sacred flame" which must be continually tended—rested on notions of "good breeding" that straddled conceptions of nurture and nature and held open consensual, forward-looking possibilities for social advance, while simultaneously attributing linguistic performance to the "natural"—an inherent contradiction, of course. "The speech of a well-bred woman" thus becomes highly valued by White because it reconciles conflicting views of language and gender (as basically opposed products of "nurture" and "nature") within a larger naturalized category of "good breeding" that casts women as conservators of language.

This Lamarckian view of language presented acquired or performable traits of linguistic behavior (speech) as inheritable and stabilized them to "secure" a place for hegemonic interests through the gendered and naturalized process of "good breeding." Indeed, as Thorstein Veblen put it in *The Theory of the Leisure Class* (1899), manners and breeding were a kind of conspicuous leisure for the leisure classes to assert their standing: "It is significant," says Veblen with a characteristic satiric edge, "[. . .] as indicating that their activity to a good extent falls under that category of conspicuous leisure known as manners and breeding, that the learned class in all primitive communities are great sticklers for form, precedent, gradations of rank, ritual, ceremonial vestments and learned paraphernalia generally" (367). Such an obsession with form, Veblen further recognizes, was linguistically manifest in specific obsessions with "classic speech," "elegant diction," or "great purity of speech," which also "goes to show [the speaker's] leisure-class antecedents. Great purity of speech is presumptive evidence of several successive lives spent in other than vulgarly useful occupations" (398–99).

While Veblen ironically saw "manners and breeding" and "purity of speech" as archaic, primitive survivals within the leisure class, many Americans of his time saw them as long-standing markers of a "civilization" to which women were the natural partners. Wells' *Manners, Culture, and Dress of the Best American Society* (c. 1890), for instance, claims that manners *toward* and *of* women indicate the extent of the country's civilization:

> Good manners were perhaps originally but an expression of submission from the weaker to the stronger, and many traces of their origin still remain; but a spirit of kindliness and unselfishness born of a *higher order of civilization* permeates for the most part the code of politeness.
>
> As an illustration of this, we cannot do better than cite the requirements of *good breeding in regard to women*. It is considered perfectly proper in the more barbarous forms of society to treat women with all contumely. In polite society great deference is paid to her and certain seemingly arbitrary requirements are made in her favor. (Wells 26, my emphasis)[14]

Given this centrality of women to good breeding—and specifically, to good *linguistic* breeding—women's language manners are central to American civilization in Mrs. Burton Kingsland's chapter on "Conversation" in *Correct Social Usage: A Course of Instruction in Good Form, Style and Deportment* (1903, 1907). Kingsland points out that Americans are disparaged by Europeans for speaking through their noses, observing that

"A pleasing inflection of the voice is the hallmark of gentlehood," noting that the "peculiarly reposeful, well-modulated, silvery tones come from a long continued association with people who have, perhaps through generations, imposed a *well-bred control* upon their speech, as well as actions, whose refinement of nature has affected even the physical organs of language" (46, my emphasis), and prescribing that "Women should produce their voices from midway between the throat and chest, not far up in the head. A shrill voice is as unpleasant as the squeak of a pencil on slate" (45). Here again, the Lamarckian idea is that qualities of speech such as "well-modulated silvery tones" are traits "imposed" through generations of women, such that they become inheritable forces uniting those who are "well-bred." Kingsland's commentary firmly places gendered metalinguistic notions—notions about women's "well-bred control" of vocal tone—within the evolutionist discourse of civilization.

As Kingsland's observations on manners suggest and as White's verbal criticism foreordained, women as good linguistic breeders were linguistic leaders, broadly tasked with sustaining conversation and regulating their vocal tone. Thus gendered verbal criticism like White's could be seen in the etiquette manuals of the day, some of which quoted White and bore similar titles—for instance, Marion Harland's and Virginia Van De Water's manual *Everyday Etiquette: A Practical Manual of Social Usages* (1905, 1907) and Martha Louise Rayne's chapter on "Every-Day Etiquette" in *Gems of Deportment and Hints of Etiquette* (1882), a collection billed as *"the* [sic.] standard work upon social etiquette, containing as it does gems of knowledge from the best acknowledged authorities of the world" (Rayne 3–4). Women were charged with taking the lead in the conversational arena: "The truth is, conversation, as a fine art, needs to be made the fashion again. Women set the social mold, and it is for them to begin the reform. Men will be glad to follow their example, and the effect will be mutually stimulating" (Rayne 37). Even speculations about "The Conversation of the Future" end up resting with women's regenerative and reformative conversational roles in American society, as in the *Social Mirror* (1888), which devotes an entire section to the importance of conversation in the home: "Nothing in the home life needs to be more carefully watched and more diligently cultivated" (*Social Mirror* 196, 378; see also 376–82).

Etiquette books suggested not only *what* comprised suitable subjects for conversation, but they also outlined *how* to converse, giving detailed instructions for modulating pronunciation and governing tone of voice. Thus, beyond leading in conversation, women were charged with regulating their vocal tone as an extension of their domestic roles.[15] *Correct Social Usage: A Course of Instruction in Good Form, Style and Deportment* gives a particularly forceful example of how women's vocal tone is given a central place in the upholding of the laws of civilization to which etiquette is compared.[16] In his chapter on "Good Manners in the Society and the Home," Reverend C. W. de Lyon Nichols stresses the importance of parents' well-regulated voices for their children's success: "It is a commonplace to premise that a child whose parents possess well-modulated, correct speaking voices and use polite English, is more apt to excel" (*Correct* 29). More explicitly, Rayne's *Gems of Deportment* places women squarely in the role of vocal training when she propounds that "The foundation for a good voice should be laid in childhood by the mother and teacher, who instructs the child how to use the voice in its strength and purity, avoiding nasal tones, studying a true, clear pronunciation, and giving every word its full value" (387). Harcourt's *Good Form for Women* (1907) echoes Rayne's pronouncements on women's governing their vocal tone as a sign of good breeding:

> A gentlewoman is marked no less by the quality of her voice than by that of her words. Well modulated tones, soft accent and correct pronunciation are the surest indications of good breeding and education. When one has had the advantage of refined associations from childhood these qualities of speech are acquired naturally and unconsciously, but they are attainable by almost anyone who will take the trouble to acquire them. And it is surely worth while to do so, for few are insensible to the magnetism of a melodious voice and the effect of proper speech. It is no uncommon thing to find pleased listeners to platitudes delivered in musical accents, whilst on the other hand the wisest thoughts and the most beautiful word pictures lose much of their charm when the vehicle of expression is repulsive. (121)

With Harcourt again sounding much like White in highlighting *women's* vocal strengths and faults throughout her verbal criticism, writers like Wilcox, Rayne, and Harcourt gave women—namely mothers—the task of carrying and imparting vocal quality, working to naturalize acquired vocal habits through notions of "good breeding" by which "qualities of speech are acquired naturally and unconsciously," a phrase again denoting how the gendering of language practices naturalized them. Not only were women "marked," in Harcourt's words, by the quality of their voices; but also as mothers and teachers, they were responsible for "marking" others—for imparting, as Rayne put it, "the foundation for a good voice" in childhood.

Granting women's conversational voices and vocal tone a central place in upholding American civilization, these manners manuals reflect how gendered discourse on language worked in complex ways to locate ideal women by regulating *how* they should speak, rather than (or, as well as) *that* they should speak—a complex way of delimiting their civilizing influence. While, as some scholars have noted, such discourse on manners could work in some ways to expand women's roles, others have noted how it did so in limited ways, often confining women's roles to the parlor.[17] Indeed, as *Harper's Bazar*'s Mary Elizabeth Wilson Sherwood's popular *Manners and Social Usages* observed in 1884, although the American woman does "all the social work" in this country, she "has almost no position in the political world. [. . .] is not a leader, an *intrigante* in politics, as she is in France" (14). Moreover, discourse on women's manners could subtly absorb anxieties about America's standing in the world, and about increased immigration in America. For, as Sherwood also states, there are "faults and inelegancies of which foreigners accuse us which we may do well to consider. One of these is the greater freedom allowed in the manners of our young women—a freedom which, as our New World fills up with people of foreign birth, cannot but lead to social disturbances" (5). Here, Sherwood's aptly-put concerns about "social disturbances," caused by the new freedom allowed young women and by "people of foreign birth" filling up "our New World," are enveloped by commentary regulating women's voices in the home.

As verbal criticism and manners manuals did, Henry James' writings were immersed in concerns about national speech and women's vocal "tone." Specifically, James' Bryn Mawr speech "The Question of our Speech" and *The Bostonians* entered into discourses of gendered linguistic domestication. In a sense, then, we need to read Basil Ransom's comments in *The Bostonians* as "about" "The Question of Our Speech," and, reciprocally, "The Question of Our Speech" as "about" *The Bostonians*.

There is a historical basis for considering the relationship between these works. As James recounts in "The Speech of American Women" (1906–07), his impressions of "hooting," "howling," "shrieking," and "bawling" Boston schoolgirls some 25 years earlier—impressions predating the publication of *The Bostonians*—remained with him and spawned his later contemplations on American women's speech after he had gathered "a wider view and more evidence" of "the crudity of tone of my countrywomen in general" and, even more, of "the immunity from comment, from any shadow of criticism, that it [this crudity of tone] serenely enjoys" ("Speech" 70). In his recollection of bawling Boston schoolgirls, James reflects upon his three-month springtime stay in Boston in the early 1880s and his daily, late-morning walk across the Common and Mount Vernon Street, where he regularly passed a young ladies' seminary at the hour of "recess." These Boston schoolgirls, he relates, were quite "in possession of the public scene [. . .]—so that the vociferous pupils (those of the 'most fashionable school in Boston,' as I heard their establishment described,) had the case all in their hands. My point is simply that, being fashionable, they yet *were* vociferous, and in conditions that, as they ingenuously shrieked and bawled to each other across the street and from its top to its bottom, gave the candid observer much to think of" (69). It is not far-fetched to imagine that this occasion of young women's vocal "possession of the public scene" in the early 1880s gave James "the candid observer much to think of" for many years to come, years spanning the composition and publication of both *The Bostonians* and his essays on American women, speech, and manners—such that, in "The Question of our Speech," James observes that the collective *vox Americana* is in trouble: "The *vox Americana* then, frankly, is for the spectator, or perhaps I should say for the auditor of life, as he travels far and wide, one of the stumbling blocks of our continent [. . .]" ("Question" 51). As James continues, "I cannot but regard the unsettled character and the inferior quality of the colloquial *vox Americana*—and I speak here but of the poor dear distracted organ itself—as in part a product of that mere state of indifference to a speech-standard and to a tone-standard on which I have been insisting" (52).

As we discover in James' essays, these "questions of speech" such as "tone" and a "tone-standard" in fact become much the measure of American civilization. As James says:

> All life therefore comes back to the question of our speech, the medium through which we communicate with each other; for all life comes back to the question of our relations with each other. These relations are made possible, are registered, are verily constituted, by our speech [. . .].
>
> [. . .] Of the degree in which a society is civilized the vocal form, the vocal tone, the personal, social accent and sound of its intercourse, have always been held to give a direct reflection. That sound, that vocal form, the touchstone of manners, is the note, the representative note—representative of its having (in our poor, imperfect human degree) achieved civilization. Judged in this light, it must frankly be said, our civilization remains strikingly *un*achieved; the last of American idiosyncrasies, the last by which we can be conceived as 'represented' in the international concert of culture, would be the pretension to a tone-standard, to our wooing comparison with that of other nations. ("Question" 44–45)

As James defines it in "The Question of Our Speech," and again in "The Speech of American Women," vocal *tone* is *how* the voice is used in speaking:

> I shall go so far as to say that there is no such thing as a voice pure and simple: there is only, for any business of appreciation, the voice *plus* the way it is employed; an employment determined here by a great number of influences than we can now go into—beyond affirming at least, that when such influences, in general, have acted for a long time we think of them as having made not only the history of the voice, but positively the history of the national character, almost the history of the people. ("Question" 51)

Tautologically here, the issue of vocal tone as a question of American civilization expresses the national character. As James puts it: "The interest of tone is the interest of manners, and the interest of manners is the interest of morals, and the interest of morals is the interest of civilization," distinctly opposed to barbarism ("Speech" 78). Thus those language manners expressed generally through speech, and particularly through tone, are representative signs of a society's having "achieved civilization," and they importantly weave together the layers of civil society. It follows that, for James, the utmost means of guarding civilization is the consciousness of speech—a consciousness kept up through attention to what James calls a "tone-standard." Such a "tone-standard" is "a clear criterion of the best usage and example: which is but to recognize, once for all, that avoiding vulgarity, arriving at lucidity, pleasantness, charm, and contributing by the mode and degree of utterance a colloquial, a genial value even to an inevitably limited quantity of intention, of thought, is an art to be acquired and cultivated, just as much as any of the other, subtler, arts of life" (James, "Question" 46). While it may be "easier," says James, to ignore the question of speech, doing so simply locates us among "the beasts, who prosper as well without a vocabulary as without a marriage-service. It is easier to overlook any question of speech than to trouble about it, but then it is also easier to snort or neigh, to growl or to 'meaow,' than to articulate and intonate" (55).[18]

Taken together, James' writings moreover reveal how ideas about vocal "tone" and a "tone-standard" as crucial facets of American civilization and national character are gendered—such that women become as much a part of America's vocal problem as they are its solution. Basil Ransom's famous comment in *The Bostonians* again comes to mind: "The whole generation is womanized," he says, "the masculine tone is passing out of the world; it's a feminine, a nervous, hysterical, chattering, canting age [. . .]" (322). *The Bostonians* here anticipates James' cultural criticism, in which James echoes Basil in his damning the age's feminization, noting that "the women, on our side of the world [. . .] are encamped on every inch of the social area that the stock-exchange and the football-field leave free [. . .]," and in bringing such criticism down to questions of speech such as vocal tone ("Speech" 66). Furthermore, James' essays unequivocally depict American women, namely "well-bred women," as responsible for upholding agreeable speech and a tone-standard in America because "it is in their [vocal] chords to give more effect to the intention": "No one can doubt it who has listened to the speech of a succession of well-bred women—well bred in the sense that an incalculable amount of thought has been taken for their manners, and that their native organization and social piety, as it were, have enabled them to justify it" ("Speech" 67). As James reiterates again and again in his reflections—reflections that conceivably unfolded from his early impressions of Bostonian schoolgirls—women's speech is central to national civilization.[19]

Perhaps, then, it makes sense that, in *The Bostonians,* James places the subject of the struggle over one woman's *voice* at the center of a novel whose historical context is the fight for women's *votes.* Because *The Bostonians* pivots on the conflict between the politicization and domestication of its democratic heroine's voice, I read the novel as "alluding to" (to use Althusser's phrase again), and indeed illuminating, the gendered language politics of James' day. James' *Bostonians* (1886) has in fact often been read, alongside his *Princess Cassamassima* (1886), as one of the sociopolitical novels of James' middle period, and its backdrop is the ongoing agitation for women's suffrage at the end of the 19th century. Though set in Boston, James regarded the novel's story as "very national, very typical [. . .] very American [. . .], a tale very characteristic of our social conditions"—"the situation of women, the decline of the sentiment of sex, the agitation on their behalf" (*Notebooks* 19–20).[20] He notes that the story "relates an episode connected with the so-called 'woman's movement'" and that its characters—namely Olive Chancellor and her protégée, the novel's heroine and "gifted" public speaker Verena Tarrant—"are for the most part persons of the radical reforming type, who are especially interested in the emancipation of women, giving them the suffrage, releasing them from bondage, co-educating them with men, etc." (18). The foil, of course, to Olive and Verena is transplanted Southerner and Bostonian outsider Basil Ransom, "who falls in love with her [Verena] and in whom she also becomes much interested, but who, being of a hard-headed and conservative disposition, is resolutely opposed to female suffrage and all similar alterations. The more he sees of the heroine the more he loves her, and the more determined he is to get her out of the clutches of her reforming friends [especially Olive], whom he utterly abominates" (19).

Central to the conflict between Basil and Olive is the fact that it is Verena's *voice* with which they both fall in love, and their ensuing struggle to contain or to release it becomes a central conflict of the novel, highlighting the gendered language politics of the day. Basil, for example, metonymizes Verena through her "clear, bright, ringing voice" (James, *Bostonians* 249), which is described as "golden" (251) and rings "like silver" (411), with a "native sweetness" (214). He listens not to Verena's ideas but to her *tone*, "so pure and rich, and yet so young, so natural, [which] constituted in itself a talent" (253); he sees Verena's voice as a form separable from the content of "her ridiculous, fantastic, delightful argument[s]" (254). Indeed, Basil and Olive both believe that Verena's voice, with its "pure and rich" tones, "had magic in it" (364).

Ultimately, *The Bostonians* shows how Basil's and Olive's opposing efforts to regulate the "magic" of Verena's voice—and their gendered commentary about language—emerge to manage larger questions of the political participation not only of "native" Bostonian/American women such as Verena and Olive, but also that of migrant outsiders, like Basil himself, who is consistently figured as "alien" to them. With Basil as a figure for masculinity and foreignness in relation to the novel's vocally charming suffragist Verena Tarrant, *The Bostonians* tells a story about how gendered discourses of vocal regulation could play out ideological struggles over women's and aliens' presence in the public arena, a story that James then extends in his cultural criticism. In the end, *The Bostonians* alludes to one particular late-19th-century answer to these struggles: a domestication of women's voices that confined them to what Basil Ransom would call dining-table platforms.[21]

One of the complexities of reading *The Bostonians,* noticed by its first reviewers, is its identifiably, indubitably open ending.[22] Indeed, Basil Ransom's final "victory" in the novel's last pages—his "wrenching" Verena and her lovely voice away from her eagerly awaiting audience at Boston's new Music Hall—is at best a dubious victory, one that works not by mental persuasion but by what James describes as sheer "muscular force" (*Bostonians* 434). Verena exits the hall (and the novel) in tears and, in fact, as one perceptive reviewer put it in 1886, we gain "no sense of real strength anywhere" (*Contemporary Review* 50 [Aug. 1886], 300–01, rpt. in Hayes 171). With such an ambiguous ending, James seems less to take "sides" on the Woman Question than to give us a portrait of competing narratives at work, in a sense committing himself in two directions at once—as Verena herself had done when she "threw herself upon [Basil] with a protest which was all, and more than all, a surrender" (*Bostonians* 429). In one direction, considering his characterization of Basil as a conservative white man who seeks to domesticate Verena's voice, James shows us in *The Bostonians* how discourses of gendered linguistic domestication, epitomized in Basil's commentary on Verena's voice, work to manage concerns about women's suffrage. Yet in another direction, if Basil is read as a figure for foreignness, this initial story is complicated and begins to suggest how gendered commentary about language could also manage uneasiness about the public presence of immigrants, as well as women—ultimately showing how the Woman and Alien Questions were intertwined in and through gendered commentary about language.

The more evident narrative in *The Bostonians,* as Gavin Jones and Caroline Levander both argue, is a story of gendered linguistic conquest. This is a story of the accession of masculine control over a feminized political voice on the lecture platform. In this conquest, Basil, by "muscular force," wrests Verena "from the mighty multitude," hurries her out of Boston's Music Hall, and thrusts her cloak over her head, thereby winning an uncertain victory over the public and political circulation of Verena's voice (*Bostonians* 413, 434–35). For it is Verena as *vox Americana*—Verena as "a flower of the great Democracy" (104) coupled with the "charming notes of her voice" (57)—that Olive and Basil, from a mixture of personal and political motives, both desire to possess, if only to cast in divergent directions. As we learn early on, Olive wants to publicize Verena's voice, which she sees as a power for good in the woman's movement, while Basil wants to privatize it. At the same time that Olive is personally taken with Verena's democratic leanings, her "bright, vulgar clothes, her salient appearance" (74), Olive is committed to the development of Verena's voice for "the redemption of women," professedly "the only thing in all the world she cared for" (80). When Basil asks Olive "whether she supposed the girl would come out in public," Olive replies:

> "Come out in public!" Olive repeated, "in public? Why, you don't imagine that pure voice is to be hushed?"
> "Oh, hushed, no! it's too sweet for that. But not raised to a scream; not forced and cracked and ruined. She oughtn't to become like the others. She ought to remain apart."
> "Apart—*apart?*" said Miss Chancellor; "when we shall be looking to her, gathering about her, praying for her!" There was an exceeding scorn in her voice. "If *I* can help her, she shall be an immense power for good."
> "An immense power for quackery, my dear Miss Olive!" (90)

At the center of this struggle between Basil and Olive to possess Verena are, then, Basil's and Olive's opposing linguistic perceptions, whether Verena's voice should "remain apart" or be "an immense power for good" in public.

In this first narrative of Basil's victorious "hushing" of Verena's political voice, James perceptively places the timely question of American women's voices, and thus gendered commentary about language, at the core of the sociopolitical milieu of *The Bostonians*. James circuits Olive's and Basil's opposing personal and political agendas through their commentary about, and regulation of Verena's voice, the voice of the "flower of the great Democracy." We see this circulation perhaps most clearly in Basil's opinions about Verena's voice, opinions that are visibly invested in a larger discourse of "civilization" that has clear linguistic elements. In striking contrast to Olive's vision of "the suffering of women" through the ages (79), Basil's "conviction" was "strong that civilization itself would be in danger if it should fall into the power of a herd of vociferating women" (45). Basil thought his age "talkative, querulous, hysterical, maudlin, full of false ideas, of unhealthy germs, of extravagant, dissipated habits, for which a great reckoning was in store. He was an immense admirer of the late Thomas Carlyle, and was very suspicious of the encroachment of modern democracy" (181)—an encroachment signified to him largely by the public and overtly political uses to which Olive deigns to put Verena's voice. Thus when Basil hears Verena's voice, he is struck with the fact that "her apostleship [in the women's movement] was all nonsense, the most passing of fashions, the veriest of delusions, and that she was meant for something divinely different—for privacy, for him, for love" (258; see also 352). James writes that, for Basil:

> all he could feel was that to *his* [sic.] starved senses she irresistibly appealed. He was the stiffest of conservatives, and his mind was steeled against the inanities she uttered—the rights and wrongs of women, the equality of the sexes, the hysterics of conventions, the further stultification of the suffrage, the prospect of conscript mothers in the national

Senate. It made no difference; she didn't mean it, she didn't know what she meant, she had been stuffed with this trash by her father, and was neither more nor less willing to say it than to say anything else; for the necessity of her nature was not to make converts to a ridiculous cause, but to emit those charming notes of her voice, to stand in those free young attitudes, to shake her braided locks like a naiad rising from the waves, to please everyone who came near her, and to be happy that she pleased. (56–57)

While Olive, then, seeks to politicize Verena's voice to make converts to a cause that Basil sees as "ridiculous," Basil romanticizes Verena's voice (it spurs his figuration of Verena as "a naiad rising from the waves") and seeks to privatize it in the interest of recouping what he believes American civilization has lost—or will lose—with the "equality of the sexes" and "the prospect of conscript mothers in the national Senate." Thus when Verena herself points out to Basil that "It's a remarkable social system that has no place for *us*," Basil responds by saying, "No place in public. My plan is to keep you at home and have a better time with you there than ever" (323).

In another fascinating scene—an exchange between Verena and Basil over Verena's voice that is central to the text—the question of what to do with Verena's vocal "facility" absorbs the larger question of women's "place" in American life. In this scene, the novel reveals how Basil's gendered commentary about Verena's voice intervenes in the Woman Question. Here, Verena questions Basil's marriage-plot to privatize her voice, a plan that is central to his agenda to rescue American "civilization" from feminization:

> "I should like to know what is to become of all that part of me [Verena's vocal facility, her 'gift'], if I retire into private life, and live, as you say, simply to be charming for you. I shall be like a singer with a beautiful voice (you have told me yourself my voice is beautiful), who has accepted some decree of never raising a note. Isn't that a great waste, a great violation of nature? Were not our talents given us to use, and have we any right to smother them and deprive our fellow-creatures of such pleasure as they may confer?" (375)

To Verena's inquiries, Basil's "sportive" reply is, "My dear young woman, it will be easy to solve the difficulty: the dining-table shall be our platform, and you shall mount on top of that" (375). Basil's ideal location of Verena's voice in the home—specifically, in the dining room—could not be clearer here. He continues, more seriously:

> We shall find plenty of room for your facility; it will lubricate our whole existence. Believe me, Miss Tarrant, these things will take care of themselves. You won't sing in the Music Hall, but you will sing to me; you will sing to every one who knows you and approaches you. Your gift is

indestructible; don't talk as if I either wanted to wipe it out or should be able to make it a particle less divine. I want to give it another direction, certainly; but I don't want to stop your activity. Your gift is the gift of expression, and there is nothing I can do for you that will make you less expressive. It won't gush out at a fixed hour and on a fixed day, but it will irrigate, it will fertilize, it will brilliantly adorn your conversation. Think how delightful it will be when your influence becomes really social. Your facility, as you call it, will simply make you, in conversation, the most charming woman in America." (376)

As Basil states so plainly here, achieving his goal of saving the age from the "most damnable feminization" (322) ultimately revolves around the socialization—indeed, the domestication—of Verena's voice. This domestication is spatially and rhetorically symbolized by Basil's fantasy in which Verena's lecture platform is converted into the "dining-table," and her lectures themselves are transformed into private "conversations." These rhetorical-spatial conversions, in the end, relocate women's "real," "social" influence within the home and resonate with manners manuals' emphasis on women's domesticating linguistic influence.

As such, this particular narrative of *The Bostonians* shows us how commentary on women's voices like Verena's could plot a course for the restriction of women's votes. Through Basil's commentary in particular, the novel perceptively reveals the limits imposed on Verena's interrelated vocal, rhetorical, and political success by traditional patriarchal forces. *The Bostonians*, then, illuminates how women's votes can be contained by gendered vocal regulation. James reinforces this point by depicting this control as both verbal and physical: Basil makes Verena *his* auditor by the end of the novel ("A woman that listens is lost, the old proverb says; and what had Verena done for the last three weeks but listen?" [388]); and, as we have seen, Basil fulfills his fancy and finally succeeds in "kidnapping" Verena at the end of the novel (379). Basil's protest against "the damnable feminization of the age" is thus finally enacted and taken to its logical ends. Through it, he seems to have restored "the masculine tone" to the age. But, at the same time, the novel's dénouement implies that Basil's restoration of "masculine tone" is an uneasy and unstable one.

The instability of Basil's final "victory" is evident in the novel's final implication that Verena's professed "gladness" was fated to be compromised by tears. Moreover, Basil's "victory" is unstable because the story of masculine linguistic conquest over the age's vocal feminization is itself intertwined with an understated second narrative, in which Basil emerges as an uneasy presence not simply because of his masculinity, but also because of his foreignness. In this second narrative, the novel suggests how regulation of women's voices might also "soothe" anxieties about aliens in America.

Interestingly, Basil's foreignness rises to the surface when we focus on the novel's descriptions of Basil's *own* speech, rather than Basil's ideas *about* speech. The novel's second page reveals the outstanding characteristic of Basil's speech as not its masculinity but its foreignness relative to the speech of the Bostonians:

> [Basil Ransom] came, in fact, from Mississippi, and he spoke very perceptibly with the accent of that country. It is not in my power to reproduce by any combination of characters this charming dialect; but the initiated reader will have no difficulty in evoking the sound, which is to be associated in the present instance with nothing vulgar or vain. This lean, pale, sallow, shabby, striking young man, with his superior head, his sedentary shoulders, his expression of bright grimness and hard enthusiasm, his provincial, distinguished appearance, is, as a representative of his sex, the most important personage in my narrative; he played a very active part in the events I have undertaken in some degree to set forth. And yet the reader who likes a complete image, who desires to read with the senses as well as with the reason, is entreated not to forget that he prolonged his consonants and swallowed his vowels, that he was guilty of elisions and interpolations which were equally unexpected, and that his discourse was pervaded by something sultry and vast, something almost African in its rich basking tone, something that suggested the teeming expanse of the cotton-field. (2–3)

James does not represent Basil's speech as literary dialect, perhaps because, as we know from his thoughts in "American Letter" (1898), James would come to see literary dialect as a faddish infatuation with the primitive. Although written after *The Bostonians*, "American Letter" suggests that James recognized how late-19th-century discourse on dialect, the subject of the previous chapter, was a manifestation of American "civilization." James reflects: "Nothing is more striking, in fact, than the invasive part played by the element of dialect in the subject-matter of the American fiction of the day. [. . .] It is a part, in its way, to all appearance, of the same great general wave of curiosity on the subject of the soul abundingly *not* civilized that has lately begun to roll over the Anglo-Saxon globe [. . .]" (18).[23]

Despite James' choice *not* to represent Basil's speech in literary dialect in his fiction, his early *description* of Basil's speech in the novel linguistically marks its central male character as outside the "civilized" world of Boston and perhaps that of many of his readers. Certainly, because he hails from Mississippi, Basil's "otherness" is *southern*ess—a fact that critics have noted.[24] However, this otherness is simultaneously exoticized and associated with foreignness. Basil's Mississippi accent is described as the accent of "*that* country" (my emphasis), a use of a demonstrative adjective that, while James does not wish to associate Basil's sound with anything "vulgar or vain," nonetheless distances it from other characters in the novel; even Olive's voice, for instance, is described as "low and agreeable—a cultivated voice," in contrast to Basil's (6). As the passage continues, James' narrator literally begs his readers to remember that Basil is set apart from "cultivated" Bostonians through his language. Basil "prolonged his consonants and swallowed his vowels" and "was guilty" of "unexpected" verbal omissions and insertions. These were vocal transgressions harped upon by critics including James, who in "The Question of Our Speech," faults American youth for eliding consonants (pronouncing "yes" as "yeheh") and inserting *r* and *s* (as in "vanilla-r" and "a good ways-on") and says that pronouncing *u* for *e* (for example, "Amurrica" instead of "America") cheapens language by substituting "limp, slack, passive tone for clear, clean, active, tidy tone" (51). Perhaps most significantly, Basil's discourse was "pervaded," a word choice that suggests complete saturation and thorough permeation, by "something" vaguely suggestive of Africa "in its rich basking tone," sultriness, and vastness. The association of Africa with "the teeming expanse of the cotton field" marks Basil's otherness as southern, but "African" also marks it as foreign, such that Basil's language figures him as both migrant and immigrant in Boston/America. In the late-19th-century's racially-charged context, such a description was indicative of the linguistic primitive, the linguistic other, southern and foreign. Indeed, the fact that "African" was considered "foreign" and "exotic" to the Bostonians is reinforced in the novel by Miss Birdseye's nostalgic recollections of her abolitionist days: "But they had been the happiest days, for when causes were embodied in foreigners (what else were the Africans?), they were certainly more appealing" (25). Basil's voice is finally, decidedly "exotic" to the Bostonians, as similarly seen in a later description of Verena's response to Basil's voice—"Strange I call the nature of her reflections, for they softly battled with each other as she listened, in the warm, still air, touched with the far-away hum of the immense city, to his deep, sweet, distinct voice, expressing monstrous opinions with *exotic cadences*" that cast "a spell upon her as she listened" (316, my emphasis).

Basil's otherness, thus initially introduced through descriptions of his exotic southern dialect, is pursued throughout the novel with like characterizations of his physical appearance, economic status, political views, and setting. Most obviously, as originally the object of Olive's family's charity, Basil is seen by Olive as "a personage so exotic," as "strange" (9). In physical appearance, he stands out: His complexion is brown; his eyes are "dark, deep, and glowing," or "fuliginous" ('sooty'), suggesting a kind of elemental "smouldering fire" behind them; and the fall of his black hair is physically characterized as "leonine" (2, 239)—an adjective evoking the wildcats of India or Africa. Socioeconomically, Basil has been financially forced to migrate northward to try his hand at his profession—law—in order to pay the debts occasioned by the family's ruin in the Civil War (9–10). Consistently and increasingly throughout the novel, Basil is positioned as an outsider or an "intruder" (356) to the Bostonian group, particularly to Olive and Verena (271–72). Even to the flirtatious Mrs. Luna, a New Yorker, Basil represents something distinctly "other." Mrs. Luna cares for Basil because he represents, to her, something geographically and historically distant—that is, the "fallen aristocracy (it seemed to be falling everywhere very much; was not Basil Ransom an example of it? was he not like a French *gentilhomme de province* after the Revolution? or an old monarchical *émigré* from the Languedoc?)" (197–98). And yet, even while (or perhaps because) he is an outsider, an "*émigré*," the Bostonian women see him, at one point or another in the narrative, as a potential "convert"—a perspective that places them in the position of missionaries. This perspective is epitomized by Miss Birdseye's unshakeable vision that Verena might "shake" Basil, "act on" him, "bring him round" to their progressive views (210–11). Miss Birdseye clings to this vision with "benignant perversity"—a vision in which "the stiff-necked Southerner" was "led captive by a daughter of New England trained in the right school, who would impose her opinions in their integrity" (383, 353). As the narrative clearly shows, however, this vision is an illusion, for it is only sustained through Verena's and Basil's dissimulation until Miss Birdseye's death (383). For Miss Birdseye, Basil's "exclusion from the house" of the Bostonians at Marmion—a spatialization of his otherness to them—is mitigated by the potential for his conversion and made even more dramatic through the fact of his southernness/otherness (383); presenting a great challenge for their cause, *he* is a prime target for *their* "missionary" work, as much as *Verena* is a target for *his*.

Miss Birdseye's spatialization of Basil's foreignness reinforces the earlier description of Basil's personal "setting," which is infused with foreign associations of both class and nation. Basil's habitations in New York, in stark contrast to those of Olive Chancellor's comfortable and civilized home, are comprised of "two small shabby rooms in a somewhat decayed mansion which stood next to the corner of the Second Avenue," a setting connected with, but not fully expressive of, "a rank civilization" (176–77). Here, it is an exceptional "smart, bright wagon" that grants the scene a picturesque, pastoral quality and rescues it from otherwise being fully "rank"—that is, suggestive of the staleness, stagnation, or rancidity of a civilization so profuse or excessive or corrupt it is in decline. Further, Basil's sitting-room commands a view of tenements that have "an elaborate iron lattice-work" that causes them "slightly to resemble the little boxes for peeping unseen into the street, which are a feature of oriental towns" (177). While James is careful to state in the same passage that Basil's "setting" may not have had "any particular influence" on his life or thoughts, James also notes that "a figure is nothing without a setting" (177). Indeed, Basil's indifference to his own setting might suggest that he is thoroughly "at home" among these "foreign" features. Basil's house with "oriental" features, next to a Dutch grocery, in a much-less-than-genteel neighborhood that verges on "rank" civilization become part of his character. As migrant and immigrant, Basil Ransom thus becomes, at once, a "masculine" personage and a figure for foreignness in the novel.

Through such descriptions of Basil's speech, character, and setting, then, Basil is not simply a masculine force containing a feminine American voice in the novel, but also a more complicated figure for foreignness, causing another narrative to surface in *The Bostonians*. In addition to Basil's removal of Verena's voice from the politically-charged lecture hall to his domesticated dining-table platform, an alternative story unfolds alongside and interarticulated with it: a story suggesting that such a narrative about the masculine domestication of women's voices bears within it a submerged tale about the relationship between foreign forces and a feminized *vox Americana*.

Basil's doubleness as a masculine and alien figure begins to suggest ways in which gendered language politics simultaneously managed ambivalent ideas about women and immigrants. For, strikingly, when Basil finally wrenches Verena from the stage to place her, presumably, in their dining room, he removes *both* Verena *and* himself from the public scene into their domestic space—an act that saves "civilization" from both women and im/migrants.

If we read *The Bostonians* as anticipating James' cultural criticism, in which immigrants from abroad are portrayed as threatening the American language, this ending becomes doubly provocative. As this cultural criticism reveals, anxiety about the public presence of immigrants as well as women could become deflected onto gendered commentary about language—specifically, commentary about a feminized *vox Americana* and about women's cultural mission to, as James would put it, "sound the clearer notes of intercourse as only women can." While James' criticism would not adopt Basil Ransom's perspective that women's voices ought to be confined to the home, he would give them culturally significant, domesticating social and linguistic roles—roles that anticipated women's roles in not only civilizing Americans, but moreover, in Americanizing immigrants.

3. MODELS, MISSIONARIES, AND MARTYRS: "THE QUESTION OF OUR SPEECH," WOMEN, AND THE LINGUISTIC DOMESTICATION OF IMMIGRANTS

> Imitating, yes; I commend to you, earnestly and without reserve, as the first result and concomitant of observation, the imitation of formed and finished utterance wherever, among all the discords and deficiencies, that music steals upon your ear. The more you listen to it, the more you will love it—the more you will wonder that you could ever have lived without it. What I thus urge upon you, you see, is a consciousness, an acute consciousness, absolutely [. . .]. Unconsciousness is beautiful when it means that our knowledge has passed into our conduct and our life; has become, as we say, a second nature. But the opposite state is the door through which it has to pass, and which is, inevitably, sometimes, rather straight and narrow. This squeeze is what

we pay for having revelled too much in [vocal] ignorance. Keep up your hearts, all the same, keep them up to the pitch of confidence in that "second nature" of which I speak; the perfect possession of this highest of the civilities, the sight, through the narrow portal, of the blue horizon across the valley, the wide fair country in which your effort will have settled to the most exquisite of instincts, in which you will taste all the savor of gathered fruit, and in which perhaps, at last, *then,* "in solemn troops and sweet societies," you may, sounding the clearer notes of intercourse as only women can, become yourselves models and missionaries, perhaps even martyrs, of the good cause. (Henry James, "The Question of Our Speech" [1905] 56–57)

James closes "The Question of Our Speech" by urging his Bryn Mawr auditors to so imitate "the formed and finished utterance" that it becomes internalized, "unconscious," "second nature," and "the most exquisite of instincts," and by finally commissioning them to become "models and missionaries, perhaps even martyrs" of the "good cause." While we are left to wonder what precisely "the good cause" might be (a national tone-standard? civilized speech? the "sacred flame" of good breeding? American civilization itself?), we know that, for James, speech is "the highest of civilities" and that "the good cause" is linked with "the clearer notes of intercourse" that "only women" can sound. In the closing words of this graduation address, James comes to charge these young women graduates with the cultural guardianship of an acutely conscious, civilized speech against the "forces of looseness" that, earlier in his address, he claims work against it—forces including the American common school, the American newspaper, and the "American Dutchman and Dago" (55, 53). Again, women's speech comes to indicate the degree of American civilization, and women's cultural role in guarding "our speech" also has the potential to reclaim the country from what James has identified as "the vast contingent of aliens whom we make welcome" (55): James thus ends his address above with spatial images that recast the doctrine of manifest destiny as an issue of women's now nationally domesticating speech, by which their "perfect possession of this highest of the civilities" becomes a "second nature" overreaching "the blue horizon across the valley, the wide fair country" as a whole (57).

In the same year that James gave "The Question of Our Speech" as Bryn Mawr's graduation address, Jane Addams gave a speech on "Immigration: A Field Neglected by the Scholar" as a convocation address at the University of Chicago, in which she too proposed new responsibilities for new graduates—to humanize studies of immigration. Though obviously very different in many respects, both James' and Addams' speeches touch on immigration and bear traces of the era's evolutionary discourse of civilization in contrasting "primitive" and "civilized" cultures. Moreover, while operating in different directions, James and Addams similarly theorize how women, in their roles as civilizers and educators, might provide answers to problems posed by immigration. As we have seen, James' essays, extending in part the notions of Richard Grant White and writers of manners manuals, revolve around women's conservation of the fine discriminations of civil speech, a kind of "top-down" manners education in which women play central social and linguistic roles. Addams' agenda, on the other hand, operates in a sense from the "bottom-up," not only to teach the English language to immigrants, but to bring to Americans an understanding of "the sweetness and charm which inhere in primitive domestic customs" and might be found among many immigrants—yet another educational agenda in which women became important linguistic domesticators (Addams, "Immigration" 13). For, Addams' conviction was that any threat from immigration came not from the nation's limited powers of assimilation, nor from a dilution of "American" characteristics, but from "intellectual dearth and apathy," "a tradition too provincial and limited," and a deficit of "mental energy, adequate knowledge, and a sense of the youth of the earth" ("Immigration" 3–4).

In this section, I read James' commissioning of young Bryn Mawr women in wider cultural—indeed, vocal—roles as "models and missionaries, perhaps even martyrs" of American "civilization" as forecasting women's widening social and linguistic roles to address the increased presence of immigrants in America in the early years of the 20th century. In the settlement house movement of which Addams' Hull-House was the exemplar, in the Americanization movement, and in the Home Teacher Act—all of which I will discuss below after first returning to James' criticism—women were given national places in the linguistic domestication of immigrants. These widened roles were no longer staged on Basil Ransom's dining-table platform; they were located instead in settlement houses, "homey" classrooms, and immigrant homes—settings that domesticated the voices of women even as they were charged with linguistically domesticating immigrants in preparation for American citizenship.[25]

In *The Bostonians,* the presence of Basil Ransom as a figure for foreignness, as we have seen, destabilizes the narrative and leaves the ending unsettled. In "The Question of Our Speech," the presence of aliens prompts James to commission women to guard a feminized language and reveals how gendered commentary about the English language absorbed discomforts about the alien presence in America. As noted earlier, in "The Question of Our Speech," James calls the English language an "unfriended heroine," a "transported maiden," an "unrescued Andromeda" who has become detached from her "ancestral circle" in America. James depicts this feminized English language, unmoored from her family, as "betrayed" by alien forces. He figures this "unfriended heroine," a clearly feminized English language in America, as having been "given away" or "handed over" to "the American common school, to the American newspaper, and to the American Dutchman and Dago, as the voice of the people describes them" in a quite "distracted, disheveled, despoiled, divested" state—adjectives associated with her clothing and emphasizing the debasement of the English language as having very material, bodily effects (53–54). While the school and the newspaper are not "alien" forces as such, for James they embody "forces of betrayal" (53) that become associated with a polyglot immigrant population threatening the "prosperity of our idiom"—an association that James makes explicit as he continues:

> There are many things our now so profusely imported and, as is claimed, quickly assimilated foreign brothers and sisters may do at their ease in this country, and at two minutes' notice, and without asking any one else's leave or taking any circumstance whatever into account—any save an infinite uplifting sense of freedom and facility; but the thing they may best do is play, to their heart's content, with the English language, or, in other words, dump their mountain of promiscuous material into the foundations of the American. ("Question" 54)

The fact that James has feminized the English language electrifies the claim that "our now so profusely imported and [. . .] quickly assimilated foreign brothers and sisters may [. . .] play, to their heart's content, with the English language" and "dump their mountain of promiscuous material into the foundations of the American"; James' choice of the descriptor *promiscuous* further charges it with sexual connotations. Such an interarticulation of ideas to figure the English language shows how gender could be inserted into discourse on language to manage concerns about national "civilization."

In addition to using gendered figures for language to depict sociopolitical problems, James proposes solutions that hinge on gendered linguistic roles. As antidote to the foreign debasement of a feminized English language in America, James commends a round-the-clock vigilance to protect American speech from "the innumerable aliens [who] are sitting up [. . .] to work their will on their new inheritance [our speech]":

> We should rather sit up at night with our preoccupation than close our eyes by day as well as by night. All the while we sleep the vast contingent of aliens whom we make welcome, and whose main contention, as I say, is that, from the moment of their arrival, they have just as much property in our speech as we have, and just as good a right to do what they choose with it—the grand right of the American being to do just what he chooses "over here" with anything and everything: all the while we sleep the innumerable aliens are sitting up (*they* don't sleep!) to work their will on their new inheritance and prove to us that they are without any finer feeling or more conservative instinct of consideration for it, more fond, unutterable association with it, more hovering, caressing curiosity about it, than they may have on the subject of so many yards of freely figured oilcloth, from the shop, that they are preparing to lay down, for convenience, on kitchen

floor or kitchen staircase. Oilcloth is highly convenient, and our loud collective medium of intercourse doubtless strikes these new house-holders as wonderfully resisting "wear"—with such wear as it gets!—strikes them as an excellent bargain: durable, tough, cheap. ("Question" 55)

With common schools and daily papers, aliens here become agents of linguistic vulgarization. And the necessity of an alert night watchfulness against the debasing linguistic work of careless and curious aliens is reinforced by the powerful figuration of aliens' attitudes toward "our speech" as a physical "hovering, caressing curiosity" for cheap, convenient oilcloth. Because James has incorporated physical and economic metaphors throughout his cultural criticism to compare the material impact of attention to a tone-standard to dressing and eating well, we know that James wants to preserve the richness, the value, of American speech: For example, in "The Speech of American Women," James compares having a tone-standard to dining with "ivory and silver, smooth clean damask and the bowl of flowers," very "civilized" images (78). Interpreted within the logic of such a chain of metaphors, comparing aliens' attitudes toward English to their interest in a "durable, tough, cheap" oilcloth can be seen as nothing but a debasement of American "civilization" against which his Bryn Mawr auditors must guard.

Thus, perhaps not surprisingly in the context of the period's verbal criticism discussed in the previous section, James' ultimate solution to the national problem of alien degradation of American speech makes recourse to women's social and linguistic roles in sustaining civilization. In fact, he calls on his Bryn Mawr audience to imitate "articulate individuals" to shore up tradition against the forces of looseness he has described. Ultimately, as seen above, James charges them to sound "the clearer notes of intercourse as only women can" and "become yourselves models and missionaries, perhaps even martyrs, of the good cause" ("Question" 56–57).

Seemingly, James' charge was taken up in the linguistically civilizing roles adopted by women in the settlement house and Americanization movements. For, becoming linguistic "models and missionaries" was precisely what many American women—particularly young, white, middle-class women college graduates—did in the years surrounding James' Bryn Mawr address. Educated women at this time began to take on central linguistic roles in the Americanization of aliens—an importantly gendered facet of English language education within the context of heightened anxiety about immigration. While James had assigned Bryn Mawr women the linguistic task of bearing consciousness of national vocal tone, the settlement house movement and state and federal programs following it would charge women with linguistically domesticating aliens. Women's linguistically central place in the late-19th-century settlement house movement, with Addams' Hull-House as its paradigm, lay the groundwork for their linguistically domesticating role in the Americanization movement of the early 20th century. By giving women a central role in Americanizing immigrants through English language instruction—just as by giving women a central role in civilizing Americans through language manners—discourses of gendered linguistic domestication deftly tempered the era's newborn anxieties about national citizenship.[26]

Among the first of organized efforts to Americanize newcomers, partly through language instruction, were those of the settlement houses. Like many settlements, Addams' Hull-House offered, among other classes, English language classes taught predominantly by women, who became pivotal facilitators of vocal exchanges, both in Addams' theory of the aim of the settlement house and in the practice of the classes offered at Hull-House. In "The Subjective Necessity for Social Settlements," written in 1892 and later comprising much of chapter six of *Twenty Years at Hull-House* (1910), Addams uses voice to figure the aim of "communication" between the "upper" and "lower" masses of wasted lives within the settlement:

> If you have heard a thousand voices singing in the Hallelujah Chorus in Handel's "Messiah," you have found that the leading voices could still be distinguished, but that the differences of training and cultivation between them and the voices of the chorus were lost in the unity of purpose and the fact that they are all human voices lifted by a high motive. This is a weak illustration of what a Settlement attempts to do. It aims, in a measure, to develop whatever of social life its neighborhood may afford, to focus and give form to that life, to bring to bear upon it the results of cultivation and training; but it receives in exchange for the music of isolated voices the volume and strength of the chorus. (25)

Just as James and earlier verbal critics used voice to figure the gendered linguistic work of American "civilization," Addams' use of the metaphor of voice highlights the extent to which vocal exchanges—seen as choral and educational in this passage—were theoretically central to the civilizing work of settlement houses like Hull-House. Addams, significantly, theorizes how the settlement attempted to bring together the more cultivated, trained, exceptional, "upper" few and the voluminous "lower" masses around the exchange of *voices*. Through such abstract ideas about voices, Addams and other settlement movement leaders connected college-educated women like herself to the poor and immigrant populations they sought to serve.[27]

These vocal theories of how the settlement house should work played out in women's key roles as educators at Hull-House, with English language education becoming increasingly important to the settlement's civilizing mission over the years. Education at Hull-House took the form of College Extension classes, summer schools for women, Thursday evening public lectures, Sunday evening courses, and educational clubs, such as the Shakespeare Club; women became central to teaching the language and literature classes that sought to uplift their students, often immigrants.

A weekly schedule of events at Hull-House in 1895 reflects that the bulk of English language classes were taught by women—for example, Shakespeare, English, and Letter Writing by Miss Craine (Moore 43).[28] Addams reflects on the civilizing mission of Hull-House's classes and clubs, noting that the Shakespeare Club "lived a continuous existence at Hull-House for sixteen years" and recalling that

> one of its earliest members said that her mind was peopled with Shakespeare characters during her long hours of sewing in a shop, that she couldn't remember what she thought about before she joined the club, and concluded that she hadn't thought about anything at all. To feed the mind of the worker, to lift it above the monotony of his tasks, and to connect it with the larger world, outside of his immediate surroundings, has always been the object of art, perhaps never more nobly fulfilled than by the great English bard. (*Twenty Years* 249)

Addams clearly perceives that "peopling" minds with characters from "the great English bard" is uplifting; Addams' reflections thus partake to some extent in civilizing discourses of the day, which often privileged white, Anglo-Saxon language and culture.[29]

Yet English language classes at Hull-House also had practical ends in preparing immigrants for American life, a fact which Addams recognizes when she writes that "Even a meager knowledge of English may mean an opportunity to work in a factory *versus* nonemployment, or it may mean a question of life or death when a sharp command must be understood in order to avoid the danger of a descending crane" (*Twenty Years* 250). Addams also saw English language instruction as important for shoring up the traditions and authority of first-generation immigrant parents against the "dissipated young men who pride themselves upon their ability to live without working, and who despise all the honest and sober ways of their immigrant parents" who were bewilderingly not able to speak English (147).[30] And she was impatient with "bookish and remote" approaches to teaching that were detached from immigrants' experience and failed to meet "the needs of adult working people in contra-distinction to those employed in schools and colleges, or those used in teaching children" ("Educational Methods" 199–200).

Thus, as the need for English language classes at Hull-House steadily grew, so did the English language classes that were offered, as witnessed by the growth of writing classes, taught largely by Hull-House women, over the years from 1896 to 1916. Regularly offered among the secondary classes taught by women settlers such as Miss Eleanor H. Johnson and Miss Elizabeth H. Thomas in Hull-House's early years, classes such as "English Grammar and Letter Writing" and "Lessons in English Reading" were augmented in the late 1890s by a variety of additional English language classes (*Hull-House Bulletin* vols. 1.1–2.6 [Jan. 1896–Oct. 1897]). These included English Grammar and Composition, English Writing and

Composition, Lessons in English for Beginners, and Advanced Composition and Theme Work, apparently first offered in October 1898 (*Hull-House Bulletin,* vols. 3.6–3.9 [Oct. 1898-Feb. 1899]). While the Advanced Composition and Theme Work class eventually dropped out, an expanded list of English lessons—including grammar, spelling, reading, writing/composition, and rhetoric—easily came to dominate the classes offered at the secondary level by the early 1900s. For example, in mid-winter 1903–04, twelve out of fourteen classes at the secondary level involved instruction in English (*Hull-House Bulletin* vol. 6.1). By 1905–06, ten of twelve secondary classes, with the majority still taught by women, pertained to English language instruction: two sections each of Beginners' English, Second Class in English, Third Class in English, Fourth Class in English, and one section each of Rhetoric and Composition, and Grammar (*Hull-House Bulletin* vol. 7.1 [1905–06]). The ever-expanding list of course offerings in *Hull-House Bulletins* gives the impression of increasing need for English language instruction—an impression confirmed in the *Hull-House Year Books,* which replaced the Bulletins in 1906. For example, the description of classes offered in the May, 1910 *Hull-House Year Book* notes that classes were revised to better meet immigrants' needs (8–9)—a statement echoed in later yearbooks such as the 1913 *Year Book*. By 1916, in its summary of adult classes, the *Year Book* observed that "It has been found in the last few years that the demand for instruction in elementary English, grammar and rhetoric constantly increases" (7). That year, thirteen out of seventeen elementary classes offered at Hull-House were English classes; eleven instructors were women, and three were men (8). As Mary Lynn McCree Bryan and Allen F. Davis summarize, English instruction became more and more important in the life of Hull-House: "When college extension courses and lectures on Greek art did not meet the educational requirements of many of the neighbors, the Hull-House leaders added basic instruction in English language and American government to aid the immigrant who was desperately trying to learn new American ways" (7).

Women were central to the teaching and learning of English in other settlement houses besides Hull-House. For example, one magazine, the *Gary Works Circle,* published "A Message for Mothers" that emphasized the importance of the immigrant woman's English language learning at the local settlement house, not only to her own Americanization but also to the domestication of her family "as wife and mother":

> Do your best to learn English, go to the Mother's Club at the Settlement House if there is one near you. Maintain your place in the home and keep the respect of your husband and children by learning as much as you can about what is going on in the new country . . . By so doing you will not only retain the place of honor you should have as wife and mother but you will be adding to the sum of your happiness and usefulness. (Jack 6–7 qtd. in Crocker 138)

As just such domesticators, women as both teachers and learners were central to Hull-House and the settlement house movement as a whole.[31]

Women soon became similar linguistic players in the Americanization movement in the 1910s and 1920s. Despite disagreement over the precise meaning of "Americanization," most commentators agreed that English language instruction, perceived as part of the national defense and a practical solution to the problems of immigrant illiteracy, was the "first step" in the process of Americanization (Mahoney and Herlihy 3–12; Winkler and Alsberg 50). Some would see English language education as nearly identical to the process of Americanization—such as Theodore Roosevelt in his address on "Americanism" (657). And even those who may have perceived the shortcomings of the slogans of "a common language and a common citizenship" and recognized that the English language was "not necessarily [equivalent to] Americanization," still saw English as "an implement of Americanization" (Kellor 627–28; 629).[32] By the second decade of the 20th century, discourses of linguistic domestication surfaced in Americanization efforts in which white, middle-class women were central to the teaching of English to national newcomers.

Specifically, women's clubs and the home teaching movement that followed the founding of settlement houses featured women at their helm and brought English language instruction into the homes of immigrants. For example, the Federation of Women's Clubs, the Women's Municipal League of Boston, the U.S. Chamber of Commerce in New York City, and the Council of Jewish Women in New York City all issued bulletins in the late 1910s focused on what women could contribute to Americanization efforts (cited in Mahoney, Wetmore et al. 19). By 1920, when the superintendent of Boston public schools, Frank V. Thompson, published *Schooling of the Immigrant*, a book in a series of Americanization studies, and when the Department of the Interior's Bureau of Education released *Training Teachers for Americanization*, the Americanization teacher of English was strikingly, consistently gendered female. Thus taking on leadership roles of and in the Americanization movement, women became linguistic domesticators once again—they became linguistic Americanizers of immigrants, as they had been linguistic civilizers of "native-born" Americans.[33]

A closer look at Americanization training manuals and at some of the educational materials on "Schooling the Immigrant" reveals the extent to which Americanization efforts manifested gendered discourses of linguistic domestication. These manuals described the role of Americanization teachers as akin to that of missionaries and mothers and associated their language instruction with the skills and space of domesticity. Like that of White's and James' guardians of the "sacred flame," the female teacher's major task revolved around the cultivation of English *speech* in immigrant students. *First Steps in Americanization* (1918), for instance, carefully establishes the gendered linguistic expectations of the Americanization teacher: "the teacher of the immigrant" must know "what her aims should be in the task of teaching immigrants to talk English, and how this can best be done; to read English, and how this can best be done; to write English, and how this can best be done. Finally, she must appreciate that her big task is Americanization, and must understand just what this means, and how it can best be brought about" (Mahoney and Herlihy 13).[34] Throughout this manual, the repetitive use of the pronouns *she* and *her* to discuss the teacher of immigrants stands in stark contrast to the consistent gendering of the school administrator as male and the gendering of immigrants themselves as male (Mahoney and Herlihy 44–45, 69). *Training Teachers for Americanization* (1920), a bulletin put out by the Department of the Interior's Bureau of Education, likewise emphasizes the importance of the female teacher's role in the linguistic Americanization of immigrants (8). For example, the bulletin's final point among its "Fifteen Points for Workers in Americanization" calls attention to the missionary role of the American female teacher in educating the immigrant:

> In the final analysis the major part of the burden of Americanizing the immigrant rests on the shoulders of the teacher. Her task is a meaningful one, and she should approach it as one who engages not for hire. She must be an American 100 per cent pure. She must be sane, and sympathetic, and able to see things whole. She must be ready to give and give, and reckon not the return. But the return will come, if she remembers—as she must remember—that she may not give over giving. (Mahoney, Wetmore et al. 16)

Here, the Americanization teacher is elevated in importance through her "100 per cent pure" American identity. Moreover, her work is that of an American "model, missionary, and martyr" who "may not give over giving," along the lines James forecasted in "The Question of Our Speech." The passage makes clear that the teacher must be ready to assume the "major part of the burden of Americanizing the immigrant" as a job akin to domestic labors: "she should approach it as one who engages not for hire" and "be ready to give and give, and reckon not the return"—a mission with predominantly spiritual rather than material rewards.

Attesting strikingly to women's roles as linguistic domesticators, in some Americanization efforts, women were commissioned to teach not only the English language, but also domestic skills such as personal hygiene and American values, ultimately highlighting how Americanization brought together both native-born and foreign-born women through linguistic domestication. One of the most fascinating aspects of Americanization efforts, echoing those of women settlers, was the domesticating role assigned the teacher of immigrants in the classroom. *First Steps in Americanization* emphasizes this role, advocating that the skillful teacher make her classroom space "homey"—in fact so "homey" that she converts the space to a "club-room," an attractive alternative to the street-corner or saloon:

> If we are really to Americanize the immigrant, we must take cognizance of the immigrant's social nature. The school should become his meeting-place. The school center and the evening school should supplement each other. And the evening school itself, where attention is directed primarily to the matter of classroom teaching, should be shot through with the school-center idea. The experienced teacher appreciates this. She knows that however skillful she may be, and however earnest her class, the spirit of the room is greatly improved if occasionally she breaks up the routine. She knows that regular attendance can be maintained only by making the atmosphere of the classroom so 'homey' that the hard-working immigrant prefers it to the street-corner or the saloon. She knows that only by getting close to her pupils, through touching their social side, can she win their confidence. And so her room becomes, now and then, a club-room. (Mahoney and Herlihy 38)

Here, in a rhetorical maneuver akin to Basil Ransom's spatial conversion of lecture platforms into dining-tables, teachers become hostesses who must make their classroom spaces so "homey" that they are converted into "meeting-places" and "club-rooms." This concept of classroom as home seems to be an extension of the social nature of women's educational work that existed at settlement houses, too. For example, when Addams describes "the relation of students and faculty to each other and to the residence," she uses the framework of hospitality, defining the relation as "that of guest and hostess" ("Objective" 36). Moreover, the English classes at Hull-House themselves boasted decidedly social elements; the 1916 *Hull-House Year Book* notes that

> Once a month the members of all the English classes are brought together for an entertainment and dance. On each occasion a program of music by the Hull-House Orchestra, a dramatic entertainment, or a lecture with stereopticon is followed by a dance. An important event of the evening is always a grand march, led by members of one of the Social Clubs, who devise a number of spirited figures that both skilled and unskilled dancers keenly enjoy. Between two hundred and four hundred young people attend each of these parties. (7–8)

As English teachers in settlements as well as in Americanization efforts, then, women as hostesses and social coordinators continued in some of their traditional domestic roles. While the classroom ostensibly provides a space to teach and learn English, in these passages, it is "homey-ness" and socialization that become a significant part of that teaching and learning—another relocation of women's linguistic exchanges, from home dining tables to classrooms.

Not only settlement houses and "homey" classrooms, but also immigrants' homes and neighborhoods—that is, the domestic spaces of both

American women and their "alien sisters" (Winkler and Alsberg 53)—were important sites of the work of gendered linguistic domestication. Forcefully demonstrating the ideal teacher of language as a domesticator was California's Home Teacher Act (1915), which legislated the domesticating linguistic role of women educators in the creation of the Home and Neighborhood Teacher.[35] Under the Home Teacher Act, "domestic educators" were appointed by local boards of election "to go from house to house, especially in the foreign sections, for the purpose of training the mothers and children in the rules of health, sanitation, and hygiene, the principles of buying food and clothing, the English language and civics, and other appropriate subjects" (Wheaton 573). The Home and Neighborhood Teacher thus worked to shift "the emphasis from the child to the mother, bringing to the mother a knowledge of English and of those fundamentals necessary to American standards of living" (Winkler and Alsberg 52). The fact that the Home and Neighborhood Teacher was responsible for teaching English side-by-side with hygiene, health, and sanitation, underscores the extent to which these women educators were "domesticators" as well as the extent to which teaching and learning English was a "domesticating" pursuit: "Through the friendly contact established in the individual *homes,* mothers' groups especially *organized for the study of English* become by their very nature the Americanizing centers of the neighborhood [. . .]" (53, my emphasis); primary among the suggestions was that "speaking English should be the constant aim of the home and neighborhood teacher" (55).

With her dual qualifications as specially-trained language instructor and sympathetic, tactful social worker, the home and neighborhood teacher was finally seen as an "interpreter": "the home and neighborhood teacher, with English as her first objective, imperceptibly and persistently interprets to the mothers the American point of view without causing undue conflict in their mental attitude" (Winkler and Alsberg 55–56), a figuration that suggests the importance of women's *language* as a bridge between native-born and foreign-born. As just such a bridge, the gendered language education of immigrants domesticated in two directions, aiming, in "the interest of the community," to bring "the native-born women" into the affairs of "the foreign-born women," and to bring "the non-English-speaking women [. . .] into closer neighborhood relations" ("The Immigrant and the State" 487). This goal, as "The Immigrant and the State" succinctly put it, equally involved "education and protection for the foreign-born women, and education for the native-born woman concerning her foreign-born neighbor" (487).

As such descriptions of the Home and Neighborhood Teacher show, Americanization texts gave women pivotal, linguistically domesticating roles and participated in the wider discourse of civilization that expressed the era's anxieties about American citizenship—for, as one text put it, by "systematic home visiting," Americanization efforts ultimately aimed to "secure," "the interest in citizenship of all the adults in the family" (Winkler and Alsberg

53). A clear manifestation of gendered linguistic domestication, the Home and Neighborhood Teacher aimed to "secure" an interest in American *citizenship* for immigrants—an echo of the way American women were to "secure" good manners for American "civilization"—and yet another indication of the myriad ways in which gender and language might be combined to manage American citizenship.

4. CONCLUSION: LINGUISTIC BEARERS OF CITIZENSHIP

> Obviously, Americanization is something more than dealing with the immigrant in school. And obviously, too, the school is taking only the first step in Americanization when it breaks down the language barrier. The Americanization leader and the Americanization teacher must know something more than how to teach one subject or other to immigrants. She must know what Americanization really means, in its larger aspects. She must know America and what America stands for and must be able to interpret America to the immigrant in language that he will understand. She must know, too, what citizenship really means—not that citizenship which is measured in terms of the immigrant's knowledge of naturalization requirements, but that citizenship which is the expression of the American spirit that the good citizen believes in, swears by, and loves. She must know how to communicate her knowledge in such a way that good citizenship will be the actual fruit of her teaching. (Mahoney, Wetmore et al., *Training Teachers for Americanization* [1920] 10–11).

As *Training Teachers for Americanization* notes, learning English was an important "first step" in Americanization. Yet, as this passage also expresses, Americanization involved instilling an ineffable "something more," something beyond how to teach "one subject or other," something beyond requirements for naturalization. Americanization ultimately aimed to develop "that citizenship which is the expression of the American spirit that the good citizen believes in, swears by, and loves." *This* ideal citizenship is, strikingly, one built not on tangible political participation or civic engagement but on the intangibles of *affect*—faith, loyalty, and devotion—the bonds of kinship, the ties of family.

It is significant that, even as women were commissioned with ever-widening linguistic responsibilities at the end of the 19th century and the beginning of the 20th, their roles were yet grounded in their "natural" capacities of reproduction and nurturance—at this point in history, as we have seen, not simply biological reproduction, but social, linguistic, indeed *national* reproduction, the reproduction of American culture if not American children. Seen as reproducers and nurturers of culture, as in the passage above, women civilizers and Americanizers were seen to possess the special linguistic and domestic skills to interpret and communicate the "American spirit." Thus women were depicted as the bearers of good linguistic breeding in verbal criticism and manners manuals—"good breeding" without which, James says, "intercourse fails to flower into fineness" and "human relations bear but crude and tasteless fruit." Likewise, they were figured in Americanization texts such as *Training Teachers for Americanization*, above, as the bearers of the "actual fruit" of "good citizenship."

Even as early-20th-century women took on increasingly national responsibilities, then, the emphasis on their linguistic roles as reproducers of culture in manners manuals and Americanization texts continued to reflect a domestic view of them, and to circumscribe women's national participation in subtle ways. In verbal criticism and manners manuals, discourses of gendered linguistic domestication managed anxieties about American "civilization" by governing women's vocal tone in the home and family. In much the same way, in Americanization texts, discourses of gendered linguistic domestication managed anxieties about American citizenship by directing women's voices in a wider, cultural arena through ideas about language education. These discourses ultimately governed women's voices for the *national* family, such that women's teaching of English and other domestic arts to immigrant women became the dual domestication of "alien sisters," native and foreign alike. As women approached the attainment of the suffrage, gendered national language ideologies thus continued to govern their voices and to domesticate their national participation—as well as the participation of those newcomers whom they were quite "naturally" charged to nurture.

Coda
Herland and "The Future of English": Considering Language, Gender, and National Identity in Early-20th-Century America

"If we are good boys and learn our lessons well," I suggested. "If we are quiet and respectful and polite and they are not afraid of us—then perhaps they will let us out. And anyway—when we do escape, it is of immense importance that we know the language."

Personally, I was tremendously interested in that language, and seeing they had books, was eager to get at them, to dig into their history, if they had one.

It was not hard to speak, smooth and pleasant to the ear, and so easy to read and write that I marvelled at it. They had an absolutely phonetic system, the whole thing was as scientific as Esparanto yet bore all the marks of an old and rich civilization. (Charlotte Perkins Gilman, *Herland* [1915] 33)

Charlotte Perkins Gilman gave language a notable place in imagining what the nation could be in her novel of a utopian, all-female *Herland* (1915), published not quite a century after Washington Irving fantasized the founding of America as Rip Van Winkle's awakening to a new language of democracy. As Rip experiences this new language as a perfectly bewildering "Babylonish jargon" to which he must grow accustomed, Gilman's narrator Vandyck "Van" Jennings and his two adventuresome college classmates awaken in Herland as foreigners who must also "learn the language" (29)—a "clear musical fluent speech" (17)—in order to make their way around in, and perhaps out of, this land where early-20th-century gender expectations are reversed to the extent that, as Van would put it, "in Herland women were 'the world'" (135). Van reiterates the importance of language, for "as soon as we learned the language—and would agree to do no harm—they would show us all about the land" (46). In noting that the three men must "learn [their] lessons well" and be "respectful and polite" before learning further about Herland and gaining a degree of self-possession in it, Van recognizes the role of both language education and language manners—topics of the previous chapter—to national acculturation. The importance of language education to national acculturation was not missed on Gilman herself, who spent time at Addams' Hull-House in 1896 (Bryan and Davis 6–7). Nor was the importance of language to national identity missed on Gilman; underlining the centrality of language to the "national growth" of the novel's nation of women, Van remarks, "[. . .] with their sublimated mother-love, expressed in terms of widest social activity, every phase of their work was modified by its effect on the national growth. The language itself they had deliberately clarified, simplified, made easy and beautiful, for the sake of the children" (*Herland* 103). The need to learn the Herlanders' phonetic, Esperanto-like, civilized language, which Gilman makes the very expression of Herland's matriarchal national culture, binds the Herlanders themselves together as much as it marks the three Americans as outsiders in Herland.

In conceiving language as just such an extension of this utopian national community and as a means of acculturation to it, Gilman shares a set of beliefs with those of Irving's day who had likewise imagined the nation as an ideal speech community. Noah Webster returns to mind: Webster figured American English, with its own lexicon and orthography, as "a band of *national union*" fusing the young patriarchal nation, much as the Herlanders' language unites their ancient matriarchal civilization.[1] Gilman's gendered reformulation of some of Webster's linguistic and national ideals thus provides a logical endpoint for the trajectory of this project: Gilman's imagination in *Herland* of a matriarchal nation with its own unique "band of *national union*" in many ways represents the culmination of the prior century's practice of combining notions of gender and language to recast the idea of the American nation and to reframe who might become an American citizen in the historical moment when women finally gained the franchise.

At the same time, in this coda, I am interested in connecting Gilman with another early-20th-century theorist of language—H.L. Mencken—whose work similarly engages constructions of language, nation, and gender in ways that help us look forward to the 20th-century implications of this project. Fittingly, Mencken's and Gilman's day marked the waning of 19th-century nation building and the fading of views of American English as a dialect of British English, as well as the ending of the fight for women's suffrage that began in Webster's lifetime. Moreover, with their varying degrees of prescience, Mencken and Gilman together highlight the continuing force of interarticulated ideas about language, gender, and nation into the 20th century. Both writers imagine globally-situated national utopias similarly bound by visions of gender and language, such that Gilman's *Herland* and Mencken's "The Future of English" begin to suggest that gendered language ideologies may contribute not only to conceptions of national citizenship, but also to fantasies of America as a global citizen, and not simply in Gilman's and Mencken's day, but in our own day as well.

Herland reaffirms how a national language signals political unity, both within Herland and in opposition to other nations. Yet, because the whole of *Herland* is saturated with awareness of gender ideologies,

Gilman's utopian romance and social reform novel also shows us how national language ideologies may be pervaded by gender—specifically, how gender may surface in discussions of language to mediate national identity. In doing so, *Herland* compels us to look not only to the "voicing" of America in Webster's day, but also to its gendered rearticulation in Gilman's own day. For example, *Herland's* discussion of different understandings of the words *men* and *women*—a conversation about gender and language—strikingly highlights national differences. In this conversation, Van comments:

> When we say *men, man, manly, manhood,* and all the other masculine derivatives, we have in the background of our minds a huge vague crowded picture of the world and all its activities. To grow up and "be a man," to "act like a man"—the meaning and connotation is wide indeed. That vast background is full of marching columns of men, of changing lines of men, of long processions of men; of men steering their ships into new seas, exploring unknown mountains, breaking horses, herding cattle, ploughing and sowing and reaping, toiling at the forge and furnace, digging in the mine, building roads and bridges and high cathedrals, managing great businesses, teaching in all the colleges, preaching in all the churches; of men everywhere, doing everything—"the world."
>
> And when we say *Women,* we think *Female*—the sex.
>
> But to these [Herland] women, in the unbroken sweep of this two-thousand-year-old feminine civilization, the word *woman* called up all that big background, so far as they had gone in social development; and the word *man* meant to them only *male*—the sex.
>
> Of course we could *tell* them that in our world men did everything; but that did not alter the background of their minds. That man, "the male," did all these things was to them a statement, making no more change in the point of view than was made in ours when we first faced the astounding fact—to us—that in Herland women were "the world." (135)

These observations about words calling up a "big background" in the mind certainly attest to the complex relationship between language and thought in general. They also, for Van, indicate national affiliation and invite comparison across the national borders of America—where *man* calls up "the world"—and Herland—where *woman* does. Gilman's novel thus suggests the ways in which gender could surface in conversations about language and nation in an international context. In this sense, Gilman shares a set of beliefs with not only Webster, but also H. L. Mencken, who likewise envisioned language in the early 20th century as a national emblem in an international context and used notions of gender to heighten his comparisons of nations' languages.

That Gilman and Mencken might have shared some beliefs about language might very well seem strange, particularly since they could be seen as taking opposite positions on "The Woman Question" in the years when women finally won the right to vote. Gilman was a political progressive whose *Women and Economics* (1898) influenced generations of American women and became known across the globe, as one reviewer put it, "as the outstanding book on Feminism."[2] Considered liberal in the 1920s and conservative in the 1930s, Mencken's politics have been difficult to pinpoint, although he was dependably notorious for his caustic, ruthless criticism of everything—including democracy and women, as seen in his 1918 *In Defense of Women*. Originally written as "a *pastiche* of proverbs," in Mencken's words, to avoid the subject of international politics after his antidemocratic wartime essays had been greeted with "antipathy," *In Defense of Women,* if a defense of women at all, is a convoluted one (*Defense* xxi, xix).[3] Given the vast differences between these two contemporary autodidacts, their commentary comprises an excellent illustration of how gendered, national verbal hygiene could come from across the sociopolitical spectrum. Moreover, Gilman's awareness of how ideas about gender pervade the relationship between language and nation fascinatingly calls our attention to her contemporary's explicit use of gender to figure the relationship between language and nation—and, eventually, to propose the global superiority of American English.

One hundred years after Irving published "Rip Van Winkle," in the same year that Congress approved the Nineteenth Amendment granting women the right to vote, Mencken published the first edition of his monumental *The American Language* (1919), whose popularity extended beyond the almost-thirty years over which he added to it. As Mencken announced and as Webster predicted, in the century-plus following Webster's *Dissertations* and ending in *The American Language,* America grew from a former colony to a world power, and American English moved from a dialect of British English to a global language (Webster, *Dissertations* 22–23; Webster, Intro to *An American Dictionary* in Babbidge 172–73). When Mencken finished the first edition of *The American Language,* it pivoted on three main ideas: (1) that American English and British English had diverged and were becoming separate languages, an announcement that fulfilled Webster's vision in his *Dissertations;* (2) that nationalism was the source of the new American language; and (3) that the brilliance of the American language lies in the lawlessness of "vulgar" speech in opposing Standard English—or, as others such as Whitman had put it before him, that the creative force of language came from the "common people." By the significantly enlarged fourth edition of the text in 1936, Mencken had expanded his thesis: Not only had American English diverged from British, but it now subjugated British English—a formulation that achieved widespread critical and popular response.[4] American English, he claimed, became recognizably different from British English in the age of Andrew Jackson—the

American president, in fact, whose policies provoked women to petition. Not insignificantly for Mencken's ideas about national language, Jackson was Mencken's "archetype of the new American who appeared after 1814—ignorant, pushful, impatient of restraint and precedent, an iconoclast, a Philistine, an Anglophobe in every fiber" (*American Language* 132). In the plain-speaking, uproarious, expansionistic Jacksonian age, Mencken wrote, "America began to stand for something quite new in the world—in government, in law, in public and private morals, in customs and habits of mind, in the minutiae of social intercourse. And simultaneously the voice of America began to take on its characteristic tone-colors, and the speech of America began to differentiate itself unmistakably from the speech of England" (133). When reevaluating the language in his own day, Mencken even suggested that American English "maintained [its general characteristics] unbrokenly since Jackson's day, though there was a formidable movement to bring it into greater accord with English precept and example during the years following the Civil War," a movement led by "purists" such as Edward S. Gould and Richard Grant White and supported by "Anglomaniacs" and "schoolmarms" (164).

In characterizing the growth of American English over the 19th century, Mencken rallied notions of gender. Perhaps most memorably revealing Mencken's gendered discussion of national language is his invocation of this priggish schoolmarm, whom the American language had successfully resisted over the century. For Mencken, the "average American schoolmarm" is "the chief guardian of linguistic niceness in the Republic" (*American Language* 326-27). These schoolmarms, Mencken says, create "most of the gratuitous rules and regulations that afflict schoolboys and harass the writers of the country" and "are the chief discoverers and denouncers of 'bad English' in the books of such men as Whitman, Mark Twain and Howells" (326-27). Though priggish pedagogues of Mencken's day were, as he notes, both male and female (164), Mencken's pedagogue is nonetheless persistently figured, in opposition to the schoolboys and (male) writers mentioned above, as a *schoolmarm,* a thoroughly feminized figure, 'a woman teacher, especially one who is regarded as strict, old-fashioned, or prudish' (*American Heritage Dictionary,* 3rd ed.). And Mencken's long introduction of pedagogues in his volume—an introduction in which his pedagogues are associated with Mother's Day, then morph into the General Federation of Women's Clubs, then become reforming schoolmarms—strongly attests to his feminization of these forces of standardization (*American Language* 51). Again, he repeats: "For many years the indefatigable schoolmarm has been trying to put down the American vulgate, but with very little success. At great pains she teaches her pupils the rules of what she conceives to be correct English, but the moment they get beyond reach of her constabulary ear they revert to the looser and more natural speech-habits of home and work-place" (417). For Mencken, much of the genius of

American English, unlike British English, is that it resists the feminizing forces of the reforming schoolmarm.

Mencken extends these ideas in his chapter "The Future of the Language" and in his April 1935 *Harper's Magazine* article, "The Future of English," in which he explicitly invokes notions of gender to cement American language and national identity and to extend the reach of American language around the globe. Notably, Mencken quotes extensively from Danish linguist and English grammarian Otto Jespersen—who stated that "It [English] seems to me positively and expressly masculine. It is the language of a grown-up man, and has very little childish or feminine about it" (*Growth and Structure* 2 qtd. in "Future of English" 87; also qtd. in "Future of the Language" 599).[5] Jespersen, as Mencken notes, sees the language as "masculine" because "it is grounded chiefly upon clarity, directness, and force" and because its "grammatical baldness" is a "chief source" of its "vigor": "The prevalence of very short words in English, and the syntactical law which enables it to dispense with the definite article in many constructions 'where other languages think it indispensable, *e.g.,* "life is short," "dinner is ready"'—these are further marks of vigor and clarity, according to Dr. Jespersen" (Mencken, "Future of the Language" 599–600).

Based on its simplicity, clarity, logic, and economy, Mencken and Jespersen, then, both figure English as "masculine." In addition, the fact that Mencken often quotes Jespersen is noteworthy because elsewhere Jespersen, likewise, infuses his study of language with notions of gender, as when he states:

> Men will certainly with great justice object that there is a danger of the language becoming languid and insipid if we are always to content ourselves with women's expressions, and that vigour and vividness count for something. [. . .] Men thus become the chief renovators of the language, and to them are due those changes by which we sometimes see one term replace an older one, to give way in turn to a still newer one, and so on. [. . .] This is not invalidated by the fact that quite recently, with the rise of the feminist movement, many young ladies have begun to imitate their brothers in that as well as in other respects. (Jespersen, "The Woman" [1922] 212)[6]

In the context of his reference to "the rise of the feminist movement," it is difficult not to read Jespersen's recourse to gender and language here as co-opting women's political voices as mere mimicry of men's, a strategy for recognizing their new political voices without allowing "real" ownership of or access to a masculine national, political language. Jespersen's gesture to this sociopolitical context for his metalinguistic commentary equally illuminates Mencken's insistence that American English is "masculine" because it resists standardization. As Mencken notes in *The American Language:* "Every successful effort at standardization, as

Dr. Ernest Weekley has well said, results in nothing better than emasculation. 'Stability in language is synonymous with *rigor mortis*.' It is the very anarchy of English, adds Claude de Crespigny, that has made it the dominant language of the world today" (*American Language* 607). For Mencken, standardization is paramount to linguistic emasculation, a clear combination of notions of language and gender.

Given Jespersen's influence on Mencken's ideas about language and gender, it was a short leap for Mencken, in "The Future of English," to call on gender to cast American English as superior to British English and to explain the language's imperial capacity. Mencken again invokes the gendered figure of the schoolmarm, cunningly evaded by an agile, masculine American English: "The school-ma'am has been trying since the Revolution to bring American English to her rules, but it goes on sprouting and coruscating in spite of her, like the vigorous organism it is. My guess is that it will eventually conquer the English of England, and so spread its gaudy inventions round the globe" ("Future of English" 89). English, Mencken continues, meaning British English, "has been yielding to American for fifty years past, and since the turn of the century it has been yielding at a constantly accelerated rate" (89). Here, Mencken's repetition of the term "yielding" emphasizes the activity of "American" in contrast to the passivity of British English—a feminized, if not sexualized, passivity that Mencken further accentuates when he notes that "American" has almost colonized "English": "it is really too late for the English to guard the purity of their native tongue, for so many Americanisms have already got into it that, on some levels at least, it is now almost an American dialect" (90). Mencken imagines American English itself as a kind of virile young bachelor, able to resist the feminizing, standardizing forces of the schoolma'am and, unlike British English, to embrace change and to proliferate with abundance. For he pronounces that "English [and here again Mencken means British English], subjected to a violent policing in the Eighteenth Century, has scarcely recovered; it is still a bit tight, a bit stiff, more than a little artificial. But American, having escaped that policing and become quickly immune to the subsequent school-ma'am, has gone on developing with almost Elizabethan prodigality" (90). In rallying ideas about gender in his rhetoric on nation and language, Mencken at once unifies national identities, gendered identities, and attitudes about language. "Plainly enough," Mencken predicts in his final sentence, "the conquest of the world by English, if it ever comes off, will really be a conquest by American" (90), a prediction that some would argue has come true today—but less because of the *language's* inherent masculinity than because of the economic and military might of those who speak it.[7] Yet Mencken's strongly gendered rhetoric to imagine this global linguistic conquest disguises such economic and political factors as language's "natural" reach.

Mencken's impact on American linguistics has been difficult to assess, although no one would disagree that *The American Language* was, and is, monumental. In part, it is difficult to evaluate because Mencken's linguistics lean more toward the literary inspiration of the 19th century than the scientific inquiry of the 20th, as Raymond Nelson notes: "One of his [Mencken's] peculiar philological strengths lay in his ability to extend nineteenth-century attitudes to his own concerns of language and history" (688, 669). This, perhaps, makes Mencken even more relevant to this study, for Mencken's *American Language* "is closer in kind to nineteenth-century scholarly enterprises on a grand scale, which aspired to be definitive rather than incremental. Mencken's contribution to his discipline, then, comes from an ancestral distance and is not so much practical as it is spiritual, if we may allow ourselves so unmenckenian a concept" (688). Nelson and others have traced this "ancestral distance" to Noah Webster. But, as I hope to have shown, we might also consider tracing it to a host of 19th-century historical contexts and intellectual predecessors who likewise used commentary about language as a forum for ideas about the nation—or who, in Nelson's words, "used philology as a way of expressing a personal vision of national and civilized values" (689).

Mencken was the product of a 19th- and early-20th-century American culture that put an enormous amount of energy toward the study of language—evidenced not only by the wide-reaching, popularly-consumed commentary on language in periodicals, congressional records, grammar books, pronunciation manuals, slang dictionaries, dialect studies, and treatises on linguistic etiquette by those from James Fenimore Cooper and Seth Hurd to William Dwight Whitney and Richard Grant White, but also by the successive founding of professional philological organizations between 1869, when the American Philological Association was created, and 1924, when the Linguistics Society of America was formed. Perhaps more importantly, Mencken inherited a kind of linguistic essentialism, wherein language expressed essential identity, gendered or otherwise—a linguistic essentialism that was situated within heightened anxiety about American identity and national citizenship. Given these inheritances, Mencken calls attention to the ways in which conceptions of gender could be coupled with discussions of language to promote national identity in yet another key moment for examining national citizenship: the moment when women won the right to vote. Commentary about language like Mencken's could thus become a theater for masculinity in a national culture that, many had claimed, had become "feminized" and was still becoming "American."

Gilman and Mencken, in rallying ideas about language, gender, and nation, help us to reconsider Webster's moment and the 19th century. As the utopian *Herland* ultimately reveals, using gendered notions of language to achieve national political unity may only be possible in the philological fantasy worlds imagined by writers like Gilman. But Gilman and Mencken moreover prompt us to consider the ways in which gender ideologies might be invoked or expressed in and through American language to govern voices in today's national, international, and global contexts. Together looking forward to our day in their own distinct ways, Gilman's and Mencken's works suggest that interarticulated expressions of language, gender, and nation continue to be relevant in our contemporary moment, as the American "nation" mightily propagates ideas about democratic citizenship around the world, and as Mencken's "sprouting and coruscating" American language continues to achieve a global reach.

Notes

NOTES TO INTRODUCTION

1. Webster inherited the idea that a nation should have what Thomas Wilson called a "good language," a sign of the People's "Genius" and the nation's legitimacy (3–4). An independent American language was also, for Webster and many of his contemporaries, a means of declaring cultural independence from Great Britain, where many considered American English "a colonial dialect, with a corrupt and barbarous pronunciation, and a vocabulary, interspersed with strange and unknown terms of transatlantic manufacture" (Silliman 2: 227–28 qtd. in Bailey, *Images* 129).
2. R. Smith clearly describes the contested nature of the terms *citizen* and *citizenship* in *Civic Ideals;* see esp. 13–14. Smith's argument that U.S. citizenship is the product of multiple traditions (not only liberalism and republicanism, but also a strong ascriptive tradition that exists alongside these and embraces nativist, sexist, and racist thinking) has fundamentally shaped my thinking. I thank Joshua Miller for directing me to Smith's work. I also thank Christine DiStefano for recommending Holland's *The Body Politic,* which persuasively argues that the ascriptive tradition Smith identifies exists *within* liberalism and has been maintained there through the figure of the human body.
3. For Sollors, American ideology has navigated the tension between the two terms *descent* and *consent,* "between the rejection of hereditary old-world hierarchies [. . .] and the vision of a new people of diverse nativities united in the fair pursuit of happiness," and ethnic American texts tell stories expressing the persistent conflict between the two terms (4–5). As I draw on Sollors' paradigm, I similarly build on scholarship (e.g., Crane and Thomas) that emphasizes the importance of the opposing discourses of contract and identity in American literature and culture. For a discussion of the potential of contract to refigure social and political relations in terms of assent and practice rather than identity, see esp. Crane 185–90. I hope, then, in part, to bring a consideration of contract into discussions of language, and conversely, conversations about language into discussions of contract.
4. Or, in R. Smith's useful formulation, supporting a model of citizenship based on ascribed characteristics of race, gender, or one's nationality or religion of birth (3).
5. See again Webster, *Dissertations* 22–23. See also Webster's introduction to his *American Dictionary,* considered the pinnacle of his philological career, in which he observed that "No person in this country will be satisfied with the English definitions of the words *congress, senate* and *assembly, court,* &c., for although these are words used in England, yet they are applied in

this country to express ideas which they do not express in that country" (excerpted in Babbidge 170).
6. While I find Bederman's description of *gender* persuasive, I have also been influenced by similarly constructionist accounts of gender by Butler, Crawford, Foucault, Fuss, and Jehlen.
7. A contributor to *The North American Review,* Walter Channing, like Webster, sees a national *language* as the first step toward a national *literature,* a first step to declaring cultural independence from England. See also William Ellery Channing's "Remarks on American Literature" (1830), also published in the *Review*. Mid-19th-century literary nationalists such as John O'Sullivan ("The Great Nation of Futurity" [1839]) and Evert Duyckinck ("Nationality in Literature" [1847]) might likewise be seen as inheritors of Webster's comprehensive cultural nationalism.
8. I am grateful to Molly Wallace for suggesting Althusser's "A Letter on Art" for a formulation of literature's relationship to ideology that I worked to articulate. Unlike Althusser, I do not make a distinction between "authentic art" (he cites, for example, Balzac, Solzhenitsyn, and Tolstoy) and "works of an average or mediocre level" (222); I see both "authentic" and "average" art as "bathed in" and "alluding to" ideology. In some sense, then, I follow Tompkins' choice of both canonical authors and "popular" authors "to explore the way that literature has power in the world, to see how it connects with the beliefs and attitudes of large masses of readers so as to impress or move them deeply" (*Sensational* xiv).
9. Elsewhere, Althusser (in "Ideology and Ideological State Apparatuses") and Zizek (in "The Spectre of Ideology") have carefully defined *ideology* and delineated its modes of circulation. I have found particularly useful Zizek's extension of *ideology* in three directions: "ideology as a complex of ideas (theories, convictions, beliefs, argumentative procedures); ideology in its externality, that is the materiality of ideology, Ideological State Apparatuses [such as Althusser's church, school, family, etc.]; and finally, the most elusive domain, the 'spontaneous' ideology at work at the heart of social 'reality' itself" (9). While I am interested in the interplay among these three senses of *ideology,* when I speak of national language ideologies, I most often refer to the first of these senses. And in speaking of national language ideolog*ies,* I mean to make the distinction that Althusser does in "Ideological State Apparatuses" when differentiating between *ideologies*—particular, historically situated ideologies that demand a kind of diachronic approach—and *ideology* in general, which demands a kind of synchronous, structural approach.
10. Cameron is interested "in the possibility that verbal hygiene [commentary about language] in the abstract is as basic to the use of language as vowels are to its phonetic structure, and as deserving of serious study" (1). In addition to Cameron and Lippi-Green, Bailey and Baron are among those who take attitudes about language as a serious part of linguistic study, with Bailey's cultural histories of the English language particularly rich resources.
11. Cameron's term captures equally prescriptive and anti-prescriptive aspects of "a single (and normative) activity: a struggle to control language by defining its nature" (8). *Verbal hygiene* thus includes a wide spectrum of metalinguistic behaviors, both "liberal" and "conservative," that evaluate language—including noninstitutional activities, such as mimicking people's accents or commenting on people's profanity, and institutional ones, such as participating in dialect preservation or spelling reform societies, taking courses in the arts of communication, reading conversational improvement literature, editing prose to suit house style, or producing (or opposing) non-sexist usage guidelines (9).

12. For example, I draw together studies of the English language, such as Baron's *Grammar and Good Taste* and *Grammar and Gender,* that often separate histories of national language reform (which tend to exclude gender as a significant concern) from studies of gender and language (which tend to exclude nation as a salient feature). While diverse languages have long existed in America—see Sollors, *Multilingual America*—my focus here is on the English language.
13. I cite here Looby's reading of Irving's Mustapha letters in *Salmagundi* (1807–08) (Irving, *History* 144 qtd. in Looby 79).
14. Levander focuses not on women orators or women's writing, but on the cultural significance of the female voice, suggesting that novels centering on the female voice deconstruct the bourgeois distinction between public and private spheres and intervene in public discourse more than has been recognized (5). I concentrate at least in part on discussions about women's voices, as Levander does, and I similarly understand that commentary about the female voice "assumed a public function, despite theories that argued women lacked the capacity for public activity" (Levander 2–3). My views often coincide with Levander's observations, in her first chapter, that fictional and historical depictions of women's voices often correlated with the creation and reinforcement of a masculine public sphere. This argument likewise resembles N. Johnson's rhetorical study, which illustrates that postbellum rhetorical codes located women in the domestic sphere. Yet I depart from both Levander and Johnson in a couple of significant ways: first, by situating these discussions and representations of women's voices within a wider national context of commentary about gender and language—with an emphasis on both *gender* (as masculinity *and* femininity) and *language* (as writing as well as speech); and, second, by arguing that such gendered commentary about language, even if perhaps most visible in commentary about women's voices, could effectively marginalize not only *women* but also, as I discuss below, Native Americans, African Americans, and immigrants from public and, notably, *political* life, tempering expanding ideas of citizenship.
15. In addition to Looby's and Levander's books, there have been a host of works in literary studies and composition-rhetoric studies, among other fields, titled after and/or engaged in making sense of the vague concept of "voice." I cue off of these works but also differ from them by reading rather abstract notions of voice in the context of multiple, material concerns with the vote in American literature and culture. My interest in the plural *voices* is intended to emphasize this fact, versus the use of the singular *voice* which veers toward a more monolithic notion of "voice" (as seen in titles by Cutter, Linkon, Portelli, and Schueller). In composition-rhetoric studies, "voice" has long been a metaphor associated with authentic subjectivity (i.e., the idea of helping students find their "voice" through writing instruction). Bowden extends J. Harris' critique of such expressivist notions of voice as positing a kind of authenticity and critiques voice as a metaphor that has "outlived its usefulness" (viii). Yet in focusing on voice in the 1970s, 80s, and 90s, Bowden misses crucial 19th-century background for the metaphor; the historical embeddedness of the metaphor is an argument less for its elimination than for its illumination. From this perspective, then, *Language, Gender, and Citizenship in American Literature* might be seen as an attempt to write a literary-historicist version of the language-oriented trope of voice through exploration of ideas about voic*es*.
16. Although the term *franchise* can invoke a range of citizenship rights and privileges granted by a government, I use it in its fullest and most general sense, as the right to vote. Likewise, while *suffrage* can have subtle

connotations (e.g., the distinction between sufferance and suffrage, see Crane 157), I use the term in its most basic sense as the right or privilege of voting.
17. Particularly helpful for an understanding of the former are Kerber and De Hart's *Women's America* and J. Baker's *Votes for Women*.
18. While these topics are worthy grounds for another project, a cursory consideration of geography might lead to observations that ideas about gender and language could help to unite geographic regions (as shown in chapters one and three, in which gendered ideas about, respectively, petitioning and dialect forged connections across North and South) and could work to define places more clearly (such as the urban and domestic spaces discussed in chapters two and four).

NOTES TO CHAPTER 1

1. Hereafter, I refer to Native American Indians as *Indians,* as this is the terminology used by the writers of the period.
2. One of the nation's first and most influential periodicals, *The North American Review* gives us a sense of the attitudes and public discussion circulating around the complexly overlapping topics of women, Indians, language, American literature, and national boundaries in the 1820s and 30s. For more on the mission, circulation, and national standing of this publication, see Nourie and Nourie 333–34; Mott, *History* 1: 514; Mott, *American* 207. The periodical peaked during the period that is the focus of this chapter—the 1830s—particularly between 1830 and 1836, when it focused on American political problems (Mott, *History* 2: 234).
3. See Wills 35–43 for a vivid sketch of the relatively stable social world of the founding fathers, based largely on inheritance.
4. In addition to Connors, Bizzell's "Praising Folly" and Cmiel's *Democratic Eloquence* reveal how the study of rhetoric was traditionally and rather strictly limited to males. Kerber's *Toward an Intellectual History of Women* helpfully discusses conflicting ideas about women's education in post-Revolutionary America—the need to educate women for republican motherhood alongside the contradictory yet longstanding association of intellectual activity with masculinity—as well as ideas about masculine citizenship in various historical contexts.
5. According to Connors in his first chapter, between 1830 (when there were no women on college campuses) and 1890 (when three-quarters of American colleges were admitting women), there was unprecedented change in the educational culture; he argues that rhetoric, which entered the 19th century as an argumentative discipline, primarily oral and civic, exited the century as composition, primarily written and privatized.
6. This chapter is indebted to a few excellent studies on U. S. women's petitioning in the fields of history and rhetoric and works to extend them into literary and language study: Hershberger's "Mobilizing Women, Anticipating Abolition: The Struggle Against Indian Removal in the 1830s," Portnoy's *Their Right To Speak: Women's Activism in the Indian and Slave Debates,* hereafter cited as *Their Right,* as well as her *"A Right to Speak on the Subject": The Development of Women's Political Expression in the United States,* hereafter cited as *A Right,* and Zaeske's *Signatures of Citizenship: Petitioning, Antislavery, and Women's Political Identity*. While my project builds on these works, it also departs from them by explicitly bringing petitioning into historicist study of 19th-century American literature. Despite

the historical importance of women's antebellum petitioning, the topic has received little attention among literary scholars. I thank Gail Stygall for initially calling my attention to Portnoy's work, which is singular in its nuanced integration of gender, race, and nation in the study of debates over the rights of women, Native Americans, and African Americans during this period.
7. For more on the novel's implications for Puritan historiography and historical romance, see Arch; Baym, *American Women Writers* 152–86; Bell; and Gould.
8. Perhaps it comes as no surprise that *Hope Leslie* received almost unanimously positive reviews—the novelistic form allowed Sedgwick to envision situations that neither "genuine history" nor overtly political writing could entertain in Jacksonian America. In fact considered "the queen of American letters" in the first half of the 19th century, Sedgwick was extremely successful both popularly and critically, and by the 1830s most critics ranked her with James Fenimore Cooper, Washington Irving, and William Cullen Bryant (Beach 1). *Hope Leslie* received almost unanimously positive reviews at home and in England, where Jacksonian Americans looked for literary approval. In reviews of the novel, *Western Monthly Review* was singularly tepid. The London *Athanaeum, The Ladies' Magazine,* and *The North American Review* all gave warm reviews. As Sarah J. Hale's *Woman's Record* put it, *Hope Leslie* "continued to be [Sedgwick's] most popular tale; and, indeed, no novel written by an American, except, perhaps, the early works of Cooper, ever met with such success" (777). Attesting to Sedgwick's favor with general readers, a penciled inscription on the last page of a first edition of *Hope Leslie* reads: "Miss Sedgwick the author of this tale is an old maid of about 40 years of age. I have seen her and was [illegible] pleased with her intelligence and unvanity" (Kroupa). While the bulk of early-20th-century literary critics neglected Sedgwick's work, *Hope Leslie* has experienced a critical revival since Kelley's 1987 edition of the novel and her 1993 publication of Sedgwick's autobiography and journal. For additional biographical materials, see E. Foster's biography as well as Sedgwick's *Life and Letters* and *Power of Her Sympathy.*
9. Jackson's policies worked hand-in-hand with Georgia's rulings. In his first Annual Message to Congress on December 8, 1829, Jackson made clear that there would be no possibility for independent Indian existence within states (Prucha, *Documents* 47–48). For accessible summaries of Jacksonian Indian removal policies, see Takaki 84–105 and Zinn 102–46. For an in-depth analysis, see Rogin.
10. For more on the William Penn essays, see Evarts, *Cherokee Removal* and Portnoy, *Their Right* 26–27, 29–43.
11. Beginning on October 1, 1838, their own petitions to Congress ignored, the roughly 17,000 Cherokees who remained—much like the Chocktaws, Chickasaws, and the Creeks in the years before them—were marched from Georgia to lands west of the Mississippi on what has become known as the Trail of Tears (Takaki 96–98; 129). This massive removal was supported by rhetoric that offered only an either/or choice for the Indians—that they would either be civilized (as a true "nation") or become extinct (as a "tribe" or "race"); Maddox shows that the authors who engaged the Indian Question, whether sympathetic to removal, unsympathetic to removal, or simply ambivalent, were all contained by this dualistic discourse of civilization or extinction, which also limited Jacksonian Indian policies (11).
12. Sedgwick's hesitancy could have come in part, as Kelley and Garvey both suggest, from her sensitivity about publicity and ambivalence about her

own expression of political opinion. Sedgwick's "lingering elitism combined with support for egalitarian democracy" made her see a cultural role, versus an outright political one, for elite women in a democracy (Kelley, *Hope Leslie* xv). For a good discussion of the tension between Sedgwick's aristocratic inheritances and egalitarian impulses, see D. Nelson, "Sympathy as Strategy."
13. In addition, after her separation from the Calvinism and conversion to the more "rational Christianity" of Unitarianism in 1821, Sedgwick was greatly influenced by the Unitarian minister William Ellery Channing, who, in his speeches and writings, reveals an astuteness about the repercussions of American imperialist doctrines of "manifest destiny" for Indians (Sedgwick, *Life and Letters* 181; Sedgwick, *Power of Sympathy* 119; W. E. Channing, "On the Annexation of Texas to the United States" 210). In July 1827 Sedgwick likewise corresponded with Lydia Maria Child (*Life and Letters* 187), who actively campaigned against Indian removal by 1828 with husband David Lee Child (Karcher, *Hobomok* 153). On Child's increasingly deliberate defense of Indian rights from *Hobomok* (1824) and her short stories (1827–29) to her "Appeal on Behalf of the Indians" (1868), see Karcher, *First Woman* 87, 553, 548.
14. While Davidson argues that "the concept of separate spheres is self-perpetuating in a way that is implausible and unhealthy whether inside or outside those spheres," Kerber concludes that the metaphor still resonates because it has at least "some superficial vitality" (Davidson, "No More" 456; Kerber, "Separate Spheres" 39). The pervasiveness of the separate spheres trope attests to its importance as well as to the necessity of seeing it, in a tempered fashion, as a historically-situated discursive product intertwined with multiple ideologies. Kaplan's "Manifest Domesticity" provides a first-rate example of this perspective; Kaplan calls attention to the double meaning of *domestic* as opposed not only to the *political* but also to the *foreign,* showing how the discourses of domesticity, nationalism, and imperialism overlap, as the development of domestic discourse, contemporaneous with the discourse of Manifest Destiny, had an "imperial reach," particularly in antebellum women's novels (584).
15. Thanks to Gregg Crane for leading me to this formulation. See Malsheimer, for example, for women's proto-feminist activity in benevolent societies. See Bloch on the Republican Mother.
16. Women were not allowed to speak in public throughout the 18th century; it was in the 19th century that women first began to speak in public—and not until the 1820s and 1830s did women appear on speakers' platforms in very limited numbers, and when they spoke in public on controversial or political topics, they elicited doubly disapproving responses (Cmiel 15, 70–71). In 1828, for example, when Frances Wright gave the first lecture series by a woman in Cincinnati, she captured the nation's attention with newspaper reports that claimed Wright had "ceased to be a woman" and had become "a female monster" (qtd. in Cmiel 70). For further fascinating commentary about Wright, see R. Smith 185–86 and Bode *Lyceum* 127. Abolitionist women like Angelina Grimké elicited similar commentary. Speaking publicly to audiences of both men and women called "promiscuous audiences" (Cmiel 71; Zaeske "Promiscuous"), Grimké's voice was the subject of newspaper commentary throughout the country, much of which attacked her "for violating feminine standards of decorum despite the refinement of her speech" (Cmiel 71; see also R. Smith 231). This censure, however, may have come as much because of the controversial national topics about which she spoke (slavery) as because of her gender.

17. I am grateful to Baron's *Grammar and Gender* for pointing out this shift in Cooper's characterization of the speech of American women upon his return to America after ten years in Europe (74). Certainly, Cooper's time in Europe could have contributed to his shift in attitude toward American women's speech. Yet, when coupled with cultural conversations in American periodicals about women's roles and women's use of language during this period, Cooper's changing attitude seems also to reflect a larger shift in popular attitudes about women and language over these years. As numerous historical linguists, critical linguists, and sociolinguists have shown, women's language has been contradictorily characterized for centuries. Scholars in language studies as diverse as Bailey, Baron, Cameron, T. Crowley, and Mugglestone, to name a few, have repeatedly noted such vexed and contradictory characterizations of "women's language."
18. The reviewers also highly praise Child's *Girl's Book* and *Mother's Book,* as each "takes up the child in at the nursery, and carries her through to matrimony,—a very important part of the female pilgrimage" (143).
19. This prescription seems to become particularly acute around 1835, when women's antislavery petitions significantly increased. Thomas Dew's severe "Dissertation on the Characteristic Differences between the Sexes, and on the Position and Influence of Woman in Society" (1835) clearly drives home this point. From a less vitriolic perspective, see Caleb Cushing's "The Social Condition of Women" (1836), 512–13. Cushing's views are notable because he was one of the few congressmen who supported the right to petition against slavery in the 1838 debates over antislavery petitions, yet he still clearly objects to women's political access.
20. Because *The Democratic Review* was first issued in late 1837, near the end of the period I explore in this chapter, I focus less on it than on *The North American Review,* which had been in circulation since 1815. Nevertheless, *The Democratic Review* is an important archive of fairly independent antebellum attitudes. See Mott, *History* 1: 677–84 and Nourie and Nourie 99–102, for background on the nationalistic niche of *The Democratic Review.*
21. See Pss. 20, 34 and 1 John 5:15 Revised Standard and King James Versions; Zaeske, *Petitioning* 4; Webster, *Compendious;* Buck 403. This sense of *petition* is characterized by the *OED,* 2nd ed. as 'a supplication or prayer; an entreaty; *esp.* a solemn and humble prayer to the Deity, or to a sovereign or superior.'
22. King *Ahasuerus* (in Hebrew) is also known as *Xerxes,* the transliteration of the Greek form of the Persian name *Khshayarshan* (Barker 720). Through her petition, Esther's people were spared, and Ahasuerus/Xerxes issued an edict granting them the right to assemble and to defend themselves (Esther 8:11). Other important, but perhaps less familiar, Biblical women petitioners include the five daughters of Zelophehad, who collectively petitioned Moses for property after their father's death (Num. 27), and Hannah, who petitioned God for a son and is sometimes credited with originating silent prayer (1 Sam. 1); thanks to Alicia Ostriker for these observations. Zaeske discusses how Esther was the most important example of several Jewish women who risked their lives to save their people (including Miriam, Deborah, Jael, and Huldah); Esther was especially invoked by Angelina Grimké in her appeals and addresses to women against slavery in 1836 (Zaeske, *Petitioning* 171). See also Portnoy 49–50, 203–05, 242–43 on Beecher's invocation of Esther.
23. See Portnoy 64 for a useful summary of ways, in addition to prayer, in which the petition was well-suited for women's appeals.
24. Petitioning gained unprecedented popularity during the years surrounding the English Revolution, a transatlantic context of which Sedgwick is aware in

Hope Leslie, when Everell and Sir Philip debate the question of "declar[ing] for King or Parliament," referring to Parliament's use of petitioning to gain popular rights from the king and the events that established the right of petition in British law (*Hope Leslie* 125). For an account of the events affecting the right of petition in England, see N. Smith 1153–70 and Zaeske, *Signatures* 13–15.

25. See S. Higginson for further discussion of how colonial petitions "assured a seamlessness of public and private governance" and originated more bills than any other process of legislation (145–56).
26. N. Smith notes that the founding fathers did not claim that petitioning itself had been punished, but that colonists' petitions had not been responded to favorably (1174).
27. Scholars today continue to disagree whether the Constitution's petition clause includes only the basic right to voice grievances to Congress, or whether it also entails the obligation to receive and consider those petitions. For example, N. Smith argues that the first amendment right to petition does not impose an obligation to listen or to respond, although it does protect the right to speak freely and petition freely. Hodgkiss, on the other hand, argues for the importance of the duty to *respond* to make petitioning a means of participating in democratic decision making—without response, she argues, the right to petition amounts to nothing more than freedom of speech (577).
28. As Bellah argues, Rousseau's thinking, as seen in the *Second Discourse* and *The Social Contract,* reflects the tension between classical liberalism and civic republicanism (279–80). For a good discussion of the tensions between liberal individualism and republicanism within the multifaceted philosophical inheritances of early- and mid-19th-century Americans (not only the republican and liberal traditions, but also an inegalitarian ascriptive tradition, a strong religious vision, belief in human progress, and a budding cosmopolitanism), see Crane 18–40.
29. Arguing that collective petitioning provides a lens into popular politics in 16th-century England, Hoyle observes that petitioning in large numbers to question the *status quo* could easily be seen as "a seditious activity" and "could prove dangerous for the activists behind the petitions" (367). My thanks to Robert Stacey for sharing Hoyle's work.
30. While the scope of this project unfortunately precludes my examination of them, it is worth mentioning that Indians themselves submitted petitions that were published in periodicals of the era, although their petitions were not submitted in the high numbers that women's antiremoval petitions were.
31. Esther Downing, Mrs. Winthrop's "perpendicular niece" (*Hope Leslie* 114) and Sir Philip Gardiner's young page Roslin/Rosa also petition at different occasions on behalf of their "sister" Hope. Yet their prayers are much more religious and much less political than Hope's or Magawisca's. In addition, their uplifted voices are problematic because these characters are temporarily or finally erased from the narrative via a kind of *deus ex machina* (Esther leaves the country, and Rosa dies in an explosion aboard Gardiner's escape vessel). Therefore, I focus on Hope's and Magawisca's petitions in my exploration.
32. Several scholars have explored themes of republican citizenship and the legitimate resistance to authority in *Hope Leslie* and in Sedgwick's work more broadly—themes in which I would situate the specific form of women's petitions. See esp. S. Harris; see also Garvey; Gould; and Karafilis. Another way of thinking about the novel's depiction of justified resistance to authority is in its proposing what Fetterley calls a "Republican Sisterhood," in which

sister and brother inhabit the same subject positions, and in which women like Hope and Magawisca have access to the same "American" virtues as men—independence, self-reliance, self-determination, and a willingness to challenge authority ("'My sister! My sister!'" 496–98).

33. Portnoy E-mail to author. Given her ambivalent position on women's political activism, it might be surprising if Sedgwick did sign such a petition. Yet, interestingly, Sedgwick *did* sign a petition for international copyright law in April 1838, indicating that, at least by then, she did not oppose the idea of petitioning herself and perhaps saw it as appropriate political action on certain issues ("Memorial of a Number of Citizens of New York, Praying the passage of an international copyright law"). I thank Melissa Homestead for calling this petition to my attention.

34. In England between 1641 and 1655, the Leveler women, seeking increased democracy in government, collectively petitioned with men, setting a precedent for women's political activism (Zaeske, *Signatures* 14).

35. Indian Memorial, 27 May 1762, Lynch Collection, Stockbridge Library Historical Room, Stockbridge, Mass., as cited in Woods Weierman, "Reading and Writing" n18.

36. See C. Sedgwick, "Slavery" 421–22 and H. Sedgwick 13–18. As historians such as Zilversmit have shown, Freeman's appeal was submitted within the context of the Massachusetts legislature's consideration of several other petitions on slavery. And as Kelley proposes in her introduction to Sedgwick's autobiography, Sedgwick in many additional ways recasts her own family history in *Hope Leslie* (31).

37. Sedgwick's interest in Freeman's interposition appears again in her unfinished antislavery manuscript, "Some pages of a Slave story I began and abandoned." Here once more, the fictional slave Meta "interposed her arm in time to receive" a blow aimed by her mistress at a weaker slave named Izzy (Sedgwick, "Some pages" 121). For more on this manuscript and Sedgwick's antislavery views, see Woods Weierman, "'A Slave Story.'" Sedgwick specifically uses the term *interposed* in both slave pieces. Clearly, Freeman's interpositions on behalf of her sister Lizzy/Izzy held strong imaginative hold over Sedgwick and others in the Sedgwick family—her brother recounts the same event, featuring "Mum Bett" and invoking the same language of interposition, in his lecture on the abolition of slavery (H. Sedgwick 15–16). In reading petitioning as one form of political intervention or "interposition" in the novel—one that in this case leads to Magawica's more dramatic "interposition" of her arm—I suggest that Magawisca's body works in conjunction with other "forms" in *Hope Leslie* to convey what Sedgwick apparently viewed as justified intervention on behalf of others. I thus supplement Stadler's reading of Magawisca's injury as evidence of her position as a racialized figure mediating "public" and "private" spheres of individual and national identification such that *Hope Leslie* "attempts to ensure a place for corporeality, for embodied struggle, in the history of the nation" (42).

38. Winthrop's power was in fact somewhat limited, as seen in colonial histories; colonial assemblies could and did use petitions to limit executive/gubernatorial powers (S. Higginson 152). Yet, at the same time, Winthop's response bears similarities to removal policies under Jackson, when the disavowal of executive power could excuse the federal government's inaction. On this point, see particularly Prucha, *Documents* and Rogin.

39. In addition to ignoring Everell's sympathetic advice, Magawisca rejects the advice of John Eliot, the "apostle to the Indians," to "speak humbly" because it "will grace thy cause with thy judges" (*Hope Leslie* 286). Sedgwick paints a sympathetic picture of both Everell Fletcher and John Eliot, who was a

Congregational clergyman called the "apostle of New-England" and was feminized by Anglophiles for his association with the Indians (8, 282). Such gendered depictions resembled characterizations of Jeremiah Evarts and British abolitionist George Thompson, who visited the U.S. in the mid-1830s: See *Register of Debates in Congress,* 23 Dec. 1835, 2067; and Rice 28, qtd. in Zaeske, *Petitioning* 156–57.

40. Crane's study is again apt here, as it recounts the higher law arguments made by 19th-century literary and cultural figures in an effort to sway the nation's "ethical consensus" and revise the nation's higher law jurisprudence. This court scene makes just such an argument in an attempt to sway the courtroom through Magawisca's access to ethical claims and revolutionary rhetoric.

41. Henry's famous, rallying words at the Virginia Convention on March 23, 1775 are interesting here in the context of ongoing petitioning efforts of some colonists who, at the convention, still continued to hold out hope that King George III would address their grievances, listed in the form of petitions. Even when the petitions of the First Continental Congress (1774) were ignored, the Second Continental Congress signed the Olive Branch petition on July 5, 1775 in a last-ditch effort to keep the peace with Great Britain (Wills 10, 17). Historically resonant, this scene also revisits the trials of antinominian Anne Hutchinson, who challenged Puritan orthodoxy and whose supporters refused to rally against the Pequods in the 1630s. See Kelley, *Hope Leslie* 356n3b and Fetterley, "'My sister! My sister!'" 513.

42. As several critics have pointed out, both Child and Cooper, like Sedgwick, tell similarly sympathetic tales of Indians and their eventual, presumably inevitable, disappearance from the North American landscape. All three writers were immensely popular, well-respected, and regularly reviewed in *The North American Review,* and their novels ranked among the founding fictions of American literature, answering the call for a national culture in the 1820s and 30s. Child and Sedgwick, however, depart from Cooper, whose *Wept of Wish-Ton-Wish,* though having similar interests in Puritan history and interracial relations, has different thematic emphases on the challenges of settling and civilizing the continent rather than on rewriting historical or patriarchal perspectives about these problems. While, as Simpson has asserted, Cooper's texts are much more complex than he is generally given credit for, Cooper generally leaves out an analysis of gender; thus there are greater similarities between Child's *Hobomok* and Sedgwick's *Hope Leslie.* As Karcher has suggested in her introduction to *Hobomok,* both use a romantic plotline to offer sensitive portraits of Indians, allying white women and Indians to mobilize public opinion against Indian dispossession, and both portray their female protagonists resisting the patriarchal structures that work to determine their fates. Yet Sedgwick's novel departs from Child's in more radically portraying the consensual and political nature of alliances between whites and Indians in the novel—a portrayal that reinforces Sedgwick's attention to the importance of a consensual language of petitioning to equal rights for all. *Hope Leslie's* Indian-white alliances are not only romantic but also sociopolitical alliances made by choice, while Child's alliances are decidedly more domestic arrangements made under duress or unsound mind, as is Mary Conant's marriage to Hobomok. See particularly Opfermann for more on the intertextual connections, especially the theme of intermarriage, among *Hobomok, Hope Leslie, Last of the Mohicans,* and *The Wept of Wish-Ton-Wish.*

43. "But one, who with a spirit-glance / Hath moved her country's heart, // And bade, from dim oblivion's trance / Poor Magawiska start, // Hath won a

fame, whose blossom rare / Shall fear no blighting sky, // Whose lustrous leaf grow fresh and fair, / Though Stockbridge bowl be dry" (Sigourney, "The Stockbridge Bowl" 201). Biographical materials reveal Sedgwick's various connections with women who opposed Indian removal: Sedgwick, *Life and Letters* 187–88, 261; Karcher, *Hobomok* xi; Stowe, *Life and Letters* 62; and E. Foster 20, 114–15.

44. Beecher reflects in her *Educational Reminiscences and Suggestions* on a conversation with Evarts about intervening on behalf of the Indians that "excited" her and other women of Hartford, including Sigourney, to write the circular, distributed through a network of benevolent societies throughout the country (62–64). See also Hershberger 24–25; Portnoy, *Their Right* 1, 43–51, 242–43. Among those who participated was Harriet Beecher Stowe, a student and teacher at her sister Catharine's Hartford Female Seminary from 1824 to 1834 (Hedrick 58–60). Angelina Grimké and her sister Sarah Moore Grimké opposed Indian removal, but it appears to be inconclusive whether they petitioned against it or not (Lerner 92).

45. Zaeske, *Signatures* 23; Hershberger 25; Portnoy 1, 54. Zaeske provides a useful historical overview of women's petitioning as a prelude to her examination of, primarily, women's antislavery petitions (*Signatures* 11–28); see also Portnoy 54 and 62–64 on petitioning in the U.S. prior to the antiremoval campaign. Portnoy's examination of women's antiremoval petitions further extends our account of U. S. women's activism. And although, as Zaeske observes, the women's antiremoval petitioning campaign was relatively short-lived and involved fewer numbers of women than the antislavery campaign, it established an important U. S. precedent. See also Hershberger on the import of the antiremoval campaign in the history of U. S. popular politics. Remarkably, all but four antiremoval petitions were separately submitted according to gender, and these four appear to be anomalies (Portnoy 66).

46. Regarding the Steubenville petition, in its February 20, 1830 issue, *Niles' Weekly Register* reported that "Some conversation arose as to what disposition should be made of this petition, when, finally, it having been read by the clerk, it was ordered to be printed—ayes 86, noes 40" (37: 432). The Steubenville petition, though the second submitted to Congress from a group of women, was the first petition submitted to the House of Representatives, where, according to congressional records, the bulk of the debate over them occurred. Portnoy examines numerous petitions submitted by women against Indian removal, many of which (like the Hallowell petition) are only available at the National Archives. Some of these petitions, however, such as the Steubenville petition, were ordered to be printed and were filed congressional documents, available in the U.S. Serial Sets. In addition to the Steubenville petition, my analysis includes two more petitions signed solely by women, one signed by men, and one that is undistinguishable by gender: "Memorial of Certain Inhabitants of Pennsylvania, Praying that the Indians may be protected in their rights, &c." (7 Jan. 1830); "Memorial of the Ladies of Burlington, New Jersey, Praying that Congress would protect the Indians in their rights, and in the possession of their lands" (23 Feb. 1830); "Memorial of Ladies, Inhabitants of Pennsylvania, Praying that the Indians may be protected in their rights, and in the possession of their lands" (3 Mar. 1830); and "Memorial of Inhabitants of Burlington County, New Jersey, Praying that the Indians may be protected in their rights by the Government" (3 Mar. 1830). The largest single petition came from Pittsburgh, where 670 women signed it and submitted it to the Senate (Hershberger 27). As Portnoy notes, *petitions* were almost always submitted to the House and *memorials* to the Senate (63–64).

47. From a similar position of respectful entreaty, see "Memorial of the Ladies of Burlington County, New Jersey" 2. While this petition makes the case for women's gendered entrée in a national political debate (Portnoy 67), even in such an early petition, we see the seeds of the citizenship arguments to which, Portnoy argues, women will later turn.
48. My analysis here substantiates Portnoy's wider rhetorical analysis of women's antiremoval petitions, the bulk of which justified women's right to enter the discussion of Indian removal. While there were some similarities in men's and women's rhetorical strategies, women's early arguments, in focusing on their gendered status, duties, and influence as women, largely differed from those of their male counterparts, which were mainly historical and legal (Portnoy 67–78). Not until the late 1830s and the antislavery petitions does women's rhetoric shift, taking on the more legalistic arguments and the assumption of citizenship of their male counterparts. For more on this point, see Portnoy 11–12, 84–86.
49. *Niles' Weekly Register* (*Niles' National Register* in its last dozen years) had a respectable circulation and a large influence in national affairs throughout the first half of the 19th century, especially during Hezekiah Niles' term as editor from its first issue in 1811 to 1836 (Schmidt 296 qtd. in Nourie and Nourie 331). The *Register,* which printed the news, documents, and speeches on both sides of congressional debates, including the debate over Indian removal, is therefore useful for understanding the early 19th century (Mott *History* 1: 268–69).
50. Thompson soon abandons this tactic for tactic three, but he returns to this argument later in the debate, boosted by tactic one, a charge against the petition's "indecorous language" (611).
51. For example, Representative Rollin Mallary (VT) volleys back in defense, using a similar string of rhetorical questions (611).
52. In addition, Forsyth's response to continued petitions against Indian removal echoes the charges of nonseriousness and intermeddling in reactions to the New York memorial just months before. Yet another of Forsyth's objections to the petitions is the *manner* in which they were circulated; he complains that the popular, widespread dispersal of petitions among clergy, laity, lawyers, and ladies is inherently underhanded and reprehensible (535).
53. Because they were specifically and repeatedly admonished not to oppose slavery by petitioning or public speaking, women signed relatively few antislavery petitions in the years before 1834; they first chose more acceptable activities such as boycotting products of slave labor or educating free blacks (Zaeske, *Signatures* 41–42). However, after abolitionists like American William Lloyd Garrison and British George Thompson began calling on women to exercise the right of petition to oppose slavery in 1834–35, Congress was flooded with more exclusively women's antislavery petitions than ever before. These initially adopted a gendered rhetorical stance of humility and prayer, like the Indian removal petitions preceding them, making arguments on moral grounds (47–48).
54. In the first session of the 26th Congress, in January 1840, William Cost Johnson introduced a permanent gag rule, which passed 114–108 and, as Zaeske explains, became the most extreme measure of silencing petitions (*Signatures* 152–53). The previous gags were resolutions that sent petitions to the table after receiving them, but, as resolutions, they expired after each session. Yet the Johnson gag rule, as a House Rule, was sustained throughout the first and second sessions of the 26th Congress; in addition, it stated that no petitions would be received or entertained, thereby prohibiting them from being introduced at all. Similar rules were enacted by every Congress through 1844. As Zaeske demonstrates, the gag rule was passed in response to petitioning drives, and one can see that each time women's petitions to Congress increased, the question of reception was debated, and the "gag" on

them was renewed; in turn, the gag rule also stimulated women's political discourse (*Signatures* 73–74, 153, 156).
55. See, for example, the responses of Representatives Glascock and Underwood, which echo Garland's and others' responses to antiremoval petitions, but to greater extremes (*Register of Debates* 1316, 1322).
56. From May 9–12, 1837, the New York convention was the first national assembly of women on a controversial political issue and stimulated women's organized petitioning against slavery (Zaeske, *Signatures* 82, 84–86). According to both Portnoy and Zaeske, 1837 also marked an important strategic change in women's rhetorical strategies; they began to justify their right to petition by invoking natural rights arguments versus gendered arguments, losing the language of prayerful supplication and shifting to the more legalistic arguments that men used in their petitions. This rhetorical shift was arguably more threatening to southern congressmen's perceptions of a masculinized political language, giving yet additional justification for the heightened tension over women's petitions in the second session of the 25th Congress.
57. Bynum's remarks may come as no surprise: Bynum proudly avowed that his goal from his first day in Congress was to suppress any discussion of the divisive subject of slavery. Bynum pursues the proverbial silencing strategies to this end, including the charges of intermeddling and stalling tactics used by Glascock and Underwood against the receipt of the petitions. He also claims that Congress has no obligation to receive the petitions because the "insolent, intermeddling fanatics" (*Register of Debates* 1333) have no right to petition on the issue of slavery in the District of Columbia (1330), and he argues that slavery in the District of Columbia is not under the House's jurisdiction. What is fascinating is that Bynum calls on gender and language together to stifle debate about slavery.
58. In fact, Adams devoted four consecutive mornings between June 26 and June 30 to addressing women as yet "another class" slighted by the gag rule (Adams 64–65). The "other class" that Adams also initially, though only briefly, mentions as being slighted by the gag rule is the slave class: On the morning of Saturday, June 23, Adams suggests slaves are not excluded from the right to petition and is quickly told he is out of order (58–59; 63).
59. Other women like Sigourney and Angelina Grimké, who publicly refuted Beecher's position in her *Letters to Catherine E. Beecher* (1838), defended women's right to petition Congress on any matter. While most contemporary scholars have interpreted the disagreement between Grimké and Beecher as an early feminist debate, Portnoy astutely reads it as indicative of the period's two competing antislavery organizations: the American Colonization Society (advocating gradual emancipation through slaves' emigration to Africa, a position supported by Beecher) and the American Anti-Slavery Society (which favored immediate abolition over colonization, the stance of Grimké) (Portnoy 13–15). What I find fascinating about the Beecher-Grimké exchange is that, first, women's petitions—with the issue of gender and language—remain central to the larger national debate about slavery. Second, the fact that contemporary scholars tend to read the exchange as a confrontation of different ideas about women's roles substantiates the extent to which ideas about gender and language *continue* to intervene in larger discussions of nation and race.

NOTES TO CHAPTER 2

1. Kirkham's comparison of "*good readers*" and "*bad readers*" is a long-winded, hyperbolic indication of the extent to which reading and speaking were

entwined with moral character and social position (17–20). For example, he compares a "*good reader*" to "the stately magnolia" and lists a host of disagreeable sounds to which he would rather listen than "an *affected* speaker or a *bad* reader"—among them, "the jingling of broken glass upon a pavement, or the trampling of feet through crusted snow, or a group of madcap boys bellowing after a fire-engine, or a refusal of a friend to lend me money [. . . or] a woman scold or a child squall" (17–19, Kirkham's emphasis).

2. Each of McGuffey's readers directly and indirectly promotes good elocution. *McGuffey's First Eclectic Reader* introduces children to the basic elements of reading, including the presentation of phonics—a progressive pedagogy for the time. *McGuffey's Second Eclectic Reader* emphasizes oral presentation, an emphasis that continues in the third through sixth readers (Gorn 27). Directions for pronunciation and elocution accompany selections throughout the readers, such as instructions for reading "The Sands O' Dee" "in a low key and with a pure, musical tone" (*McGuffy's Fifth Reader* 72 in Minnich 202). Individual didactic stories, such as "Mr. Post and the Little Girl," in which a man raises an orphaned baby girl who, in turn, reads the Bible aloud to him in his old age, also celebrate the value of oral reading (*McGuffey's First Eclectic Reader* 57–58 in Minnich 6–7). Although precise figures for McGuffey's sales are unavailable, even conservative sales estimates suggest that they were the most popular American schoolbooks. The readers, from their first publication in 1836 through the two major revisions of 1857 and 1879 (around when sales peaked), outsold all the other textbooks, with conservative total sales estimates at over 50 million copies. Given the fact that they were passed down within schools and among friends and families, Gorn suggests that, with the exception of the King James Bible, the McGuffeys were the most widely read books in 19th-century America; they may have sold so well because, while somewhat pedagogically progressive in their emphasis on general reading, they "captured a broad middle ground" and were socially conservative (2, 16–17). Gorn sees the McGuffey readers as teaching a kind of secular morality, expressing both religious values to be instilled in children and social and economic values to prepare children for an urban-industrial America (11–12).

3. Sedgwick's *Means and Ends* (1839) similarly proposes that a woman's discussion of books could make her reading a "blessing" to society (244 in Ashworth 153); Ashworth notes how the emphasis on reading *aloud* set reading within a social (most often domestic) sphere, taking away any privacy a woman might claim in the activity (153). See also Carr for a useful overview of 19th-century girls' literacy (reading and writing) and its representations; opportunities for girls to read and write generally expanded in this era, although often their literacy education prepared them for marriage and motherhood, for participation in the "cult of domesticity" or "cult of true womanhood" (64–65). Certainly, not all females participated in the "cults" of domesticity and true womanhood, but these cults reflected and shaped important ideologies of linguistic—and vocal—propriety. As Carr details, an entire mid-19th-century market produced textbooks with titles aimed particularly at girls and boys (67–68). Such gendered ideas about vocal propriety held sway for many white, middle-class, Protestant women and men, and girls and boys, in the mid-19th-century U.S. Indeed, several stories from the McGuffey readers reflect such gender socialization, if not through ideas about gendered linguistic roles. See the stories "True Courage," "True Manliness," "House-Cleaning," "A Place for Every Thing," "My Mother's Bible," and "Rock Me to Sleep" in Gorn 102–13. Additionally, see "Mrs. Caudle's Lecture," which depicts a stereotypical

tongue-wagging, henpecking, Dame-Winklesque housewife (*McGuffey's Fifth Reader* in Minnich 268–69).
4. My use of quotation marks above is intended to call attention to the terms *grammar* and *slang* as discursive constructions; while my awareness of them as such will permeate the chapter, my punctuation will not. I take from Gorn the observation that piety and property "formed the foundations of civilization and the cornerstones of American society" (13). As well, however, 19th-century discourses of *propriety* incorporated both of these very "American" values. A wide variety of literate activities—such as reading, letter writing, and penmanship—were regulated by discourses of *linguistic* propriety. However, by focusing in this chapter on *vocal* propriety as a subset of linguistic propriety, I want to call attention to discourses that worked to regulate speech, such as discourses on elocution, conversation, pronunciation and the discourses of "good grammar" that came to be equated with "good speech." I use the term *vocal*, then, to emphasize the oral elements of ideas about linguistic propriety, although there were certainly writerly and readerly elements of propriety outside the scope of this chapter.
5. Elbert, for example, points out that recent accounts of women in urban spaces, such as Deborah Epstein Nord's *Walking the Victorian Streets* and Christine Stansell's *City of Women*, examine women's presence on streets "as both spectacle and participant" (13). Ryan's *Women in Public,* esp. 58–94, also establishes that a host of women made their way into public spaces such as city streets between 1825 and 1880.
6. In the 1850s, from October to April, Holmes lectured almost every evening throughout the Northeast; he taught anatomy during the day (Martensen 1294). Because Holmes was "an advocate for a social space—the conservative and genteel middle ground" (1294), his commentary is valuable to an examination of mid-19th-century perceptions of speech. His first collection of essays and verse, Holmes' *The Autocrat of the Breakfast Table* is especially so—it sold 10,000 copies during its first three days of publication (1294).
7. See Mugglestone's *Talking Proper,* which focuses on accent as social symbol in late 18th- and 19th-century Great Britain, for a prime example of a historically-focused study of language and language attitudes.
8. In literary studies, grammar as a topic of relevant study has been altogether under-explored. Contemporary studies of grammar in composition-rhetoric have tended to stress the historical practices of grammar instruction, while often missing the changing significations of grammar with respect to American notions of propriety and its implications for ethnic, class, gender, and national identities. Hartwell's dissection of the multivalent meanings of the term *grammar* is an exception to much scholarship on grammar that, rather than consider the semantic and symbolic weight of the term, traces the changes of grammar instruction within the teaching of rhetoric and composition (e.g., Berlin and Connors), or deliberates whether or not such instruction is beneficial (e.g., Shaughnessy). In historical treatments of language, scholars have attended to historical and theoretical aspects of grammar, however. For example, Baron's two books use the term *grammar* to stand in for larger topics of codified language use and historicized attempts to change it—though, revealingly, his two books separate the topics of language and gender, and language and nation, which I attempt to bring together in this project. Critical-linguistic works like Cameron's *Verbal Hygiene* is another exception in its interrogation of the ideological force of the great grammar crusade.
9. Of course, the expansion of the suffrage to white males occurred even as Chief Justice Roger Taney's *Dred Scott* decision denied citizenship to

African Americans in 1857—the same year that a financial panic and its ensuing depression devastated many American families.
10. The first forum for women to announce their own grievances rather than those of the poor, slaves, orphans, or widows, Seneca Falls led to the first truly national convention on Woman's Rights in Worcester, Massachusetts in 1850, followed by ten national and numerous local woman's rights conventions by 1860 (Lerner, "Meanings" 203–04).
11. Additionally, a long list of grievances established the systematic "tyranny" of man (or patriarchy) over woman: She was made "civilly dead" upon marriage; stripped of her property and wages; discriminated against in divorce cases; kept from the professions (theology, medicine, law) that man "considers most honorable to himself"; subordinated in Church and State; circumscribed to the domestic sphere; and made to be "willing to lead a dependent and abject life" (Declaration of Sentiments 207).
12. During this era, some state laws and judicial decisions—such as the Married Women's Property Act passed by seventeen states between 1839 and 1850—expanded women's rights in limited (here, economic) ways, but these decisions did not acknowledge female political equality. Since the first Married Women's Property Act passed in Mississippi in 1839 secured women's rights over slaves, it arguably reinforced racial inequality more so than gender equality. Further, none of the laws established full female equality in financial matters (R. Smith 233). Another case in point is the 1855 Naturalization Act, which automatically naturalized all women who married U.S. citizens, whether they wished it or not, as well as all children born overseas to fathers (but not mothers) who were U.S. citizens: It was defended on the grounds that it cost little to anyone because women had no political rights anyway (and could therefore lose nothing by a change of citizenship) and on the grounds that, if naturalized, women would be better republican mothers (234–35).
13. For a pertinent theoretical account of how issues of gender, propriety, and property are intertwined with national identity and nationalism in non-U.S. contexts, see Bannerji, Shahrzad, and Whitehead.
14. The era's self-improvement activities also included the lyceum and common schools movements. Although the American lyceum movement has occasioned little scholarly comment beyond Bode's foundational work, the lyceum was called "an institution which was so peculiarly American, and which served so well the American spirit and American life" (G.W. Curtis, *Harper's* "Editor's Easy Chair," April 1887, qtd. in Bode, *Lyceum* 252). Heavily promoted in newspapers and educational journals, it brought lectures on a wide variety of subjects to people throughout the country from the late 1820s to the Civil War (12, 252). For a summary of McGuffey's role in the common schools movement, powerful in the Midwest in the 1850s, see Gorn 9–10, 18–22.
15. See Gorn 7–9 on McGuffey's ties to the Beecher family and how L. Beecher's essay contained many of McGuffey's themes.
16. Dedicated to American teachers, Peabody's collection gathered, according to Peabody, "the principles which should govern Conversation among persons of true refinement of mind and character, and to point out some of the most common and easily besetting vulgarisms occurring in the colloquial English of our country and day" (7). Gwynne writes for what he calls bad speakers of the educated sort, interestingly saying, "We laugh at the blunders of a foreigner, but perpetrate our own offences with so much gravity that an observer would have a right to consider them—what they really are—*no laughing matter*" (62, Gwynne's emphasis). In addition to Peabody's address

and Gwynne's "Word to the Wise," the collection contains other selections, adapted for American readers, including "Mistakes and Improprieties in Speaking and Writing Corrected," assembling 379 mistakes in list form, many about pronunciation and word choice, and almost all expressed in the form, "Never say x" or "Say y."

17. According to Lyman's foundational dissertation, *English Grammar in American Schools Before 1850* (1922), grammar instruction in early America had grown out of the desire to foster Biblical literacy and to train well-spoken leaders. Grammar instruction was supported by the educational theories of John Locke and Benjamin Franklin, who influenced the teaching of grammar in America as laying the foundation for the vocal training of the nation's orators (Lyman 11–12, 38, 41). Thus a national concern with grammar was not new, although its expression as "propriety" may have been. While there was a flood of grammar textbooks published after Webster's "Plain and Comprehensive Grammar" in 1784, it was not until the second quarter of the 19th century that grammar really flourished, peaking at the middle of the century. The year 1860 marked what Lyman calls "the heyday of grammar," and the second quarter of the 19th century, Lyman suggests, "was by far the most interesting and important period in grammar instruction" (9, 133).

18. Lyman cites an estimate from 1812 that Murray's grammar, which came out in 1795, sold 35,000 copies annually in America; in 11 years, it went through over 40 editions in the states (80). Including the grammars produced by Murray's followers and abridgers, Lyman puts a conservative estimate of the total number of Murray's grammars before 1850 at 200 editions, amounting to between 1.5 and 2 million total copies (80). Murray's popular grammar not only "cornered the market," but also contributed to the perception that grammar is the art of judging right and wrong forms, bearing religious underpinnings that were echoed in later grammars (Finegan 374).

19. Put another way, 19th-century grammars became about clarifying "correct" usage as *socially acceptable* usage—not about grammatical structure itself. Baron similarly reads 19th-century grammars as usage guides, imparting not a body of knowledge but rules of etiquette—rules of linguistic propriety—as normative rules of "correctness" (*Good Taste* 169). Interestingly, although linguists today do not regard grammar in this light, much of the population still does, attesting to the ongoing ideological importance of these 19th-century ideas about language.

20. Hurd, who lectured during the winters over a series of years on the grammar of the English language, visited, in his own words, almost every section of the U.S., where he noted common errors and peculiarities of speech "for the purpose of correction and comment in the lecture-room" as well as "a source of amusement to himself" (v). Over several years, he collected more than 2,000 errors and claimed that "no list of the common errors of speech in this country, at all approaching in completeness, the present collection, has ever been published" (v). His volume includes tables with titles like false pronunciation, wrong collocation, tautology and redundancy, words requiring certain prepositions, and Americanisms. Among Hurd's 190 "authorities consulted" in cataloging these errors were numerous British and American dictionaries, glossaries, and grammars dating from Samuel Johnson's dictionary (1755) to Joseph Chandler's *American Grammar* (1847). Bearing endorsements from educators like Chandler himself, the *Grammatical Corrector* thus carried hefty self-proclaimed authoritative weight, making itself the benchmark sanctioning "general good usage," primarily through its prohibitions against general "bad" usage.

21. Kirkham's popular *English Grammar in Familiar Lectures,* first published in 1825, gave Murray's grammar serious competition and passed through 94 editions between 1829 and 1851 (Downey 5).
22. With the abolitionist and women's suffrage movements gaining momentum after the Seneca Falls convention in 1848, more and more women gained the speaking platform, so that their voices were increasingly subject to public commentary. Public speaking, however, was still considered unladylike and neither encouraged nor generally socially accepted (Cmiel 71). Although it was generally accepted that women would speak in public by the end of the 1850s, they did so in small numbers. For example, of the 203 lyceum lecturers that the *New York Tribune* listed for 1859, only 12 of them were women (283n53).
23. For the perpetuation of sex differences in language as early as the 6th century, see Baron, *Grammar and Gender* 90.
24. The popularity of *The Wide, Wide World* has become somewhat of a commonplace in literary criticism. When it first appeared, Warner's book sold better than had any other novel written in the United States, going through fourteen editions in two years. For more on its reception, see Tompkins, Afterword 584 and Bode, *Anatomy* 172.
25. Although scholars such as Carafiol on *Ragged Dick* and O'Connell, Hovet and Hovet, and Ashworth on *The Wide, Wide World* have pointed to concerns with linguistic style, silencing, feminine voice, or reading practices in these texts, to my knowledge, no studies offer a sustained probing of the politics of language in them. Perhaps coming closest to my discussion of *The Wide, Wide World's* shaping of the ideal female *speaker* is Ashworth's investigation of the novel's figuration of the ideal female *reader* who, responding to regulatory advice in the era's conduct books, could read her way into purity, piety, and selflessness, thus concretizing the (class, gender, nation) ideals of Victorian American culture. Like reading and writing, speech practices were important vehicles to ideal womanhood, and they amplified the political implications of women's other literate activities such as reading. On the threatening potential of women's reading in the early 19th century, see Davidson, *Revolution and the Word*.
26. Discipline and power are noted concerns of sentimental fiction. As Baym suggests, Warner particularly stands out as a sentimental writer who deals with power (*Woman's Fiction* 144 cited in Dobson, "Subversion" 241n24). Brodhead and Tompkins focus on *The Wide, Wide World's* obsession with submission as either a reinforcement of patriarchy (Broadhead, "Sparing") or possible empowerment for women (Tompkins, *Sensational*). Others, like Dobson (in "Subversion") or Noble (in *Masochistic Pleasures*), take the themes of submission and discipline in the novel as something more ambiguous or conflicted. I tend to fall with Noble in adopting a both/and view, seeing "grammar" in the novel as a means of *both* vocal empowerment (linguistic advancement, self-possession) *and* vocal suppression (linguistic confinement).
27. Indeed, the fact that *McGuffey's Second Eclectic Reader* condenses Ragged Dick's narrative into a story—"Henry, the Boot Black," Lesson 14 (35–37)—attests to the narrative's popularity with a wide swath of American readers and to its importance in disseminating values similar to McGuffey's.
28. It is interesting to note that, despite their shorthand associations with these "American" characteristics, these books have occasioned little serious analysis from literary critics—at least not until relatively recently. Warner's novel received little critical attention until feminist efforts of the 1970s—in 1978, Baym's *Woman's Fiction* marked its first serious critical consideration, which

Tompkins extended in *Sensational Designs* (1985); Alger's story, while the common object of both popular and critical allusion, still seems to have occasioned relatively little serious critical attention.

29. Foucault's ideas about self-surveillance in *Discipline and Punish* are obviously relevant here; see Noble 114–15 for a particularly clear discussion.
30. Such an ethic of submission can be read as both a top-down strategy for keeping women down, and as a bottom-up, self-willed act of conquering one's own passions, wherein self-mastery and self-denial is, Tompkins states, "paradoxically, an assertion of autonomy," and "the dutiful woman merges her own authority with God's" (*Sensational* 162–63). Within a Christian ethic of and submission, as Tompkins suggests, self-denial must be acknowledged as a survival strategy for women to overcome tyranny; yet it also clearly has its social and political limits.
31. Other examples of good voices in the novel belong to the respectively sweet, kind, and good-humored characters Mrs. Montgomery, the old gentleman who helps Ellen shop, and Mr. Van Brunt (64, 48, 93).
32. Dobson has questioned John's character as a model of morality, citing as support the novel's references to John's violence or his less-than-favorable nicknames. Yet, as Noble notes, Warner seems to discount these observations by placing them in the mouths of unreliable characters in the novel (120). Goshgarian traces the incestuous implications of Alice and John's relationship in her wry and readable book on Victorian America's obsession with incest under the semblance of true womanhood in bestselling 1850s women's domestic fiction; see particularly 76–119.
33. See V. Stewart for a relevant examination of Nancy Vawse in a trickster role as an important counterpoint to Ellen's suppressed nature in the novel.
34. As Damon-Bach observes, in this domestic "battle," the parlor becomes a space where Ellen can speak most publicly, gaining a male audience, a space both freeing and confining. Indeed, in this scene, Ellen becomes one of Ralph Waldo Emerson's "parlor soldiers" ("Self-Reliance" 161 qtd. in Damon-Bach 29). Damon-Bach argues that "While Emerson seems to condemn those (men) who stay home, who are only 'soldiers' in 'parlors,' Warner's novels highlight the moral courage and strength of those who had to stay home, who had no choice" (47).
35. See B. Johnson and Swaim for studies of the ways in which *Pilgrim's Progress* referenced a constellation of Protestant, American values.
36. Here I would depart from Carafiol, who sees Dick's "personal linguistic style" as differentiating him equally from his lower-class and middle-class companions (173). While Dick does have a "personal linguistic style," it distinguishes him much less from other boys of his class than from his middle-class acquaintances.
37. That Alger calls attention to Dick's *retention* of slang indicates how "essential"—in Alger's words, how "natural"—it was seen to Dick's identity and underscores his mobility. For a contrasting interpretation, see Carafiol, who suggests that when Dick, in the process of assuming a middle-class life, "puts on a new identity and a new language," he "gives up the most characteristic, the most interesting, entertaining, and powerful part of himself" (174).
38. G. Foster collected his *Tribune* sketches of urban sociology, including descriptions of the Newsboy and the B'hoy, in *New York in Slices*. The diction of the title interestingly resurfaces in Allen's recent *The City in Slang*, which Allen describes as "a *slice* of the history of popular speech through the development of the modern metropolis, specifically New York, and it is a *slice* of the social and cultural history of New York through the material of popular speech" (ix, my emphasis). Allen's discussion of "The Cycle of New

York Metropolitan Life" (20–26) is a good overview of how, in the context of new industrialization, capitalism, migration, immigration, public transportation, urban poverty, and increasing social diversity, lexical innovation in New York rose rapidly after 1850 then declined rapidly after about 1950 (20). *The City in Slang* is also remarkable with respect to this chapter's ensuing discussion of slang, in that it reinforces, from the point of view of modern scholarship, the associations of slang with urban settings from the mid 19th to mid 20th century.

39. Says Lighter, "The existence—the experience—of slang *as* slang requires the currency, within a language community, of quite specific sociolinguistic assumptions and expectations about stylistic norms and their nonobservance" (Intro xviii). On slang's perceived impiety, Mencken among others notes how slang—particularly American slang as characterized by British critics—is sometimes "belabored as intolerably vulgar, indecent and against God [. . .]" (*AL* 571).

40. I want to reiterate that what I mean here is not "grammar" in the linguistic sense of the systematic study of language or descriptions dealing with the syntax and morphology of language, but in the popular sense of social and linguistic propriety, a sense that rose to prominence during the middle of the 19th century. Much as *grammar* has become an overarching term for linguistic propriety in popular circles, *slang* has become a useful "catch-all" term for linguistic impropriety—an aspect of slang that has frustrated linguists because it leads to difficulty in defining slang and collecting it. As Eble says, slang does not easily align itself with either style labels (formal/informal) or status labels (standard/nonstandard). I thus differentiate the popular senses of both *grammar* and *slang* in this chapter from their linguistic senses. As Eble points out, from today's *linguistic* perspective, unlike the popular perspective, slang is not an "improper" grammatical construction (such as "between you and I") or an objectionable form (such as "ain't" or "irregardless"); "objections to the use of slang are matters of social appropriateness and not grammar" (21).

41. The "b'hoy" was a recasting of antebellum humor's "frontier screamer," such as the "ring-tailed roarer" or the loud backwoods braggart, which could be found in humorists' tall tales, like the Davy Crockett papers, published between 1835 and 1856 in many cities across the country (Reynolds 463, 449–50). Both the "frontier screamer" and the "b'hoy" had female sidekicks—the screamer woman, who was the "ultimate adventure feminist" (450), and the "g'hal." I read these figures, whether male or female, as commonly-perceived "masculine" types in this era, posed in their verbal unboundedness against the ideal femininity of domesticated grammar and the image of the proper female speaker of popular domestic fiction. For more on frontier and urban humorists and their broad influence on American culture, see especially Reynolds 441–83. See also Lighter's "Slang" for a short but helpful survey of the role of literature by humorists like Artemus Ward, Joe Strickland, Seba Smith, Thomas Haliburton, and George Washington Harris in the propagation of American slang.

42. See "The Needlewomen," in which Foster urges the young rural female to avoid coming to the city, and if she is a "real Woman," to stay in the country to preserve her "moral purity" (53).

43. This interdependence arguably replicates the 18th-century beginnings of perceptions of English itself as standard/nonstandard. For the most comprehensive and scholarly overview of slang, see Lighter's introduction to the *Random House Historical Dictionary of American Slang*. For background on English slang and transatlantic conversations about slang, particularly from the 18th to early 20th century, see J. Green, esp. 402–39.

44. See also Partridge 322. Webster defined *slang* rather generally as 'low, vulgar unmeaning language.' According to Lighter, Whitney's definition in the *Century Dictionary* (1889–90) was "perhaps the first comprehensive treatment of the term" (Lighter, Intro xxxviiin1). Many still attempt to define slang terms, although "to define a slang term is, in strictness, impossible. The defining process kills at a blow the aura, the characteristic shading of the original" (Scott 118–19). According to Lighter, *slang* "is a term that conveniently designates words and phrases diverging markedly in social ambiance, use, and style from those in the standard lexicon," and may be briefly defined, not as whatever is new or popular in language but as "an informal, nonstandard, nontechnical vocabulary composed chiefly of novel-sounding synonyms for standard words and phrases" and that has a "vital social dimension as well" (Lighter, Intro xi-xii; see also xiv-xvi). See also Eble's first chapter for an extensive and accessible definition of slang, including a clear and relevant delineation of what slang *is* and what it *is not*.
45. See Bailey, *Nineteenth* 193–210. Hall compiled the first edition of his collection of college slang "during the leisure hours of the last half-year of a Senior's collegiate life" and presented it anonymously to the public (Hall iii).
46. For further discussions of both popular and scholarly attitudes about slang, see Lighter, Intro xxvi-xxviii; Mencken, *AL* 568; Bailey, *Nineteenth* 178–85, 213–14.
47. Slang grew out of criminal *cant*, "a private language of the underworld, [which] was the earliest form of nonstandard language to be condemned by critics" (Lighter, Intro xvi). The wider but equally condemned category of *slang* that arose in the 17th and 18th centuries was once synonymous with *cant* (Intro xxii-xxiv). On both military and civilian sources of slang, see Lighter, Intro xxviii-xxxii. For the only contemporary book-length work that systematically examines both formal and social features of college slang, see Eble. One fascinating aspect of Eble's study is that her corpus of slang comes largely from white, *female* students, age 19–23, seeking teacher certification at the University of North Carolina at Chapel Hill between 1972 and 1993. That this receives little comment from Eble suggests, perhaps, that gender is becoming less a variable in slang, especially among current-day college students.
48. Flexner's comments above are part of an extended description of slang as confined to "primarily masculine use" (xii). While coming a century after the first slang studies, Flexner's overtly masculinized characterizations of slang arose within some similar historical conditions, such as second-wave feminism. Such stereotyped perceptions of slang as a male linguistic characteristic continue today—although they may be changing. Lighter, in his more recent discussion of slang, hypothesizes that "American men in general have traditionally known and used a more extensive slang repertory than have women of the same socioeconomic class, especially upper- and middle-class women. (*Slang,* as used here, does not mean 'general informal or nonstandard language.' Common experience suggests that the speech of both sexes is comparably informal.) If this hypothesis proves true, Flexner's explanation could be a valid one: until the recent past, relatively few women were involved with exceptionally slang-productive activities and subcultures" (Lighter, Intro xxxii). As Lighter also notes, "The interesting questions of 'women and slang,' 'men and slang,' 'minorities and slang,' 'power and slang,' etc., are complicated ones, and current 'answers' rest mainly on unanalyzed assumptions. Careful investigation is required from more than one discipline" (Intro xxxii). De Klerk has investigated the stereotyping of slang, leading her to conclude that "the expected differences between males

and females in this area are not as striking as one is led to believe by literature in the field" (589).
49. Consider even Lighter's recent description of the effect of slang: "the use of slang undermines the dignity of verbal exchange and charges discourse with an unrefined and often aggressive informality. It pops the balloon of pretense. There is often a raw vitality in slang, a ribald sense of humor and a flip self-confidence; there is also very often locker-room crudity and toughness, a tawdry sensibility" (xii).
50. A complexly plot-driven, rags-to-riches adventure novel about an orphan girl who becomes the ward of wealthy Warfield and who proves the value of standing up for herself, much like Sedgwick's Hope Leslie, *The Hidden Hand* was extremely popular with male and female readers on both sides of the Atlantic. As Baym suggests, Southworth may have been the most widely-read novelist in the 19th century, even though she has been largely critically invisible ("Melodramas" 124). Between 1859 and 1883, the *New York Ledger* published *The Hidden Hand* at full length three times to satisfy both male and female readers, and it was dramatized 40 times, including internationally (Dobson, Intro xiv). Its eventual book publication in 1888 came after numerous requests from book publishers for publication rights (xiv). The plot was apparently based on true story of a 9-year-old girl dressed in boy's clothing and selling newspapers, a story that Southworth discovered in a New York newspaper and that appealed to her conceptually. Dobson claims that "an aberrant gender socialization, significantly, is Capitola's salvation. [. . .] her education on the streets where she works as a newsboy—allows her to develop the saving characteristics of self-reliance, irreverence, and active, rather than passive, courage" (xxxi). See also Dobson, "Subversion" 233–35.
51. Race-charged issues are also "hidden" in this novel. For example, Southworth herself held a strong antislavery stance, but the policy of the *Ledger,* the popular story magazine in which *The Hidden Hand* was first serialized, was to remain neutral on the divisive subject of slavery in order to appeal to both northern and southern readers. For more on Southworth's antislavery position, see P. Jones. Despite her antislavery stance, Southworth often uses racial stereotypes, although she often uses them as she does gendered ones—to reveal their absurdity (Dobson, Intro xxiv-xxv).

NOTES TO CHAPTER 3

1. Indeed, the Fourteenth Amendment was the culmination of what Crane identifies as antebellum higher law constitutionalism, lawmaking guided by a mixture of consent and conscience (135, 169).
2. Saks describes how the writers of the Fourteenth Amendment incessantly talked about miscegenation and how, at both federal and state levels, the Civil War Amendments and Civil Rights Acts resulted in the increased passage of antimiscegenation laws because they "threatened the white South with the potential legal legitimation of interracial sex and intermarriage" and "threatened the sovereignty of the individual Southern state courts that adjudicated miscegenation cases, since the empire of federal power was expanding [. . .]" (44). See also Bardaglio, esp. 176–213, for a legal discussion of how the "Old South's" conceptions of race, blood, and gender persisted in the "New South's" southern appellate court decisions vis-à-vis sexuality and marriage, such as the court's reevaluations of miscegenation, rape, and incest. See

Thomas, Intro for a comprehensive analysis of the legislation of this period and its implications for the Plessy case.
3. Although Linke's observations apply to a European context, her analysis pertains to the late-19th-century American context examined here. As one metaphor of descent that I explore in this chapter, "blood" in recent years has come to be seen as a central trope in 19th- and early-20th-century Euro-American scientific discourse, inseparable from discourses of both race and gender. On the denaturalization of kinship and its representation by "blood," see Yanagisako and Delaney 1–22; on blood as a signifier of gender as well as race, located within multiple 19th-century discourses, see Kassanoff, esp. 165; Spillers; and Weston, esp. 103; and on the extension of 19th-century ethnology and theories of blood associated with racialist discourse and racist social objectives into 20th-century American culture, see Michaels, *Our America*.
4. My thanks to Mark Patterson for offering this formulation and for suggesting Doyle's helpful work.
5. While many states soon allowed women to practice law, the theory of *Bradwell* was sustained until *Reed v. Reed* (1971), when the Court began to undermine sex discrimination by using the Fourteenth Amendment (Finkelman and Urofsky 88). *Bradwell*, like antimiscegenation cases, anticipated the descent-based logic that would be used in the "separate but equal" legislation of *Plessy* (1896). The *Slaughterhouse Cases* (1873) and the *Civil Rights Cases* (1883) also undermined the protections of the Civil War amendments but more subtly, by distinguishing between national and state citizenship (Crane 170–71).
6. For this chapter's discussion, pertinent recent studies on language in late-19th-century American literature include G. Jones' *Strange Talk*—which, while importantly broadening our understanding of dialect and language politics, tends to isolate race and gender with respect to dialect and does not consider issues of enfranchisement—and Nettels' two important studies, yet ones that likewise segregate issues of language and race from issues of language and gender. As throughout the study, this chapter's argument is influenced by work on consent/descent and contract/identity in American culture; my analysis of Chesnutt's notions of consensual language in "The Dumb Witness" and *The Colonel's Dream* tends to follow Crane's understanding of Chesnutt as invested in the promise of contract.
7. See also Van Evrie 140–41 for a similar essentialization of linguistic differences. My thanks to Crane for drawing Van Evrie's work to my attention.
8. While this chapter focuses on the retention of descent-based metaphors in discussions of language, it is worth noting—and relevant with respect to the previous chapter's discussion of linguistic propriety—that American Dialect Society members, Whitney, and Howells also retained ideas about propriety in their discourse on language. See, for example, Phipson's authoritative judgments about linguistic propriety ("British vs. American English" 436) and Whitney's rather hierarchical notions of "deviations" from standard speech that maintained distinctions between barbaric and cultivated speech (*Life and Growth* 155–56; "Dialect and Languages" 62, 64–65; and Rev. of White's *Words and Their Uses* 469, 476). Howells recognized the cultural obsession with propriety alongside his tendency to conceive of "good natural English," as Nettels puts it, as "not Whitman's idiosyncratic melding of standard English, slang, technical, and foreign words, but the language of Henry James" (*Language, Race* 25). Pertinent to this retention of propriety is Warren's argument that realism "failed"

in fulfilling its "dual promise" of offering both an aesthetic and a liberal politics because it was incompatibly wedded to notions of propriety (*Black and White* 51, 65). Discussions of language at this time could also register the discourse of civilization addressed in the next chapter (e.g., Whitney, "Dialect and Languages" 62).

9. Attesting not only to the increased, and ever-increasing, interest in American letters, but also to the push to validate, to professionalize, and eventually to institutionalize this interest, the formation of the American Dialect Society was situated within the founding of a number of other professional organizations. For example, the American Philological Society (formed in 1869) was soon followed by the Spelling Reform Association (1876), the Modern Language Association (1883), the American Folk-Lore Society (1888), and the American Institute of Arts and Letters (1898), whose original members brought together, among others, America's leading men of letters, including Henry Adams, Samuel Clemens, John Hay, Joel Chandler Harris, William Dean Howells, Henry James, and Charles Edward Norton. The slew of organizations dedicated to American "letters" was capped in the early 20th century with the formation of the Linguistic Society of America (1924), which marked the achievement of the scientization of language begun in the late 19th century—a time which Shumway identifies as the beginning of the institutionalization and creation of "American civilization" that culminated in the 1930s-60s. In these organizations, such "men of letters" came together to study and to promote American language and literature, with the avowedly political ends of promoting national identity. The phrase "men of letters" itself denotes not only the fluidity of language and literary study (across fields such as philology, dialectology, linguistics, literature, rhetoric, etc.) at the time but also the early masculinization of the "letters" profession predominantly in the hands of elite white men.

10. For example, in addition to several works on "Americanisms," "provincialisms," "Southernisms," and professional "lingos," the bibliography for the first year of the society includes works titled "The philosophy of dialect" from *Modern English Notes* and "Waste-basket of words" from the *Journal of American Folk-Lore;* proceedings and publications from the American Philological Association; Alexander Melville Bell's multiple works on "visible speech," with a review of his primer by Edward S. Sheldon of the American Dialect Society; James Murray's "A new English dictionary on historical principles"; Richard Grant White's "Some alleged Americanisms"; William Dwight Whitney's *The Elements of English pronunciation* and *The Century Dictionary;* and James A. Harrison's "Negro English," now acknowledged to be the first description of AAE (African American English).

11. Refer, for example, to the membership lists of 1890 (*Dialect Notes* I: 30–32, 179–83); 1895 (*Dialect Notes* I: 406); and 1901, 1902, and 1903 (*Dialect Notes* II: 282–88, 365–71, 432–38). Jewett and her sister Mary are also listed as members in 1899 and 1900 (*Dialect Notes* II: 84, 194).

12. Fascinatingly evidencing the mutual investments of language study and literature in dialect, the Society worked to compile material for the American Dialect Dictionary—as stated in its 1895 circular, "*a complete record of American speech-forms in our day*"—for which members used the OED method in soliciting contributions of American usage, calling on public volunteers to collect notes not only from their experience but particularly from dialect stories (*Dialect Notes* I: 360; II: 77). The sheer mass of submissions that were received from volunteer readers of dialect literature not only reflects the wide public interest in dialect, but also indicates the interdisciplinary nature of dialect study at the end of the century (II: 129–30, 275). For more

on then the fate of the early Dialect Dictionary, see McDavid, "Linguistic" 5 and Bailey, "Ideologies" 123.
13. In our own day, *dialect* remains a somewhat contested term that tends to convey a sense of regional or racial identity and linguistic inferiority, despite the fact that *dialect* and *language* are linguistically, if not politically, synonymous terms. While *dialect* does not necessarily denote race—19th-century writers of literary dialect such as Stephen Crane, Sarah Orne Jewett, Mary Murfree certainly represented a range of dialects, including those of region and class—black dialect, now called AAE, is "the dialect that has had the strongest influence on 20th-century literature" and thus, perhaps, the widest cultural influence (G. Jones 12–13). For more on this 20th-century influence, see North. For more on the origins, history, salient linguistic features, or oral traditions of AAE, consult Mufwene, Rickford, Smitherman, and Wolfram.
14. For Sheldon, *dialect,* "with special reference to America," signified a wide range of differences in speech, demarcating differences among speakers of varying trades, professions, ages, and genders (*Dialect Notes* I: 287–88, 289–90). Like Sheldon in the 19th century, G. Jones today highlights how understandings of the term *dialect* have consistently broadened "to regional speech divisions, to the neologisms of popular culture, to the distinctive speech of American women, to creole languages, to urban slang, and to the so-called broken English of recent immigrants" (12; see also 34–35).
15. The American Dialect Society sought to study dialect scientifically, as opposed to value-laden public perception. What members considered an objective focus on "natural" speech was at the heart of the American Dialect Society's aims in the very first pages of their proceedings (*Dialect Notes* I: 4). Society members worked hard to differentiate their point of view from public perceptions and ideas about linguistic standards, recognizing the problem addressed in the previous chapter—namely, that the history of English standard pronunciation "has not yet been touched by the spirit of scientific investigation" such that "the good people of this country look upon a variation from some so-called standard almost as a mark of illiteracy, though it would be quite impossible for them to give any rational explanation of their horror [. . .]" (*Dialect Notes* II: 273–74).
16. Generally regarded as the first American linguist but also a scholar who wrote for academic journals and general interest magazines, Whitney also helped to form the American Philological Society, the Spelling Reform Association, and the Modern Language Association (Silverstein xiii). Whitney was innovative in locating linguistics as "historical science," cutting across late-19th-century controversies about whether the study of language belonged in the "moral/historical sciences" or "physical/natural sciences." As Hockett explains in his introduction to Whitney's most popular work, *The Life and Growth of Language* (1875), those who argued for the latter saw languages as living organisms; Whitney, on the other hand, saw languages as *analogical* to living organisms and as a historical force, recognizing the role of the human will as fundamental to the development of languages (xii–xiii). Whitney had a long-term impact on the study of language in the U.S. and, perhaps even more so, in Europe, laying the groundwork for sociolinguistics, neogrammarians, and semioticians, like Saussure, who appreciated Whitney's view that there is no internal correlation between the vocal sign and the idea—or as Whitney himself would say repeatedly, there is "merely an extraneous and unessential" tie "which connects the meaning of a word with its form" (*Life and Growth* 77). Indeed, according to Saussure, Whitney's "great originality" was his "higher and general view of language" (qtd. in Jakobson xxxi); and according to Jakobson, Whitney's "latent intuition" about language

must have planted the seed for the later subdivision of the study of language into its abstract and concrete, general and special, synchronic and diachronic aspects (xliii). For good summaries of Whitney's thought and his legacies for 20th-century linguistics, see Hockett, Jakobson, and Silverstein. Many today would call Whitney a philologist—for example, G. Jones sees both Whitney and White (discussed in the following chapter) as philologists, but with different emphases (he terms Whitney a "scientific" philologist and White an "armchair" philologist). While recognizing the usefulness of a term like "philologist," I tend to consider Whitney an early linguist, as Whitney himself saw the study of language as linguistic science.

17. See also *Life and Growth* 146 for comparison of tendency in language to political institutions. In "Languages and Dialects," Whitney further discusses the fluidity of the concept of community and matters of consent in language (38).
18. "The force of analogy" itself, Whitney said, "is, in fact, one of the most potent in all language-history; as it makes whole classes of forms, so it has the power to change their limits" (*Life and Growth* 75).
19. For more on the professionalization of American literature at this time, and the role of "men of letters" like Howells in it, see Shumway. For pieces attesting to Howells' familiarity with late-19th-century writings on language while he was at *The Atlantic,* see "Recent Literature" 394–95; "Literary and Philological Manuals" 355–61; and selections from *The Atlantic Monthly's* "The Contributor's Club," begun by Howells in January 1877, which calls on Whitney, Muller, and White, three well-known philologists, for a gender-neutral singular pronoun. Nettels, *Language, Race* also gives a historically rich overview of Howells as a writer about language (2–9).
20. While thorough discussion of the regional implications of Howells' linguistic logic is beyond the scope of this chapter, geography was likewise an essentialized marker of identity in Howells' day. As evident in Howells' criticism above, the essentialization of language could also occur on the basis of *place,* by which country, region, or city became an essential trait attributed to language practice as well as race or gender. For instance, in the passage quoted above, Howells not only emphasizes the importance of dialect in the "representation of our national life," but he also clearly equates the use of dialect with particular places—Tennessee, Philadelphia, Boston, New York.
21. As Gates suggests, Howells' essay on Dunbar's *Majors and Minors* made Dunbar "the veritable father of a 'pure' or an 'authentic' black literary tradition, a tradition that Howells, remarkably, defined by the absence of miscegenation in the author's ancestry, as if the writings of mulattos such as Frederick Douglass or Harriet Jacobs had not really counted. Howells' review made Dunbar a star in the nation's literary firmament, in the very same year in which the Supreme Court decided the infamous Plessy v. Ferguson 'separate-but-equal' case" (Gates, Foreword xiii). Since Howells' enthusiastic praise for Dunbar's "Minors," many writers, including Dunbar, have questioned the desirability of his use of dialect, and some have used it to bolster their readings of Dunbar as a "plantation school accommodationist" (Martin and Primeau xxii, 165). Dunbar himself recognized the complexity of dialect representations and their potential to subordinate "black" poetry to "American" poetry. In an 1898 interview, when pressed by a reporter to claim for black poetry a kind of "tropic warmth, a cast of temperament that belongs of right to the African race [. . .] if it is to be genuine, a thing apart," Dunbar raises the point that the environment of blacks, for 250 years, has been *American,* and "in every respect the

same as that of all Americans" and expresses disdain for those "who would hold the negro down to a certain kind of poetry—dialect and concerning only scenes on plantations in the south" (Dunbar, "Negro in Literature" 205–06). What is often neglected in characterizations of Dunbar's writing, too, is the fact that Dunbar depicts a range of dialects in his poems and stories—not only African American dialects, but also German American and Irish American dialects, and Western dialects reminiscent of Bret Harte. See Braxton xxiii–xxiv for more on Dunbar's experimentation with a range of dialects and ix–xxxiv on the complexities of Dunbar's dialect poetry.

22. See Nettels, *Gender* 5–26 for a useful contextualization of such attitudes about gender and language.
23. Howells' own fiction also tended to illustrate the contradictory characterizations of women and language at the time: Not only were female characters expected to be social arbiters and guardians of the language, but they were also criticized as subordinate to men in language matters ("Our Daily Speech" cited in Nettels, *Gender* 28; see also 29–30, 34).
24. See Birnbaum for more on the relationships among early phonology, dialect writing like Harris', and race. As Birnbaum shows, and as I elaborate above, the work of late-19th-century linguists helped to certify fictional dialect as "real."
25. See Fruit 196–98, for an example of how one member of the American Dialect Society used the Uncle Remus tales as specimens for dialect study. From the *Atlanta Constitution,* whose editorial staff Harris joined in November 1876, Harris' tales were quickly reprinted in northern newspapers like the *Springfield Republican* and the *New York Evening Post,* where they attracted more attention and established Harris as a leading writer of dialect folklore. Collected in November 1880 in the volume that made Harris, Uncle Remus, and the Brer Rabbit legends famous, titled *Uncle Remus, His Songs and His Sayings,* the tales were published by D. Appleton and Company—the same company that published works by Noah Webster, Charles Darwin, and Lewis Carroll (Brasch 65). The collection was comprised of 34 "Legends of the Old Plantation" (these were slave tales, mostly animal trickster tales, told by Uncle Remus); 9 songs and 21 sayings (short dialect sketches featuring Uncle Remus and other human characters); and 1 short story (titled, "A Story of the War," discussed below). Within two weeks after publication, *Uncle Remus' Songs and Sayings* had sold two printings of 1500 each, and Charles A. Dana, editor of the *New York Sun,* predicted it would "not only have a large, but a permanent, and enduring sale" (qtd. in Brasch 82). Dana was right. Within six months about 10,000 copies were sold; by mid-1881, it was read in England (Kipling read it to his daughter). The book was immensely, nationally, popular, praised by reviewers for its contributions to literature of the South and American folklore, and Harris' later collections never matched it. See J. A. Miller on the national popularity of the Uncle Remus tales at the turn of the century; see Brasch xxv, 82–83, for more on their reception and popularity throughout the 20th century.
26. See Levine 81–83, 112–14 on Harris' treatment of the animal tales. As Levine suggests, while Harris' stories were faithful to the slave folklore from which Harris collected the tales, they focused on Brer Rabbit at the expense of other slave tales. Much of the scholarly material on Harris' animal tales, as Levine notes, centers on their origins (as African, Native American Indian, or Euro-American) rather than their meanings (82). Other scholarly work on Harris explores the intricacies of Harris' use of dialect (e.g., Ives and Pederson) or the relationships between Harris and his contemporaries, like Thomas Nelson Page, Mark Twain, or George Washington Cable (e.g., English). I am

less interested in the authenticity of Harris' dialect representations than in the conceptions of language, oriented toward consent or descent, reflected by representations of dialect and of gender and language. Although the animal legends are less relevant to this chapter, it is worth noting that these legends, too, create a masculinized and often aggressive world of dialect speakers—a fact that underscores the cultural interest in the black male voice in an era negotiating the black man's vote. In the animal legends, female characters are scarce, and when they do appear, they figure as a supporting cast to the male animals, signaled as male by their names ("Brers" Fox, Rabbit, Possum, Bear, Terrapin, Bull-Frog, Wolf). These few female animals (Miss Partridge, Miss Brune, Miss Brindle, Sis Cow, Molly Cottontail) rarely speak, while their male counterparts consistently exchange verbal banter.

27. See Keely on the trope of romantic reconciliation and marriage plots in post-bellum literature.
28. Mugglestone also deals with the term *eye dialect* (139, 212–13, 218). For yet another useful discussion of the dynamics of eye dialect, see Birnbaum 42. An understanding of eye dialect lends linguistic insight into Borus' characterization of realism as a way of seeing. Eye dialect is used extensively in the animal fables narrated by Uncle Remus, as we see in the very beginning of the famed "Wonderful Tar-Baby Story," when Harris writes that Brer Fox fixed up "a *contrapshun wat* he *calla* Tar-Baby, en he tuck dish yer Tar-Baby en he sot 'er in de big road, en den he lay off in de bushes fer to see *wat* de news *wuz* gwineter be" (*Uncle Remus* 7, my emphasis).
29. "Sound-blindness" is a term from Franz Boas' "On Alternating Sounds" that Sundquist uses to discuss the vernacular language of black spirituals long woven into but ignored in American culture. According to Sundquist, the challenge of revising the canon calls for rethinking patterns of value, patterns of "sound-blindness," that have helped to segregate American literature throughout the 20th century (22–23). From this perspective, writers like Harris were forward-looking. As Broadhead notes, Harris' *Uncle Remus* and Thomas Nelson Page's *In Ole Virginia* (1887) paradoxically had to make a progressive move by handing "the role of dialect speaker to a black character, and so made a literary place for an authentic-sounding black voice" even while delivering a regressive social message (Intro 5). And, Dunbar, when asked in an 1898 interview, "Which one of the current writers of negro stories best represents the race?" responded that Harris himself, along with Ruth McEnery Stuart, "shows the most intimate sympathy" (qtd. in Martin and Primeau 207). (Dunbar notably omits Thomas Nelson Page, whose attitude he sees as "condescending, always" [207]. Chesnutt would echo Dunbar's sentiments about Page in Chesnutt's "Post Bellum—Pre Harlem," which describes Page as "disguising the harshness of slavery under the mask of sentiment" [103].)
30. Thomas Nelson Page's "Meh Lady: A Story of the War" is another story that functions like Harris' "A Story of the War"; the titles of the two stories indicate the remarkable similarities in their plots, both told by eyewitness black male storytellers. Similarly, their black narrators' voices are *heard*, in the first paragraphs of the stories, before their characters are *seen*—a strategy that emphasizes the importance of black male dialect in framing these nostalgic tales and in making them "authentic" linguistic reconstructions. Much like Harris' story, although longer and more complex, Page's "Meh Lady" revolves around the southern white woman's (Meh Lady's) nursing an injured Union soldier (Captain Wilton) back to health and eventually marrying him and naming their children, children of the New South, after the story's narrator Uncle Billy, Page's version of Uncle Remus.

31. The argument that Chesnutt's stories offered an alternative to the plantation tale and to the Uncle Remus stories is not new (e.g., Church). Chesnutt himself had explicitly contrasted his Uncle Julius tales with Harris' Uncle Remus tales on more than one occasion—see his "Superstitions and Folklore of the South" (95) and "Post Bellum—Pre Harlem" (103). For more on the conventionality and unconventionality of Chesnutt's conjure tales, see Broadhead, Intro; for more on Chesnutt's relationship to Harris, see Sundquist.
32. While Chesnutt's initial dialect stories were enthusiastically accepted, those stories interested in racial mixing and not written in dialect were repeatedly refused publication in the 1890s. In October 1897, Walter Hines Page tentatively accepted "The Dumb Witness" for publication, but it was never separately published within Chesnutt's lifetime. Page asserted that the tales "Dave's Neckliss" and "The Dumb Witness" were excluded from the original *Conjure Woman* collection, begun in 1897 but published in 1899, because they worked against coherence and did not deal with conjure. But the excluded works were also somewhat dark and threatening tales, unwelcome to readers who were hungry for the nostalgia of Harris (Broadhead, Intro 18). In Stepto's view, the editors' rejection of tales that seemed to imply the possibility of bringing whites into an understanding of blacks constituted an official curbing of Chesnutt's subversive meanings (Broadhead, Intro 20).
33. As Broadhead notes, "The Dumb Witness" exists in two manuscript versions in the Chesnutt Papers at Fisk University Library—one version of 21 pages and another of only 8 (Intro 25–26). The second is a revision of the first, but is incomplete; we don't know how Chesnutt further intended to revise it. The edition in the Broadhead collection, which I use, follows the text of the second typescript where it exists, using the first typescript to fill in the rest. Passages from the first version but later deleted are printed in notes. A third version of the story is the version in Chesnutt's novel *The Colonel's Dream*, which I discuss below.
34. Similar to his praise of Dunbar's dialect poems, Howells praises Chesnutt's conjure tales, yet responded in measured fashion to Chesnutt's nondialect stories, unavoidably grappling with the relation of Chesnutt's descent to his writing. Despite the fact that Howells claims that "It is not from their racial interest that we would first wish to speak of [Chesnutt's writings], though that must have a very great and very just claim upon the critic," Howells praises Chesnutt's *Conjure Woman* as his "most important work" (Howells, "Chesnutt's Stories" 113–14). Howells' ambivalence about Chesnutt may partially reflect cultural attitudes toward the mulatta/mulatto figures whom Chesnutt worked to recast in his nondialect stories that rejected the vernacular plantation tale; the mulatta/mulatto "constituted a cultural anomaly whose story inevitably resulted in sentimental or melodramatic tragedy" (Wohnam 56). Refer to Andrews for a comparison of the Howells-Dunbar and Howells-Chesnutt relationships.
35. See Broadhead, Intro 12–13 for further discussion of Chesnutt's mixed feelings about the dialect tale formula as it appealed to the dominant literary system at the time; see C. Foster for an analysis of Chesnutt's phonological depictions.
36. Broadhead, Stepto, and Wohnam have primarily focused on the dynamics of the tale's narration by John, rightly noting Chesnutt's powerful reversals of narrative conventions in the story of revenge, but not bringing—though Chesnutt himself does bring—the significant question of gender into the discussion of race and dialect. We need to look not merely at Chesnutt's representation of Julius' or John's language, but of *Viney's* speech, to find the "secret" of "The Dumb Witness."

37. Chesnutt is unclear here as to the cause of Viney's objections, but the passage, when read on the heels of descriptions of her, seems to imply that her "blood" lay some claim to the Murchison's household. While this could be interpreted as an essentialist reference to the Indian or black blood in her veins—"passionate strains" that speak out—the fact that Chesnutt has already deconstructed "blood" and that Viney shares the family's blood complicates such a reading.
38. Here, Murchison's fortune "eludes his grasp," and Chesnutt's hand imagery throughout the story fascinatingly traces the ways in which Viney's and Murchison's fates are linked. For example, Viney withdraws her hand from his in the story's initial frame; he does not stay his hand in punishing her; she "might as well have been without hands" in his attempts to teach her to write (168). This imagery becomes equally significant in light of the ending of the story in *The Colonel's Dream*, discussed below.
39. It is at this point that Chesnutt "apparently hesitated as to whether Viney should speak 'perfect' English or black dialect English. In the first version she replies, 'Yes, sir, I'll call him'" (171n3). In *The Colonel's Dream* (1905), as we will see, Viney also speaks Standard English.
40. *The Colonel's Dream* is thus politicized in a way that "The Dumb Witness" is not. Throughout the novel, Chesnutt's protagonist learns of all of the ways in which Clarendon's predominantly white supremacist society works "to keep the Negro down," including the corruption in the prison system, through which black prisoners are brought in on trumped-up charges and sold cheaply as convict labor in proceedings reminiscent of the slave trade. French is a man of sincere but still-limited ideals concerning race relations—limited with respect to his inability to recognize how deeply entrenched racism is in Clarendon and his own retention of aristocratic values and ideas about blood, that "blood did tell" (*Colonel's Dream* 37, 77); his capitalist assumptions that the town could be stimulated simply with an inflow of cash; and his nostalgia for the South of his youth. Yet these shortcomings are counterbalanced by the fact that, while he is aristocratic in feeling, French is "an ardent democrat" in principle (81); he works against the corruption epitomized by his rapacious antagonist, appropriately named Bill Fetters (a "vampire bat, sucking the life-blood of the people" [117]), to complicate the contrived sociopolitical lines drawn in Clarendon (156, 165).
41. While Twain's *Pudd'nhead*, set in antebellum Dawson's Landing, is obviously relevant to the issues in this chapter, I have focused instead on Chesnutt's stories, which, while reflecting on the antebellum era and the Civil War, are set in the Reconstruction era and published in the wake of *Plessy*, alongside Chesnutt's contemplations about the law.
42. Twain's view of speech as a social institution, like manners or clothing, is reinforced at the end of the novel when "The real heir suddenly found himself rich and free, but in a most embarrassing situation. He could neither read nor write, and his speech was the basest dialect of the negro quarter" (*PW* 225). See Fishkin for more on Twain's use of dialect.
43. See Doyle esp. 21–28.

NOTES TO CHAPTER 4

1. While Matthews can be said to have written for a different audience than White, whose collected essays were originally published in *The Galaxy* in the late 1860s-80s, Matthews, White, and James shared more than simply their

criticism of American speech: Matthews cited both White and James in *Parts of Speech* (1901) and was a member of the prestigious Author Club with James. For more on the era's social and literary clubs that revolved around Matthews, see Ashton 91–126.
2. It is noteworthy that Matthews' writings about language (e.g., "The Stock that Speaks the Language" [1901], *Parts of Speech* 4–6, 17) also often exemplify the collocation of ideas about blood, gender, race, and nation in commentary about language as addressed in the previous chapter. Matthews' writings likewise manifest the era's rhetoric of Anglo-Saxonism, which joined notions of gender, race, and language and gained fuel from its coupling with scientific racial theories over the second half of the century. On Anglo-Saxonism, see Horsman and S. Anderson.
3. The "old" immigrants were from Northern and Western Europe and presumably more easily assimilated. M. Jones refutes the classic "new"/"old" distinction in immigration trends established by the Dillingham Commission and subsequently emphasized by historians, arguing that it was a "completely artificial distinction" that joined very unlike groups of 19th-century immigrants. While M. Jones acknowledges that there was a shift in the geographic origin of American immigration at the end of the 19th century, he claims it occurred later and less suddenly than is often rehearsed; not until 1896 did the "new" immigration outgrow the "old" (179). As R. Smith corroborates, the rate of immigration relative to the population was highest between 1901 and 1910 (441). Regardless of when precisely the "new" immigration occurred, what is relevant here is that immigration continued to increase and that many turn-of-the-century Americans *perceived* it as distinct from earlier in the century. See M. Jones 177–206, 207–46, 247–77, for an overview of immigration in this era. See R. Smith 347–409, 410–69 for an excellent description of the era's citizenship laws.
4. See also Newman 36 on the relation between responses to immigration and to women's rights.
5. As Gere notes, while this was not the first bill that curbed immigration, "it was the first to identify literacy as a characteristic of 'admissable aliens'" (21). Gere's first chapter, 17–53, explores how clubwomen from various social positions developed understandings of literacy to counter those posed in the 1917 bill (22).
6. Additionally highlighting the turn to language to manage anxiety about immigration were the remarks in "Immigration—A Review" (1900) of Senator Henry Cabot Lodge (MA), who sponsored the 1896 Literacy Bill, and of Brander Matthews in his address to the American Library Association, "The American of the Future" (July 4, 1906). See esp. Lodge 54–55; Matthews, *American* 4–5, 9–10, 12–13, 22. Although, as Gere and others have shown, *literacy* became an ever more important term in discussions of American citizenship, I am less concerned with ideas about literacy in this chapter than with ideas about language education, broadly conceived, which paved the way for the notions of literacy as a distinct marker of American culture that were legislated in 1917, the end of the period I examine here. While the 1917 bill focused on a narrow conception of literacy as *reading*—as Gere points out, a consuming mode of literacy unlike writing's producing mode—I focus on conceptions of language education that were largely oral or "vocal" and that can not easily be classed as either consumptive or productive.
7. Similar to the discourse of civilization, Americanization too was "an effort to secure cultural and ideological hegemony through configuration of the symbolic order" (Olneck 399).

8. I again borrow a dual understanding of *domestic* from Kaplan, "Manifest Domesticity." In a sense, through commentary about gender and language, women were both co-opted *by* "civilization" and *themselves* co-opted "civilization" to their own ends (for example, in advocating women's rights, an argument that Newman cogently makes). Late-19th-century *linguistic* notions of uplifting American "civilization" operated, as did the wider discourse of civilization, on the assumption that, as vocal guardians of American "civilization," white, middle-class women were racially superior—a formulation I take from Newman 16–19.
9. For example, Bederman references Basil Ransom's lament in *The Bostonians* that "the masculine tone is passing out of the world" (*Manliness* 16). Yet while Bederman's emphasis is on the word *masculine* here—on reading Ransom's comments as reflective of the era's conceptions of manhood, manliness, and masculinity—I want to emphasize "masculine *tone*," reading Basil Ransom's comments, as I do other characters' verbal commentary throughout this project, as part of the era's gendered commentary on language.
10. See again my introductory discussion for an elaboration of Althusser's formulation and my view of the place of literature in this project.
11. See Goodman 2–4 and Schlesinger 27–34 for helpful summaries of the increased interest in manners over the course of the 19th and early 20th centuries.
12. The apparent difference between mid-century propriety and late-19th-century manners as a facet of "civilization" could further be seen by larger historical trends: Manners were taken up across the board by schools, magazines, newspapers, and independent publishers and were increasingly described as "art." An example of an etiquette manual that secured a place in late-19th-century schools, *The Primer of Politeness: A Help to School and Home Government* (1883), demonstrates the way in which manners were considered part and parcel of a liberal education, a key contribution to American "civilization." Its "Hints to Teachers" advertises that it might be used "as a text-book, or, preferably, as a class-book for study by the pupils" (Gow 4); and its title page bears the quote "Scholarship without good breeding is only half an education." In addition to etiquette conceived as education, etiquette was now conceived broadly as art, a description that reflects the desire to uphold an advanced civilization via manners, as seen in titles such as *The Art of Pleasing, The Art of Good Manners, The Art of Good Behavior, The Art of Being Agreeable, The Art of Dining,* and *The Art of Speech and Deportment* (Schlesinger 35).
13. Bentley demonstrates how "propriety" developed into "manners" at the end of the century through her analysis of Edith Wharton's social metaphors, such as Wharton's figurations of the "tribes" of the New York rich, which compared drawing-room culture to ethnographic culture (7), and she discusses the "deeply political" and institutional nature of manners as "the personalized, bodily absorption of social habits and decorum" (2). I aim to highlight in this section how ideas about vocal regulation regulate bodies no less than ideas about posture or table manners.
14. See also Harrison 178 on women's manners as a measure of American civilization.
15. Rayne's *Gems of Deportment,* for example, compares the voice—a "perfectly modulated voice, clear, resonant, and with no guttural tones to make it harsh"—to "all the charm of a strain of music to the educated ear" (41). Echoing White, who likewise compares the voice to a musical instrument and advocates voice training in *Every-Day English,* Rayne devotes an

entire chapter of her book to "Elocution—Reading and Speaking—Culture of the Voice—Value of Words—Pronunciation." While women were especially urged to regulate their tone, men and even children were also regularly instructed to do so. Gow's *Primer of Politeness* offers an example of a manners manual addressed to schoolchildren and, as such, is written in question-and-answer format. See especially his section titled "An Agreeable Voice," which centers on the tone (59). Wells addresses his tonal pointers to those aspiring to be gentlemen (67); *Etiquette for Americans* addresses its vocal instructions more broadly (13; see also 154), as does M. Cooke's *Social Etiquette* (1896) (37), whose chapter "Art of Conversation" is devoted to conversational regulations.

16. This collection, compiled by "eighteen distinguished authors," emphasizes the importance of vocal regulation, as signified by the fact that one of its "distinguished authors" was Lillie d'Angelo Bergh, "World-famed as a musician and voice teacher" and "Author of several text-books on the voice" (1). In the collection, Ella Wheeler Wilcox declares that "The True Etiquette" is akin to the legal code ("Ignorance of the law excuses no offender, and ignorance of etiquette is without excuse, always, if opportunities for learning are neglected"), and she stresses the importance of a young girl's rearing "in a kind and loving home" to developing the "instincts of a gentlewoman" that "will prompt her to do and say the right thing" in any society (25).

17. The focus on etiquette in some ways carved out a new public role for women beyond the home (Goodman 3–4). Yet, as N. Johnson convincingly shows, "parlor" traditions of rhetoric, in which I would locate manners manuals' advice, also worked to sustain domesticity as an extension of ideal womanhood.

18. Without attention to tone, James believes, we threaten our very bodies and cheapen our society. James consistently, throughout his essays, uses very material metaphors to underline the import of attention to a tone-standard (or lack thereof) on American civilization. For example, James compares "vowel-cutting" to "gem-cutting," and he compares speech to "the motion, the food, or the clothing of intercourse," which must be pursued "lightedly," with "neatness and completeness," to prevent "groping, helplessly, empirically, almost dangerously (perilously, that is, to life and limb), in the dark" ("Question" 47–49). James wants to keep words "expensive" and valuable, rather than making indifferent substitutions for sounds and words; the varied quality of our sounds retains the *parts* of our language, and he wants to retain these differentiated parts for the benefit of *interest,* for the aesthetic sense, for amusement, for the beauty of life ("Speech" 77–78). He thus pleads against simply useful speech, which he compares to "cheap, innutritive food" at the expense of tasteful, discriminating, differentiating attention to tone (79). For still more on James' conception of tone, see also his "Manners" 84–85, 92–93, 104–05.

19. See also James, "Manners" 88–89.

20. Reviewers of the time, not surprisingly, likewise saw the subject of *The Bostonians* as "the situation of women," and as particularly American (Hayes 153–72). See S. Davis for an exploration of historical feminist sources in *The Bostonians* that attest to the relevance of the women's movement to James' novel.

21. Again, I want to be clear here that my argument is not about reading *The Bostonians* in order to position James as a feminist or anti-feminist, or racist or anti-racist, writer—questions that other critics have explored with nuance but that continue to remain open. On feminism, for example, see Fetterley's timeless chapter on *The Bostonians* in *Resisting,* esp. 113–15;

Posnock's incisive pages on James' androgyny in *Trial,* 200–01; Person's examination of Basil Ransom's shifting subject positions—racial, gendered, and sexual; and Daugherty's discussion of James' representations of women as they respond to other authors' treatments of women. On the question of race, see especially the exchange among Blair, Posnock, and Warren in *The Henry James Review* 16.3 (1995), and in the same issue, see Michaels, "Jim Crow." On the question of sexual dynamics in James, Esteve's analysis of James' "anerotics" in *The American Scene* usefully illuminates Fetterley's interest in James' lesbianism and Posnock's in James' androgyny. What Posnock identifies as a pragmatist position of marginality central to understanding James, whether in terms of gender, race, or sexuality, is what I believe makes James particularly attentive to dynamics of discourse and power, and to politics of language. Thus I am less interested in pinning James down on questions of gender, race, or sexuality than in exploring what James' writings might tell us about the politics of language within the context of the Woman Question he foregrounds. In this sense, my reading most overlaps with those who focus on James' concern with "voice" and its 19th-century contexts in the novel—G. Jones, Levander, and Wardley. Yet my interests also diverge from theirs. For instance, Wardley is interested in Verena's voice as an extension of "democracy's body," a springboard from which to examine anxieties surrounding feminine openings—oral, gustatory, sexual, and spatial apertures—where social differences may be erased in a democracy; I am interested, however, in locating Verena's voice within turn-of-the-century discourses on language education rather than physiology. While G. Jones locates James' concern with voice in *The Bostonians,* as I do, within late-19th-century linguistic contexts, Jones is less interested in how commentary on language might manage the historical and political context of the women's movement and immigration, than in how ideas about linguistic decay were linked to 19th-century neurasthenia. Levander's reading of *The Bostonians,* which she compares to Sarah J. Hale's *The Lecturess, or Woman's Sphere* (1839), perhaps most overlaps with mine in her interest in how James' narrative of Basil Ransom's need to privatize Verena's speech shows how 19th-century language theories are disguised as "'essential truths' in order to marginalize women from the public sphere" (Levander 14). Yet, in addition to this, I am interested in another possible, overlooked narrative in the novel—about how the regulation of Verena's voice also effectively removes im/migrants from the public sphere.

22. As one reviewer of "Mr. Henry James' New Novel" in England's *Pall Mall Gazette* rightly observed about James' dénouement: "Mr. James dismisses his heroine in tears [. . .]. How different from the flourish with which the heroine generally leaves the stage!" (15 March 1886 rpt. in Hayes 156).

23. James incisively came to locate the interest in dialect within wider cultural interests in what he called "the preference for the study of the primitive" that flourished at the end and turn of the century and observed that the answer to the "Why?" of dialect stories "would probably take us far, land us even perhaps in the lap of an inquiry as to what cultivation the human plant, in the country at large, *is* under" ("American Letter" 18).

24. On this point, see C. Anderson 48–52, who suggests that James mixes the narrator's point of view with his own impressions of the South as a location for difference, exoticism, and aristocracy.

25. While *The American Scene* (1907), published around the same time as James' essays, shares many ideas with them, I focus here on the essays—particularly "The Question of Our Speech" but also "The Manners of American Women"

and "The Speech of American Women"—because they more explicitly foreground interest in women's voices.
26. I read the settlement movement, as some historians do, as a precedent for the Americanization movement; both partook in the turn-of-the-century discourse of civilization and featured women as language educators to help immigrants assimilate. Women were key educators in other areas—for example, by the 1880s, two-thirds of public school teachers nationwide were white middle-class women, and by 1892 five-sixths were (Newman 28). My focus here, however, is on those efforts to Americanize immigrants through language instruction.
27. Addams founded Hull-House on September 18, 1889, when she and her friend Ellen Gates Starr moved into an old mansion in a run-down Chicago neighborhood hoping to "settle" there and become good neighbors to the poor, since, for Addams, the waste of the life and talent of educated youth was as wasteful as that of the destitute ("Subjective" 22). Settlers like Addams noticed the social inequalities brought about by industrialization, immigration, and national expansion and hoped their projects would bridge the gaps between rich and poor, between "American" and "foreigner." American settlements, like their English counterparts, were thus motivated to serve both the urban poor and middle-class college graduates. In the U.S., the movement caught on quickly: Settlements were founded within years of one another in New York (Neighbourhood Guild 1886, College Settlement 1889), Chicago (Hull-House 1889), and Boston (Andover House 1891, Denison House 1891) (Carson 34–35; Garbus 549); there were 411 settlements across the U.S. by 1911 (Woods and Kennedy vi cited in Garbus 549). Like other settlement houses of the era, Hull-House gave a central mission to women—not only Addams and Starr and the women who lived there, but also the group of wealthy Chicago women who gave their time and money to the project (Addams, "Subjective" 20; Bryan and Davis 7; Hurt xvii). More widely, American settlement houses bore gendered aspects; given the limitation of women's spirituality to the domestic sphere in American culture more generally, settlement houses provided an outlet, ratified by middle-class American culture's sentimental conventions, for women's religious and moral positions to "leak" into social life (Carson 37). At the same time, however, the new "civic duties" (Addams, "Objective" 32) adopted by these women could reform women's experience and their wider sociopolitical roles. These wider roles may have been recognized by J. Edgar Hoover, Founding Director of the FBI, who called Addams "The Most Dangerous Woman in America," and by the FBI, which stated in a report dated March 20, 1928, that Addams "is directly responsible for the growth of the radical movement among women in America" for her support of women's right to vote at the Progressive Party Convention of 1912 (Jane Addams Hull-House Museum).
28. Of the instructors listed for Evening Clubs and Classes in this schedule of events, there were twenty-five women to fourteen men. If the kindergarten classes that met every morning are included, these twenty-five women taught or led fifty-three classes or clubs, compared with eighteen taught or led by men—over twice as many (Moore 43). In addition, the instructors cited in Addams' personal reflections on Hull-House education were women (Addams, *Twenty Years* 249).
29. Thus some contemporary scholars see Hull-House's classes and clubs as part of "a larger assimilatory vision" that tacitly believed in a superior Anglo-American culture and failed to honor immigrant cultures (Lissak 90–91 qtd. in Carson 40). To be fair, Addams did seem to sense the imbalance in such a vision. While Hull-House did offer classes emphasizing "the best"

of Western culture, such as the class in advanced literature, which featured readings from Austen, Boswell, Cervantes, Goethe, Lamb, Tolstoy and "the best contemporary dramas" (*Hull-House Year Book* [1916] 8), at the same time, Addams' educational philosophy held up the settlement's inter-national ideal of lateral connection and fellowship among diverse people ("Snare of Preparation" 50). In her later writings, Addams distinctly espoused a broad inter-nationalism, valuing an *alternative* conception of civilization as "a method of living, an attitude of equal respect for all men" ("Aspects of the Women's Movement" 287); she disdained what she called "institutionalized" and "dogmatized" nationalism in a 1919 essay titled "Americanization" (241) and derided what she called "our national self-righteousness" in a forward-looking 1933 essay of this title. As a practical extension of this human solidarity, Addams and her fellow settlers were often legal advocates for immigrants (see "Objective" 43). When reading settlers' writings, the well-intentioned earnestness and expansiveness of their project, despite the settlement movement's shortcomings, are thus inescapable. On this point, see Garbus 557.

30. The centrality of being able to read, write, or speak English to assessing the family status of immigrants also becomes apparent in a "Family Schedule" questionnaire from 1893, issued by the U. S. Department of Labor, of which roughly 12% of the total questions deal explicitly with language abilities (*Hull-House Maps and Papers* 2).

31. See Crocker on settlement house night schools as early and important Americanizers (54). American Settlement in Indianapolis and Campbell House in Gary, Indiana also offered English classes helping to Americanize immigrants (Crocker 61, 128).

32. Prompted by the First World War, interest in national defense, a focus on industrialization, and fears of national disloyalty in war time, the Americanization movement gained national attention and federal support by 1920 and resulted in Americanization Conferences, such as the one held from May 12–15, 1919 in Washington, D.C. ("National Americanization Conference" 702–40). On *Americanization* itself as a debated and evolving term, see Brandeis 639–40; Claxton 621–22; Kellor 623–25; and Thompson, "School" 595.

33. While my concern here is how discourses of Americanization placed women, Gere's chapter "Constructing and Contesting Americanization(s)," 54–92, shows how clubwomen reworked these discourses, both corroborating and contesting them. Gere's analysis also addresses the generally condescending relationship between white middle-class women and working class women in projects that echoed Americanization's gendered family structure; and she shows how working women created a broader definition of America themselves.

34. On the primary importance of *speaking* English over articulation and pronunciation, see Mahoney and Herlihy 119–20; Thompson, *Schooling* 183; and Winkler and Alsberg 54–55. See Mahoney and Herlihy 49–51 for the teacher's need for "frequent self-examination," a list of accompanying questions she should ask herself, and suggested lessons for her "program-book"; see 60–61 for suggestions for conversation and reading lessons calling on the teacher's ingenuity.

35. This act answered the need to focus on, as Kate Waller Barrett, Special Agent of the U.S. Immigration Service, put the problem in 1915, "the alien mother who is often an uncrowned heroine" (Barrett 227). The recognition of the need for close cooperation between the home and the school to overcome the immigrant mother's "greatest handicap—illiteracy" led to experiments

in various cities from which the idea of the home and neighborhood teacher, connected to the public-school system, was developed (Winkler and Alsberg 51). Thus in 1915, the California legislature, prompted by the State Commission of Immigration and Housing of California, passed the precedent-setting Home Teacher Act, leading by 1919 to several types of home and neighborhood classes in Los Angeles and becoming the national model for bringing American and immigrant women together through the home. Attesting to its wide influence, at its annual meeting in April 1919, the Chairman of Education of the national General Federation of Women's Clubs (an organization that represented 2 million women and was dedicated to Americanization work) urged all states to inform themselves of the act and "*inaugurate a movement looking toward similar legislation in their own states* [sic.]" (qtd. in "The Immigrant and the State" 466). See Gere for an account of the work of women's clubs during this era.

NOTES TO CODA

1. Of course, *civilization* was a loaded word for Gilman, as it was for many late-19th- and early-20th-century Americans; as Newman states, Gilman's feminism, "while dismissing sexual difference as crucial to evolutionary progress, nonetheless continued to encode assumptions of white racial superiority. Gilman's discursive tactics, formulated in response to the racial anxieties (and in light of the assimilationist policies) of whites during the progressive era, were based on an ongoing denigration of the 'primitive' as the antithesis of 'civilization'" (Newman 136). See also Bederman 123–24. While a full consideration of Gilman's work is beyond the scope of this coda, which aims to be suggestive and to indicate new directions for the study of language, gender, and nation, scholars have written in-depth on racial and other tensions in Gilman's life and work in recent years. Refer, for instance, to Bederman's biographical analysis (124–34) and to Newman's examination of Gilman's intellectual affinities with sociologists Lester Ward and Edward A. Ross (132–51).
2. *New York City Review of Literature* (1933) qtd. in Bederman 135. By 1915, *Women and Economics* had eight American printings and was published in translation in Japan, Hungary, Holland, Denmark, Italy, Germany, and Russia (Bederman 135).
3. As the editors of Mencken's *In Defense of Women* put it, "Although he [Mencken] approved of the vote for women on the ground that women would have sense enough to abolish democracy, he despised active suffragettes" (xiii). Mencken derided much, including women, blacks, Jews, Indians, politicians, Catholics, Protestants, democracy, and the "booboisie," his term for "the vast herd of human blanks" (Fecher 124). Mencken himself was said to elicit more vigorous denunciations than "any other American of his time, not even excepting Henry Ford, Robert M. LaFollette, Clarence Darrow, and Sacco and Vanzetti" (Prefatory Note, *Menckeniana*). For more on Mencken's anti-Semitism, see Kanigel; on his anti-feminism, see Schaum. It is fascinating that, in contrast to his irascibility in just about every other arena, Mencken's wide philological correspondence with linguists such as Louise Pound appeared to be always polite and congenial; see McDavid, "H.L. Mencken."
4. Edmund Wilson and William Carlos Williams were among this edition's serious reviewers. Its extraordinary readership established it as Mencken's masterpiece, and though Mencken swore he was finished after this volume,

his philological collections grew by leaps and bounds, leading to two Supplements—"works of grumpy heroism"—that were published in 1945 and 1948 and were "repositories more than compositions" (R. Nelson 685–87). R. Nelson gives a very lucid summary of the themes and tensions in *The American Language*. For Mencken biography, see Hobson. For an excellent analysis of Mencken's nationalist philology and an analysis of all five editions of *The American Language* in the context of 20th-century ideas about monolingualism, see J. L. Miller, Part I.
5. Jespersen saw English as "masculine" in part because it had lost grammatical gender, which he, like Mencken, considered an "affliction" (Mencken, "Future of English" 88). Besides using ideas about gender to support American English's superiority, Mencken uses numbers—he works to establish it as superior through sheer mass as a language spoken by at least 20 million people throughout the world.
6. Throughout Jespersen's piece "The Woman" in *Language: Its Nature, Development, and Origin* (1922), he catalogues differences between men's and women's speech in essentialist ways. For example, men are responsible for linguistic growth and innovation; women are responsible for "weakening" in language (206, 208). Jespersen believes women have a smaller vocabulary, use punctuation in a weak manner, and speak more rapidly than men—but this rapid readiness of speech, Jespersen makes sure to add, "is no proof of intellectual power," only proof of their smaller vocabularies (217–18).
7. See again Kahane, who charts the many factors at work in the development of American English from a "colonial substandard" to a "prestige language" (217).

Bibliography

Adams, John Quincy. "Speech of John Quincy Adams, of Massachusetts, Upon the Right of the People, Men and Women, to Petition; on the Freedom of Speech and of Debate in the House of Representatives of the United States; on the Resolutions of Seven State Legislatures, and the Petitions of more than One Hundred Thousand Petitioners, Relating to the Annexation of Texas to this Union." U.S. House of Representatives. 16 June–7 July 1838. Washington, D.C.: Gales and Seaton, 1838.

Addams, Jane. "Americanization." In *American Sociological Society Publications* 14 (1919). Rpt. in Elshtain 240–47.

———. "Aspects of the Women's Movement." In *The Second Twenty Years at Hull-House, September 1909 to September 1929 with a Record of Growing World Consciousness.* New York: Macmillan, 1930. Rpt. in Elshtain 275–93.

———. "Educational Methods." *Democracy and Social Ethics.* New York: Macmillan, 1902. 178–220.

———. "Immigration: A Field Neglected by the Scholar." University of Chicago Convocation Address. *The Commons* 10.1 (Jan. 1905). Rpt. in P. Davis 3–22.

———. "The Objective Value of a Social Settlement." In Henry C. Adams, ed. *Philanthropy and Social Progress, Seven Essays by Miss Jane Addams, Robert A. Woods, Father J.O.S. Huntington, Professor Franklin H. Giddings and Bernard Bosanquet. Delivered before the School of Applied Ethics at Plymouth, Mass., during the Session of 1892.* New York: Thomas Y. Crowell, 1893. Rpt. in Elshtain 29–45.

———. "Our National Self Righteousness," *University of Chicago Magazine,* vol. 26 (Nov. 1933). Rpt. in Elshtain 442–47.

———. "The Snare of Preparation." Ch. 4 in *Twenty Years at Hull-House with Autobiographical Notes.* 40–53.

———. "The Subjective Necessity for Social Settlements." In Henry C. Adams, ed. *Philanthropy and Social Progress, Seven Essays by Miss Jane Addams, Robert A. Woods, Father J.O.S. Huntington, Professor Franklin H. Giddings and Bernard Bosanquet. Delivered before the School of Applied Ethics at Plymouth, Mass., during the Session of 1892.* New York: Thomas Y. Crowell, 1893. Rpt. in Elshtain 14–28.

———. *Twenty Years at Hull-House with Autobiographical Notes.* 1910. Intro. and notes by James Hurt. Illus. by Norah Hamilton. Urbana and Chicago: U of Illinois P, 1990.

———. "Votes for 'Ignorant Women.'" *Survey* 23 (Oct. 1915): 85.

———. "Women's Conscience and Social Amelioration." In Charles Stelzle et al., *Social Application of Religion.* Merrick Lectures, Ohio Wesleyan University. Cincinnati: Jennings and Graham, 1908. Rpt. in Elshtain 252–63.

Alger, Horatio, Jr. *Ragged Dick; Or, Street Life in New York with the Boot Blacks.* 1867. New York: Signet, 1990.

Allen, Irving Lewis. *The City in Slang: New York Life and Popular Speech.* New York: Oxford UP, 1993.

Althusser, Louis. "Ideology and Ideological State Apparatuses (Notes towards an Investigation)." *Mapping Ideology.* Ed. Slavoj Zizek. New York: Verso, 1994. 100–40.

———. "A Letter on Art in Reply to André Daspre." In *Lenin and Philosophy and Other Essays by Louis Althusser.* Trans. Ben Brewster. New York: Monthly Review, 1971. 221–27.

"American Women." *U.S. Magazine and Democratic Review* 6.20 (Aug. 1839): 127–43.

Anderson, Benedict. *Imagined Communities: Reflections on the Origin and Spread of Nationalism.* Rev. ed. New York: Verso, 1991.

Anderson, Charles R. "James's Portrait of the Southerner." Budd and Cady, *On Henry James* 30–52.

Anderson, Stuart. *Race and Rapprochement: Anglo-Saxonism and Anglo-American Relations, 1895–1904.* Madison: Farleigh Dickinson UP and London: Associated UP, 1981.

Andrews, William L. "William Dean Howells and Charles W. Chesnutt: Criticism and Race Fiction in the Age of Booker T. Washington." Budd and Cady, *On Howells* 232–44.

Arch, Stephen Carl. "Romancing the Puritans: American Historical Fiction in the 1820s." *ESQ* 39 (1993): 107–32.

Argersinger, Jana L. "Susan Warner." Knight, *Writers* 384–91.

Ashton, Susanna. *Collaborators in Literary America, 1870–1920.* New York: Palgrave Macmillan, 2003.

Ashworth, Suzanne M. "Susan Warner's *The Wide, Wide World,* Conduct Literature, and Protocols of Female Reading in Mid-Nineteenth-Century America." *Legacy: A Journal of American Women Writers* 17.2 (June 2000): 141–64.

Babbidge, Homer D., Jr., ed. and intro. *On Being American: Selected Writings, 1783–1828.* By Noah Webster. New York: Praeger, 1967. 3–15.

Bailey, Richard. "Democracy in American Speech." Fred Newton Scott Lecture. University of Michigan. Ann Arbor, Michigan. 2002. Ed. Richard Bailey. 9 Jan. 2005. <http://www-personal.umich.edu/~rwbaily/ScottFN.htm>. 1–19.

———. "Ideologies, Attitudes, and Perceptions." *Needed Research in American Dialects,* ed. Dennis R. Preston. Publication of the American Dialect Society 88. Durham, NC: Duke UP, 2003. 123–50.

———. *Images of English: A Cultural History of the Language.* Ann Arbor: U of Michigan P, 1991.

———. *Nineteenth-Century English.* Ann Arbor: U of Michigan P, 1996.

Baker, Houston A. *Modernism and the Harlem Renaissance.* Chicago: U of Chicago P, 1987. 41–47. Rpt. in Wohnam 130–34.

Baker, Jean H., ed. *Votes for Women: The Struggle for Suffrage Revisited.* New York: Oxford UP, 2002.

Bannerji, Himani, Mojab Shahrzad, and Judith Whitehead, eds. *Of Property and Propriety: The Role of Gender and Class in Imperialism and Nationalism.* Toronto: U of Toronto P, 2001.

Bardaglio, Peter W. *Reconstructing the Household: Families, Sex, and the Law in the Nineteenth-Century South.* Chapel Hill: U of North Carolina P, 1995.

Barker, Kenneth, ed. *The NIV Study Bible.* New International Version. Grand Rapids: Zondervan, 1985.

Baron, Dennis. *Grammar and Gender.* New Haven: Yale UP, 1986.

———. *Grammar and Good Taste: Reforming the American Language*. New Haven: Yale UP, 1982.
Barrett, Kate Waller. "The Immigrant Woman." Printed by the American Sociological Society and the Committee of One Hundred, Federal Council of Churches in America. Aug. 1915. Rpt. in P. Davis 224–30.
Baym, Nina. *American Women Writers and the Work of History, 1750–1860*. New Brunswick: Rutgers UP, 1995.
———. "Melodramas of Beset Manhood: How Theories of American Fiction Exclude Women Authors." *American Quarterly* 33.2 (Summer 1981): 123–39.
———, ed. *Norton Anthology of American Literature*. Shorter 5th ed. New York: Norton, 1999.
———. *Woman's Fiction: A Guide to Novels By and About Women in America, 1820–1870*. Ithaca: Cornell UP, 1978.
Beach, Seth Curtis. *Daughters of the Puritans: A Group of Brief Biographies*. Boston: American Unitarian Association, 1905.
Bederman, Gail. *Manliness and Civilization: A Cultural History of Gender and Race in the United States, 1880–1917*. Chicago: U of Chicago P, 1995.
Beecher, Catharine E. *Educational Reminiscences and Suggestions*. New York: J.B. Ford, 1874.
———. *An Essay on Slavery and Abolitionism, with Reference to the Duty of American Females*. 1837. Freeport, NY: Books for Libraries Press, 1970.
Beecher, Lyman. "Necessity of Education." *McGuffey's Sixth Eclectic Reader*. Ed. William Holmes McGuffey. New York: American Book, 1879. 228–31. Rpt. in Gorn 99–101.
Bell, Michael Davitt. "History and Romance Convention in Catharine Sedgwick's *Hope Leslie*." *American Quarterly* 22 (Summer 1970): 213–21.
Bellah, Robert N. "Rousseau on Society and the Individual." *Rousseau* 266–87.
Bentley, Nancy. *The Ethnography of Manners: Hawthorne, James, Wharton*. Cambridge: Cambridge UP, 1995.
Benton, Thomas Hart. *Abridgment of the Debates of Congress, from 1789 to 1856. From Gales and Seaton's Annals of Congress; From Their Register of Debates; and From the Official Reported Debates, by John C. Rives. By the Author of the Thirty Years' View*. Vols. 10 (1828–1830) and 11 (1830–1832). New York: D. Appleton, 1857–61.
Berlant, Lauren. *The Anatomy of National Fantasy: Hawthorne, Utopia, and Everyday Life*. Chicago: U of Chicago P, 1991.
Berlin, James A. *Writing Instruction in Nineteenth-Century American Colleges*. Carbondale: Southern Illinois UP, 1984.
Birnbaum, Michele. "Dark Dialects: Scientific and Literary Realism in Joel Chandler Harris's *Uncle Remus* Series." *New Orleans Review* 18.1 (Spring 1991): 36–45.
Bizzell, Patricia. *Academic Discourse and Critical Consciousness*. Pittsburgh: U of Pittsburgh P, 1992.
———. "Praising Folly: Constructing a Postmodern Rhetorical Authority as a Woman." *Feminine Principles and Women's Experience in American Composition and Rhetoric*. Ed. Louise Wetherbee Phelps and Janet Emig. Pittsburgh: U of Pittsburgh P, 1995. 27–41.
Blair, Sara. "Documenting America: Racial Theater in *The American Scene*." *The Henry James Review* 16.3 (1995): 264–72.
———. "Response: Writing Culture and Henry James." *The Henry James Review* 16.3 (1995): 278–81.
Bloch, Ruth. "Commentary" on "The Republican Mother: Women and Enlightenment—An American Perspective." *Locating American Studies: The Evolution of a Discipline*. Ed. Lucy Maddox. Baltimore: Johns Hopkins UP, 1999. 162–65.

234 Bibliography

Bode, Carl. *The American Lyceum: Town Meeting of the Mind*. New York: Oxford UP, 1956.

———. *The Anatomy of American Popular Culture, 1840–1861*. Berkeley: U of California P, 1959.

Borus, Daniel H. *Writing Realism: Howells, James and Norris in the Mass Market*. Chapel Hill: U of North Carolina P, 1989.

Bowden, Darsie. *The Mythology of Voice*. Portsmouth, NH: Boynton/Cook, 1999.

Bradwell v. State of Illinois. 1873. Rpt. in Kerber and De Hart 242–43.

Brandeis, Louis D. "True Americanism." Oration. Faneuil Hall, Boston. 5 July 1915. In *Boston City Record* 10 July 1915. Rpt. in P. Davis 639–44.

Brandt, Deborah. *Literacy in American Lives*. New York: Cambridge UP, 2001.

Brasch, Walter. *Brer Rabbit, Uncle Remus, and the 'Cornfield Journalist': The Tale of Joel Chandler Harris*. Macon: Mercer UP, 2000.

Braxton, Joanne M., ed. and intro. *The Collected Poetry of Paul Laurence Dunbar*. Charlottesville: U of Virginia P, 1993. ix-xxxvi.

Broadhead, Richard, ed. and intro. *The Conjure Woman and Other Conjure Tales*. By Charles W. Chesnutt. Durham: Duke UP, 1993. 1–21.

———. "Sparing the Rod: Discipline and Fiction in Antebellum America." *Representations* 21 (Winter 1988): 67–95.

Brody, Miriam. *Manly Writing: Gender, Rhetoric, and the Rise of Composition*. Carbondale: Southern Illinois UP, 1993.

Brooks, Florence. Interview. "Henry James in the Serene Sixties." *New York Herald* 2 Oct. 1904, sec. 4: 1. Rpt. in Walker 35–41.

Brown, Goold. *The Institutes of English Grammar, Methodologically Arranged; with Examples for Parsing, Questions for Examination, False Syntax for Correction, Exercises for Writing, Observations for the Advanced Student, and A Key to the Oral Exercises: To Which are Added Four Appendixes. Designed for the Use of Schools, Academies, and Private Learners*. New York: Samuel S. & William Wood, 1849.

Bryan, Mary Lynn McCree and Allen F. Davis, eds. *100 Years at Hull-House*. Bloomington: Indiana UP, 1990.

Buck, Charles. *Theological Dictionary, Containing Definitions of all Religious Terms, Etc.* 5th American ed. Philadelphia: W. W. Woodward, 1818.

Budd, Louis J. and Edwin H. Cady, eds. *On Henry James: The Best from American Literature*. Durham: Duke UP, 1990.

———. *On Howells: The Best from American Literature*. Durham: Duke UP, 1993.

Buntline, Ned [Edward Zane Carroll Judson]. *The B'hoys of New York; a Sequel to The Mysteries and Miseries of New York*. New York: Dick and Fitzgerald, 1850.

———. *The G'hals of New York: A Novel*. New York: Dewitt and Davenport, 1850.

Butler, Judith. *Bodies that Matter: On the Discursive Limits of "Sex."* New York: Routledge, 1993.

———. *Excitable Speech: A Politics of the Performative*. New York: Routledge, 1997.

———. *Gender Trouble: Feminism and the Subversion of Identity*. New York: Routledge, 1990.

Cameron, Deborah, ed. *The Feminist Critique of Language*. New York: Routledge, 1990.

———. "Performing Gender Identity: Young Men's Talk and the Construction of Heterosexual Masculinity." *Language and Gender: A Reader*. Ed. Jennifer Coates. Malden: Blackwell, 1998. 270–84.

———. *Verbal Hygiene*. New York: Routledge, 1995.

Carafiol, Peter. "The Nationalist Model for American Ethnic Narrative." *'Writing' Nation and 'Writing' Region in America*. Ed. Theo D'haen and Hans Bertens. Amsterdam: Vu UP, 1996. 166–85.

Carr, Jean Ferguson. "Nineteenth-Century Girls and Literacy." *Girls and Literacy in America: Historical Perspectives to the Present*. Ed. Jane Greer. Oxford: ABC-CLIO, 2003. 51–77.

Carson, Mina. "American Settlement Houses: The First Half Century." *Settlements, Social Change, and Community Action: Good Neighbors*. Ed. Ruth Gilchrist and Tony Jeffs. London: Kingsley, 2001. 34–53.

Channing, Walter. "Essay on American Language and Literature." *North American Review* 1 (Sept. 1815): 307–14.

Channing, William Ellery. "On the Annexation of Texas to the United States." *The Works of Rev. Dr. William E. Channing*. 12th ed. Vol. 2. Boston: Crosby, Nichols and New York: C. S. Francis, 1853. 181–260. 6 vols.

Chesnutt, Charles W. *The Colonel's Dream*. 1905. Upper Saddle River, NJ: Gregg, 1968.

———. *The Conjure Woman and Other Conjure Tales*. 1899. Ed. Richard H. Broadhead. Durham: Duke UP, 1993.

———. "The Courts and the Negro." Speech delivered c. 1908. Rpt. in Thomas, *Plessy* 149–60 and McElrath, Leitz, and Crisler 262–70.

———. "The Disfranchisement of the Negro." *The Negro Problem*. New York: James Pott, 1903. 79–124. Rpt. in McElrath, Leitz, and Crisler 179–95.

———. "The Dumb Witness." Chesnutt, *Conjure Woman* 158–71.

———. "The Future American: What the Race is Likely to Become in the Process of Time." *The Boston Evening Transcript* 18 Aug. 1900: 29. Rpt. in Wohnam 93–94.

———. "Liberty and the Franchise." c. 1899. Rpt. in McElrath, Leitz, and Crisler 101–08.

———. "The Negro's Franchise." *Boston Evening Transcript* 11 May 1901: 18. Rpt. in McElrath, Leitz, and Crisler 161–68.

———. "Post-Bellum—Pre-Harlem." *Crisis* 49 (June 1931): 193–94. Rpt. in Wohnam 102–07.

———. "Superstitions and Folklore of the South." *Modern Culture* 13 (1901): 231–35. Rpt. in Wohnam 95–101.

———. "What Is a White Man?" *New York Independent* 30 May 1889: 693–94. Rpt. in Wohnam 89–92.

———. "Women's Rights." *Crisis* 10 (Aug. 1915): 182–83. Rpt. in McElrath, Leitz, and Crisler 383–84.

Cherniavsky, Eva. *That Pale Mother Rising: Sentimental Discourses and the Imitation of Motherhood in 19th-Century America*. Bloomington: Indiana UP, 1995.

Child, Lydia Maria. *Hobomok and Other Writings on Indians*. 1824. Ed. Carolyn L. Karcher. New Brunswick: Rutgers UP, 1986.

Church, Joseph. "In Black and White: The Reader's Part in Chesnutt's 'Gray Wolf's Ha'nt.'" *The American Transcendental Quarterly*. 13.2 (June 1999): 121–36.

"Circular, Addressed to Benevolent Ladies of the U. States." Anon. Attrib. to Catharine E. Beecher. *Christian Advocate and Journal and Zion's Herald*. 173 (25 Dec. 1829).

Claxton, P. P. "Americanization." P. Davis 621–22.

Cmiel, Kenneth. *Democratic Eloquence: The Fight over Popular Speech in Nineteenth-Century America*. New York: Morrow, 1990.

Colton, C. "The Right of Petition." *The Democratic Review* 7.28 (Apr. 1840): 326–41.

Connors, Robert J. *Composition-Rhetoric: Backgrounds, Theory, and Pedagogy*. Pittsburgh: U of Pittsburgh P, 1997.

"The Contributors' Club." *The Atlantic Monthly* 42.253 (Nov 1878): 639–40.

Cooke, Alistair. "Mencken and the English Language." *On Mencken*. Ed. John Dorsey. New York: Knopf, 1980. 84–113.

Cooke, Maud C. *Social Etiquette or Manners and Customs of Polite Society, Containing Rules of Etiquette for All Occasions [. . .] Forming a Complete Guide to Self-Culture*. Boston: G. M. Smith, 1896.
Cooper, James Fenimore. *The American Democrat*. 1838. Intro. H. L. Mencken. New York: Liberty, 1981.
———. *Notions of the Americans: Picked up by a Travelling Bachelor*. 1828. Ed. Gary Williams. New York: State U of New York P, 1991.
———. *The Prairie*. 1827. *The Leatherstocking Tales, Vol. I: The Pioneers, The Last of the Mohicans, The Prairie*. New York: Library of America, 1985.
———. *The Wept of Wish-Ton-Wish*. 1829. New York: G. P. Putnam's Sons, n.d.
Correct Social Usage: A Course of Instruction in Good Form, Style and Deportment. By Eighteen Distinguished Authors. 8th ed. New York: New York Society of Self-Culture, 1907.
Crane, Gregg D. *Race, Citizenship, and Law in American Literature*. New York: Cambridge UP, 2002.
Crawford, Mary. *Talking Difference: On Gender and Language*. London: Sage, 1995. 1–48.
Crocker, Ruth Hutchinson. *Social Work and Social Order: The Settlement Movement in Two Industrial Cities, 1889–1930*. Urbana: U of Illinois P, 1992.
Crowley, Tony. *Standard English and the Politics of Language*. Urbana: U of Illinois P, 1989.
Cushing, Caleb. "The Social Condition of Women." *The North American Review* 42.91 (Apr. 1836): 489–513.
Cutter, Martha J. *Unruly Tongue: Identity and Voice in American Women's Writing, 1850–1930*. Jackson: UP of Mississippi, 1999.
Dahlgren, Madeleine Vinton. *The Social-Official Etiquette of the United States*. 6th ed. Baltimore: J. Murphy, 1894.
Damon-Bach, Lucinda. "To Be a 'Parlor Soldier': Susan Warner's Answer to Emerson's 'Self-Reliance.'" *Separate Spheres No More: Gender Convergence in American Literature, 1830–1930*. Ed. Monika M. Elbert. Tuscaloosa: U of Alabama P, 2000. 29–49.
Damon-Bach, Lucinda L. and Victoria Clements, eds. *Catharine Maria Sedgwick: Critical Perspectives*. Boston: Northeastern UP, 2003.
Daugherty, Sarah B. "James and the Representation of Women: Some Lessons of the Master(')s." *Questioning the Master: Gender and Sexuality in Henry James's Writings*. Ed. Peggy McCormack. Newark: U of Delaware P and London: Associated UP, 2000. 176–95.
Davidson, Cathy N. "No More Separate Spheres!" *American Literature* 70.3 (Sept. 1998): 443–63.
———. *Revolution and the Word: The Rise of the Novel in America*. New York: Oxford UP, 1986.
Davis, Philip, comp. and ed. *Immigration and Americanization: Selected Readings*. Boston: Ginn and Co., 1920.
Davis, Sara deSaussure. "Feminist Sources in *The Bostonians*." Budd and Cady, *On Henry James* 209–26.
Declaration of Sentiments. *History of Woman Suffrage*. Ed. Elizabeth Cady Stanton, Susan B. Anthony, and Matilda Joslyn Gage. Vol. 1. New York: Fowler and Wells, 1881. 70–71. Rpt. in Kerber and De Hart 207–09.
De Klerk, Vivian. "Slang: A Male Domain?" *Sex Roles* 22.9–10 (1990): 589–606.
Dew, Thomas. "Dissertation on the Characteristic Differences between the Sexes, and on the Position and Influence of Woman in Society." *Southern Literary Messenger I* (1835): 493–691.
Dialect Notes. Vol. I (1889–1896). Norwood, MA: American Dialect Society, 1896.

———. Vol. II (1900–1904). New Haven, CT: American Dialect Society, 1904.
Dobson, Joanne. "The Hidden Hand: Subversion of Cultural Ideology in Three Mid-Nineteenth-Century Women's Novels." *American Quarterly* 38.2 (1986): 223–42.
———. Introduction. *The Hidden Hand. Or, Capitola the Madcap.* By E. D. E. N. Southworth. New Brunswick: Rutgers UP, 1988. xi-xlii.
Douglas, Ann. *The Feminization of American Culture.* New York: Knopf, 1977.
Downey, Charlotte. Introduction. *English Grammar in Familiar Lectures.* By Samuel Kirkham. 1834. 63rd ed. Delmar, NY: Scholars', 1989.
Doyle, Laura. *Bordering on the Body: The Racial Matrix of Modern Fiction and Culture.* New York: Oxford UP, 1994.
Dunbar, Paul Laurence. "Negro in Literature." Interview with Dunbar. *New York Commercial* (1898). Paul Laurence Dunbar Collection, Reel IV, Box 16, OHS. Rpt. in Martin and Primeau 205–07.
Duyckinck, Evert. "Nationality in Literature." *The United States Magazine and Democratic Review.* 20.105 (Mar. 1847): 264–72.
Eble, Connie. *Slang & Sociability: In-Group Language among College Students.* Chapel Hill: U of North Carolina P, 1996.
Elbert, Monika M., ed. and intro. *Separate Spheres No More: Gender Convergence in American Literature, 1830–1930.* Tuscaloosa: U of Alabama P, 2000. 1–25.
Eley, Geoff and Ronald Grigor Suny, eds. "Introduction: From the Moment of Social History to the Work of Cultural Representation." *Becoming National: A Reader.* New York: Oxford UP, 1996. 3–37.
Elshtain, Jean Beth, ed. *The Jane Addams Reader.* New York: Basic, 2002.
Emerson, Ralph Waldo. "Eloquence." 1867. *Letters and Social Aims.* Boston: Houghton, 1884. 109–29.
———. "Self-Reliance." *Selections from Ralph Waldo Emerson.* Ed. Stephen E. Whicher. Boston: Houghton, 1960.
English, Thomas H., ed. *Mark Twain to Uncle Remus, 1881–1885.* Emory University Publications, Sources and Reprints Series VII, No. 3. Emory: Emory U Library, 1953.
Esteve, Mary. "Anerotic Excursions: Memory, Celibacy, and Desire in *The American Scene.*" *Questioning the Master: Gender and Sexuality in Henry James's Writings.* Ed. Peggy McCormack. Newark: U of Delaware P and London: Associated UP, 2000. 196–216.
Etiquette for Americans, By a Woman of Fashion. Chicago: H. S. Stone, 1898.
Evarts, Jeremiah. *Cherokee Removal: The 'William Penn' Essays and Other Writings.* Ed. Francis Paul Prucha. Knoxville: U of Tennessee P, 1981.
Fecher, Charles A. "The Comfortable Bourgeois: The Thought of H. L. Mencken." *On Mencken.* Ed. John Dorsey. New York: Knopf, 1980. 114–27.
Fetterley, Judith. "'My sister! My sister!': The Rhetoric of Catharine Sedgwick's *Hope Leslie.*" *American Literature* 70.3 (Sept. 1998): 491–516.
———. *The Resisting Reader: A Feminist Approach to American Fiction.* Bloomington: Indiana UP, 1978.
Finegan, Edward. "Usage." *The Cambridge History of the English Language.* Vol. 6. *English in North America.* Ed. John Algeo. New York: Cambridge UP, 2001. 358–418.
Finkelman, Paul and Melvin I. Urofsky, eds. *Landmark Decisions of the US Supreme Court.* Washington, D.C.: Congressional Quarterly, 2003.
Fishkin, Shelley Fisher. *Was Huck Black?: Mark Twain and African-American Voices.* New York: Oxford UP, 1993.
Flexner, Stuart Berg. Preface. *Dictionary of American Slang.* Comp. and ed. Harold Wentworth and Stuart Berg Flexner. Supp. ed. New York: Thomas Y. Crowell, 1967. vi-xv.

Forgie, George. *Patricide in the House Divided: A Psychological Interpretation of Lincoln and His Age.* New York: Norton, 1979.
Foster, Charles W. "The Phonology of the Conjure Tales of Charles W. Chesnutt." *Publication of the American Dialect Society* 55 (Apr. 1971): 1–43.
Foster, Edward Halsey. *Catharine Maria Sedgwick.* New York: Twayne, 1974.
Foster, George A. *New York in Slices: By An Experienced Carver: Being the Original Slices Published in the N. Y. Tribune. Revised, Enlarged, and Corrected By the Author. With Splendid Illustrations.* New York: William H. Graham, 1849.
Foucault, Michel. *Discipline and Punish: The Birth of the Prison.* Trans. Alan Sheridan. New York: Vintage, 1995.
———. *The History of Sexuality.* Vol. 1: *An Introduction.* 1978. Trans. Robert Hurley. New York: Vintage, 1990.
———. *Power/Knowledge: Selected Interviews & Other Writings, 1972–1977.* Trans. Colin Gordon, Leo Marshall, John Mepham, and Kate Soper. Ed. Colin Gordon. New York: Pantheon, 1980.
Franklin, Benjamin. "The Idea of the English School." 1751. *Ben Franklin: Writings.* New York: Library of America, 1987. 348–54.
Fruit, J. P. "Uncle Remus in Phonetic Spelling." *Dialect Notes* I: 196–98.
Fullerton, Hugh S. Preface. *Old Favorites from the McGuffey Readers.* Ed. Harvey C. Minnich. Cincinnati: American Book, 1936. v-vi.
Fuss, Diana. *Essentially Speaking: Feminism, Nature, and Difference.* New York: Routledge, 1989.
Garbus, Julie. "Service-Learning, 1902." *College English* 64.5 (May 2002): 547–65.
Garvey, Gregory T. "Risking Reprisal: Catharine Sedgwick's *Hope Leslie* and the Legitimation of Public Action by Women." *ATQ* New Series 8.4 (Dec. 1994): 287–98.
Gates, Henry Louis, Jr. "Dis and Dat: Dialect and the Descent." *Figures in Black: Words, Signs, and the 'Racial' Self.* New York: Oxford UP, 1987. 167–95.
———. Foreword. *In His Own Voice: The Dramatic and Other Uncollected Works of Paul Laurence Dunbar.* Ed. Herbert Woodward Martin and Ronald Primeau. Athens: Ohio UP, 2002. xi–xiv.
Gere, Anne Ruggles. *Intimate Practices: Literacy and Cultural Work in U. S. Women's Clubs, 1880–1920.* Urbana: U of Illinois P, 1997.
Gilman, Charlotte Perkins. *Herland.* 1915. *Herland, The Yellow Wall-Paper, and Selected Writings.* Ed. Denise D. Knight. New York: Penguin, 1999.
Goodman, Susan. *Civil Wars: American Novelists and Manners, 1880–1940.* Baltimore: Johns Hopkins UP, 2003.
Gorn, Elliott, ed. and intro. *The McGuffey Readers: Selections from the 1879 Edition.* Boston: Bedford/St. Martin's, 1998.
Goshgarian, G. M. *To Kiss the Chastening Rod: Domestic Fiction and Sexual Ideology in the American Renaissance.* Ithaca: Cornell UP, 1992.
Gould, Philip. "Catharine Sedgwick's 'Recital' of the Pequot War." *American Literature* 66 (Dec. 1994): 641–62.
Gow, Alex. M. *The Primer of Politeness: A Help to School and Home Government.* Philadelphia: J. B. Lippincott, 1883.
Greeley, Horace. Introduction. *Tribune Essays: Leading Articles Contributed to The New York Tribune from 1857–1863.* By Charles T. Congdon. New York: J. S. Redfield, 1869. xix–xxiv.
Green, Jonathon. *Chasing the Sun: Dictionary Makers and the Dictionaries They Made.* New York: Holt, 1996.
Greenough, James Bradstreet and George Lyman Kittredge. *Words and Their Ways in English Speech.* New York: Macmillan, 1901.

Greer, Jane, ed. *Girls and Literacy in America: Historical Perspectives to the Present.* Oxford: ABC-CLIO, 2003.
Grimké, Angelina. *Letters to Catherine E. Beecher, in Reply to an Essay on Slavery and Abolitionism.* 1838. New York: Arno Press and the New York Times, 1969.
Gustafson, Thomas. *Representative Words: Politics, Literature, and the American Language, 1776–1865.* New York: Cambridge UP, 1992.
Gwynne, Parry. "A Word to the Wise, or Hints on the Current Improprieties of Expression in Writing and Speaking." *Conversation, Its Faults and Its Graces.* Comp. and ed. Andrew P. Peabody. Rev. ed. Boston: James Monroe, 1856.
Habegger, Alfred. "W. D. Howells and the 'American Girl.'" *Texas Quarterly* 19 (1976): 152.
———. "A Well-Hidden Hand." *Novel* 14 (1981): 197–212.
Hale, Sarah J. *Woman's Record; or, Sketches of All Distinguished Women from the Creation to A.D.* New York: Harper and Bros., 1855.
Halfmann, Ulrich, ed. *Interviews with William Dean Howells.* Arlington: U of Texas, 1973.
———. "Interviews with William Dean Howells." *American Literary Realism* 6 (1973): 326–27.
Hall, B. H. *A Collection of College Words and Customs.* Cambridge: John Bartlett, 1856.
Halttunen, Karen. *Confidence Men and Painted Women: A Study of Middle-Class Culture in America, 1830–1870.* New Haven: Yale UP, 1982.
Harcourt, Mrs. Charles [pseud.]. *Good Form for Women, A Guide to Conduct and Dress on All Occasions.* Philadelphia: J. C. Winston, 1907.
Harland, Marion and Virginia Van De Water. *Everyday Etiquette: A Practical Manual of Social Usages.* Indianapolis: Bobbs-Merrill, c. 1905.
Harris, Joel Chandler. "A Story of the War." In Harris, *Uncle Remus, His Songs and His Sayings* 201–12.
———. *Uncle Remus, His Songs and His Sayings.* 1880. New York: D. Appleton, 1910.
Harris, Joseph. *A Teaching Subject: Composition Since 1966.* Upper Saddle River, NJ: Prentice Hall, 1997.
Harris, Susan. "The Limits of Authority: Catharine Maria Sedgwick and the Politics of Resistance." Damon-Bach and Clements 272–85.
Harrison, Constance. *The Well-Bred Girl in Society.* Philadelphia: Curtis and New York: Doubleday and McClure, c. 1898.
Hartwell, Patrick. "Grammar, Grammars, and the Teaching of Grammar." 1985. *Cross-Talk in Comp Theory: A Reader.* Ed. Victor Villanueva, Jr. Urbana: NCTE, 1997. 183–211.
Hayes, Kevin J., ed. *Henry James: The Contemporary Reviews.* New York: Cambridge UP, 1996.
Hedrick, Joan D. *Harriet Beecher Stowe: A Life.* New York: Oxford UP, 1994.
Hershberger, Mary. "Mobilizing Women, Anticipating Abolition: The Struggle Against Indian Removal in the 1830s." *The Journal of American History* 86 (June 1999): 15–40.
Higginson, Stephen A. "A Short History of the Right to Petition Government for the Redress of Grievances." *Yale Law Journal* 96 (1986): 142–66.
Higginson, Thomas Wentworth. *Women and the Alphabet.* 1881. New York: Arno, 1972.
Hobsbawm, E. J. *Nations and Nationalism Since 1780: Programme, Myth, Reality.* 2nd ed. New York: Cambridge UP, 1990.
Hobson, Fred C. *Mencken: A Life.* New York: Random, 1994.

Hockett, Charles F. Introduction. *The Life and Growth of Language: An Outline of Linguistic Science.* By William Dwight Whitney. 1875. New York: Dover, 1979. v-xxiii.
Hodgkiss, Anita. "Petitioning and the Empowerment Theory of Practice." *Yale Law Journal* 96 (1987): 569–92.
Holland, Catherine A. *The Body Politic: Foundings, Citizenship, and Difference in the American Political Imagination.* New York: Routledge, 2001.
Holmes, Oliver Wendell. *The Autocrat of the Breakfast Table.* Philadelphia: Henry Altemus, 1858.
Homestead, Melissa. E-mail to author. 17 Jan. 2003.
Rev. of *Hope Leslie; or Early Times in Massachusetts,* by Catharine Maria Sedgwick. *The Athanaeum. Journal of Literature, Science, and the Fine Arts* 411 (London, Sept. 1835): 693–94.
———. "Miss Sedgwick's Novels: Redwood, New England Tale, Hope Leslie, &c." *The Ladies' Magazine* 2 (1829): 234–38.
———. *The North American Review* 26.59 (Apr. 1828): 403–20.
———. *Western Monthly Review* I (1828): 289–95.
Horsman, Reginald. *Race and Manifest Destiny: The Origins of American Racial Anglo-Saxonism.* Cambridge: Harvard UP, 1981.
Hovet, Grace Ann and Theodore R. Hovet. "Identity Development in Susan Warner's *The Wide, Wide World:* Relationship, Performance, and Construction." *Legacy* 8.1 (1991): 3–16.
Howells, William Dean. "American English; W. H. White; Balzac; American Criticism." *Harper's Monthly* (Feb. 1886). Howells, *Selected Literary Criticism* 2: 7–12.
———. "Mr. Charles W. Chesnutt's Stories." *The Atlantic Monthly* 85 (May 1900): 699–700. Rpt. in Wohnam 113–16.
———. *Criticism and Fiction.* 1891. Howells, *Selected Literary Criticism* 295–354.
———. "Dialect in Literature." *Harper's Weekly* (8 June 1895). Howells, *Selected Literary Criticism* 223.
———. "The Grasshopper: The Simple, the Natural, the Honest in Art." Howells, *Selected Literary Criticism* 71–75.
———. Introduction. *Lyrics of Lowly Life.* 1896. By Paul Laurence Dunbar. *The Complete Poems of Paul Laurence Dunbar.* New York: Dodd, Mead, 1913. vii-x.
———. Rev. of *Majors and Minors,* by Paul Laurence Dunbar. "Life and Letters." *Harper's Weekly* 27 (June 1896): 630.
———. "A National American Literature." *Harper's Monthly* (Nov. 1891). Howells, *Selected Literary Criticism* 189–92.
———. "The New 'Study' and the Use of American English." *Harper's Monthly* (Jan. 1886). Howells, *Selected Literary Criticism* 2: 3–6.
———. "Our Daily Speech." *Harper's Bazaar* 40 (1906): 931.
———. *Selected Literary Criticism: William Dean Howells.* Ed. Donald Pizer et al. Vol 2. Bloomington: Indiana UP, 1993. 3 vols.
Hoyle, R. W. "Petitioning as Popular Politics in Early Sixteenth-Century England." *Historical Research* 75.190 (Nov. 2002): 365–89.
Hull-House Bulletins. Vols. 1 (1896)–7 (1906). Hull-House Association Records. Hull-House Collection. Box 1, Folders 425–432. Jane Addams Memorial Collection. U of Illinois at Chicago Library Special Collections, Chicago.
Hull-House Maps and Papers: A Presentation of Nationalities and Wages in a Congested District of Chicago, together with Comments and Essays on Problems Growing Out of the Social Conditions. 1895. By Residents of Hull-House. New York: Arno Press and The New York Times, 1970.
Hull-House Year Book. Sept. 1, 1906–Sept. 1, 1907. Hull-House Association Records. Hull-House Collection. Box 43, Folder 434. Jane Addams Memorial

Collection (hereafter cited as JAMC). U of Illinois at Chicago Library Special Collections (hereafter cited as UIC Spec Coll), Chicago.

———. May 1, 1910. Hull-House Association Records. Hull-House Collection. Box 43, Folder 435. JAMC. UIC Spec Coll, Chicago.

———. Jan. 1, 1913. Hull-House Association Records. Hull-House Collection. Box 43, Folder 436. JAMC. UIC Spec Coll, Chicago.

———. May 1, 1916. Hull-House Association Records. Hull-House Collection. Box 43, Folder 437. JAMC. UIC Spec Coll, Chicago.

Hurd, Seth T. *A Grammatical Corrector; Or, Vocabulary of the Common Errors of Speech: Being a Collection of Nearly Two Thousand Barbarisms, Cant Phrases, Colloquialisms, Quaint Expressions, Provincialisms, False Pronunciation, Perversions, Misapplication of Terms, and Other Kindred Errors of the English Language, Peculiar to the Different States of the Union. The Whole Explained, Corrected, and Conveniently Arranged for the Use of Schools and Private Individuals.* Philadelphia: E. H. Butler, 1847.

Hurt, James. Introduction and Notes. *Twenty Years at Hull-House.* Urbana: U of Illinois P, 1990. ix-xix.

"The Immigrant and the State." P. Davis 440–501.

Irving, Washington. *History, Tales and Sketches.* New York: Library of America, 1983.

———. "Rip Van Winkle." 1819. Baym, *Norton* 428–40.

Ives, Sumner. "The Phonology of the Uncle Remus Stories." *Publication of the American Dialect Society* 22 (Nov. 1954): 3–59.

Jack, Hugh. "A Message to Mothers. Written Especially for the Mothers Who Have Recently Come with Their Husbands and Children from Foreign Lands, to Make Homes in America." *Gary Works Circle* 14 (Aug. 1920): 6–7.

Jakobson, Roman. "The World Response to Whitney's Principles of Linguistic Science." *Whitney on Language: Selected Writings of William Dwight Whitney.* Ed. Michael Silverstein. Cambridge: MIT P, 1971. xxv-xlv.

James, Henry. "American Letter." *Literature* 3.38 (9 July 1898): 17–19.

———. *The Bostonians.* 1886. Ed. R. D. Gooder. New York: Oxford UP, 1984.

———. *The Complete Notebooks of Henry James.* Ed. Leon Edel and Lyall H. Powers. New York: Oxford UP, 1987.

———. "The Manners of American Women." *Harper's Bazar* 41.4 (Apr.1907): 355–59; 41.5 (May 1907): 453–58; 41.6 (June 1907): 537–41; 41.7 (July 1907): 646–51. Rpt. in Walker 82–112.

———. "The Question of Our Speech." *The Question of Our Speech; The Lesson of Balzac: Two Lectures.* Boston: Houghton, 1905. Address to the graduating class at Bryn Mawr College. 8 June 1905. Rpt. in Walker 42–57.

———. "The Speech of American Women." *Harper's Bazar* 40.11 (Nov. 1906): 979–82; 40.12 (Dec. 1906): 1103–06; 41.1 (Jan. 1907): 17–21; 41.2 (Feb. 1907): 113–17. Rpt. in Walker 58–81.

Jane Addams Hull-House Museum Exhibit. U of Illinois at Chicago. 2 Nov. 2007.

Jehlen, Myra. "Gender." *Critical Terms for Literary Study.* Ed. Frank Lentricchia and Thomas McLaughlin. 2nd ed. Chicago: U of Chicago P, 1995. 263–73.

Jespersen, Otto. *Growth and Structure of the English Language.* 3rd ed. Leipzig: Teubner, 1919.

———. "The Woman." *Language: Its Nature, Development and Origin.* London: Allen and Unwin, 1922. Rpt. in *The Feminist Critique of Language.* Ed. Deborah Cameron. New York: Routledge, 1990. 201–19.

Johnson, Barbara A. *Reading Piers Plowman and The Pilgrim's Progress: Reception and the Protestant Reader.* Carbondale: Southern Illinois UP, 1992.

Johnson, Nan. *Gender and Rhetorical Space in American Life, 1866–1910.* Carbondale: Southern Illinois UP, 2002.

Jones, Gavin. *Strange Talk: The Politics of Literature in Gilded Age America*. Berkeley: U of California P, 1999.
Jones, Maldwyn Allen. *American Immigration*. Chicago: U of Chicago P, 1960.
Jones, Paul Christian. "'This Dainty Woman's Hand . . . Red With Blood': E. D. E. N. Southworth's *The Hidden Hand* as Abolitionist Narrative." *American Transcendental Quarterly* 15.1 (Mar. 2001): 59–80.
Kachru, Braj B., ed. and intro. *The Other Tongue: English Across Cultures*. 2nd ed. Urbana: U of Illinois P, 1992. 1–15.
Kahane, Henry. "American English: From a Colonial Substandard to a Prestige Language." Kachru 211–19.
Kanigel, Robert. "Did Mencken Hate the Jews?" *Menckeniana* 73 (Spring 1980): 1–7.
Kaplan, Amy. "Manifest Domesticity." *American Literature* 70.3 (Sept. 1998): 581–606.
Karafilis, Maria. "Catharine Maria Sedgwick's *Hope Leslie*: The Crisis between Ethical Political Action and U.S. Literary Nationalism in the New Republic." *American Transcendental Quarterly* 12 (Dec. 1998): 327–44.
Karcher, Carolyn L. *The First Woman in the Republic: A Cultural Biography of Lydia Maria Child*. Durham: Duke UP, 1994.
———, ed. and intro. *Hobomok and Other Writings on Indians*. By Lydia Maria Child. New Brunswick: Rutgers UP, 1998. ix–xlvi.
Kassanoff, Jennie A. "'Fate Has Linked Us Together': Blood, Gender, and the Politics of Representation in Pauline Hopkins's *Of One Blood*." *The Unruly Voice: Rediscovering Pauline Elizabeth Hopkins*. Ed. John Cullen Gruesser. Urbana: U of Illinois P, 1996. 158–81.
Keely, Karen. "Marriage Plots and National Reunion: The Trope of Romantic Reconciliation in Postbellum Literature." *The Mississippi Quarterly* 51.4 (Fall 1998): 621–48.
Kelley, Mary, ed. and intro. *Hope Leslie; Or, Early Times in the Massachusetts*. By Catharine Maria Sedgwick. New Brunswick: Rutgers UP, 1995. ix–xxxvii.
———, ed. and intro. *The Power of Her Sympathy: The Autobiography and Journal of Catharine Maria Sedgwick*. Boston: Massachusetts Historical Society, Dist. Northeastern UP, 1993. 3–40.
Kellor, Frances A. "What is Americanization." *Yale Review* (Jan. 1919). Rpt. in P. Davis 623–38.
Kerber, Linda K. "The Republican Mother." *Locating American Studies: The Evolution of a Discipline*. Ed. Lucy Maddox. Baltimore: Johns Hopkins UP, 1999. 143–61.
———. "Separate Spheres, Female Worlds, Woman's Place: The Rhetoric of Women's History." *The Journal of American History* 75.1 (June 1988): 9–39.
———. *Toward an Intellectual History of Women*. Chapel Hill: U of North Carolina P, 1997.
———. *Women of the Republic: Intellect and Ideology in Revolutionary America*. Chapel Hill: U of North Carolina P, 1980.
Kerber, Linda K. and Jane Sherron De Hart, eds. *Women's America: Refocusing the Past*. 5th ed. New York: Oxford UP, 2000.
Kirkham, Samuel. *English Grammar in Familiar Lectures*. 1834. 63rd Facsim. ed. Delmar, NY: Scholars', 1989.
———. *An Essay on Elocution, Designed for the Use of Schools and Private Learners*. 1833. 5th ed. New York: Sheldon, 1867.
Knight, Denise D., ed. and intro. *Herland, The Yellow Wall-Paper, and Selected Writings*. By Charlotte Perkins Gilman. New York: Penguin, 1999. ix–xxiv.
———, ed. *Writers of the American Renaissance*. Westport: Greenwood, 2003.

Krapp, George Philip. "Is American English Archaic?" *Southwest Review* 12 (Summer 1927): 302.
Kroupa, Sandra. University of Washington Archivist and Book Arts Librarian. Personal interview. Seattle, WA. 17 Dec. 2002.
Kruman, Marc W. "Suffrage." *The Reader's Companion to American History*. Ed. Eric Foner and John A. Garraty. Boston: Houghton, 1991. 1043–47.
Lang, Amy Schrager. "Class and the Strategies of Sympathy." *The Culture of Sentiment*. Ed. Shirley Samuels. New York: Oxford UP, 1992. 128–42.
"Language and Ethnicity: The Case of African-American English." *Language Files: Materials for an Introduction to Language and Linguistics*. Ed. Nick Cipollone, Steven Hartman Keiser, and Shravan Vasishth. 7th ed. Columbus: Ohio State UP, 1998. 386–92.
Lerner, Gerda. *The Grimké Sisters from South Carolina: Rebels against Slavery*. Boston: Houghton, 1967.
———. "The Meanings of Seneca Falls, 1848–1998." *Women's America: Refocusing the Past*. Ed. Linda K. Kerber and Jane Sherron De Hart. 5th ed. New York: Oxford UP, 2000. 200–06.
Levander, Caroline Field. *Voices of the Nation: Women and Public Speech in Nineteenth-Century American Literature and Culture*. New York: Cambridge UP, 1998.
Levine, Lawrence W. *Black Culture and Black Consciousness: Afro-American Folk Thought from Slavery to Freedom*. New York: Oxford UP, 1977.
Lighter, Jonathan E. "Slang." *The Cambridge History of the English Language*. Vol. 6. *English in North America*. Ed. John Algeo. New York: Cambridge UP, 2001. 219–49.
———, ed. and intro. *Random House Historical Dictionary of American Slang*. Vol. 1. New York: Random, 1994. xi-xxxix.
Linke, Uli. *Blood and Nation: The European Aesthetics of Race*. Philadelphia: U of Pennsylvania P, 1999.
Linkon, Sherry Lee, ed. *In Her Own Voice: Nineteenth-Century American Women Essayists*. New York: Garland, 1997.
Lippi-Green, Rosina. *English with an Accent: Language, Ideology, and Discrimination in the United States*. New York: Routledge, 1997.
Lissak, R. S. *Pluralism and Progressives: Hull House and the New Immigrants, 1890–1917*. Chicago: U of Chicago P, 1989.
"Literary and Philological Manuals." *The Atlantic Monthly* 45.269 (Mar. 1880): 355–61.
Lloyd, John Uri. "The Language of the Kentucky Negro." *Dialect Notes* II: 179–84.
Locke, John. *Second Treatise of Government*. Ed. Thomas P. Peardon. Indianapolis: Library of Liberal Arts, 1952.
Lodge, Henry Cabot. "Immigration—A Review." Address. Boston City Club. 20 Mar. 1900. Rpt. in P. Davis 50–60.
Looby, Christopher. "Phonetics and Politics: Franklin's Alphabet as a Political Design." *Eighteenth-Century Studies* 18.1 (Fall 1984): 1–34.
———. *Voicing America: Language, Literary Form, and the Origins of the United States*. Chicago: U of Chicago P, 1996.
Lyman, Rollo La Verne. *English Grammar in American Schools Before 1850*. Diss. University of Chicago, 1922. U.S. Bureau of Education Bulletin, 1921, No. 12. Washington, D.C.: Government Printing Office, 1922.
Maddox, Lucy. *Removals: Nineteenth-Century American Literature and the Politics of Indian Affairs*. New York: Oxford UP, 1991.
Mahoney, John J. and Charles M. Herlihy. *First Steps in Americanization: A Handbook for Teachers*. Boston: Houghton, 1918.

Mahoney, John J., Frances K. Wetmore, Helen Winkler, and Elsa Alsberg. *Training Teachers for Americanization: A Course of Study for Normal Schools and Teachers' Institutes.* U.S. Bureau of Education Bulletin, 1920, No. 12. Washington, D.C.: Government Printing Office, 1920.

Maier, Pauline. *American Scripture: Making the Declaration of Independence.* New York: Knopf, 1997.

Malsheimer, Lonna M. "Daughters of Zion: New England Roots of American Feminism." *The New England Quarterly* 50.3 (Sept. 1977): 484–504.

Marshall, John. "Seven Lectures on Female Education, Inscribed to Mrs. Garnett's Pupils." *The North American Review* 20.47 (Apr. 1825): 444–46.

Martensen, Robert L. "Oliver Wendell Holmes, MD: An Appreciation." *JAMA, The Journal of the American Medical Association* 272.16 (26 Oct. 1994): 1249.

Martin, Herbert Woodward and Ronald Primeau, eds. *In His Own Voice: The Dramatic and Other Uncollected Works of Paul Laurence Dunbar.* Athens: Ohio UP, 2002.

Mathews, William. *Words: Their Use and Abuse.* 1876. Chicago: S.C. Griggs, 1882.

Matthews, Brander. *The American of the Future and Other Essays.* New York: Scribner's, 1909.

———. *Parts of Speech: Essays on English.* New York: Scribner's, 1901.

Matossian, Lou Ann. "A Woman-Made Language: Charlotte Perkins Gilman and *Herland*." *Women and Language* 10.2: 16–20.

McClintock, Ann. *Imperial Leather: Race, Gender, and Sexuality in the Colonial Contest.* New York: Routledge, 1995.

McDavid, Ravin I., Jr. "H. L. Mencken and the Linguistic Atlas Project." *Menckeniana* 73 (Spring 1980): 7–9.

———. "Linguistic Geography." *Needed Research in American English (1983).* Publication of the American Dialect Society 71. University: U of Alabama P, 1984. 4–28.

McElrath, Joseph R, Jr. "W. D. Howells and Race: Charles W. Chesnutt's Disappointment of the Dean." *Nineteenth-Century Literature* 51.4 (1997): 474–99.

McElrath, Joseph R., Jr. and Robert C. Leitz, III, eds. *"To Be an Author": Letters of Charles W. Chesnutt, 1889–1905.* Princeton: Princeton UP, 1997.

McElrath, Joseph R., Jr., Robert C. Leitz, III, and Jesse S. Crisler, eds. *Charles W. Chesnutt: Essays and Speeches.* Stanford: Stanford UP, 1999.

McGuffey, William Holmes. "The Good Reader." *McGuffey's Fifth Eclectic Reader.* Rev. ed. New York: Van Antwerp, Bragg, 1879. 39–43. Rpt. in Greer 177–79.

———, ed. *McGuffey's Second Eclectic Reader.* Chicago: American, 1879.

McWilliams, Dean. "*The Colonel's Dream*: 'Sho Woul 'a' Be'n a 'Ristocrat.'" *Charles W. Chesnutt and the Fictions of Race.* Athens: U of Georgia P, 2002. 166–82.

"Memorial of Certain Inhabitants of Pennsylvania, Praying that the Indians may be protected in their rights, &c." *Cong. Rec.* 7 Jan. 1830. 21st Cong., 1st sess. S. Doc. 25. S. Docs., vol. 1, no. 1–40, serial 203, 1–4.

"Memorial of Inhabitants of Burlington County, New Jersey, Praying that the Indians may be protected in their rights by the Government." *Cong. Rec.* 3 Mar. 1830. *Cong. Rec.* 21st Cong., 1st sess. S. Doc. 77. S. Docs., vol. 2, no. 50–146, serial 193, 1.

"Memorial of the Ladies of Burlington, New Jersey, Praying that Congress would protect the Indians in their rights, and in the possession of their lands." *Cong. Rec.* 23 Feb. 1830. 21st Cong., 1st sess. S. Doc. 66. S. Docs., vol. 2., no. 50–146, serial 193, 1–2.

"Memorial of Ladies, Inhabitants of Pennsylvania, Praying That the Indians may be protected in their rights, and in the possession of their lands." *Cong. Rec.* 3 Mar. 1830. 21st Cong., 1st sess. S. Doc. 76. S. Docs., vol. 2, no. 50–146, serial 193, 1–2.

"Memorial of the Ladies of Steubenville, Ohio, Against the forcible removal of the Indians without the limits of the United States." *Cong. Rec.* 15 Feb. 1830. 21st Cong., 1st sess. H. Doc. 209. H. Rpts., vol. 2, no. 176–298, with gaps, serial 200, 2.

"Memorial of a Number of Citizens of New York, Praying the passage of an international copyright law." *Cong. Rec.* 24 Apr. 1838. 25th Cong., 2nd sess. S. Doc. 399. S. Rept., vol. 5, serial 318, 1–4.

Mencken, H. L. *The American Language: An Inquiry into the Development of English in the United States.* 4th ed., 10th printing. New York: Knopf, 1946.

———. "The Future of English." *Harper's Magazine* (Apr. 1935). Rpt. in *Harper's Magazine* 299.1792 (June 1999): 86–90.

———. "The Future of the Language." Chapter 12 in *The American Language: An Inquiry into the Development of English in the United States.* 4th ed. New York: Knopf, 1946. 590–615.

———. *In Defense of Women.* 1918, 1922. Alexandria: Time-Life, 1982.

———. Introduction. *The American Democrat.* By James Fenimore Cooper. New York: Liberty, 1981. ix-xxi.

Menckeniana, A Schimpflexicon. New York: Knopf, 1928.

Michaels, Walter Benn. "Jim Crow Henry James?" *The Henry James Review* 16.3 (1995): 286–91.

———. *Our America: Nativism, Modernism, and Pluralism.* Durham: Duke UP, 1995.

Miller, James A. "The Other Fellow: Joel Chandler Harris." *The Nation* 244 (9 May 1987): 614–17.

Miller, Joshua L. *Lingual Politics: The Syncopated Accents of Multilingual Modernism, 1919–1948.* Diss. Columbia U, 2001. Ann Arbor: UMI, 2001. 3005760.

Miller, Thomas P. *The Formation of College English: Rhetoric and Belles Lettres in the British Cultural Provinces.* Pittsburgh: U of Pittsburgh P, 1997.

Minnich, Harvey C., ed. *Old Favorites from the McGuffey Readers.* Cincinnati: American Book, 1936.

Minnick, Lisa Cohen. *Dialect and Dichotomy: Literary Representations of African American Speech.* Tuscaloosa: U of Alabama P, 2004.

"Miss Sedgwick's Novels: Redwood, New England Tale, Hope Leslie, &c." Rev. of *Hope Leslie; or Early Times in Massachusetts,* by Catharine Maria Sedgwick. *The Ladies' Magazine* 2 (1829): 234–38.

Moore, Dorothea. "A Day at Hull House." *American Journal of Sociology* (Mar. 1897): 629–32, 634–36, 638–40. Rpt. in Bryan and Davis 42–49.

Mott, Frank Luther. *American Journalism. A History: 1690–1960.* 3rd ed. New York: Macmillan, 1962.

———. *A History of American Magazines.* Vol. 1. New York: Appleton, 1930. 5 vols.

———. *A History of American Magazines.* Vol. 2. Cambridge: Harvard UP, 1938–1968. 5 vols.

Mufwene, Salikoko S., John R. Rickford, Guy Bailey, and John Baugh, eds. *African-American English: Structure, History, and Use.* New York: Routledge, 1998.

Mugglestone, Lynda. *"Talking Proper": The Rise of Accent as Social Symbol.* London: Oxford UP, 1996.

Murray, Lindley. *English Grammar, Adapted to the Different Classes of Learners.* 1795. 9th ed. Philadelphia: Marot and Watter, 1826.

———. *English Grammar. Adapted to the Different Classes of Learners*. 1824. Delmar: Scholars', 1981.

"National Americanization Conference: Digest of Program Addresses Made Before Conference of Americanization Specialists and Workers Held in Washington, May 12–15, 1919." Rpt. in P. Davis 702–40.

Nelson, Dana D. *National Manhood: Capitalist Citizenship and the Imagined Fraternity of White Men*. Durham: Duke UP, 1998.

———. "Sympathy as Strategy in Sedgwick's *Hope Leslie*." *The Culture of Sentiment: Race, Gender, and Sentimentality in Nineteenth-Century America*. Ed. Shirley Samuels. New York: Oxford UP, 1992. 191–202.

Nelson, Raymond. "Babylonian Frolics: H. L. Mencken and *The American Language*." *American Literary History* 11.4 (Winter 1999): 668–98.

Nettels, Elsa. *Language and Gender in American Fiction: Howells, James, Wharton, and Cather*. Charlottesville: UP of Virginia, 1997.

———. *Language, Race, and Social Class in Howells's America*. Lexington: UP of Kentucky, 1988.

Newman, Louise Michele. *White Women's Rights: The Racial Origins of Feminism in the United States*. New York: Oxford UP, 1999.

Niles' Weekly Register. Containing Political, Historical, Geographical, Scientific, Statistical, Economical, and Biographical Documents, Essays and Facts; together with Notices of the Arts and Manufactures, and a Record of the Events of the Times. Vols. 37 (Sept. 1829-Mar. 1830), 38 (Mar. 1830-Sept. 1830), 53 (Sept. 1837-Mar. 1838), 54 (Mar. 1838-Sept. 1838), and 55 (Sept. 1838-Mar.1839). Baltimore: Niles and Sons.

Noble, Marianne. *The Masochistic Pleasures of Sentimental Fiction*. Princeton: Princeton UP, 2000.

North American Review. "Contents." 26.59 (Apr. 1828): 3–4.

North, Michael. *The Dialect of Modernism: Race, Language, and Twentieth-Century Literature*. Oxford: Oxford UP, 1994.

Nourie, Alan and Barbara Nourie. *American Mass-Market Magazines*. New York: Greenwood, 1990.

O'Connell, Catharine. "'We must sorrow': Silence, Suffering, and Sentimentality in Susan Warner's *The Wide, Wide World*." *Studies in American Fiction* 25.1 (Spring 1997): 21–40.

Olneck, Michael R. "Americanization and the Education of Immigrants, 1900–1925: An Analysis of Symbolic Action." *American Journal of Education* 97 (Aug. 1989): 398–423.

Opfermann, Susanne. "Lydia Maria Child, James Fenimore Cooper, and Catharine Maria Sedgwick: A Dialogue on Race, Culture, and Gender." *Soft Canons: American Women Writers and Masculine Tradition*. Ed. Karen L. Kilcup. Iowa City: U of Iowa P, 1999. 27–47.

O'Sullivan, John L. "The Great Nation of Futurity." *The United States Magazine and Democratic Review*. 6.23 (Nov. 1839): 426–30.

Page, Thomas Nelson. *In Ole Virginia. Or, Marse Chan and Other Stories*. 1887. Nashville: J. S. Sanders, 1991.

Parker, Andrew, M. Sommer, A. Russo, and P. Yaegar, eds. *Nationalisms and Sexualities*. London: Routledge, 1992.

Partridge, Eric. *Slang, To-Day and Yesterday: With a Short Historical Sketch; and Vocabularies of English, American, and Australian Slang*. 3rd ed. New York: Bonanza, c.1950.

Peabody, Andrew P. "An Address Delivered Before the Newburyport Female High School, Dec. 19, 1846." *Conversation, Its Faults and Its Graces*. Comp. and ed. Andrew P. Peabody. Rev. ed. Boston: J. Munroe, 1856.

———, comp. and ed. *Conversation, Its Faults and Its Graces*. Rev. ed. Boston: J. Munroe, 1856.
Pederson, Lee. "Language in the Uncle Remus Tales." *Modern Philology*. Vol 82. Chicago: U of Chicago P, 1984–1985. 292–98.
Person, Leland S. "In the Closet with Frederick Douglass: Reconstructing Masculinity in *The Bostonians*." *The Henry James Review* 16.3 (1995): 292–98.
Phipson, Evacustes. "British *vs.* American English." *Dialect Notes* I: 428–36.
Pizer, Donald. "Introduction: The Problem of Definition." *The Cambridge Companion to American Realism and Naturalism*. New York: Cambridge UP, 1995. 1–20.
Plessy v. Ferguson. 1896. Rpt. in Thomas, *Plessy* 41–60.
Portelli, Alessandro. *The Text and the Voice: Writing, Speaking, and Democracy in American Literature*. New York: Columbia UP, 1994.
Portnoy, Alisse [Theodore]. E-mail to author. 28 Jan. 2003.
———. "'Female Petitioners Can Lawfully Be Heard': Negotiating Female Decorum, United States Politics, and Political Agency, 1829–1831." *Journal of the Early Republic* 23 (2003): 573–610.
———. "*A Right to Speak on the Subject*": The Development of Women's Political Expression in the United States. Diss. U of Maryland, 1999. Ann Arbor: UMI, 1999. 9926763.
———. "'A Right to Speak on the Subject': The U.S. Women's Antiremoval Petition Campaign, 1829–1831." *Rhetoric and Public Affairs* 5.4 (Winter 2002): 601–23.
———. *Their Right to Speak: Women's Activism in the Indian and Slave Debates*. Cambridge: Harvard UP, 2005.
Posnock, Ross. "Henry James and the Limits of Historicism." *The Henry James Review* 16.3 (1995): 273–77.
———. *The Trial of Curiosity: Henry James, William James, and the Challenge of Modernity*. New York: Oxford UP, 1991.
Pound, Louise. "The American Dialect Society: A Historical Sketch." *Publication of the American Dialect Society* 17 (Apr. 1952): 3–28.
Prucha, Francis Paul. *American Indian Policy in the Formative Years: The Indian Trade and Intercourse Acts, 1790–1834*. Cambridge: Harvard UP, 1962.
———, ed. *Documents of United States Indian Policy*. 2nd ed. Lincoln: U of Nebraska P, 1990.
———. "Protest by Petition: Jeremiah Evarts and the Cherokee Indians." *Proceedings of the Massachusetts Historical Society* 97 (1985): 42–58.
Quackenbos, G. P. *First Lessons in Composition, In Which the Principles of the Art are Developed in Connection with the Principles of Grammar; Embracing Full Directions on the Subject of Punctuation; With Copious Exercises*. 1851. New York: D. Appleton, 1870.
Rayne, Martha Louise. *Gems of Deportment and Hints of Etiquette: The Ceremonials of Good Society, Including Valuable Moral, Mental, and Physical Knowledge, Original and Compiled from the Best Authorities, with Suggestions on All Matters Pertaining to the Social Code. A Manual of Instruction for the Home*. Detroit: Tyler, 1882.
"Recent Literature." *The Atlantic Monthly* 27.161 (Mar. 1871): 394–95.
Register of Debates in Congress. Washington, D.C.: Gales and Seaton, 1825–37.
Reynolds, David S. *Beneath the American Renaissance: The Subversive Imagination in the Age of Emerson and Melville*. New York: Knopf, 1988.
Rice, C. Duncan. "The Anti-Slavery Mission of George Thompson in the United States, 1834–35." *Journal of American Studies* 2 (April 1968): 13–31.
Rickford, John R. *African American Vernacular English: Features, Evolution, Educational Implications*. Malden: Blackwell, 1999.

Riis, Jacob. *How the Other Half Lives: Studies among the Tenements of New York*. New York: Scribner's, 1890.
Rogin, Michael Paul. *Fathers and Children: Andrew Jackson and the Subjugation of the American Indian*. New York: Knopf, 1975.
Roosevelt, Theodore. "Americanism." Address. Knights of Columbus, Carnegie Hall, New York. 12 Oct. 1915. Rpt. in P. Davis 645–60.
Ross, Edward Alsworth. "The Political Consequences of Immigration." *The Century Magazine* (Jan. 1914). Rpt. in P. Davis 319–25.
Rousseau, Jean-Jacques. *The Social Contract and The First and Second Discourses*. Ed. Susan Dunn. New Haven: Yale UP, 2002.
Ryan, Mary P. *Women in Public: Between Banners and Ballots, 1825–1880*. Baltimore: Johns Hopkins UP, 1990.
Saks, Eva. "Representing Miscegenation Law." *Raritan* 8 (1988): 39–69.
Schaum, Melita. "H. L. Mencken and American Cultural Masculinism." *Journal of American Studies* 29 (1995): 379–98.
Schele de Vere, M. *Americanisms: The English of the New World*. New York: Scribner's, 1872.
Schlesinger, Arthur M. *Learning How to Behave: A Historical Study of American Etiquette Books*. New York: Macmillan, 1946.
Schmidt, Philip R. *Hezekiah Niles and American Economic Nationalism*. New York: Arno, 1982.
Schueller, Malini Johar. *The Politics of Voice: Liberalism and Social Criticism from Franklin to Kingston*. Albany: State U of New York P, 1992.
Scott, Fred Newton. "American Slang." *Society for Pure English* Tract No. 24 (1926): 118–27.
Sedgwick, Catharine Maria. *Hope Leslie; Or, Early Times in the Massachusetts*. 1827. Ed. Mary Kelley. New Brunswick: Rutgers UP, 1995.
———. *Life and Letters of Catharine M. Sedgwick*. Ed. Mary E. Dewey. New York: Harper and Bros., 1871.
———. *Live and Let Live; or, Domestic Service Illustrated*. 1837. New York: Harper and Bros., 1861.
———. *Means and Ends, or Self-Training*. London: Charles Tilt, 1839.
———. *The Power of Her Sympathy: The Autobiography and Journal of Catharine Maria Sedgwick*. Ed. Mary Kelley. Boston: Massachusetts Historical Society, 1993.
———. "Slavery in New England." *Bentley's Miscellany* 34 (1853): 417–24.
———. "Some pages of a slave story I began and abandoned." Catharine Maria Sedgwick Papers I, Massachusetts Historical Society. Rpt. in Damon-Bach and Clements 119–21.
Sedgwick, Henry Dwight. *The Practicability of the Abolition of Slavery: A Lecture, Delivered at the Lyceum in Stockbridge, Massachusetts, February 1831*. New York: J. Seymour, 1831.
Shaughnessy, Mina. *Error and Expectation: A Guide for the Teacher of Basic Writing*. New York: Oxford UP, 1977.
Sheldon, E. S. "What is a Dialect?" *Dialect Notes* I: 286–97.
Sherwood, Mary Elizabeth Wilson. *Manners and Social Usages*. New York: Harper and Bros., 1884.
Shumway, David R. *Creating American Civilization: A Genealogy of American Literature as an Academic Discipline*. Minneapolis: U of Minnesota P, 1994.
Sigourney, Lydia Howard Huntley. Introduction. *Noble Deeds of American Women: With Biographical Sketches of Some of the More Prominent*. Ed. J. Clement. Buffalo: G. H. Derby, 1851.
———. "The Stockbridge Bowl." *Scenes in My Native Land*. Boston: J. Munroe, 1845. 200–01.

Silliman, Benjamin. *A Journal of Travels in England, Holland, and Scotland, and of Two Passages over the Atlantic, in the Years 1805 and 1806.* Boston: T. B. Wait, 1812. 2 vols.
Silverstein, Michael, ed. and intro. "Whitney on Language." *Whitney on Language: Selected Writings of William Dwight Whitney.* Cambridge: MIT P, 1971. x–xxiii.
Simpson, David. *The Politics of American English, 1776–1850.* New York: Oxford UP, 1986.
"Slavery." *The North American Review* 41.88 (July 1835): 170–94.
Smith, Norman B. "'Shall Make No Law Abridging . . . ': An Analysis of the Neglected, but Nearly Absolute, Right of Petition." *University of Cincinnati Law Review* 54 (1986): 1153–96.
Smith, Rogers M. *Civic Ideals: Conflicting Visions of Citizenship in U.S. History.* New Haven: Yale UP, 1997.
Smitherman, Geneva. *Black Talk: Words from the Hood to the Amen Corner.* New York: Houghton, 1994.
———. "Ebonics, *King,* and Oakland: Some Folk Don't Believe Fat Meat is Greasy." *Journal of English Linguistics* 26.2 (1998): 97–107.
———. *Talkin' and Testifyin'.* Boston: Houghton, 1978.
Social Mirror: A Complete Treatise on the Laws, Rules, and Usages that Govern Our Most Refined Homes and Social Circles. St. Louis: L. W. Dickerson, 1888.
Sollors, Werner. *Beyond Ethnicity: Consent and Descent in American Culture.* New York: Oxford UP, 1986.
———, ed. *Multilingual America: Transnationalism, Ethnicity, and the Languages of American Literature.* New York: NYU P, 1998.
Southworth, E. D. E. N. *The Hidden Hand. Or, Capitola the Madcap.* 1859. Ed. Joanne Dobson. New Brunswick: Rutgers UP, 1992.
Spillers, Hortense. "Notes on an Alternative Model: Neither/Nor." *The Year Left 2: An American Socialist Yearbook.* Ed. Mike Davis, Manning Marable, Fred Pfiel, and Michael Sprinkler. Stony Brook: Verso, 1987. 176–94.
Spivak, Gayatri Chakravorty. "The Making of Americans, the Teaching of English, and the Future of Culture Studies." *New Literary History* 21.4 (Autumn 1990): 781–98.
Stadler, Gustavus. "Magawisca's Body of Knowledge: Nation-Building in *Hope Leslie.*" *The Yale Journal of Criticism* 12.1 (1999): 41–56.
Stepto, Richard. "'The Simple but Intensely Human Inner Life of Slavery': Storytelling and the Revision of History in Charles W. Chesnutt's 'Uncle Julius Stories.'" *History and Tradition in Afro-American Culture.* Ed. Gunter Lenz. Frankfurt: Campus, 1984. 29–55.
Stewart, Susan. "Letter on Sound." *Close Listening: Poetry and the Performed Word.* Ed. Charles Bernstein. New York: Oxford UP, 1998. 29–52.
Stewart, Veronica. "The Wild Side of *The Wide, Wide World.*" *Legacy* 11.1 (1994): 1–16.
Stowe, Harriet Beecher. *Life and Letters of Harriet Beecher Stowe.* Ed. Annie Fields. Boston: Houghton and London: Sampson, 1897.
Sundquist, Eric J. *To Wake the Nations: Race in the Making of American Literature.* Cambridge: Harvard UP, 1993.
Swaim, Kathleen M. *Pilgrim's Progress, Puritan Progress: Discourses and Contexts.* Urbana: U of Illinois P, 1993.
Takaki, Ronald. *A Different Mirror: A History of Multicultural America.* Boston: Little, 1993.
Thomas, Brook. *American Literary Realism and the Failed Promise of Contract.* Berkeley: U of California P, 1997.

———, ed. "Introduction: The Legal Background." *Plessy v. Ferguson: A Brief History with Documents*. Boston: Bedford, 1997. 1–38.
Thompson, Frank V. *Schooling of the Immigrant*. New York: Harper and Bros., 1920.
———. "The School as the Instrument for Nationalization Here, and Elsewhere." P. Davis 582–99.
Tompkins, Jane. Afterword. *The Wide, Wide World*. By Susan Warner. New York: Feminist, 1987. 584–608.
———. *Sensational Designs: The Cultural Work of American Fiction, 1790–1860*. New York: Oxford UP, 1985.
Trachtenberg, Alan. Introduction. *Ragged Dick: Or, Street Life in New York with the Boot-blacks*. By Horatio Alger, Jr. New York: Signet, 1990. v–xx.
Twain, Mark. *Pudd'nhead Wilson and Those Extraordinary Twins*. 1894. Ed. Malcolm Bradbury. New York: Penguin, 1969.
———. "The Temperance Crusade and Women's Rights." 1873. *Europe and Elsewhere*. New York: Harper and Bros., 1923. 24–30.
Van Evrie, John H. *White Supremacy and Negro Subordination; or, Negroes a Subordinate Race, and (So-Called) Slavery its Normal Condition*. 1868. New York: Negro UP, 1969.
Vasquez, Mark G. "'Your Sister Cannot Speak to You and Understand You as I Do': Native American Culture and Female Subjectivity in Lydia Maria Child and Catharine Maria Sedgwick." *The American Transcendental Quarterly* 15.3 (Sept. 2001): 173–90.
Veblen, Thorstein. *The Theory of the Leisure Class*. 1899. New York: Penguin, 1994.
Wald, Priscilla. *Constituting Americans: Cultural Anxiety and Narrative Form*. Durham: Duke UP, 1995.
Walker, Pierre, ed. *Henry James on Culture: Collected Essays on Politics and the American Social Scene*. Lincoln: U of Nebraska P, 1999.
Wardley, Lynn. "Woman's Voice, Democracy's Body, and *The Bostonians*." *ELH* 56.3 (Autumn 1989): 639–65.
Warner, Susan. *The Wide, Wide World*. 1850. New York: Feminist, 1987.
Warren, Kenneth. *Black and White Strangers: Race and American Literary Realism*. Chicago: U of Chicago P, 1993.
———. "Still Reading Henry James?" *The Henry James Review* 16.3 (1995): 282–85.
Webster, Noah. *A Compendious Dictionary of the English Language*. New Haven: Sidney's Press for Hudson, and Goodwin of Hartford, 1806.
———. *Dissertations on the English Language*. 1789. Gainesville: Scholars', 1951.
———. *Letters of Noah Webster*. Ed. Harry R. Warfel. New York: Library, 1953.
———. *On Being American: Selected Writings, 1783–1828*. Ed. Homer D. Babbidge, Jr. New York: Praeger, 1967.
Weierman, Karen Woods. "Reading and Writing *Hope Leslie*: Catharine Maria Sedgwick's Indian 'Connections.'" *The New England Quarterly* 75 (Sept. 2002): 415–44.
———. "'A Slave Story I Began and Abandoned': Sedgwick's Antislavery Manuscript." Damon-Bach and Clements 122–38.
Wells, Richard A. *Manners, Culture, and Dress of the Best American Society, Including Social, Commercial and Legal Forms, Letter Writing, Invitations, &c., also valuable suggestions on Self Culture and Home Training*. c. 1890. Springfield: King, Richardson, 1894.
Weston, Kath. "Forever is a Long Time: Romancing the Real in Gay Kinship Ideologies." *Naturalizing Power: Essays in Feminist Cultural Analysis*. Ed. Sylvia Yanagisako and Carol Delaney. New York: Routledge, 1995. 87–110.

Wheaton, H. H. "Education of Immigrants." P. Davis 567–81.
White, Richard Grant. *Every-Day English: A Sequel to "Words and Their Uses."* Boston: Houghton and Cambridge: Riverside, 1880.
———. *Words and Their Uses, Past and Present. A Study of the English Language.* 1870. 3rd ed. Boston: Houghton and Cambridge: Riverside, 1880.
Whitman, Walt. *Leaves of Grass.* 1855. Baym, Norton 1005–19.
———. "Slang in America." 1885. *The English Language, 1858–1964.* Ed. W. F. Bolton and David Crystal. Cambridge: Cambridge UP, 1969. 54–58.
———. *Words; The Primer of Words; and Other Notebooks, &c on Words.* [c. 1856]. *The Collected Writings of Walt Whitman, Vol. 3: Diary in Canada, Notebooks, Index.* Ed. William White. New York: NYU P, 1977.
Whitney, William Dwight. "Languages and Dialects." *North American Review* 104.214 (Jan. 1867): 30–64
———. *Language and the Study of Language: Twelve Lectures on the Principles of Linguistic Science.* New York: Scribner's, 1867.
———. *The Life and Growth of Language: An Outline of Linguistic Science.* 1875. New York: Dover, 1979.
———. Rev. of *Words and Their Uses*, by Richard Grant White. *The North American Review* 112.231 (Apr. 1871): 469–76.
Wills, Garry. *Inventing America: Jefferson's Declaration of Independence.* Garden City, NY: Doubleday, 1978.
Wilson, Thomas. *The Many Advantages of a Good Language to Any Nation, with An Examination of the present State of our own; As also, An Essay towards correcting some Things that are Wrong with it.* 1724. Yorkshire, Eng.: Scolar, 1969.
Winkler, Helen and Elsa Alsberg. "The Home and Neighborhood Teacher." *Training Teachers for Americanization: A Course of Study for Normal Schools and Teachers' Institutes.* Mahoney et al. 49–58.
Wolfram, Walt. "Language Ideology and Dialect: Understanding the Oakland Ebonics Controversy." *Journal of English Linguistics* 26.2 (1998): 108–21.
Wohnam, Henry B., ed. *Charles W. Chesnutt: A Study of the Short Fiction.* New York: Twayne, 1998.
Wolfram, Walt and Natalie Schilling-Estes. *American English: Dialects and Variation.* Malden: Blackwell, 1998.
Woods, Robert and Albert J. Kennedy. *Handbook of Settlements.* New York: Arno, 1970.
"Works of Mrs. Child." *North American Review.* 37.80 (July 1833): 138–65.
Yanagisako, Sylvia and Carol Delaney, eds. "Introduction: Naturalizing Power." *Naturalizing Power: Essays in Feminist Cultural Analysis.* New York: Routledge, 1995. 1–22.
Zaeske, Susan. *Petitioning, Antislavery, and the Emergence of Women's Political Consciousness.* Diss. U of Wisconsin-Madison, 1997. Ann Arbor: UMI, 1997. 9727430.
———. "The 'Promiscuous Audience' Controversy and the Emergence of the Early Woman's Rights Movement." *Quarterly Journal of Speech* 81 (1995): 191–207.
———. *Signatures of Citizenship: Petitioning, Antislavery, & Women's Political Identity.* Chapel Hill: U of North Carolina P, 2003.
Zilversmit, Arthur. "Quok Walker, Mumbet, and the Abolition of Slavery in Massachusetts." *William and Mary Quarterly* 25 (1968): 614–24.
Zinn, Howard. "*A People's History of the United States, 1492–Present.* New York: Harper, 1995.
Zizek, Slavoj, ed. and intro. "The Spectre of Ideology." *Mapping Ideology.* New York: Verso, 1994. 1–33.

Index

A

Addams, Jane, 171, 172, 174–82, 227n27. Works: "Educational Methods," 176; "Immigration," 171–72; "Objective Value of a Social Settlement, The," 180; "Subjective Necessity for Social Settlements, The," 175; *Twenty Years at Hull-House*, 176
Addams, John Quincy, 58
African American English: first description of, 216n10; and literary dialect, 217n13
Alger, Horatio: background of, 79; *Ragged Dick*, 13, 64, 77–79, 89–97
"Alien Question," 163. *See also* immigrants
Alsberg, Elsa, 148
Althusser, Louis: "Letter on Art, A," 7–8, 152, 194n8
American Anti-Slavery Society, 55, 205n59
American Board of Commissioners for Foreign Missions, 21
American Colonization Society, 205n59
American Democrat, The (Cooper), 22–23
American Dialect Society, 108–09, 111–14, 216nn9–14
American Dictionary of the English Language, An (Webster), 3, 97
American Language, The (Mencken), 1, 85, 99–100, 187, 188, 190–91
American literature: ideology and, 7–8; national identity and, 3, 7; relation to language, 7
American Philological Society, 191

"'American' Speech" (White), 145–46, 154–55
Americanisms (Bartlett), 97
Americanization, discourse of: English instruction and, 171–84; relation to discourse of civilization, 145–46, 148–53, 170; role of settlement houses in, 172–80, 227n26; training manuals for, 179–82
Anatomy of National Fantasy, The (Berlant), 9–10
Anderson, Benedict, 5–6
Anglo-Saxonism, 130, 167, 176, 223n2
anxiety: over Civil War Amendments, 127, 139; over immigrants, 147, 148, 166, 174–75; over national civilization, 151, 152, 173
Appeal in Favor of that Class of Americans Called Africans, An (Child), 25
Archer, William, Representative, 51
ascriptive tradition in U.S. citizenship, 108, 193n3, 200n28
Atlanta Constitution, 122
Atlantic, The, 126, 153
Atlantic Monthly, The, 117, 218n19
Autocrat of the Breakfast Table, The (Holmes), 65–66, 99

B

Bailey, Richard, 72, 94, 97, 194n10
Baron, Dennis E., 194n10, 195n12, 199n17
Bartlett, John, 98; *Americanisms*, 97
Baym, Nina, 197n7, 214n50
"becoming American," 5
Bederman, Gail, 6, 146–47, 224n9; *Manliness and Civilization*, 147–48

Index

Beecher, Catharine, 43–45, 203n44; "Circular, Addressed to Benevolent Ladies of the U. States," 43–45, 46; *Essay on Slavery and Abolition with Reference to the Duty of American Females*, 60
Beecher, Lyman, "Plea for the West, A," 70
Bell, John, Representative, 51
Bentley, Nancy, 224n13
Benton, Thomas Hart: *Congressional Debates*, 48–55
Berlant, Lauren: *Anatomy of National Fantasy, The*, 9–10
Berlin, James, 207n8
B'hoy, the, 93–97, 212n41
blood, figure of: critique of, 142–44; as metaphor of descent, 107–08, 110, 111, 115–17, 118, 128–29, 130, 131, 137, 139, 155, 193n3; in anti-miscegenation discourse, 106–07; relation to race, 106, 107, 110–11, 115–16, 118, 130; to gender, 119–20; to sexuality, 116
Bordering on the Body (Doyle), 107
Borus, Daniel H., 220n28
Bostonians, The (James), 14, 149, 151–53, 159, 161–70, 172
Bradley, Joseph P., Chief Justice, 107–08, 125
Bradwell v. Illinois, 107, 125, 215n5
Brodhead, Richard, 130, 220n29, 221n33
Brown, Goold, 74; *Institutes of English Grammar*, 72–73
Bryn Mawr College, 150, 159, 171
Bynum, Representative, 56–58, 205n57

C

Cable, George Washington, 220n26
California Home Teacher Act of 1915, 181, 229n35
Cameron, Deborah: *Verbal Hygiene*, 8–9, 194n10
Channing, Walter, 7, 194n7
Channing, William Ellery, 198n13
Cherokee removal, 21; *See also* Indian removal
Chesnutt, Charles, 13, 221nn31–32. Works: *Colonel's Dream, A*, 13, 109, 122, 126, 137–42, 222n40; *Conjure Woman, The*, 126, 128, 129–30; "Courts and the Negro, The," 127; "Disfranchisement of the Negro," 134; "Dumb Witness, The," 13, 109, 122, 126, 130–37; "Future American, The," 130; "Liberty and the Franchise," 136; "Women's Rights," 127–28
Child, Lydia Maria, 24, 202n42; *Appeal in Favor of that Class of Americans Called Africans*, 25; *Hobomok*, 42
Chinese Exclusion Act, 147
Christian Advocate and Journal and Zion's Herald, 43–44
"Circular, Addressed to Benevolent Ladies of the United States," 43–45
citizenship, 30, 60, 67, 146, 183–84; anxiety about, 147, 148; contestations of, 2–3, 193n2; and English, 178; and gender, 74; and language, 77–78; and Reconstruction, 105–06, 107. *See also* language: gender and nation
civilization, discourse of: and Americanization, 145–52, 154, 161 (*see also* Americanization); and manners, 153–58; role of settlement houses in, 174–82; and tone of voice, 159–61
Civil Rights Act of 1866, 106–07
classroom: as home, 179–80
Cmiel, Kenneth, 17
Colonel's Dream, A (Chesnutt), 109, 122, 126, 137–42, 222n40
Congressional Debates (Benton), 48–55
Conjure Woman, The (Chesnutt), 13, 126, 128, 129–30
Connors, Robert, 17, 70, 196n5
consent, paradigm of, 2–3, 122, 126, 132, 133, 136, 140–42, 193n3
Constitution, U.S.: Civil War Amendments, 105–07, 127, 129, 132, 139, 143; Fifteenth Amendment, 13, 105, 109, 127, 138; First Amendment, 28; Fourteenth Amendment, 106, 110, 214n; Nineteenth Amendment, 14, 187; Thirteenth Amendment, 59, 106
contractual view of language, 122, 126, 132, 133, 140–42
conversation: relation to "civilization," 156–57; women's role in, 156–58

Cooper, James Fenimore, 42, 199n17. Works: *American Democrat, The*, 22–23; *Notions of the Americans*, 22; *Wept of Wish-Ton-Wish*, 42
Correct Social Usage, 156–58; *See also* manners, manuals about
"Courts and the Negro, The" (Chesnutt), 127
Crane, Gregg D., 193n3, 200n28, 202n40, 215n6
Criticism and Fiction (Howells), 117–18
"cult of domesticity," 206n3. *See also* true womanhood; "woman's sphere"

D

Damon-Bach, Lucinda, 211n34
Darwin, Charles, 114–15
Davidson, Cathy, 198n14
Declaration of Independence, 34, 68
Declaration of Sentiments, 11, 68; and vocal propriety, 74–75. *See also* Seneca Falls
Defense of Women, In (Mencken), 187, 229n3
Democratic Review, The, 22, 25, 199n20
descent, paradigm of: 2–3, 107–08, 110, 111, 115–17, 118, 128–29, 130, 131, 137, 139, 155, 193n3. *See also* blood
dialect, 13, 108, 111–13; 116, 121, 136–37, 167, 217nn13–15; Americanisms, 117, 216n10; critique of, 129–30, 142–44; and Darwin, 114–15; eye, 123–24; and literature, 117–18, 120–21.
"Dialect in Literature" (Howells), 117
Dialect Notes, 112–13
Dictionary of American Slang (Flexner), 98, 213n48
Dillingham Commission, 146, 223n3
discourse: political, 16–17, 19–20
"Disfranchisement of the Negro, The" (Chesnutt), 134
Dissertations on the English Language (Webster), 1, 3, 187
Dobson, Joanne, 103, 210n26
domesticity, ideology of, 71. *See also* true womanhood; "woman's sphere"
Douglas, Ann, 67; *Feminization of American Culture, The*, 53

Doyle, Laura, 107
Drayton, William, Representative, 50
Dred Scott, 207n9
"Dumb Witness, The" (Chesnutt), 13, 109, 122, 126–27, 130–37
Dunbar, Paul Laurence: Works: *Lyrics of Lowly Life*, 119; *Majors and Minors*, 118–19, 218n21

E

"Editor's Study" (Howells), 117, 120
"Educational Methods" (Addams), 176
Eley, Geoff, 6
English: British vs. American, 1, 185–87, 193n1; as masculine, 189–90
English with an Accent (Lippi-Green), 8
English Grammar (Murray), 72
English language education, 174–82
"English Language in the United States, The" (Matthews), 145–46
English, Standard, 137, 141, 154
Essay on Elocution (Kirkham), 63, 80
Essay on Slavery and Abolition with Reference to the Duty of American Females (C. Beecher), 60
essentialism: in/of language, 3, 106–07, 111–12, 116–17, 118–20, 191
Esther, Queen, 27
ethic: of submission, 81, 211n30
etiquette, books of, 153–58
Etiquette for Americans, 153
Evarts, Jeremiah, 21
Every-Day English (White), 145, 154
Expatriation Act of 1907, 147
eye dialect, 123–124, 220n28

F

family: gendered structure of, 148, 151, 228n33; representations of, 6, 124; traditional American, 148–49
feminization: of language, 161, 165–66, 170, 173, 188–90
Feminization of American Culture, The (Douglas), 53
Fetterley, Judith, 4, 200n32, 225n21
First Steps in Americanization, 178–80
Fishkin, Shelly Fisher, 222n42
Flexner, Stuart: *Dictionary of American Slang*, 98, 213n48
Forsyth, John, Senator, 52–53, 204n52
Foster, George A.: *New York in Slices*, 93–97, 211n38

franchise, 107, 109, 195n16; and African-Americans, 127–29, 134, 136–39, 142; and commentary about language, 10–11; expansion of to non-propertied white men, 67–68; and women, 58, 68–69, 128, 147, 162, 185, 187
Freeman, Elizabeth, 34, 35, 201n37
Fruit, J.P., 113
"Future American, The" (Chesnutt), 130
"Future of English, The" (Mencken), 14, 185, 189
"Future of the Language, The" (Mencken), 189

G

gag rule, the, 55–60, 204n54
Garland, Representative, 53–55
Garrison, William Lloyd, 204n53
Gary Works Circle, 177
Gates, Henry Louis, 218n21
Gellner, Ernest, 5
Gems of Deportment (Rayne), 157–58, 224n15
gender, 6; and language, 1–2, 11–12, 119–20, 122, 126–27, 140–42, 144, 152, 230n6; and politics, 24–26, 30, 42, 43–59; and race, 142–44; and "Rip Van Winkle," 4–5; and slang, 93–100; and speech, 153–61; spheres of, 65, 107–08. *See also* language: gender and nation; true womanhood
Gere, Anne Ruggles, 148, 228n33
Gilman, Charlotte Perkins, 229n1; *Herland*, 14, 184–86, 191–92; *Women and Economics*, 187
Good Form for Women (Harcourt), 153, 155, 158
"Good Reader, The" (McGuffey), 62–64, 65, 70
grammar, 12, 13, 64, 209nn17–20; and character, 79–80; grammar books, 72–74, 80; and manners, 154; and piety, 73, 74, 92; and property, 73–74; relation to 19th-century self-improvement, 69–70, 73–74, 91. *See also* vocal propriety
Grammatical Corrector, A (Hurd), 73, 85
Grammatical Institute of the English Language, A (Webster), 7

"Grasshopper: The Simple, the Natural, the Honest in Art, The" (Howells), 118
Grimké, Angelina, 55, 205n59
Gwynne, Parry, 71, 208n16; "Word to the Wise, A," 72

H

Halttunen, Karen, 24
Harcourt, Mrs. Charles: *Good Form for Women*, 153, 155, 158
Harper's Bazar, 158
Harris, Joel Chandler: and gender, 125, 219nn25–26; "Story of the War, A" 109, 122–25; *Uncle Remus, His Songs and His Sayings*, 120–21, 124–25, 219nn25–26
Herland (Gilman), 14, 184–86, 191–92
Hershberger, Mary, 196n6
Hidden Hand, The (Southworth), 101–04
Higginson, Stephen, 55
history: and fiction, 19–20
Hobsbawm, Eric, 5
Holmes, Oliver Wendell: *Autocrat of the Breakfast Table, The*, 65–66, 99
Home and Neighborhood Teacher, the, 181–82
Home Teacher Act, 172, 181
Hope Leslie (Sedgwick), 12, 18, 19–20, 24, 31–42, 60–61, 197n8
Hotten, John Camden: *Slang Dictionary*, 97–98
Howells, William Dean, 108, 111, 118–20, 215n8, 221n34; and realist aesthetic, 118. Works: *Criticism and Fiction*, 117–18; "Dialect in Literature," 117; "Editor's Study," 117, 120; "Grasshopper: The Simple, the Natural, the Honest in Art, The," 118; "New 'Study' and the Use of American English, The," 117
Hoyle, R. W., 30
Hull-House, 172, 174–82, 185, 227nn27–29
Hull-House Bulletin, 176–78
Hull-House Year Book, 177, 180
Hurd, Seth, 73, 85

I

immigrants, 151, 223n3; linguistic domestication of, 170–82; and

Index 257

literacy, 147–48; and motherhood, 149; "new," 146–47
"Immigration" (Addams), 171–72
Indian removal, 20, 21–22, 197nn9–11. *See also* petitioning: antiremoval and antislavery
"Indian Question," 16, 21–22, 26–27, 43–54; in *Hope Leslie*, 32–42
Institutes of English Grammar (Brown), 72–73
Irving, Washington: Works: Mustapha letters, 10; "Rip Van Winkle," 3–5, 6–7, 184

J

Jackson, Andrew, 21, 43–44, 187–88, 197n9
Jakobson, Roman, 217n16
James, Henry, 13–14, 149; and tone standard, 160, 161, 174, 225n18. Works: *Bostonians, The*, 14, 149, 151–53, 159, 161–70, 172; "Manners of American Women, The," 14, 225n18; *Notebooks*, 162; *Princess Cassamassima, The*, 162; "Question of Our Speech, The" 14, 150–51, 155, 159–60, 168, 171–74, 179; "Speech of American Women, The," 14, 159, 160–61, 174
Jespersen, Otto, 189, 230n6
Jim Crow era, 108, 137, 146
Jones, Gavin, 163, 215n6

K

Kaplan, Amy, 23, 198n14, 224n8
Kellor, Frances, 148, 178
Kerber, Linda, 196n4, 198n14
Kirkham, Samuel, 74: *Essay on Elocution*, 63, 80
Krapp, George Philip, 99–100

L

language: commentary about, 85, 148, 150, 151, 163, 170, 172, 195n14; and gender and nation, 1–5, 6–7, 11–12, 14–15, 18, 59–61, 63–64, 66, 185–92; and identity, 111, 113, 116–17, 118–20, 121–22, 131; ideologies of, 7–9, 77, 191–92, 194n9; manners, 155, 156, 161; and politics of speech, 48–59, 105, 109, 137, 142, 150, 161–62; prescriptivism in, 194n11; and race, 109–26, 129–32, 140–42; and social position, 65; standardization, 76, 85, 190–91; woman and, 22–24
language education, 72–74, 80, 83–85, 172–82; relation to national acculturation, 76, 85–89, 170–82, 184–85. *See also* vocal propriety
"Language of the Kentucky Negro, The" (Lloyd), 113
language politics, 8, 11; gendered, 150, 161–62, 170
Leaves of Grass (Whitman), 99
"Letter on Art, A," (Althusser), 7–8, 152, 194n8
Levander, Caroline, 10, 163, 195n14
Levine, Lawrence, 219n6
"Liberty and the Franchise" (Chesnutt), 136
Lighter, Jonathan, 97, 212n39
linguistic: domestication and women, 149–50, 159, 163–64; essentialism (*see* essentialism: in/of language); otherness, 166–70; propriety, 65–66, 69–89; vulgarization, 173–74
Linguistic Society of America, 191
Linke, Uli, 106–07
Lippi-Green, Rosina, 7; *English with an Accent*, 8
literature: and history, 7, 19–20; and language, 7–8, 112; and politics, 14; relation to ideology, 7–8, 15
Lloyd, John Uri, 113
Locke, John, 29
Looby, Christopher, 4, 9–10
lyceum movement, 34, 198n16, 208n14
Lyman, Rollo, 77, 209n17
Lyrics of Lowly Life (Dunbar), 119

M

McGuffey, William Holmes, 206n2; "Good Reader, The," 62–64, 65, 70; *McGuffey's Sixth Eclectic Reader*, 70, 73
McGuffey's Sixth Eclectic Reader (McGuffey), 70, 73
Maddox, Lucy, 197n11
Maier, Pauline, 28
Majors and Minors (Dunbar), 118–19, 218n21

Manliness and Civilization (Bederman), 147–48
manners: and conversation, 156–59; good breeding, 155, 156; manuals about, 153–58, 224n12. *See also* vocal tone
"Manners of American Women, The" (James), 14, 225n18
Manners, Culture, and Dress of the Best American Society (Wells), 153, 156
Manners and Social Usages (Sherwood), 158–59
Married Women's Property Act, 208n12
Marshall, John, Chief Justice, 23
masculinity, 151–52, 186; and congressional debates over petitioning, 56–58; and the English language, 189–90; and slang, 98–100
Matthews, Brander, 222nn1–2; "English Language in the United States, The," 145–46
Means and Ends (Sedgwick), 25
Mencken, H. L.: on language, gender, and nation, 1–2, 185–92. Works: *American Language*, 1, 85, 99–100, 187, 188, 190–91; *Defense of Women, In*, 187, 229n3; "Future of English, The," 14, 185, 189; "Future of the Language, The," 189
miscegenation laws, 106–07, 214n2
"mixed blood," 116, 126
Modern Language Association (MLA), 113
Mugglestone, Lynda, 220n28
Murray, Lindley, 72, 74

N

nation: and language, 5–6, 69–70, 146–82, 185–86, 194n7; and slang, 99–100
National Americanization Committee, 148
nature, as metaphor of descent, 107–09, 110, 111, 156
Negroes and Negro 'Slavery' (Van Evrie), 110
Nelson, Raymond, 191
Nettels, Elsa, 119–20, 123–24, 215n6
"New 'Study' and the Use of American English, The," (Howells), 117
Newman, Louise Michele, 148

Newsboy, the, 95–97
"New Woman," 146–47
New York in Slices (Foster), 93–97, 211n38
New York Picayune, 94
New York Tribune, 93, 101, 210n22
Niles' Weekly Register, 48–49, 203n46, 204n49
North American Review, The, 16, 18, 22, 23–24, 196n2
Notebooks (James), 162
Notions of the Americans (Cooper), 22

O

"Objective Value of a Social Settlement, The" (Addams), 180
otherness: in *Bostonians, The*, 166–70

P

Pace v. Alabama, 107
Page, Thomas Nelson, "Meh Lady: A Story of the War," 220n30
Partridge, Eric, 97
patriarchy, 6, 37, 38, 41; racial, 106–07, 124, 126–27
Peabody, Andrew P., *Conversation, Its Faults and Its Graces*, 71, 80
petitioning, 62, 199nn24–27; antiremoval and antislavery, 12, 16, 17–18, 20–21, 31, 43–59; collective, 29–30, 45, 204n53; congressional reactions to, 48–59, 199n19, 205n57; female justification of, 46–47, 205n56; history of, 27–29; in *Hope Leslie*, 31–43; male, 48; and prayer, 26–27; and Steubenville, 46–47, 203n46
"Plea for the West, A" (L. Beecher), 70
Plessy v. Ferguson, 107, 127, 138
Portnoy, Alisse, 12, 18, 47, 205n56
Posnock, Ross, 226n21
Primer of Politeness, The (Gow), 80
Princess Cassamassima, The (James), 162
propriety, 69–70. *See also* vocal propriety
Pudd'nhead Wilson (Twain), 142–43, 222n42
Puritans: relations with Indians, 19, 31–32, 35–42

Q

"Question of Our Speech, The" (James), 14, 150–51, 155, 159–60, 168, 171–74, 179

R

racism, 106, 107, 110–11, 130
Ragged Dick (Alger), 13, 64, 77–79, 89–97
Rayne, Martha Louise: *Gems of Deportment*, 157–58, 224n15
reading, good, 62–63
realist aesthetic, 118
Reconstruction, 108; and Constitutional amendments, 105–06, 127; in literature, 122–25, 127; post-, 127, 128, 132, 137–38
Register of Debates in Congress, 54, 56
republican motherhood, 23, 24, 69, 146, 196n4
representation: crisis of, 106, 107; by the victor, 19; and reproduction, 106, 107
reproducer, woman as, 143, 144
Retribution (Southworth), 101
rhetoric: and the early American republic, 16–17; and the 1830s, 17
"Rip Van Winkle" (Irving), 3–5, 6–7, 184
romantic reconciliation: trope of in 19th-century literature, 123, 220n27
Rousseau, Jean Jacques, 29, 200n28

S

Saks, Eva, 106, 107, 214n2
Saussure, Ferdinand de, 217n16
Schooling of the Immigrant (Thompson), 178
schoolmarm: figure of in Mencken's writing, 188–90
Schele de Vere, M., 105
Sedgwick, Catharine Maria, 42; history and fiction, 19–20; *Hope Leslie*, 12, 18, 19–20, 24, 31–42, 60–61, 197n8; on *Means and Ends*, 25; and politics, 21–22, 198n12, 201n33; "Slavery in New England," 34, 35; "Some pages of a slave story," 201n37
Sedgwick, Theodore, 34
Seneca Falls Convention, 13, 67; and Declaration of Sentiments, 11, 68, 74–75
Sensational Designs (Tompkins), 79, 81, 194n8
sentimental novel, 76; heroine in, 11, 77, 103–04
sentimentalism: in culture, 67; in literature, 79, 81, 103; relation to trope of romantic reconciliation, 123, 220n27
separate spheres, trope of, 22, 23, 24, 54, 57, 69, 198n14
settlement houses: English language instruction in, 174–82; Hull-House as exemplar, 172, 174–82; Jane Addams' role in, 171, 172, 174–82. *See also* Americanization, discourse of
Sheldon, Edward S., 112–13
Sherwood, Mary Elizabeth Wilson: *Manners and Social Usages*, 158–59
Sigourney, Lydia, 43, 44; "Stockbridge Bowl, The," 43, 44
slang, 64, 90–91, 93–97, 99–100, 213nn44–49; and cant, 97–98, 105
"Slang in America" (Whitman), 99
Slang Dictionary (Hotten), 97
slavery, 17, 18, 25, 34–35, 48–60. *See also* petitioning: antiremoval and antislavery
"Slavery in New England" (Sedgwick), 34, 35
"Slavery Question," 12, 26
Smith, Norman B., 27–28
Smith, Rogers, 68, 69, 108, 193n2
Social Mirror, 157
Sollors, Werner, 2–3, 193n3
"Some pages of a slave story" (Sedgwick), 201n37
Southworth, E.D.E.N.; *Hidden Hand, The*, 101–04; *Retribution*, 101
speech: American, 151, 154–55, 171–74; and manners, 153–55; and social position, 65. *See also* vocal propriety
"Speech of American Women, The" (James), 14, 159, 160–61, 174
Spivak, Guyatri, 14
standardization of language, 76, 85; resistance to by American English, 76, 85, 189–91
Stanton, Elizabeth Cady, 11, 67, 68, 75
"Stockbridge Bowl, The" (Sigourney), 43, 44
"Story of the War, A" (Harris), 109, 122–25
Storrs, William, Representative, 51
Stowe, Harriet Beecher, 43

260   Index

"Subjective Necessity for Social Settlements, The" (Addams), 175
suffrage, 58, 105, 162, 195n16. See also franchise
Sundquist, Eric J., 220n29
Suny, Ronald Grigor, 6

T
Taney, Roger, Chief Justice, 207n9
Theory of the Leisure Class, The (Veblen), 156
Thompson, Frank V., 178
Thompson, George, 204n53
Thompson, Wiley, Representative, 51
Tompkins, Jane, 13, 76; and "ethic of submission," 81, 211n30; *Sensational Designs*, 79, 81, 194n8
tone of voice: and discourse of national civilization, 149, 158–61; and manners manuals, 154–55; masculine, 151–52, 224n9; regulation, 157–58, 225n16; and tone standard, 160, 161, 174; women's role in sustaining, 157–59
Tourgée, Albion, 129
Training Teachers for Americanization, 178, 179, 182–83
true womanhood, ideology of, 63, 66, 69; and vocal propriety, 71, 74
Twain, Mark: *Pudd'nhead Wilson*, 142–43, 222n42
Twenty Years at Hull-House (Addams), 176

U
Uncle Remus, His Songs and His Sayings (Harris), 120–21, 124–25, 219nn25–26
University of Chicago, 171

V
Van Evrie, John H.: *Negroes and Negro 'Slavery'*, 110; theory of language and race, 110–11; *White Supremacy and Negro Subordination*, 109–11
Veblen, Thorsten, 156
verbal criticism, 153–59
verbal hygiene, 8–9, 187, 194n10. See also language: commentary about; verbal criticism
Verbal Hygiene (Cameron), 8–9, 194n10

vocal propriety, 64–65, 69–70, 76–77, 79–85, 89–93, 207n4; gendered, 66, 71–72, 74–75, 87–89, 93–100, 101–04; and impropriety, 93–100, 101–03
vocal tone. See tone of voice
voice: domestication of women's, 162–66; loss of, 133–36; public vs. private, 163–65, 198n16; relation to vote, 10–11, 127, 128, 134–35; trope of, 10, 62, 82–83, 195nn14–15
vote: relation to voice, 10–11, 127, 128, 134–35. See also franchise
vox Americana, 159–60, 163, 170

W
Wald, Priscilla, 148
Warner, Susan: background on, 78–79; *Wide, Wide World, The*, 13, 64, 75–89
Webster, Noah, 1, 185; *American Dictionary of the English Language, An*, 3, 97; *Dissertations on the English Language*, 1, 3, 187; *Grammatical Institute of the English Language, A*, 7; on language and nation, 1, 3, 187
Weinreich, Max, 5
Wells, Richard A.: *Manners, Culture, and Dress of the Best American Society*, 153, 156
White, Richard Grant: "'American' Speech," 145–46, 154–55; *Every-Day English*, 145, 154; *Words and Their Uses*, 153–54
White Supremacy and Negro Subordination (Van Evrie), 109–11
White Women's Rights (Newman), 148
Whitman, Walt, 99; *Leaves of Grass*, 99; "Slang in America," 99
Whitney, William Dwight, 108, 111, 112, 114, 215n8, 217n16; *Life and Growth of Language, The*, 114; theory of language, 114–17
Wide, Wide World, The (Warner), 13, 64, 75–89
Wills, Gary, 28
Wilde, Richard, Representative, 50, 52
Winkler, Helen, 148
Winthrop, John, 37–38, 201n38

"Woman Question," 16, 20, 22, 26, 163–65, 187
"woman's sphere," 22–24, 54, 57, 69, 198n14
women: as linguistic domesticators, 149–50; as linguistic domesticators of immigrants, 170–82; as means of refinement, 96–97; and politics, 24–26, 30, 42, 43–60; as protectors of American speech, 173–74; as reproducers, 143, 144
Women and Economics (Gilman), 187
"Women's Rights" (Chesnutt), 127–28
Women's Rights Movement, 68–69, 208n10, 210n22
Women's Studies, 8, 11
women's suffrage, 17
Woods Weierman, Karen, 20, 201n37
"Word to the Wise, A" (Gwynne), 72
Words and Their Uses (White), 153–54
Wright, Frances, 198n16

Z

Zaeske, Susan, 12, 203n45, 204n54, 205n56
Zizek, Slavoj, 194n9

For Product Safety Concerns and Information please contact our EU representative GPSR@taylorandfrancis.com
Taylor & Francis Verlag GmbH, Kaufingerstraße 24, 80331 München, Germany

www.ingramcontent.com/pod-product-compliance
Lightning Source LLC
Chambersburg PA
CBHW071814300426
44116CB00009B/1310